JOURNAL FOR THE STUDY OF THE OLD TESTAMENT
SUPPLEMENT SERIES
376

Editors
David J.A. Clines
Philip R. Davies

Executive Editor
Andrew Mein

Editorial Board
Richard J. Coggins, Alan Cooper, J. Cheryl Exum,
John Goldingay, Robert P. Gordon, Norman K. Gottwald,
John Jarick, Andrew D.H. Mayes, Carol Meyers,
Patrick D. Miller

Reading the Latter Prophets

Toward a New Canonical Criticism

Edgar W. Conrad

T & T CLARK INTERNATIONAL
A Continuum imprint
LONDON • NEW YORK

Copyright © 2003 T&T Clark International
A Continuum imprint

Published by T&T Clark International
The Tower Building, 11 York Road, London SE1 7NX
15 East 26th Street, Suite 1703, New York, NY 10010

www.tandtclark.com

British Library Cataloguing-in-Publication Data
A catalogue record for this book is available from the British Library

Typeset and edited for Continuum by Forthcoming Publications Ltd
www.forthcomingpublications.com

Printed on acid-free paper in Great Britain by MPG Books Ltd, Bodmin, Cornwall

ISBN 0-8264-6652-4 (hardback)
    0-5670-8452-3 (paperback)

In celebration of the eighty-fourth birthday
of my mother, Violet M. Conrad

CONTENTS

This book grows out of and builds on my previous studies on reading prophetic books in two ways. First, it extends my reader response and intertextual approach to prophetic books by drawing on the semiotic theory of Umberto Eco, especially as that relates to his ideas concerning the limits of interpretation. While I agree with the recent redactional critical goal to interpret prophetic books as literary wholes, it is not my aim to build on these studies. Rather, as in my previous work, my perspective is synchronic rather than diachronic.

Second, this study is also different from my previous work in its focus on reading the prophetic corpus rather than focusing on a single prophetic book. One aspect of my study is attention to the significance and implications of the order and arrangement of prophetic books for reading. However, my interest in order assumes the existence of different canons with different implications for reading. Although I select a particular canonical order as a basis for my reading, I do not assume the authority of any particular one.

I am thankful for the many people who have given me assistance in carrying out this study. I was elected as a Visiting Research Fellow by the Institute for Advanced Study in the Humanities, the University of Edinburgh, for the period January–June 2001. I am grateful for the fruitful discussions on semiotics that I had with Professor John Frow, the Director of the Institute, and the stimulating weekly seminars shared by all members of the institute. Professor Graeme Auld welcomed me at the weekly seminars at New College and I appreciated the feedback I received from the paper I delivered at that seminar. Philip Davies' work has always been thought provoking and has given me insight into my research for this study, especially as that relates to matters of canon. I am also grateful for his work as editor of this series and for Sheffield Academic Press/Continuum's acceptance of the book for publication. Roland Boer, of Monash University, co-chair with me of the Bible and Critical Theory Seminar, has been a major support in discussing the implications of contemporary critical theory for the study the Bible. I am also indebted to the members of the seminar who have listened to and given me feedback on papers I have presented, especially on the implications of semiotics for my readings of prophetic books. I have also received support from the Faculty of Arts at the University of Queensland and the Office of Research, which have recognized the Bible and cultural studies as a research strength at the University and so supported it with a research infrastructure grant for 2001 and 2002.

My postgraduate students have given me sage advice as we have discussed our mutual research projects in 'Ed's Group', a gathering of Higher Degree Research students under my supervision at the University of Queensland. Thanks to Johnson, Man Soo, Patricia, Michael, Sehoon, Marie, Julie, Scott, David, Graeme, Andrew, Katie, John, Carol, Won Ju, Harold, Myoung, Joel, Jason and Glen. I also want to thank Doug Nykolaishen and Lydie Kucova, two postgraduate students at the New College, University of Edinburgh, who met with me weekly to listen and respond to me during the time that the bulk of this material was written.

I also am grateful to my colleagues in Studies in Religion in the School of History, Philosophy, Religion and Classics at the University of Queensland, whose mutual support has helped create a productive research culture: Philip Almond, Michael Lattke, Rod Bucknell, Richard Hutch, Lynne Hume, Rick Strelan, Hereward Tilton, Roxanne Marcotte, Primos Pecenko and Tamara Dittrich.

Above all, however, I have received strong support in developing my ideas from my wife, Dr Linda Conrad, who has listened, read and critiqued my ideas as they were developing.

I dedicate this book to my mother, Violet M. Conrad, in celebration of her eighty-fourth birthday on 5 March 2003 and gratitude for her care and concern through the years.

ABBREVIATIONS

AB	Anchor Bible
ABD	David Noel Freedman (ed.), *The Anchor Bible Dictionary* (New York: Doubleday, 1992)
ANET	James B. Pritchard (ed.), *Ancient Near Eastern Texts Relating to the Old Testament* (Princeton: Princeton University Press, 1950)
AOAT	Alter Orient und Altes Testament
BJS	Brown Judaic Studies
BZAW	Beihefte zur *ZAW*
ConBOT	Coniectanea biblica, Old Testament
CRBS	*Currents in Research: Biblical Studies*
Int	*Interpretation*
JAAR	*Journal of the American Academy of Religion*
JQR	*Jewish Quarterly Review*
JSOT	*Journal for the Study of the Old Testament*
JSOTSup	*Journal for the Study of the Old Testament*, Supplement Series
NRSV	New Revised Standard Version
OTL	Old Testament Library
OTS	*Oudtestamentische Studiën*
PMLA	*Publications of the Modern Language Association of America*
SBLSS	SBL Semeia Studies
THL	Theory and Hisory of Literature
VT	*Vetus Testamentum*
ZAW	*Zeitschrift für die alttestamentliche Wissenschaft*

Introduction

It is my aim in this study to read the Latter Prophets as a continuation of
the Former Prophets. I understand prophetic books to be scribal constructions in which material was collected, ordered and arranged. Therefore, to
read these books as literary wholes it is necessary to understand them in
terms of their compilational rather than their compositional unity. I am
assuming that these books were compiled with the purpose of communicating. They construct prophetic worlds, which their scribal authors
assumed could convey meaning for those intended to read them or for
whom they were intended to be read. To understand prophetic books as
books from a past world, I am also assuming that it is necessary to respect
their textual limits. In this way my present study follows my previous
research on prophetic literature and takes a different direction from that of
the traditional historical-critical approach. Historical criticism rather than
reading prophetic books as givens, as compilational wholes, has attempted
to interpret the prophetic books by ignoring textual limits and by focusing
on earlier reconstructions of the life and times of the prophet, underlying
sources or the history of their redaction. Rather than read prophetic books
as compilational wholes, historical critics have used source analysis, form
criticism, redaction criticism and other techniques to create different compilations of the material.

I understand my role in interpretation to be that of a reader. For the last
quarter of a century or so it has become increasingly clear in literary theory
that meaning can only emerge from a text in the activity of reading. The
active role of the reader in producing meaning has sometimes been taken
to extremes so that it is assumed that the reader is in complete control. My
approach does not represent this radical form of reader response criticism.
I am interested in the role of the text as well as the role of the reader in the
production of meaning. It is for this reason that I am concerned with
respecting textual limits rather than the more radical approach represented

by conventional biblical studies, which, in most instances, ignores present textual boundaries by reconstructing new texts.[1]

I outline my methodological approach to reading prophetic books in Chapter 1, in which I draw on the insights of Umberto Eco's theory of semiotics for understanding my role as a reader of prophetic books. Semiotics concerns the way in which communication takes place between an addresser and an addressee. To simplify a bit, semiotics understands communication to take place through writing when the reader brings to the text information that the author assumed the reader had in his or her possession. For example, if my mother left me a note as a child 'to red up the room', I, as a reader from a Pennsylvania Dutch community, brought information about the meaning of 'red' or 'redd'. I knew that I was asked to tidy up the room. All texts are filled with codes that authors expect their readers to know for communication to take place.

I bring this discussion of semiotics in conversation with the way form criticism, advocated by Hermann Gunkel, has functioned in biblical studies. Rather than see form criticism as providing information about an oral *Sitz im Leben*, I understand that the form critic's concern for convention can be used as important information for reading. In this way I have tried to heed Muilenburg's challenge, made in the late 1960s, to move beyond form criticism in order to see how the typical and conventional can be used to yield important insights for understanding the particularities of a text. In short, I am concerned as a reader with identifying coded information, which scribal authors expected their readers to possess in order to read the texts.

I understand that the task of reading ancient texts from alien cultures is replete with problems, and I have no illusions that I will understand prophetic books as did the readers for whom they were intended. I do, however, make it a goal or aim of my reading to identify and understand, insofar as possible, the semiotic codes in prophetic books. In particular I am concerned with the openings of prophetic books, and I take this up in Chapter 4. For example, Isaiah, Jeremiah and Ezekiel all open in very different ways. Isaiah opens, 'the vision (חֲזוֹן) of Isaiah', Jeremiah with 'the words of' (דְּבָרֵי) Jeremiah, and Ezekiel with 'and it happened' (וַיְהִי). These different openings of prophetic books, I suggest, provide important semiotic information for reading what follows. Each of these three books

---

1.   While it is not traditional to think of historical criticism, with its evocation of objectivity to be 'reader response criticism', this is how it looks from a semiotic perspective.

represents a different genre, which means that they must be read in different ways. The significance of these openings of the 'Major Prophets' achieves clarity when the openings are read in conjunction with the openings of the books of the 'Minor Prophets'. To ignore important information at the beginning of prophetic books about how to read the compilation that follows, disregards compilational unity.

To read prophetic books as compilations aimed at conveying a meaning requires that the reader also be concerned with the constructed whole. I understand that a prophetic book represents a kind of collage, but it is this very collage as a whole that creates a literary world. To understand the meaning of a prophetic book means that we must read it according to its order and arrangement.

In my reading of the prophetic corpus I am also concerned with canonical order and the significance of that order for arriving at meaning. I take up this issue in Chapter 3. My interest in canonical order is not a theological one, for I realize that there are many different canonical outcomes. For example, in Christian Bibles, to read Isaiah, Jeremiah, Ezekiel and the Twelve at the end of the canon, separated from the former prophets (Joshua, Judges, Samuel and Kings), is different from reading the Latter Prophets as a continuation of the Former Prophets (as in the rabbinic tradition). In this study I have chosen to read in a particular canonical order not because I think that it is normative or original, but simply because I think that canonical order does make a difference to the meaning a reader derives from a text. I have chosen to read the prophetic corpus according to the Talmudic order: Joshua, Judges, Samuel, Kings, Jeremiah, Ezekiel, Isaiah and the Twelve. I found reading in this order to be an interesting exercise because it solves (or identifies as marginal or irrelevant) some questions of interpretation in traditional critical biblical studies.[2]

In Chapter 2, I deal with the question of history and its significance for reading prophetic books. My view is that prophetic books are themselves artifacts of the ancient world. I contend that these books cannot be used as data in the positivistic sense in which they have so often been used in biblical studies for reconstructing the world as it actually was. The view that we can somehow get behind these texts to reconstruct the world of the prophets is highly problematic. The literary worlds of the prophetic books

2. For example, a recurring question in traditional historical-critical studies has been, 'Why are only two of the Latter Prophets (Jonah and Isaiah) mentioned in the book of Kings?' In Chapter 3, I discuss this and other similar questions in light of my reading of the text with attention to canonical order.

themselves are important for knowing about the prophetic past. To know, for example, if there was an actual Isaiah or what an actual Isaiah actually said is something we cannot determine from a prophetic book alone. What we can know and experience is the literary world of the prophetic books themselves. Those books allow us to experience as readers a prophetic world as their scribal authors constructed it.

In Chapter 5, I offer an intertextual reading of Amos and Jeremiah. Both of these books open with the phrase 'the words of'. In Chapter 6, I read together the two books that begin with the phrase 'and it happened': Jonah and Ezekiel. In Chapter 7, I read Isaiah along with the other prophets of 'vision' (Joel, Micah, Obadiah, Nahum, Habakkuk and Zephaniah). In Chapter 8, I read the scroll of the Twelve as a compilational whole. These readings are not intended to be definitive or exhaustive but to be illustrative. I show how a reading of a canonical collection as a compilational whole can proceed from a semiotic perspective.

Chapter 1

PROPHETIC BOOKS: TOWARD A SEMIOTICS OF READING

> Above all, however, if contemporary readers wish to understand the prophets, they must entirely forget that the writings were collected in a sacred book centuries after the prophets' wrote. The contemporary reader must not read their words as portions of the Bible but must attempt to place them in the context of the life of the people of Israel in which they were first spoken.[1]

> For the more deeply one penetrates the formulations as they have been transmitted to us, the more sensitive he is to the roles which words and motifs play in a composition; the more he concentrates on the ways in which thought has been woven into linguistic patterns, the better able he is to think the thoughts of the biblical writer after him.[2]

In *Reading Isaiah*[3] and *Zechariah*[4] I attempted to bring my strategies of reading prophetic books in line with developments in contemporary critical theory. Prophetic books were deemed to be problematic when treated as data for reconstructing the history behind the texts, including the biography of the prophets, as well as the origins and redactional history of the prophetic books themselves. Contemporary theoretical notions regarding language, text and history suggest that books like the prophetic books do not simply mirror the external world but participate in its construction.

Furthermore, I argued that reading a prophetic book, like any text, involves the active role of the reader in constructing textual meaning.

For these reasons I chose to sever ties with the traditional historical-critical approach to reading prophetic books. Instead I identified with developments in hermeneutics associated with the broader field of the

1. Hermann Gunkel, 'The Prophets as Writers and Poets', in *idem*, *Prophecy in Israel: Search for Identity* (trans J.L. Schaaf; ed. D.L. Petersen; Issues in Religion and Theology, 10; Philadelphia: Fortress Press; London: SPCK, 1987), pp. 22-73 (24).

2. James Muilenburg, 'Form Criticism and Beyond', *JBL* 88 (1969), pp. 1-18 (7).

3. Edgar Conrad, *Reading Isaiah* (Overtures to Biblical Theology; Minneapolis: Augsburg/Fortress Press, 1991).

4. Edgar Conrad, *Zechariah* (Readings: A New Biblical Commentary; Sheffield: Sheffield Academic Press, 1999).

humanities that understood that a detached and objective stance vis-à-vis the text was impossible. The perspective of the reader will necessarily influence interpretation.

The question I want to explore in this chapter is: 'Is meaning solely dependent on the reader or do texts themselves play a role in limiting interpretation?' This question reflects what I think was a fundamental tension between my practice and the theory I appealed to in my previous studies such as *Reading Isaiah* and *Zechariah*. In both books I followed a reader response approach and, especially in *Reading Isaiah*, I appealed to the theory of Stanley Fish propounded in his book, *Is There a Text in This Class? The Authority of Interpretive Communities*.[5] I argued for the importance of the reader's explicit and active role in the development of the meaning of the book of Isaiah, and I made no claim to any determinate or normative meaning. However, I diverged from Stanley Fish's more radical reader-oriented approach by arguing that the text provides a kind of frame or structure that sets interpretive limits. In *Reading Isaiah*, I argued,

> My primary aim is to understand the text as a whole by paying special attention to its structure. My understanding of the structure of the book differs from that of redaction criticism in that I will be concerned with the text's aesthetic momentum, not its historical development.
>
> My reading does not assume the genre of the text, but it assumes the text is something as a whole and seeks to discover what that whole is. I am therefore not interested in relating parts of the text to a world external to it (its historical background or its history of literary development) but to the literary world of the text itself. I will be dealing with the 'final form' of the text, but I will be focusing on the form itself not on the process by which it became final.
>
> The structure of a text such as Isaiah is not obvious to contemporary readers of the text. This is because the text has been read customarily by biblical critics as a largely disunified collection of material of disparate origin. It is possible, however, in a close reading of Isaiah to identify recurring rhetorical techniques and patterns that suggest its unity... I look at repetition in the text as a clue to its structural unity.
>
> The Book of Isaiah contains repetition in vocabulary, motif, theme, narrative sequence, and rhetorical devices such as rhetorical questions, pronominal shifts, and forms of address. This repetition creates cohesion in the text. The repetition in the book, however, is not literal; repetition is always repetition with a difference. Variation in the recurrence of repeated elements in the text suggests movement and progression.

5.　　Stanley Fish, *Is There a Text in This Class? The Authority of Interpretive Communities* (Cambridge, MA: Harvard University Press, 1980).

The attention to these elements of repetition in the text will alert my reading to the function of its narratives, the interaction of narration and poetry, the interplay of narrative voices, the relation between the implied audience and the narrators and poetic personae. My study will concern the book's presentation of the prophet not the prophet's presentation of the book.[6]

By appealing to the role of the text in my interpretative practice, I downplayed the exclusive role of communities of interpretation in the determination of meaning. Obviously, the text was always more clearly in my class than it was for Fish.

Fish's theory, however, has made me aware of the important role of community in my own interpretive practice. My recognition of the active role of the reader in interpretation is related to my own change of community. My PhD training was in a theological community where the historical-critical approach was standard practice; the Arts Faculty community to which I now belong has challenged the author-centered approach represented by historical-critical practice and has recognized the active role of the reader in the construction of meaning. Movement in my own interpretive practice reflects an actual move from one interpretive community to another.[7]

1. *Form Criticism and Beyond*

In order to gain a clearer theoretical perspective on what I have done in my past studies, and what I propose to do in this book, I want to look again at the consequence of how the change of community effected my own interpretive practice. I see now that my interpretive agenda in *Reading Isaiah* did not completely sever ties with earlier historical-critical work represented, for example, in my book, *Fear Not Warrior: A Study of 'al tîra' Pericopes in the Hebrew Scriptures*.[8] There was continuity with this

6.   Conrad, *Reading Isaiah*, pp. 29-30.
7.   I wrote about this change of community in an earlier article, 'Changing Context: The Bible and the Study of Religion', in E.W. Conrad and T.G. Newing (eds.), *Perspective's on Language and Text: Essays in Honor of Francis I. Andersen's Sixtieth Birthday July 28 1985* (Winona Lake, IN: Eisenbrauns, 1986), pp. 393-402.
8.   Edgar Conrad, *Fear Not Warrior: A Study of 'al tîra' Pericopes in the Hebrew Scriptures* (BJS, 75; Chico, CA: Scholars Press, 1985). See Katheryn Pfisterer Darr, *Isaiah's Vision and the Family of God* (Louisville, KY: Westminster/John Knox Press, 1994), p. 228, who points out how I played down this continuity.

past research but a continuity that moved away from it and took it in a radically different direction.

My research career began in the early 1970s in the wake of James Muilenburg's well-known presidential address in 1968 to the Society of Biblical Literature, 'Form Criticism and Beyond', later published in the *Journal of Biblical Literature*.[9] In his article James Muilenburg was interested in how a biblical text used a *Gattung*. In this way he was arguing against the influence that Hermann Gunkel's form criticism had gained in the field. He wanted to go beyond form criticism's generalizations about *Sitz im Leben*, which he thought led away from the particularities of the text. He advocated the need to interpret larger literary units by employing what he called 'rhetorical criticism'. My own approach was an attempt to heed Muilenburg's challenge by focusing on the textual setting of a *Gattung*, or what I called its '*Sitz im Text*'.

In my doctoral dissertation, which I submitted in 1974,[10] I challenged Joachim Begrich's understanding of the 'Oracle of Salvation' with its characteristic 'fear not' formula as having its institutional setting in the cult as a priestly answer to lament, and I suggested in later writings that its textual setting concerned situations of warfare. I called the form a 'War Oracle'. Subsequently, I published these findings in two articles, 'Second Isaiah and the Priestly Oracle of Salvation' (1981)[11] and 'The Fear Not Oracles in Second Isaiah' (1984)[12] and a book, *Fear Not Warrior* (1985). In a later article, 'The Royal Narratives and the Structure of the Book of Isaiah' (1988),[13] I argued that the strategic use of this oracle throughout the book of Isaiah was a key to understanding what I referred to as the unity of Isaiah. My focus, then, was on how forms were suggestive for understanding not only literary units but also whole texts.

Subsequently, in my *Reading Isaiah* (1991), I had become aware of the recognition in critical literary theory of the role of the reader in constructing textual meaning. Texts did not speak for themselves. Rather, meaning

---

9.   Muilenburg, 'Form Criticism and Beyond'.

10.   Edgar Conrad, 'Patriarchal Traditions in Second Isaiah' (doctoral dissertation, Princeton Theological Seminary, 1974).

11.   Edgar Conrad, 'Second Isaiah and the Priestly Oracle of Salvation', *ZAW* 93 (1981), pp. 234-46.

12.   Edgar Conrad, 'The Fear Not Oracles in Second Isaiah', *VT* 34 (1984), pp. 126-52.

13.   Edgar Conrad, 'The Royal Narratives and the Structure of the Book of Isaiah', *JSOT* 41 (1988), pp. 67-81.

arose in the activity of reading. I found Stanley Fish's notions about how communities of interpretation shared strategies of interpretation compelling. His well-known book, *Is There a Text in This Class?*, suggested the then radical notion: that meaning does not lie embedded in the text but arises only when a reader 'authors' the text in reading. Fish's approach appealed to me because it offered me the opportunity to make sense out of the plurality of readings emerging in biblical studies, for example, feminist readings, liberation readings, Minjung readings, post-colonial readings, and so forth. It also gave me a theoretical base to support my strategies of reading in opposition to traditional historical criticism, which I identified as a community with shared interpretive strategies. Recognizing myself in a community where structuralist and post-structuralist theories formed the prevailing strategies of interpretation enabled me to acknowledge the input of the reader by reading Isaiah as a whole rather than by reconstructing underlying sources or *Sitze im Leben*. In my book, *Zechariah* (1999), in which I read Zechariah as part of the book of the Twelve, I stressed in a slightly more radical way the role of the reader in constructing prophetic books as a literary collage. At the same time, however, I emphasized an intertextual reading of the Twelve with Isaiah and the larger Old Testament. In doing this I continued to acknowledge the way a prophetic book read as a whole limited my interpretation.

In short, in the 1980s my reading of prophetic books focused on how the text as a whole opened up new opportunities when the interpreter went in a different direction than form criticism to focus on larger literary units. In the 1990s, I discovered in a kind of liberating way the role of the reader in the production of meaning and its accompanying notion of the indeterminacy of meaning. Nevertheless, even in the 1990s my strategies emphasized textual boundaries.

Interestingly, both Gunkel and Muilenburg were interested in readers and texts as limiting interpretation—something that only stood out for me after I recently re-read Gunkel's article, 'The Prophets as Writers and Poets' and Muilenburg's article, 'Form Criticism and Beyond' (mentioned above). I suspect my own interest in the relationship between readers and texts goes back to and grows out of this older discussion. I want to review these articles of Gunkel and Muilenburg as a way of looking for theoretical clarity in my present position.

In his article on prophets as writers and poets, Gunkel makes the following comment about ancient writing such as prophetic books:

Here there are many genres that are completely unknown to *modern read-ers* initially—genres to which *modern readers* can become accustomed only with a great deal of difficulty. This is especially true of the prophets, who have scarcely any parallel in contemporary literature and whose style of speaking is thus at first completely foreign to us.[14]

He goes on to maintain that a reader must know the limits of the genre,

The history of the growth of the prophetic books belongs together with the history of the gradual development of the individual units of which they are composed. It is one of the inherent laws of a genre that its *units have defi-nite limits* that are traditionally prescribed. Moreover, one of the funda-mental preconditions for aesthetically evaluating as well as for factually understanding a genre is that one keep in mind *the whole that the writer himself intended.*[15]

For Gunkel, however, the limiting or framing of genres in prophetic books had to do also with establishing the proper context for reading the genre. He observes that

in interpreting as well as in criticizing the prophetic books one must use the criterion of 'context' only with great caution; and also that in attempting to indicate the structure of prophetic books such as Amos or Deutero-Isaiah one must first investigate whether such a thing exists at all.[16]

Gunkel's concern for context led him to advise readers of prophetic books to look outside the prophetic book itself in order to locate the proper con-text for reading:

The prophets were not originally writers but speakers. Anyone who thinks of ink and paper while *reading* their writings is in error from the outset. 'Hear!' is the way they begin their works, not 'Read!' Above all, however, if *contemporary readers* wish to understand the prophets, they must entirely forget that the writings were collected in a sacred book centuries after the prophets' wrote. *The contemporary reader must not read their words as portions of the Bible but must attempt to place them in the context of the life of the people of Israel in which they were first spoken.*[17]

For Gunkel, then, reading prophetic books was a problem for contemporary readers. Readers must identify a genre in order to read it (the genre) as a whole (within its boundaries). Limits also involve the correct understand-

---

14. Gunkel, 'Prophets as Writers and Poets', p. 22. In this quotation and the ones that follow, the italics are mine unless otherwise indicated.
15. Gunkel, 'Prophets as Writers and Poets', p. 29.
16. Gunkel, 'Prophets as Writers and Poets', p. 31.
17. Gunkel, 'Prophets as Writers and Poets', p. 24.

ing of the context for interpreting the genre, which is an oral institutional setting, not the written context provided by the prophetic book.

Muilenburg in 'Form Criticism and Beyond' also speaks about readers and limits of interpretation. However, differences in the role of the reader and in the role of the text in limiting interpretation appear in his challenge to move beyond form criticism. He says that, while Gunkel never repudiated 'literary and historical criticism',[18] he nevertheless 'averred that it is insufficient for answering the most pressing and natural queries of *the* reader'.[19] Gunkel was concerned with identifying literary genres. And this, according to Muilenburg, is where Gunkel's 'influence has been greatest and most salutary because the student must know what kind of literature it is that he is *reading*, to what literary category it belongs, and what its characteristic features are'.[20] Muilenburg, however, disagrees with Gunkel about the way a genre prescribes limits for a reader. He maintains that there is too much emphasis on the typical at the expense of the particular. He says,

> The basic contention of Gunkel is that the ancient men of Israel, like their Near Eastern neighbors, were influenced in their speech and their literary compositions by convention and custom. We therefore encounter in a particular genre or *Gattung* the same structural forms, the same terminology and style, and the same *Sitz im Leben*. Surely this cannot be gainsaid. But there has been a proclivity among scholars in recent years to lay such stress upon the typical and representative that the individual, personal, and unique features of the particular pericope are all but lost to view.[21]

Later on he states this in a different way, and it is here that his notion of the role of the reader and its divergence from Gunkel's understanding of the reader begins to appear:

> To state our criticism in another way, form criticism by its very nature is bound to generalize because it is concerned with what is common to all the representatives of a genre, and therefore applies an *external measure* to the individual pericopes. It does not focus sufficient attention upon what is unique and unrepeatable, upon the particularity of the formulation. Moreover, form and content are inextricably related. They form an integral whole. The two are one. Exclusive attention to the *Gattung* may actually obscure

---

18. He means here 'source analysis'.
19. Muilenburg, 'Form Criticism and Beyond', p. 2.
20. Muilenburg, 'Form Criticism and Beyond', p. 2.
21. Muilenburg, 'Form Criticism and Beyond', p. 4. Muilenburg in this quote is clearly reflecting the dominant masculinist language of his time.

the thought and intention of the writer or speaker. *The passage must be read and heard precisely as it is spoken. It is the creative synthesis of the particular formulation of the pericope with the content that makes it the distinctive composition that it is.*[22]

While Gunkel was much more concerned with what we might call a 'passive reader informed by the constraints of genre', Muilenburg was acknowledging the more active role of the reader in determining the particularities and peculiarities of a text. Muilenburg suggests that this more active role of the reader is required by the more flexible and fluid way in which genres are employed by the prophets. He notes that many genres used by the prophets are imitated from a wide variety of institutional settings:

> in numerous contexts old literary types and forms are imitated, and, precisely because they are imitated, they are employed with considerable fluidity, versatility, and, if one may venture the term, artistry. The upshot of this circumstance is that the circumspect scholar will not fail to supplement his form-critical analysis with a careful inspection of the literary unit in its precise and unique formulation. He will not be completely bound by the traditional elements and motifs of the literary genre; his task will not be completed until he has taken full account of the features which lie beyond the spectrum of genre. If the exemplars of the *Gattung* were all identical in their formulations, the Old Testament would be quite a different corpus from what it actually is.[23]

The fluidity in the use of a genre requires a more active role on the part of the reader.

Muilenburg says that the more deeply a reader

> penetrates the formulations as they have been transmitted to us, the more sensitive he is to the roles which words and motifs play in a composition; the more he concentrates on the ways in which thought has been woven into linguistic patterns, *the better able he is to think the thoughts of the biblical writer after him.* And this leads me to formulate a canon which should be obvious to us all: a responsible and proper articulation of the words in their linguistic patterns and in their precise formulations will reveal to us the texture and fabric of the writer's thought, not only what it is that he thinks, but as he thinks it.[24]

22. Muilenburg, 'Form Criticism and Beyond', p. 5.
23. Muilenburg, 'Form Criticism and Beyond', p. 7.
24. Muilenburg, 'Form Criticism and Beyond', p. 7.

While Muilenburg was not living in a world that recognized the active role of readers in the construction of meaning, his phrase about a reader who is able 'to think the thoughts of the biblical writer after him' suggests just such an involvement of the reader. Muilenburg's attempt to defend himself against the charge of subjectivity—a charge often directed against reader response critics—further suggests the more active role he envisions on the part of the reader. He says,

> Now the objection that has been most frequently raised to our contention is that too much subjectivity is involved in determining where the accents of the composition really lie. *The objection has some force, to be sure, but in matters of this sort there is no substitute for literary sensitivity... There are many marks of composition which indicate where the finale has been reached.*[25]

This role of the sensitive reader in identifying not only genre but also other artistic marks in textual composition indicate the changed perception of the reader in Muilenberg's article. The notion of a more active reader is matched by a new way of thinking about the limits of interpretation. These limits now lie within, not outside the text:

> What I am interested in, above all, is in understanding the nature of Hebrew literary composition, in exhibiting the structural patterns that are employed for the fashioning of a literary unit, whether in poetry or in prose, and in discerning the many and various devices by which the predications are formulated and ordered into a unified whole. Such an enterprise I should describe as rhetoric and the methodology as rhetorical criticism.[26]

Both Gunkel and Muilenberg at the beginning and middle of the twentieth century made an immense contribution to biblical studies by calling scholars to move on from source analysis and historical criticism to focus on reading texts as literature. A common concern for both Gunkel and Muilenburg was to read the text so that it communicated from the past. For Gunkel this meant that

> if contemporary *readers* wish to understand the prophets, they must entirely forget that the writings were collected in a sacred book centuries after the prophets' wrote. *The contemporary reader must not read their words as portions of the Bible but must attempt to place them in the context of the life of the people of Israel in which they were first spoken.*[27]

---

25. Muilenburg, 'Form Criticism and Beyond', p. 8.
26. Muilenburg, 'Form Criticism and Beyond', p. 8.
27. Gunkel, 'Prophets as Writers and Poets', p. 24.

For Muilenburg, however, this communication from the past would take place only after the reader focused on the written text, the larger rhetorical unit in which a *Gattung* was uniquely employed. Only then will the reader be able 'to think the thoughts of the biblical writer after him'. Muilenburg's significant contribution was to call scholars to go beyond form criticism by shifting the focus from a reconstructed world behind the text to the text as it is written in its present form.

It is interesting to see how both Gunkel and Muilenburg also spoke about the role of readers and the textual limits of interpretation. Gunkel saw the constraints placed on the reader not in the written text but in the restrictions of genre when it was correctly identified and understood in its oral setting or *Sitz im Leben*. It was generalization about genre that determined the limits of interpretation. Muilenburg was calling readers to open up the strictures of generalization and focus on another set of limits—the specific textual setting in which a genre was employed. By emphasizing the larger structural patterns employed in fashioning a literary unit, Muilenburg was advocating a return to the written text that Gunkel urged readers to abandon in favor of the spoken word in its original oral setting.

My own form-critical work, in which I stressed the importance of *Sitz im Text*, was an attempt to heed Muilenburg's challenge to move from generalizations about the oral setting of a genre to focus on its particular setting in the literature. In my work, however, I began to stress the active role of the reader in interpretation and the indeterminacy of meaning. However, reader response criticism and accompanying notions of the indeterminacy of meaning, both of which are current inside and outside biblical studies,[28] were not options in Muilenburg's time.

In the present climate, therefore, it is important to reconsider Muilenburg's challenge in his presidential address, 'Form Criticism and Beyond', concerning the role of the reader and the limits of interpretation. I am especially interested in raising the question implicit in Muilenburg's rhetorical criticism: Can a prophetic text communicate from the past? Can a contemporary reader learn how to read a prophetic book so as 'to think a biblical writer's thought after him'? In particular, I want to see if this phrase about thinking 'a biblical writer's thought' can be cast in a new way to accommodate the more active role of the reader than Muilenburg anticipated.

---

28. Adele Berlin, 'The Role of the Text in the Reading Process', *Semeia* 62 (1993), pp. 143-46.

2. *Umberto Eco, Semiotics and Biblical Studies*

I propose to utilize Umberto Eco's theory of semiotics as a way of addressing these questions. As a literary theory, semiotics looks at 'literary texts as signifiers' in order 'to discover the operations and conventions by which the reader understands what is signified'.[29] In other words the theory is concerned with textual communication, and I want to see the implications of this theory for reading prophetic books as communicating from the past. I see it as a way of bringing together the notion of the reader's active role in constructing the text as well as the notion of textual limits to interpretation in the interaction between text and reader.

Eco's theory is interesting not only because it concerns communication but also because Eco himself speaks about both the active role of the reader and the text as providing a kind of frame limiting interpretation. In his *The Role of the Reader*,[30] his emphasis was on the active role of the reader in determining textual meaning, while in the 1990s he began to emphasize how the text limits interpretation in his *The Limits of Interpretation*.[31] In the 'Introduction' to the latter work, he explains this dialectic in his thought between the role of the reader and the role of the text. He says,

> I have the impression that, in the course of the last few decades, the rights of the interpreters have been overstressed. In the present essays I stress the limits of the act of interpretation. To say that interpretation (as the basic feature of semiosis) is potentially unlimited does not mean that interpretation has no object and that it 'riverruns' for the sake of itself. To say that a text potentially has no end does not mean that *every* act of interpretation can have a happy ending... Even the most radical deconstructionists accept the idea that there are interpretations which are blatantly unacceptable. This means that the interpreted text imposes some constraints upon its interpreters. The limits of interpretation coincide with the rights of the text...[32]

By re-reading my own work on prophetic books as well as the previous work of Gunkel and Muilenburg in light of Eco's theory of semiotics, I am

---

29. Mark W.G. Stibb, 'Semiotics', in R.J. Coggins and J.L. Houlden (eds.), *A Dictionary of Biblical Interpretation* (London: SCM Press; Philadelphia: Trinity Press International, 1989), pp. 618-20 (619).

30. Umberto Eco, *The Role of the Reader: Explorations in the Semiotics of Texts* (London: Hutchinson, 1981).

31. Umberto Eco, *The Limits of Interpretation* (Bloomington: Indiana University Press, 1990).

32. Eco, The *Limits of Interpretation*, pp. 6-7.

engaging in what Frederic Jameson refers to as 'transcoding'.[33] I understand this term to imply the notion that the theoretical base of an interpretive procedure will itself be limiting. The limits of a particular theory may be exposed when seen through the lens of another theory that will lay open what is blurred or left out. In particular, I will argue that from the semiotic theory of Eco one can see: (1) that it is the role of the text in limiting interpretation that is excluded by Gunkel; (2) that it is the active role of the reader in interpretation that is excluded from the rhetorical critical approach of Muilenburg. The semiotic theory of Eco also helps me to understand that, in my earlier work on Fishian reader response theory, I failed to see the inadequacy of Fish's theory to accommodate the role of the text in limiting interpretation. Both the reader and the text played a role in my interpretive practice.

I want to argue that semiotics, as it has come to expression as a theory of reading texts, provides a way of revitalizing the form criticism of Gunkel while at the same time providing the opportunity to go beyond form criticism in Muilenburg's sense to focus on the unique literary features of a text. A semiotics of reading will offer a way forward to reassess the issues of reading and the limits of interpretation evident in my own approach as a reader response critic.[34]

Umberto Eco, especially in his *The Role of the Reader* and in his *The Limits of Interpretation*, offers important insights to biblical scholars involved in negotiating strategies for reading prophetic books. Essential to any semiotic theory of communication are (1) the Sender, (2) the Message and (3) the Addressee. According to Eco,[35] however, the communication between the Sender and the Addressee is rather more complicated than the usual model proposed by information theorists in which *a Sender* codes *a Message* which is in turn decoded by *an Addressee* on the basis of a common Code shared by both the Sender and the Addressee.

In *The Role of the Reader*, Eco outlines in diagrammatic form the theory of semiotics presented in his earlier (1976) work, *A Theory of Semiotics*:[36]

33. Frederic Jameson, 'Introductory Note', in *idem*, *The Ideologies of Theory, Essays 1971–86*. II. *Syntax of History* (THL, 49; 2 vols.; Minneapolis: University of Minnesota Press, 1988), pp. viii-ix. His notion of transcoding grows out of his earlier notion of 'metacommentary'.

34. For a brief discussion of how semiotics is related to reader response criticism and how if offers a possible sequel to form criticism see Stibb, 'Semiotics', pp. 618-20.

35. Eco, *The Role of the Reader*, p. 5.

36. Umberto Eco, *A Theory of Semiotics* (Bloomington: Indiana University Press, 1976).

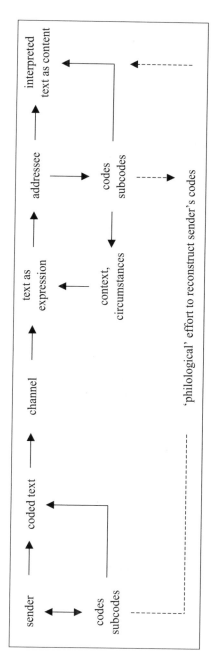

Figure 1. *Eco's Model of Communication*
(Eco, The Role of the Reader, *p. 5)*

I want to look at the following implications of this diagrammatic theory of semiotics for reading prophetic books. First, a prophetic book, according to this diagram, is a 'channel' encoded by the sender with a series of codes and subcodes (including subtexts). As a channel it is a coded text, but without an addressee (a reader), it is an 'empty form to which various senses can be attributed'.[37] It is simply ink and paper, a material object. Second, to come to expression the channel requires a reader who plays an active role in producing a text by bringing the material object to expression. The addressee (the reader) does this by employing a series of codes and subcodes, which emerge out of the addressee's 'context and circumstances' and these codes and subcodes are in turn used by the addressee to interpret the text. Third, for communication to be successful, the addressee must attempt to reconstruct the sender's codes.[38] Fourth, herein lies the problem for all texts and especially for the biblical text, which is an alien text from the past. The 'socio-cultural circumstances' surrounding the production of the text are different from those of the contemporary reader and the 'presuppositions and abductions'[39] of the addressee will inevitably lead in a different direction from that of the sender. The questions raised for reading prophetic books are: Can a prophetic book communicate at all from the past, or is it totally dependent on the response of the reader? Can a contemporary reader (addressee) read a prophetic book sharing codes its sender encoded in the text?

Both Gunkel and Muilenburg were interested in reading biblical texts in such a way as to limit meaning to what was originally intended. It is not difficult to see how *Gattungen* for Gunkel and the rhetorical features of the written text for Muilenburg can be understood as signs for a reader to utilize in order to decode biblical texts. As readers, were they employing codes drawn from their own 'presuppositions and abductions'? Did their codes share anything in common with the sender's codes? Do the *Gattungen* and rhetorical features of the text relate to the codes employed by the sender?

To gain a perspective on these questions I want to look more closely at Eco's notions of the Sender, the Message (Text) and the Reader. According to Eco, for communication to take place the reader does not decode the

---

37. Eco, *The Role of the Reader*, p. 5.

38. Reconstruction of the sender's codes should not be confused with reconstructing the author's intention. See Eco, *The Limits of Interpretation*, pp. 50-51.

39. Eco, *The Role of the Reader*, p. 5.

text in such a way as to arrive at original authorial intention.[40] The absence of the author in a written text means that the author's intentions are not available for interpretation. What are available are the codes a sender uses in sending a message, writing a text. Eco says,

> To organize a text, its author has to rely upon a series of codes that assign given contents to the expressions he uses. To make this text communicative, the author has to assume that the ensemble of codes he relies upon is the same as that shared by his possible reader. The author has thus to foresee a model of the possible reader (hereafter Model Reader) supposedly able to deal interpretatively with the expressions in the same way as the author deals generatively with them.[41]

What Eco is saying about the author here appears to be similar to the way Muilenburg conceived of the reader as one who should '*think the thoughts of the biblical writer after him*'.[42] For Eco, however, the Model Reader is not a real reader but exists in the mind of the author. What is accessible for the real reader is an encoded text, which is limited by codes employed by the sender (author) for the envisaged Model Reader. And herein lies the problem: 'In the process of communication, a text is frequently interpreted against the background of codes different from those intended by the author'.[43] This situation is precisely the case with prophetic texts whose envisaged Model Reader is imagined against a different social context than that of a contemporary reader of a prophetic text. Such texts according to Eco 'obsessively aim at arousing a precise response on the part of more or less precise empirical readers...and are in fact open to a possible "aberrant" decoding. A text so immoderately "open" to every possible interpretation will be called a *closed* one.'[44]

As closed texts, prophetic books are open, and have been open, to a seemingly infinite number of ways of decoding them. This notion of the

---

40. Eco, *The Limits of Interpretation*, p. 41.

41. Eco, *The Role of the Reader*, p. 7.

42. Muilenburg, 'Form Criticism and Beyond', p. 7.

43. Eco, *The Role of the Reader*, p. 8. And it is for this reason that Eco would say meaning is indeterminate since what an absent author intended is no longer available to a reader. What is accessible is only the encoded text.

44. Eco, *The Role of the Reader*, p. 8 (emphasis in original). Some contemporary texts are written in such a way as to 'support multiple interpretations' (Eco, *The Limits of Interpretation*, p. 40). He refers to these texts as 'open texts'. He says, 'An open text, however "open" it be, cannot afford whatever interpretation. An open text outlines a "closed" project of its Model Reader as a component of its structural strategy.'

'closed text' raises questions for Muilenburg's interpretive agenda about reading biblical texts. While Muilenburg wanted to read according to the conventions of the original readers, is it possible for him to accomplish that aim? Is he, as a modern reader, bringing the biblical text to expression by using alien codes? The questions I am posing here are similar to the issues addressed by Eco in his *The Limits of Interpretation*. Is interpretation unlimited and totally dependent on the interpreter (the addressee)? What role (if any) does the text play in interpretation? Can we read so as to employ codes employed by the sender in a 'closed text' such as the Bible?

In *The Limits of Interpretation*, Eco does not argue that meaning is either singular or determinate, but he does want to maintain that the text provides limits of interpretation. The way Eco speaks about the limits of interpretation provides a way to recast Muilenburg's 1968 programmatic essay, 'Form Criticism and Beyond', in a new way and to offer a clearer theoretical base for my own reading of prophetic books. As a reader, Muilenburg wants 'to think the thoughts of the biblical writer after him'.[45] In the light of Eco's semiotic theory, it is possible to interpret those words of Muilenburg in a new way. One can understand that Muilenburg was approaching the biblical text as an addressee wanting to read the text in such a way as to enable it to communicate from the past. As a reader, Muilenburg can be seen as utilizing codes (not only *Gattungen* but also the larger rhetorical features of the text in which the *Gattungen* appear) to read a text. 'To think the thoughts of the biblical writer after him' at first sounds problematic in an interpretive milieu in which author intention is highly suspect. But it is not too difficult to hear these words in a new way in light of Eco's notion of the Model Reader. While the Model Reader existed only in the mind of the author, the real reader can use the Model Reader heuristically as a strategy of reading. As a real reader one can attempt to reconstruct a Model Author, not the real author,[46] and the codes utilized in producing a text for a Model Reader.

The Model Reader plays a central role in Eco's discussion of the limits of interpretation and here again his theoretical discussion can provide insights into Muilenburg's agenda to move beyond form criticism to focus on the larger rhetorical units in which a *Gattung* is employed. By creating a text for a Model Reader, according to Eco, the sender (author) has created a textual world.[47] In that textual world codes are contextually

45. Muilenburg, 'Form Criticism and Beyond', p. 7.
46. Eco, *The Limits of Interpretation*, pp. 58-59.
47. Eco, *The Limits of Interpretation*, p. 23.

based. This production of the text for the Model Reader is what Eco refers to as 'the intention of the work' (*intentio operis*).[48] The 'intention of the work' is not to be confused with 'the intention of the author' (*intentio auctoris*), which is not available to the reader. What is available is a text encoded for the Model Reader, and it is the way the text works as a text that Eco identifies with 'the intention of the work'. As readers of these old texts we cannot get inside the head of the absent sender (author) to discover what the author might have had 'in mind'. As readers, however, we can get inside the text, which we bring to life as a message when we begin to read.

In calling attention away from the generalized and typical use of a *Gattung* in its oral setting to concentrate on the unique and particular way a *Gattung* functions in a larger rhetorical setting, Muilenburg is also challenging his readers to focus on what Eco refers to as the *intentio operis*. Muilenburg wants the reader to forego excursions into the oral world behind the text and focus on the rhetorical features of the text as written literature—to read and interpret the text in its particularity rather than to use the text to reconstruct the typical.

Because Eco wants to argue that the *intentio operis* limits interpretation, he makes a distinction between the *use* of a text and the *interpretation* of a text. Eco's argument is with radical reader response critics (such as Richard Rorty, and one could include Stanley Fish here)[49] who take a pragmatic approach in understanding a text's meaning. For such critics a text's meaning is dependent entirely on the intention of the reader (*intentio lectoris*).[50]

According to Eco, a pragmatic reading such as that of Rorty or Fish is 'to use a text...in order to get something else...'[51] He understands that radical reader response critics use the text in this way because they maintain that there are no limits to interpretation. When they 'use' a text, they beat it into a shape to serve their own purposes.[52] One could also argue that a form critic such as Gunkel was also using the text 'to get something

---

48. Eco, *The Limits of Interpretation*, p. 50.

49. For a taste of this debate see Umberto Eco, *Interpretation and Overinterpretation* (ed. S. Collini; Cambridge: Cambridge University Press, 1992). The exchange in this volume is with Richard Rorty, whose essay, 'The Pragmatist's Progress', appears on pp. 89-108. Eco's response is on pp. 139-51.

50. Eco, *The Limits of Interpretation*, p. 50.

51. Eco, *The Limits of Interpretation*, p. 57.

52. Eco, *The Limits of Interpretation*, p. 56.

else'. He was using the text to reconstruct oral settings outside the text (*Sitze im Leben* or institutional background). Indeed, one could argue that the historical-critical enterprise from source analysis to redaction criticism uses the text in this way. The text has been beaten into a variety of shapes for a variety of uses. Historical critics do not read or interpret a biblical text, but use it 'to get something else': underlying sources, *Sitz im Leben*, redactional intention, or a history of tradition. The text is used and left behind in search of something other than the *intentio operis*. Seen from this pragmatic perspective, historical critics ironically can be seen as radical reader response critics.

'To interpret a text', according to Eco 'is to read it in order to discover, along with our reactions to it, something about its nature'.[53] This way of speaking about interpretation is similar to Muilenburg's challenge to biblical scholars to take up the rhetorical-critical enterprise. For both Eco and Muilenburg, the interpretation of a text is limited by 'the intention of the work'. However, Eco would see that interpretations of the text will be more pluralistic and indeterminate than interpretation envisaged by Muilenburg. Perhaps this difference is due to the fact that Muilenburg was writing at a time in biblical studies when the active role of the reader in constructing meaning was not recognized.

For Eco, then, the meaning of a text is limited by the *intentio operis*. But how does one *interpret* a text? To answer this question Eco distinguishes between a *semiosic* (or *semantic*) interpretation and a *semiotic* (or critical) interpretation. At the semantic level of interpretation the reader is 'guided by the verbal strategy' of the text. To interpret texts at this level is seldom problematic and is a task undertaken by all who read. However, at the semiotic or critical level the interpretation takes place on the basis of an 'interpretive decision'. There is 'nothing in the text appearing as an explicit appeal to a second level reading'.[54] At this semiotic level of interpretation the *intentio operis* can only be discovered by a decision of the reader:

> The text's intention is not displayed by the textual surface... One has to decide to 'see' it. Thus it is possible to speak of the text's intention only as the result of a conjecture on the part of the reader. The initiative of the reader basically consists in making a conjecture about the text's intention.[55]

53. Eco, *The Limits of Interpretation*, p. 57
54. Eco, *The Limits of Interpretation*, p. 55.
55. Eco, *Interpretation and Overinterpretation*, p. 63.

But how is the reader to validate the conjecture about textual intention? Eco answers this question by saying,

> The only way is to check it upon the text as a coherent whole. This idea, too, is an old one and comes from Augustine (*De doctrina christiana*): any interpretation given of a certain portion of a text can be accepted if it is confirmed by, and must be rejected if it is challenged by, another portion of the same text. In this sense the internal textual coherence controls the otherwise uncontrollable drives of the reader.[56]

In applying this notion of internal coherence to prophetic books, I understand that internal coherence will be seen differently by different readers—an indeterminate internal coherence. It is then a control on the reader, but not a characteristic of the text in any absolute sense. An assumption of internal coherence restrains the reader, but it is not the 'nature' of the text in a real sense. It is a 'model' internal coherence, not a real internal coherence.

At this semiotic level of interpretation, however, Eco is doing something quite different from what Muilenburg envisioned in 'Form Criticism and Beyond'. Muilenburg, working in biblical studies at the end of the 1960s, did not have the opportunity to contemplate the active role of the reader in interpretation. While Muilenburg was, in a sense, looking for the *intentio operis*, the way he and his followers in rhetorical criticism understood this intention differed from Eco's later understanding. For Muilenburg this intention lay embedded in the text in ways consistent with the New Critical Theory and did not require the active role of the reader in decoding the text at this semiotic level. As a result, the meaning of a text was understood to be more singular and more determinate.

3. *Prophetic Books and the Model Reader*

Gunkel's challenge for readers to recognize community convention in the identification of *Gattungen* parallels in some sense the semiotic understanding of the role of codes and subcodes in communication. However, Gunkel called on readers to concentrate on the *Gattungen* themselves, building up what one might call an encyclopedic knowledge of a culture's codes and subcodes.[57] As a consequence, Gunkel implored contemporary readers to move away from the prophetic book and not to attempt to read

---

56. Eco, *Interpretation and Overinterpretation*, p. 65.
57. Eco, *The Role of the Reader*, p. 19.

it. His agenda, therefore, is not able to accommodate the notions of Eco's Model Reader. For Gunkel, prophetic books were not understood as texts designed to communicate 'a message'. Rather, they were collections of messages that had to be re-contextualized in a preliterary oral setting to communicate.

Muilenburg's agenda, on the other hand, can be understood as a call for readers to use the encyclopedic knowledge built up in the recognition of *Gattungen* precisely for the purpose of reading—'to read the thoughts of the writer after him'. Seen through the lens of semiotic theory, Muilenburg's agenda can be understood as a challenge for readers to concentrate on the way *Gattungen* have been employed by the author in constructing a specific text for a Model Reader. For a real reader (an addressee) of a prophetic book to focus on the Model Author as Eco has delineated that notion in his theory of semiotics, provides a way to move beyond form criticism in Muilenburg's sense. Yet to understand the Model Author as something an actual reader must construct by himself or herself,[58] recognizes that the role of the reader in interpretation is more active than Muilenburg envisaged.

Of course, to use a term such as 'the Model Author' in reading prophetic books is not unproblematic. These books themselves have long been understood to be a more or less random collection with a long redactional history. This is why the historical-critical study of these books began with a source-critical search to identify the authentic words of the prophets, which were to be separated from the inauthentic additions of redactors. Form criticism is an extension of that search by attempting to locate the prophet's words in an original oral setting.

My criticism of this historical-critical endeavor concerns my skepticism, which I will discuss in the next chapter, about using the biblical text as a source for reconstructing the actual history of ancient Israel, including the history of its literature, as it actually was—or for reconstructing the specific prophetic characters in the text as they actually were. In some ways, my own approach in reading prophetic books in their present form reflects developments within historical criticism itself. In recent years the role of the redactor has changed significantly.[59] The redactor has come to be understood not as a scribe who mechanically assembles a prophetic book into a random collection, but as an author involved in creating a prophetic

---

58. A reader does this by envisaging a Model Author.

59. See my *Reading Isaiah*, pp. 12-27.

book seen to be carefully shaped and organized into a 'unified' whole that can be understood in its final form.[60]

My concerns about redaction criticism are associated with what John Barton has called the 'trick of the disappearing redactor'.[61] The trick is that the more successful the redaction critic is in demonstrating that the redactor has created a text as a structured and unified whole, the more he or she undermines the necessity and ability to identify the underlying sources utilized by the redactor. If the redaction critic becomes too successful in elucidating the book as a whole, he or she performs the trick of making the redactor disappear as a necessary explanation for textual wholeness.

In light of the way I understand my reading of prophetic books to be illuminated by Eco's theory of semiotics, my argument with the traditional historical-critical approach to texts can be put in a different way. When historical-critical scholars concentrate on the history and development of the text, they are not reading the text or interpreting it. They are using the text 'to get something else from it'. They beat the text into shape to use it for their own agenda. They are not reading the text in order to understand the *intentio operis*. Indeed, by constructing underlying sources, oral settings, redactional stages and a history of tradition, they are engaged in creating new texts. In a sense, they are 'authoring' new texts to which they assign all sorts of intentions. These intentions are attributed to a reconstructed author's intention: a prophet, a redactor, and so on. Such a use of the text guarantees that a text cannot communicate from the past. Rather than focusing heuristically on the Model Author as providing a limit to interpretation, historical-critical scholars are real readers, constructing new texts to which intentions are credited, and these intentions surely can have nothing to do with the *intentio operis*.

From the perspective of communication theory, it is possible to see that when historical-critical scholars attempt to understand a biblical text from the past, they attempt to get behind the *message* by returning to the world of the *sender* in order to reconstruct the production of the *message*. However, they cannot return to the past from which the message originated; the

---

60. See, e.g., Roland E. Clements, 'The Unity of the Book of Isaiah', *Int* 36 (1982), pp. 117-29; Marvin A. Sweeney, *Isaiah 1–4 and the Post-Exilic Understanding of the Islamic Tradition* (BZAW, 171; Berlin: W. de Gruyter, 1988).

61. John Barton, *Reading the Old Testament: Method in Biblical Study* (London: Darton, Longman & Todd, 1984), pp. 56-58.

message has come to them.[62] For an *addressee*, the requirement is to focus on 'the intention of the work' which the *sender* encoded for the Model Reader—not the impossible act of recreating the text's production.

For me to speak about the Model Author of a prophetic book from the point of view of an addressee is itself not without its problems. Prophetic books were not authored in the same way that books are normally authored in contemporary times. They are scribal productions.[63] It is for this reason that I observed in *Zechariah* that prophetic books are like a collage:

> I would agree with redaction critics such as Terence Collins that the composition of prophetic books 'had much in common with the modern art form of collage, in which the juxtaposition of varied, even dissimilar items, is cultivated as a matter of style'. However, I will adopt a strategy for interpreting this literary collage that differs from that of redaction criticism, which has focused on diachronic history. My aim will be to understand the book of the Twelve in much the same way that one approaches a collage as a work of art in its own right apart from tracing its sources or its development. Just as a contemporary collage requires the observer to configure the parts, so a literary collage, such as the book of the Twelve, necessitates the participation of the viewer/reader in its reception.[64]

However, I do not understand a prophetic book to be a collage designed with little or no concern for an audience, or what Eco would call the Model Reader.

62. The historical-critical aim to return to the past was once illustrated graphically to me by a professor, who drew dramatically parallel lines on the blackboard and said, 'That's a river. Our task is to cross the river of time into the past in order to discover what the Bible meant. It is only when we understand what it meant that we can again cross the river and say what it means.' This river analogy illustrates the problem. We can cross no river. The text, however, has made the crossing as a communication from the past.

63. See John Barton, 'Reading the Bible as Literature: Two Questions for Biblical Critics', *Literature and Theology* 1 (1987), pp. 135-53. Barton suggests that biblical texts were scribal productions for community performance.

64. Conrad, *Zechariah*, pp. 16-17. I am here quoting Terence Collins, *The Mantle of Elijah: The Redaction Criticism of the Prophetical Books* (The Biblical Seminar, 20; Sheffield: JSOT Press, 1993), p. 29. Collins understands the origin of prophetic books to be a 'three tiered process'. He says, 'The word "redactor" will be used to refer to those who were responsible for the earlier stages of collection and organisation in the "pre-book phrase"; the term "writers" will refer to those who used this redacted material to compose the prophetical books; the term "editors" will refer to those responsible for the subsequent revisions of those books' (p. 32).

Because prophetic books are closed texts, my reading will always be open to almost inevitable aberrant decoding. I will be in no position to make absolute claims about my reading and in that way the meaning I ascribe to prophetic books will be indeterminate. However, by reading a prophetic book understood to be coded by its author/scribe (sender) for a Model Reader, I am engaging in a reading practice that recognizes the limits of interpretation associated with the intention of the text.

4. *Prophetic Books and the Sender's Codes*

I do not have the skill of a semiotician to trace the 'hierarchy of operations performed to interpret a text' as diagrammed by Eco in his *The Role of the Reader*.[65] However, I want to reflect on how features of prophetic books operate as codes and subcodes in my reading of those books. Undoubtedly, I miss many of the operations I bring to a prophetic book when I read it. Yet, to read a prophetic book in light of what Eco calls the Model Reader has made me more reflective about what I do in decoding it.

In analyzing the operations involved in the way the reader employs codes, Eco speaks about the way the reader brings what he calls 'encyclopedic knowledge' to the text for decoding it at both a semantic and semiotic level. This knowledge is often gained by the reader's experience of other texts, which Eco refers to as 'intertextual knowledge'.[66] Since the biblical text is a textual product from a culture alien to our own, however, our dictionary and encyclopedic knowledge may open prophetic books to aberrant decoding. If we are to read prophetic books with the aim of focusing on the Model Reader, we need consciously to read them intertextually to develop our intertextual knowledge of this ancient Hebrew literature at both the semantic and semiotic level.

Although Gunkel was advocating the necessity of focusing on the oral world behind the text rather than on reading, he was advocating the development of a kind of intertextual knowledge. It is precisely, however, at this level of intertextual knowledge that Muilenburg's challenge to go beyond form criticism needs to be heard. A reader of a prophetic book should not employ this intertextual knowledge to reduce everything to the generic—a kind of compacted encyclopedic article or dictionary entry. Rather, intertextual knowledge should alert a reader to the specific way in which a prophetic book has been encoded for the Model Reader.

65. Eco, *The Role of the Reader*, pp. 12-13. The diagram appears above, on p. 17.
66. Eco, *The Role of the Reader*, p. 21.

In the chapters that follow in this book, I want to focus on the way intertextual knowledge helps the reader who aims to focus on the Model Reader of a prophetic book. However, I offer the following as a way of illustrating how intertextual knowledge can aid a reader in identifying textual codes for the Model Reader of a particular prophetic book. Readers of prophetic books know that common to this genre is what biblical scholars have called the 'superscription'. These superscriptions situate a prophet in the past tense formulations and may make specific reference to events and figures.

The reader of a prophetic book with the 'intertextual knowledge' of that book as a genre encounters a superscription as a code for the model reader. However, the superscription should not be dismissed simply as if the specific formulation of that superscription has little or no significance. When reading Isa. 1.1, one encounters not just a generic superscription of a prophetic book but a very specific formulation of a superscription.

> The vision (חֲזוֹן) of Isaiah, the son of Amoz, which he saw (חָזָה) concerning Judah and Jerusalem in the days of Uzziah, Jotham, Ahaz, (and) Hezekiah, kings of Judah.

The specific formulation of this superscription incorporates codes for the Model Reader that stand out in light of the reader's 'intertextual knowledge' of other superscriptions. This superscription concerns 'the vision (חֲזוֹן) of Isaiah'. What does that encode for the reader of this book? What does it signal to the reader that is different, for example, from the superscription of Jeremiah, which begins not with 'the vision' (חֲזוֹן) but with 'the words of (דִּבְרֵי) Jeremiah'? Or, what does the formulation of past time in the superscription of Isaiah—'in the days of Uzziah, Jotham, Ahaz, (and) Hezekiah, kings of Judah'—encode for the reader compared to other superscriptions offering much more specific dates, for example, the superscription to Ezekiel: 'On the fifth of the month (it was the fifth year of the exile of Jehoiachin) the word of Yahweh came to Ezekiel...' (Ezek. 1.2)? These few comments on the superscription of prophetic books highlight how the particular formulation of superscriptions utilizes very specific codes for the Model Reader. I want to explore these in more detail later in the book.

'Intertextual knowledge' has informed my reading of prophetic books at a number of levels. In *Reading Isaiah*, I made an interpretive conjecture about how the book of Isaiah might be configured and read as a whole. I maintained that Isaiah's vision associated with the first part of the prophetic scroll was depicted as having been written down in a period of

Assyrian ascendancy, when there were kings in Judah, to be read out at a later time of emerging Persian hegemony, depicted at the end of the scroll.[67] This way of framing Isaiah as a prophetic scroll informed my understanding of a similar configuration for the scroll of the twelve Minor Prophets. In this scroll the words of the first nine prophetic figures from Hosea to Zephaniah at the beginning of the scroll can be understood as having been written down at a similar period of Assyrian ascendancy, when there were kings in Judah, to be read out at a later time of Persian hegemony, depicted at the end of the scroll.[68]

Other conventions begin to appear when the 'knowledge' from reading one text is brought to the other. For example, in both the scroll of Isaiah and the scroll of the Twelve, prophets disappear from the text in Persian times and new figures such as 'messengers' (מלאכים) appear. Furthermore, in both texts these messengers are associated with the building of the foundations of the temple.[69]

To conclude these remarks about Eco's theory of semiotics, with its notion of the Model Reader, it may be useful to emphasize the differences between prophetic books and much of the other literature to which Eco appealed in the formulation of his theory. First, I do not consider that prophetic books were authored in the contemporary sense of that term but that they are scribal compilations. However, this does not suggest that they were random collections of material. We are in debt to the significant work on redaction criticism that has helped us see a kind of organizational unity in the construction of these texts. My disagreement with redaction criticism has to do with the kind of diachronic history redaction critics want to develop on the basis of the prophetic text alone. I do not believe that the recognition of this organizational unity can give us insight into the intention of redactors viewed as authors. Rather, I see this organizational unity as the result of a text compiled for a Model Reader—with what Eco calls the 'intention of the text'.

5. *Conclusion*

In this chapter I have outlined my approach to reading prophetic books as primarily a matter of reception. If prophetic books are to communicate

---

67. Conrad, *Reading Isaiah*, pp. 130-43.

68. See my 'The End of Prophecy and the Appearance of Angels in the Book of the Twelve', *JSOT* 73 (1997), pp. 65-79, and *Zechariah*, p. 30.

69. See my 'Messengers in Isaiah and the Twelve: Implications for Reading Prophetic Books', *JSOT* 91 (2000), pp. 83-97.

as texts from the past to contemporary readers, semiotic theory such as that proposed by Umberto Eco will provide us with strategies for reading that focus heuristically on the Model Author. While we have no access to the real authors of prophetic books, we can imagine a Model Author who composed a text to communicate to readers.

To shift attention to text reception is a major move from the traditional historical-critical approach, which promoted interpretive techniques, source analysis, form criticism and redaction history, designed to uncover issues associated with the inception of the text. Biblical studies have been concerned with actual authors and their intentions, actual historical context and the actual growth and development of the biblical books themselves. In short, historical criticism has been interested in history. To shift the focus from the inception to the reception of the text, however, does not mean that I am not interested in history. It does mean, however, a different understanding of history and the way texts such as prophetic books represent the past. I want to turn to that issue in the next chapter before I begin my reading of prophetic books.

Chapter 2

Texts and History

An element of the inexplicable is in fact present in all human history and is bound to be present not merely because it is not even remotely possible to embrace the whole profusion of cause and effect even in the historical present, let alone in the past, and least of all the remote past, but above all because history is not merely a constant repetition of complicated concatenations of cause and effect if God is really active in history…as the ever present Yahweh working within the superficial interplay of cause and effect. Inevitably, therefore, there is an element of mystery, of the 'unhistorical', in all human history which makes its presence felt on the frontiers of all historical knowledge.[1]

Many scholars still write so-called histories of ancient Israel as if nothing has happened, apparently unaware of the fact that there has been a veritable upheaval in the theoretical discussion about the nature of history and the possibilities of history writing in general.[2]

Before beginning my reading of prophetic books, I want to outline my position about the current debate raging in biblical studies among those who contest the use of biblical texts in writing a history of Israel. The position one takes on this matter is important for reading prophetic books. The way one understands how a prophetic book may or may not be utilized as data for the history of Israel, including its prophetic past, has implications for the way one reads the text. Those who hold what is called a 'maximalist' position argue that one can construct a history of Israel by using the biblical text as data providing historical information about ancient Israel. Those who hold a 'minimalist' position maintain that the texts of the Bible are themselves a construction, and that one must remain

1. Martin Noth, *The History of Israel* (trans. P.R. Ackroyd; London: A. & C. Black, 2nd edn, 1960), pp. 1-2.

2. Hans M. Barstad, 'History and the Hebrew Bible', in Lester L. Grabbe (ed.), *Can a 'History of Israel' Be Written?* (JSOTSup, 245; European Seminar in Historical Methodology, 1; Sheffield: Sheffield Academic Press, 1997), pp. 37-64 (46).

skeptical about the use of the Bible in writing history from what they understand to be fictional narrative.

In this study I will side with those who take a minimalist position regarding the history of ancient Israel. In this sense I am moving in a different theoretical direction and am working with a different ideological perspective than those engaged in traditional historical-critical studies. It will be helpful if I point out these differences in theory and ideology.

1. *Fitting the Bible into the Outside World*

Historical-critical inquiry did not emerge in a 'theory free zone' but reflected the theory current in the time and place of its origin. According to Hans W. Frei in his book *Eclipse of Biblical Narrative*, 'Western Christian reading of the Bible in the days before the rise of historical criticism in the eighteenth century was usually strongly realistic, i.e., at once literal and historical, and not only doctrinal and edifying'.[3] These interpreters 'had envisioned the real world as formed by the sequence told by the biblical stories' that 'covered the span of ages from creation to the final consummation to come'.[4] As a result, biblical interpretation had as its task the imperative need to incorporate 'extra-biblical thought, experience, and reality into *the one real world* detailed and made accessible by the biblical story'.[5] With the rise of historical criticism in the eighteenth century, biblical interpreters found themselves in an age that had discovered 'the specific and irreducibly historical particularity of cultural change'.[6] In such a changed situation 'the frame of reference moved from the world inside the Bible to a world outside, and the project became one of fitting the Bible to those external data'.[7]

This need to accommodate the story of the Bible to events outside it was a challenge to the Bible's authority to narrate the one real world. Although it caused divisions within the theological community by seeking to fit the

---

3.   Hans W. Frei, *The Eclipse of the Biblical Narrative: A Study in Eighteenth and Nineteenth Century Hermeneutics* (New Haven: Yale University Press, 1974), p. 1.

4.   Frei, *The Eclipse of the Biblical Narrative*, p. 1. All other ways of reading the Bible (e.g. spiritual or allegorical) had to be done so as not 'to offend against a literal reading'.

5.   Frei, *The Eclipse of the Biblical Narrative*, p. 3 (my emphasis).

6.   Frei, *The Eclipse of the Biblical Narrative*, p. 213.

7.   Quoting Regina M. Schwartz, 'Introduction: On Biblical Criticism', in *idem* (ed.), *The Book and the Text: The Bible and Literary Theory* (Oxford: Basil Blackwell, 1990), p. 11. She summarizes Frei's point in a succinct manner.

meaning of the Bible in a world of data external to it, historical criticism gradually became accepted as a normative way of interpreting the Bible in mainstream theological seminaries and departments of Divinity. The authority of the Bible was reinscribed so that the historical-critical approach itself became normative. Regina Schwartz makes this point when she says,

> In the eighteenth and nineteenth centuries, the impression of 'foreign methods' meant that the Bible was asked to answer, for the first time, to the historical-critical examination that any other text from antiquity would. 'All that happened', in other words, is that the unchallenged authority of the Bible was challenged—powerfully and systematically. My own sense is that in the course of the critical-historical Bible scholarship that ensued, that authority was reinscribed, albeit in a disguised fashion. Whether the approach was historical or philological, the Bible was the focus of sustained, loving attention. Efforts to determine the cultic setting of psalms, to date the book of Daniel, to attribute various verses to the various hands and to correlate those hypothetical authors with events in ancient history, did not so much pose a challenge to the Bible's authority as they presupposed that authority, for only a commitment to the centrality of the Bible could authorize that exhaustive activity. Nonetheless, that authorizing motive was closeted, all the more so because scientific inquiry into the Bible became a discipline set apart—apart from questions of faith, of theology, of biblical authority, and in this way the historical approaches were unable to touch—or injure—them.[8]

The reason that historical criticism was able to be taken up and practiced so successfully and normatively in theological communities, lay squarely with the critical theory about history that informed it in the nineteenth century and continued to accompany its practice in the twentieth. I am referring here to nineteenth-century German historiography.

The central role that this theory of historiography has played in the practice of historical criticism has been argued convincingly by Robert A. Oden in his book with the somewhat provocative title, *The Bible Without Theology*.[9] I would not want to claim with Oden, however, that historical critics are somewhat peculiar in that they bring an ideology with their interpretive practice. I simply want to point out that this ideology does not

---

8. Schwartz, 'Introduction', p. 13.

9. Robert A. Oden, *The Bible Without Theology: The Theological Tradition and Alternatives to It* (San Francisco: Harper & Row, 1987). See also Schwartz ('Introduction') who also argues that 'the so-called higher criticism of the Bible...came of age in the context of nineteenth-century German historiography, sharing its assumptions, its methods, its goals' (p. 9).

sit well with the interpretive practices within a department of religion, which is the community in which my research is carried out.[10]

The attraction that historical criticism had for me, as a theological student, was its appeal 'to let the text speak for itself'. Interpretation was to be objective and free of dogmatic prescription. I found this way of doing things liberating. Coming from a conservative theological background, such an approach promised a way forward from the sometimes-bewildering notion that the Bible could mean anything that an interpreter wanted it to mean. But it is precisely these claims to be objective and theory-free that grows out of the German historiographic tradition; and it is those claims that I find to be problematic.

What then is the German historiographic tradition and how has that informed historical criticism? Oden sees the origin of this thinking in Herder (1744–1803) and traces its continuation in von Humboldt (1767–1835), Ranke (1795–1886) and Droysen (1808–84).[11] According to this tradition each nation is to be seen as an individual and the historian's task is to identify this unique character of the nation by tracing its development. By tracing this development some idea such as 'a world spirit', 'the hand of God' or some ethical world could be seen as manifesting itself in this progression toward the end. Because of the particularity of a nation's history there is to be no theorizing or abstract philosophical thinking. The task of the historian is an objective one. In human experience, then, according to this German idealism, one can gain insight into the ultimate nature of reality by paying close attention to the particularities of national development.[12]

---

10. I have reflected elsewhere on the consequences of my move from the theological community where I received my PhD to a university department of religion in an arts faculty. See my 'Changing Context', pp. 393-402.

11. Oden, *The Bible Without Theology*, pp. 8-15.

12. Regina Schwartz ('Introduction', p. 9) also summarizes in a succinct way this German historiographic tradition. She says, 'The so-called higher criticism of the Bible (as distinguished from lower, textual study) came of age in the context of nineteenth-century German historiography, sharing its assumptions, its methods, its goals. In "On the Task of the Historian" (1822) Wilhelm von Humbolt summarized many of the positions that would become characteristic: "every human epoch bears its own, uniquely individual character" and the historian's task is to chard the spiritual progress of this national individuality. Empiricism is not enough; the historian must work "as a poet" to capture the unique character of an epoch. Following suit, Leopold von Ranke wrote that the historian's task is "to portray what actually happened", but such empiricism is meant to uncover the transcendent design, "the hand of God" in history. Throughout,

Although this is a brief description of the main ideas associated with this historiographic tradition, it is not too difficult to see its inherent contradiction. The call for objectivity—'to let the text speak for itself'—is based on a theory about history and the nature of reality. It is also not too difficult to see the appeal of this tradition in historical criticism practiced by the theological community. Although the scholar was to accommodate the biblical text within a world outside of it, that very world when constructed by the historian was the source of transcendent reality. Yahweh was working in history. The very detailed work of historical criticism in presenting an objective view of the world of ancient Israel was based on a theory about ultimate reality which served very well its theological practitioners.

According to Oden, this German historiographical tradition waned after a revival in the 1900s, but it continued to influence biblical scholars who, from Wellhausen to Gunkel, shaped the historical-critical approach on the basis of this historiographic idealism that became characteristic of biblical scholarship during the twentieth century.[13] It is this theory of history underlying the historical-critical enterprise that I now see as problematic for biblical studies. Oden says,

> This tradition allowed biblical scholars to absolutize and particularize the religion of Israel beyond any meaningful comparison, on the ground that every culture was an organic individual, incomparable with any other individual. The tradition also granted legitimacy to vague and unverifiable claims about the subtlety and yet the certainty of divine guidance to Israel's history, on the ground that authentic historical reconstruction would always discover the workings of God's hand. Finally, the same historiographic tradition supported the regular affirmations by theologians engaged in biblical research that their work was once empirical and objective and yet capable of proving the unique superiority of biblical religion.[14]

This idealistic historiographic tradition is clearly evident in the remarks of Martin Noth at the beginning of his *The History of Israel*. In my

---

these histories presuppose a story of development. While Johann Gustav Droysen denies that he is Hegelian, in his *Principles of History* (1968) he speaks of the "supra-empirical level of spirit" and of the necessary logic of progressive moral development. When it is not spiritual, the development is moral. In other words, the story of nineteenth-century historiography is largely the story of an uneasy alliance between efforts toward a historical "science" and commitment to an idealistic historical philosophy.'

13. Oden, *The Bible Without Theology*, pp. 20-37.

14. Oden, *The Bible Without Theology*, p. 158.

days as a theological student Noth was a very influential scholar. The poetic idealism in Noth's approach to the history of Israel is evident in his comment that the history of Israel 'must me reconstructed intuitively'.[15] The transcendent 'hand of God' is seen in the following comment:

> The genuineness of that historical reality is not affected by the circumstance that in its history we also meet an element beyond the range of human understanding, an element that cannot be ascribed to known causes and effects. An element of the inexplicable is in fact present in *all* human history and is bound to be present not merely because it is not even remotely possible to embrace the whole profusion of cause and effect even in the historical present, let alone in the past, and least of all the remote past, but above all because history is not merely a constant repetition of complicated concatenations of cause and effect if God is really active in history…as the ever present Yahweh working within the superficial interplay of cause and effect. Inevitably, therefore, there is an element of mystery, of the 'unhistorical', in all human history which makes its presence felt on the frontiers of all historical knowledge.[16]

The individuality of Israel and the requirement to know it in that uniqueness free of any comparative study is evident in what he says a few paragraphs later:

> Yet in spite of all these historical connections and possibilities for comparison, 'Israel' still appears as a stranger in the world of its own time, a stranger wearing the garments and behaving in the manner of its age, yet separate from the world it lived in, not merely in the sense that every historical reality has its own individual character, and therefore an element of uniqueness, but rather that at the very centre of the history of 'Israel' we encounter phenomena for which there is no parallel at all elsewhere, not because the material for comparison has not yet come to light but because, so far as we know, such things have simply never happened elsewhere.[17]

I sight Noth extensively here as an example of the way this German historiographic tradition has pervaded historical criticism. In light of this historiographic theory underlying the practice of historical criticism, with its accompanying notion of transcendence revealed to the historian in a reconstructed history, it is not too difficult to see how historical-critical inquiry and its results came to play a normative and ideological role in biblical studies.

---

15. Noth, *The History of Israel*.
16. Noth, *The History of Israel*, pp. 1-2.
17. Noth, *The History of Israel*, pp. 2-3.

My ideological position is different from the historical-critical one outlined above. Traditional biblical studies follows what Norman K. Gottwald calls a 'triumphalist ideology' in which Israel is kept 'constantly at center stage'[18] and where Israel is 'persistently conceptualised as a religio-political unity continuous through time, placing priority on Israelite concepts and practices considered formative of Judaism and Christianity...'[19] To refer again to the arguments of Schwartz and Oden cited above, this triumphalist ideology has transposed the authority of the Bible to the investigation of the history of Israel external to the text whose very existence was evidence of 'the workings out of God's hand'.

My own ideological position is influenced by the location of my research in a department of religion and can be characterized in Gottwald's terms as 'anti-triumphalist'. I understand the Bible to be one sacred text among many and the status of Israel to be 'one people among many peoples in Palestine' and its religion one among many in he world. Ancient Israel is pre-Jewish and pre-Christian and is not understood as teleologically progressing toward a triumphalist Judaism or Christianity.[20] From my own ideological perspective, I find no reason to see God's hand actively involved in historical phenomena 'for which there is no parallel at all elsewhere', as did Martin Noth.

This ideological break with historical criticism is related to a different theoretical notion of history. I do not think that it is possible to gain insight through reconstruction into the life and times of the prophets as they actually were. Prophets such as Isaiah, Jeremiah, Ezekiel, Amos and others can only be encountered as characters in the text. How those texts relate to an actual Isaiah, Jeremiah or Ezekiel is a matter that cannot be resolved on the basis of the biblical texts in which they are mentioned. Was there an actual Isaiah? What did Isaiah actually say? When did Isaiah actually live? All of these are questions that cannot be answered simply on the basis of the biblical texts themselves. Prophetic books do not give us the kind of direct access to an external world of the prophets as historical-critical scholars have assumed. Therefore, my approach to reading prophetic books breaks with the earlier source critics whose analysis of prophetic books was a search for the *ipsissima verba* of the authentic prophet.

---

18. Norman K. Gottwald, 'Triumphalist versus Anti-Triumphalist Versions of Early Israel: A Response to Articles by Lemche and Dever in Volume 4 (1996)', *CRBS* 5 (1997), pp. 15-42 (30).
   19. Gottwald, 'Triumphalist versus Anti-Triumphalist', pp. 30-33.
   20. Gottwald, 'Triumphalist versus Anti-Triumphalist', pp. 30-34.

I do not accept that the history of Israel can be written by using the biblical texts as data for that reconstruction in the positivist way that biblical historians (e.g. Bright,[21] Noth[22] or Hayes and Miller[23] and others) have practiced it. Therefore, I also do not embrace the notion that prophetic books provide us with the data for constructing the history of the texts themselves. We have no way of determining how prophetic books came to be with the sort of precision redaction critics such as James D. Nogalski,[24] Terrence Collins[25] and others claim. Therefore, my approach differs from the more recent interest in redactors who are imagined to be actively involved in the diachronic development of books.

This disagreement with the practice of historical-critical inquiry does not mean that I have no interest in history. In my past studies I have expressed an interest in prophetic books as texts from the past. However, the way we gain access to that past is not in the direct referential way in which biblical books have been used as data. Our link with the past is with the textual world of the prophetic books themselves. The text is not a time machine providing the data to reconstruct the 'real' Israel as it actually was in the way Noth thought possible. In a similar world prophetic books cannot be used to reconstruct prophets as they actually were, nor can the history of prophetic books be reassembled as they actually came to be. What we find in prophetic books are textual constructions of whatever the real world was at the time these books were composed.

At the end of *Reading Isaiah*, I expressed my interest in prophetic books and the past:

> Contemporary historical-critical readers attempt to bridge the gulf between the past and the present by reconstructing the text and in that sense returning to the time of the text's inception. But the past is not something to which we can journey; we are locked into a fleeting present. It is no more possible to reconstruct the developmental history of the text of Isaiah and

---

21. John Bright, *A History of Israel* (Philadelphia: Westminster Press, 3rd edn, 1981).

22. Noth, *The History of Israel*.

23. John H. Hayes and J. Maxwell Miller, *A History of Ancient Israel and Judah* (Philadelphia: Westminster Press, 1986).

24. James D. Nogalski traces a rather complex development of the growth of the Book of the Twelve in a study that appeared in two volumes: *Literary Precursors to the Book of the Twelve* (BZAW, 217; Berlin: W. de Gruyter, 1993), and *Redactional Processes in the Book of the Twelve* (BZAW, 218; Berlin: W. de Gruyter, 1993).

25. Collins, *The Mantle of Elijah*.

uncover the intentions of its authors than it is to relive the construction of other stone monuments that are now part of our present.

This does not mean that we have no links with the past. The gap with the past has been bridged, but the text, not the reader, does the travelling. As past text, the Book of Isaiah is present to contemporary readers. It is precisely because the text has made the journey from the past that I have made the text the object of my study. The text, not its authors or original audience, is available to the contemporary reader for critical study. This does not mean that the text is to be contemporized and read as if it were a modern production. In this study I have endeavored to examine the text of Isaiah itself for clues about its structure and its implied audience in order to gain insight into how to read it.[26]

The position I take here against the normal historical-critical way of approaching biblical texts relates to the general crisis concerning the writing of history posed by postmodernism. Hans M. Barstad outlines this crisis clearly and succinctly in his article, 'History and the Hebrew Bible'.[27] I want to outline the main points of this article because I think it not only calls biblical scholars to take this challenge seriously but also proposes a way to move ahead. Barstad argues that biblical scholars must begin to acknowledge that theoretical developments now pose new problems about the possibility of writing history. However,

Many scholars still write so-called histories of ancient Israel as if nothing has happened, apparently unaware of the fact that there has been a veritable upheaval in the theoretical discussion about the nature of history and the possibilities of history writing in general. In short, the intellectual climate of the last thirty years or so appears not to have caught up on biblical studies at all. To say that historians of ancient Israel are theory weak is, in my view, the understatement of the century. As a genre, most of the so-called 'histories of ancient Israel' represent nothing more than various forms of a retelling of the biblical stories, diluted with sparse, desultory analytical remarks, not seldom with disparate references to 'archaeology'. In itself, there may be nothing wrong with this as long as the authors of these books know, or admit, what they are doing. The problem is that they themselves quite often give the impression that what they are doing is not to present us with their versions of the stories of the Hebrew Bible, but to the history of ancient Israel 'as it was'.[28]

---

26. Conrad, *Reading Isaiah*, pp. 154-55.
27. For details see above, n. 2.
28. Barstad, 'History and the Hebrew Bible', pp. 46-47.

Barstad identifies these theoretical developments challenging typical historical-critical procedures as stemming from postmodernism. The following is his summary of this critique of historical writing stated in its most extreme expression:

> In the most radical form the postmodernist critique has given a new meaning to the old discussion about objectivity. There can be no objectivity because there is no object 'the past' against which one can judge the different interpretations. And even if we do not have to deny altogether the existence of a given past, we must realise that we have no access to it. History writing, in other words, is impossible.[29]

Ignoring this problem, many biblical scholars still follow a positivist historical approach in which history is understood as a science. The task of the historical scholar is to establish the facts—what actually happened. These scholars follow the distinction between *history* = *fact* = *true* vs. *fiction* = *not true*. This distinction has been 'the chief mainstay of all history writing' since the rise of scientific history in Germany in the late eighteenth and early nineteenth century.[30] The bind for many biblical scholars is that their main source for writing the history of ancient Israel is the biblical narrative from which they attempt to separate out what is *history* = *fact* = *true* from what is *fiction* = *not true*. They want to find fact and fiction in a narrative for which this kind of distinction was not made by the authors of that narrative. As Barstad puts it,

> Apparently, very few biblical historians practising today appreciate that it is their very concept of history that is wrong. To the biblical authors there was no difference between the 'historicity' of, for instance, the Primeval Story and that of other stories in the Hebrew Bible. Subsequently, the process of cutting out bits and pieces of these stories in order to evaluate these as 'true' or 'not true' depending on whether they 'look like' history or not according to truth value standards of the twentieth century, is not only very unfair to the integrity of ancient texts, but also highly anachronistic. One simply cannot take out texts from an ancient culture which, incidentally, 'look like' modern texts and treat these as having a different semantic or cognitive status than other texts from the same culture which are not regarded as sufficiently 'historical' to be bothered with. This, in fact, is one of the main reasons why 'historical sources' as the basis for a reconstruction of the history of ancient Israel are now disappearing at such a fast rate that before long there will be no 'historical' texts at all.[31]

29. Barstad, 'History and the Hebrew Bible', p. 40.
30. Barstad, 'History and the Hebrew Bible', p. 42.
31. Barstad, 'History and the Hebrew Bible', p. 45.

Barstad's challenge in this article is to move away from this German historicism which makes the distinction between *history = fact = true* and *fiction = not true*. Significantly, however, Barstad does not conclude with the radical position that the writing of history is impossible. His argument is that all history writing comes much closer to what we understand as literature, and I would add, probably more strongly than Barstad, that all history writing is a kind of fiction.[32] What historians of ancient Israel must learn is not to separate out the facts from fiction in historical narrative in order to discover the real Israel, but to understand that the narrative itself can be understood as a representation of past reality. In this sense biblical narrative is more like a novel. He says,

> The fact that the Bible has come much closer to literature, however, does not necessarily make it less 'historical' or less a representation of past reality. Novels may provide us with some valuable insights here... Most novels are stories which *do* represent past reality, but of which one does not ask the question: did this really happen? How important is it that something really happened as along as it *might have* happened, and in this way convey important pieces of past reality? In many ways the relationship between narrative and reality in the Hebrew Bible is comparable to that of novels. A certain degree of objectivity may be obtained, and since these texts sometimes refer to realities outside themselves, a 'mild' form of realism is possible. It is most certainly true that readers create meaning, but this is not the whole story.[33]

As a consequence of all this

> We must also face the fact that history is not as important as it used to be. Our obsession with historicity must step down and give way to the recovery of the textual world itself. This does not imply that history has become obsolete, but that we must think about it in a totally different way. Furthermore, since we do not have access to past reality the way we thought we had, we should also reflect upon why and how we approach the past. How interesting is it, after all, to discuss, for example, the historicity of Abraham or whether Solomon built the temple? Are such questions really of any great importance at all? They are most certainly not as important as they used to be.[34]

---

32. Barstad prefers to use the term 'narrative history' for what we find in the Bible and understands 'narrative history' to be 'a mixture of history and fiction' ('History and the Hebrew Bible', p. 61).

33. Barstad, 'History and the Hebrew Bible', pp. 61-62.

34. Barstad, 'History and the Hebrew Bible', p. 61.

At the end of his article, Barstad challenges historians of ancient Israel to recognize what historical theorists and classical scholars have come to recognize, that is, that both narratives about the past and narratives from the past (re)present past reality.[35]

2. *Reading Prophetic Books: Toward a New Form Criticism*

Barstad's challenge for scholars to move away from the historical positivism that has characterized biblical studies for over a century is significant because it resonates with my previous research on reading prophetic books.[36] However, what is even more significant for my own approach to reading prophetic books concerns Barstad's proposal that scholars focus on 'the way these narratives make use of certain stereotypical genres'.[37]

He says that the Deuteronomistic History should be understood as

> a kind of history telling which does not pass down the past, but which actually *creates* the past. This, however, is not so unusual. We can say that in the Hebrew Bible we have an early example of 'national' history writing.[38]

While I do not want to discuss the merits of this proposal about the Deuteronomistic History as representing the genre of a 'national history',[39] I do want to speak about the consequence of this for historical inquiry. While the Deuteronomistic History 'does not tell us what Israel's history *really* looked like in ancient times', the use of this literary genre does not mean that we should conclude that the whole thing is fictional leading us to the conclusion that there was no ancient 'kingdom' of Israel at all:[40]

> We do not get a great many details from the story concerning 'what really happened', but how important is this? The main point here must be that

---

35. Barstad, 'History and the Hebrew Bible', pp. 62-63.

36. See my 'Prophet, Redactor and Audience: Reforming the Notion of Isaiah's Formation', in R.F. Melugin and M.A. Sweeney (eds.), *New Visions of Isaiah* (JSOTSup, 214; Sheffield: Sheffield Academic Press, 1996), pp. 306-26 (311-17).

37. Barstad, 'History and the Hebrew Bible', p. 64.

38. Barstad, 'History and the Hebrew Bible', p. 56.

39. Barstad draws here on the collection of essays edited by E. Hobsbawm and T. Ranger, *The Invention of Tradition* (repr.; Cambridge: Cambridge University Press, 1983), and J. Hutchinson, *The Dynamics of Cultural Nationalism: The Gaelic Revival and the Creation of the Irish Nation State* (London: Allen & Unwin, 1987).

40. Barstad, 'History and the Hebrew Bible', pp. 56-58.

even if the text makes use of stereotyped genres [Barstad had also discussed Solomon's temple building as representing a literary genre], it is not a purely fictional text, but also a 'historical' one. As a historical text it comes out of the past and it *reflects* historical reality. This is a kind of 'historical truth' which we may find in the texts of the Bible.[41]

Although prophetic books are mostly poetry and not primarily narrative history, I want to argue that they also need to be approached as literature. They will not tell us what life was actually like in the eighth century BCE during the time of Isaiah and his encounters with Ahaz and Hezekiah (or even if there were such encounters). However, to paraphrase Barstad, they are texts that come out of the past, and in that sense they do reflect historical reality. It is this textual world from the past that I encounter as a reader. I cannot use that textual world to talk about an actual Isaiah, an actual Jeremiah nor for that matter about an actual redactor of a prophetic book. Nor can I use these books to trace an actual diachronic history through which a prophetic book passed any more than a positivist historian can read a biblical narrative and tell us what actually happened in ancient Israel. My encounter with the past is with the way some ancient author (scribe) or group of authors (scribes) constructed prophetic worlds by producing prophetic books. It is that textual world that I can enter as a reader; I cannot enter the actual world of the prophet nor can I enter the world of ancient Israel so as to uncover the literary history of a prophetic book.

In reading prophetic books I am also interested in understanding how genre will assist me as a reader in interpreting them. I am calling for a return to form criticism and to take up the challenge of Gunkel to regain an interest in the literary character of the Bible. However, I want to see this form criticism in a new way and move in a different direction than the one discussed in the previous chapter. In this sense I want to return to my roots as a biblical scholar. But I now inhabit a different community in a different time and place, and so I want to proceed along a different path than either Gunkel or Muilenburg. This is not to critique Gunkel and Muilenburg for their shortcomings as if I stand in some superior position, but simply to recognize that I have journeyed into a new world where things look different to me than they could have appeared for those who got me started in biblical studies.

In some ways it is ironic to return to Gunkel as a mentor since Oden in his analysis of biblical studies identifies him more than anyone else as

---

41. Barstad, 'History and the Hebrew Bible', p. 60. His discussion of Solomon's temple is on pp. 58-60.

representing the promotion of the German historiographic tradition in biblical studies and the one who had the greatest impact on twentieth-century scholarship. Oden says,

> So plainly do his [Gunkel's] theoretical assumptions match those of the wider attempt to defend and reassert the basic postulates of the German tradition of historical understanding, that one can find evidence in his work for every one of these postulates. Just as Eichhorn had done in one of his public theses, Gunkel tirelessly repeated that to understand is to follow a phenomenon's providential growth. 'We have come to see', Gunkel wrote in a description of the origins of the History of Religions School, that the religion of Israel 'can be understood only when it is understood in its history, in its growth and becoming'.[42]

Gunkel was not only a product of his own time in advocating the German historiographic tradition but he was also skeptical of the historical positivism represented by the father of historical criticism, Julius Wellhausen.[43] In his criticism of historical positivism he shares a view of the world not totally unlike those of us who are experiencing what has been called 'the postmodern'. Looking back at others to identify what they could not see has the humbling experience of making one ask: How am I being myopic?

In the next chapter I want to look at the importance of order for reading prophetic books. There have been a number of different canonical constructions of prophetic books, and it is important that I consider how the arrangement of those books shapes one's reading. Order, arrangement and shape are important for understanding the limits of interpretation—what Eco calls the *intentio operis*.

42. Oden, *The Bible Without Theology*, p. 31.
43. Oden, *The Bible Without Theology*, p. 34.

Chapter 3

ORDERING PROPHETIC BOOKS

Our Rabbis taught: The order of the prophets is Joshua, Judges, Samuel, Kings, Jeremiah, Ezekiel, Isaiah and the Twelve Minor Prophets.[1]

In the semiotics of reading the reader plays a central role in bringing written marks to expression as a text. The order a reader gives a text is normally not problematic. The reader is guided by the progression of marks as they appear on the page. However, for anyone like myself who has been trained in biblical studies, reading biblical texts has been presented as a matter of establishing correct order. Or, perhaps better, it has been understood as a process of re-ordering.

1. *Historical Criticism, Canonical Criticism and Order*

As I argued in the last chapter, historical-critical scholars can be understood as pragmatic readers. They use the text to get at something else, and this treatment of the text often involves the active role of the historical-critical reader in re-shaping the progression of marks on a page into a different order, bringing not a singular text but a plurality of texts to expression. The instances of this practice are well known. Genesis 2.4b is not understood as the continuation of the creation account beginning in Gen. 1.1 but is re-ordered so as to read it as the beginning of a new text. Similarly, Isa. 40.1 is not read as a continuation of Isa. 39.8, but as the beginning of a new text. In the case of Isaiah, the creation of textual plurality has been reflected in the practice of producing separate commentaries on Isaiah for the new texts arising from re-ordering. The separate texts of First and Second Isaiah have even produced separate commentaries with different reader/commentators.

---

1. From *Baba Batra* 14b-15a. The translation is from Sid Z. Lieman, *The Canonization of Hebrew Scripture: The Talmudic and Midrashic Evidence* (New Haven: The Connecticut Academy of Arts and Sciences, 1991), pp. 52-53.

This historical-critical way of reading, as I maintained in Chapter 1, was a way of reading the Bible in theological communities. In recent times canonical criticism has emerged in the Christian community of scholars as a way of countering the historical-critical penchant for producing multiple texts by re-ordering and thereby creating textual plurality.[2] The most prominent proponent of this way of reading is Brevard Childs in his influential book, *Introduction to the Old Testament as Scripture*.[3] Childs challenged biblical scholars not to become bogged down in exploring the pre-history of Israel they thought they were exposing in re-ordering biblical books into a plurality of texts. Instead, he called on biblical scholars to read a biblical book in its final form. It is important to understand that Childs' own approach is largely dependent on historical-critical inquiry. However, his interest was in understanding the text as it reached its final form. This final form (the final ordered arrangement of the book) rather than underlying sources is important, he asserts, for establishing canonical authority. For example, he makes the following remarks about the final form of prophetic literature:

> The purpose of this essay is to suggest a different approach to the biblical material, which I shall try to illustrate in terms of the prophets. It begins with the recognition that a major literary and theological force was at work in shaping the present form of the Hebrew Bible. This force was exerted during most of the history of the literature's formation, but increasingly in the post-exilic period exercised its influence in the collecting, selecting, and ordering of the biblical traditions in such a way as to allow the material to function as authoritative Scripture for the Jewish community. In the transmission process, tradition, which once arose in a particular milieu and addressed various historical situations, was shaped in such a way as to serve as a normative expression of God's will to later generations of Israel who

2.   Lieman (*The Canonization of Hebrew Scripture*, p. 10) understands both historical criticism and canonical criticism as largely the work of Protestant scholars. He says: 'Canonical criticism began to flourish in the early 1970s, largely as a Protestant response to modern Bible criticism's failure to provide a biblical hermeneutic that would allow Scriptural insights to be applied to contemporary events. Committed at least in principle to *sola scriptura*, Protestants found that the mostly archaic historical insights of modern Bible criticism were at best interesting but neither important nor relevant. Canonical criticism was welcomed not so much as a rejection of modern Bible criticism (which itself is a largely Protestant enterprise), but rather as an approach that could move beyond it… In any event, canonical criticism tends to be theological and constructive.'

3.   Brevard S. Childs, *Introduction to the Old Testament as Scripture* (Philadelphia: Fortress Press, 1979).

had not shared in those original historical events. In sum, prophetic oracles which were directed to one generation were fashioned into Sacred Scripture by a canonical process to be used by another generation.[4]

While I am also interested, as is Childs, in reading biblical books as a whole, my reasons for doing that are literary, not theological. My interest is in the semiotics of reading. I am concerned with reading the texts as they have been encoded by a Model Author. For that reason I want to move away from speaking of the text in its final form, which is a canonical-critical expression that itself connotes the historical-critical predisposition to reconstruct the production of the text. The semiotics of reading enables interpretive issues to emerge in terms of text reception in which readers play an active role.

Childs' challenge to biblical scholars to move away from re-ordering biblical books as a plurality of texts by appealing to the canon raises the issue of canonical order. However, although Childs calls his approach to interpretation 'canonical criticism', he has tended to focus on individual books and has largely ignored the different number and order of books represented by a plurality of canons. The major criticism of Childs' approach has been his failure to recognize the plurality of canons and the way they are ordered.[5] Philip Davies makes this point when he says:

> Childs certainly makes many perceptive literary and ideological links within the books of the Old Testament, which make an interesting extension of the redaction-critical procedures of the 'historical critics'. But surely the crucial links for his procedure must be *between* the books. Most of Childs's analysis in fact operates at the level of individual books, and evidence that these were copied and recopied so as to reach a final theological shape (and this shape itself is often hard to verify!) does not explain the canon at all.[6]

The importance of canonical order is clearly recognized by many who read the Hebrew Bible. Even historical-critical scholars, who eagerly re-order

---

4. Brevard S. Childs, 'The Canonical Shape of the Biblical Literature', *Int* 32 (1978), pp. 46-55 (47). This quote, with its reference to a 'theological force' at work in shaping the literature, suggests that Childs' approach also represents the influence of the German historiographic tradition on his canonical criticism.

5. For an important critique of Child's canonical approach see Mark G. Brett, *Biblical Criticism in Crisis? The Impact of the Canonical Approach on Old Testament Studies* (Cambridge: Cambridge University Press, 1991).

6. Philip R. Davies, *Scribes and Schools: The Canonization of the Hebrew Scriptures* (Library of Ancient Israel; Louisville, KY: Westminster/John Knox Press, 1998), p. 52.

Genesis, do not argue for changing the order of the Pentateuch so as to read Exodus before Genesis. No one argues that Judges should be read before Joshua or that Kings should be read before Samuel. Canonical ordering of books seems to be significant for the Torah (Pentateuch) and what we call the Former Prophets. This ordering becomes consequential even for historical-critical scholars who often advocate the necessity of reading these books in order. Increasingly, scholars advocate the reading of Genesis through to 2 Kings as an ordered whole—sometimes referred to as the 'Primary History'.[7] More significantly, however, since the work of Martin Noth, it has become almost commonplace among historical-critical scholars to read Deuteronomy through to 2 Kings as a single historio-graphic work called the 'Deuteronomistic History'. This history was even understood by Noth to have been 'authored' by a lone individual living in exile.[8] Introductory classes on the Hebrew Bible/Old Testament routinely point out in discussions of the Deuteronomistic History that Ruth does not come after Kings in the Hebrew Bible. To read Ruth after Judges would disrupt the order. But the fact that Ruth does occur after Judges in Chris-tian Bibles raises the issue of canonical order. What is the significance of canonical order for reading biblical texts?

The Talmudic quotation, cited at the head of this chapter, indicates that the order of prophetic books is not just a contemporary concern. The rabbis were also concerned with the order of prophetic books. Significantly, how-ever, they extended their interest beyond the closure of what contemporary scholars have called the Deuteronomistic History to include the so-called 'Latter Prophets' and understood the second part of the Hebrew canon, 'the prophets', as an ordered whole:

> Our Rabbis taught: The order of the Prophets is, Joshua, Judges, Samuel, Kings, Jeremiah, Ezekiel, Isaiah, and the Twelve Minor Prophets. Let us examine this. Hosea came first, as it is written (Hosea 1.2): *God spoke first to Hosea*. But did God speak first to Hosea? Were there not many prophets between Moses and Hosea? R. Johanan (250–290), however, has explained that [what it means is that] he was the first of the four prophets who prophesied at the period, namely, Hosea, Isaiah, Amos and Micah. Should

---

7.   See, e.g., Peter D. Miscall, *The Workings of Old Testament Narrative* (SBLSS; Philadelphia: Fortress Press; Chico, CA: Scholars Press, 1983), p. 1. Miscall takes a literary approach to the in reading Genesis–2 Kings as a literary corpus on the basis of shared plot, themes, style, and so on.

8.   See Martin Noth, *The Deuteronomistic History* (trans. J. Doull *et al.*; JSOTSup, 15; Sheffield: Sheffield Academic Press, 2nd edn, 1991), pp. 17-26.

not then Hosea come first?—Since his prophecy is written along with those of Haggai, Zechariah and Malachi, and Haggai and Zechariah and Malachi came at the end of the prophets, he is reckoned with them. But why should he not be written separately and placed first?—Since his book is so small, it might be lost [if copied separately]. Let us see again. Isaiah was prior to Jeremiah and Ezekiel. Then why should not Isaiah be placed first?—Because the book of Kings ends with a record of destruction and Jeremiah speaks throughout of destruction and Ezekiel commences with destruction and ends with consolation and Isaiah is full of consolation; therefore we put destruction next to destruction and consolation next to consolation.[9]

The rabbis see order and continuity extending beyond Kings to include Jeremiah, Ezekiel, Isaiah and the Twelve Minor Prophets. They see progression where historical critics see closure and a disruption of order. More significantly, they also see this continuation in an order different from the one that characterizes the present order of Christian and Jewish Bibles—Isaiah, Jeremiah, Ezekiel and the Twelve—by placing Isaiah after Ezekiel and before the Twelve. Of course, Christian canons also add books to this order: Lamentations and Baruch[10] after Jeremiah, and Daniel after Ezekiel.

While historical-critical scholars have stressed the importance of order, which governs their reading of the 'Former Prophets' as the single work of a Deuteronomistic Historian, even pointing out how Ruth has disrupted that order in Christian canons, they have not shown a similar interest in the order of the Latter Prophets. The Latter Prophets are viewed simply as a collection so that the addition of Lamentations, Baruch or Daniel does not pose a problem of order. Sometimes, however, order does appear in the historical-critical discussion of these prophets, and when it does, it becomes clear that while historical critics are reading texts in Hebrew they are interpreting these texts in Christian canonical order.

An instance of this is David L. Petersen's discussion of Zechariah 9–14 and Malachi in his commentary on these passages.[11] Petersen understands this material to represent 'a tripartite collection of prophetic literature' (Zech. 9.1–11.17; 12.1–14.21; Mal. 1.1–3.24) of 'originally quite distinct material' brought together by 'a Persian period editor'.[12] For this reason he is interested in re-ordering the individual books. He, therefore, avoids the

9. Lieman, *The Canonization of Hebrew Scriptures*, p. 52.
10. In the Roman Catholic Canon.
11. David L. Petersen, *Zechariah 9–14 and Malachi* (OTL; London: SCM Press, 1995).
12. Petersen, *Zechariah 9–14 and Malachi*, pp. 3-4.

canonical labels of 'Zechariah' and 'Malachi' as denoting two separate books (Zech. 1–14 and Mal. 1–3) and the historical-critical tag of 'Deutero-Zechariah' for Zechariah 9–14.[13] Nevertheless, at the beginning and end of his commentary Petersen refers to this tripartite division as the 'concluding chapters in the Hebrew Bible', a role which he finds fitting.[14] Zechariah 9–14 and Malachi, do not, of course, conclude the Hebrew Bible; 2 Chronicles 36 does. Petersen's tripartite collection comes at the end and concludes the Protestant Old Testament. Malachi 4.5-6, with its reference to Elijah whom Yahweh will send again, is a fitting conclusion to the Old Testament from a Protestant perspective since this figure will appear in Protestant Bibles three chapters later in the character of John the Baptist (Mt. 3.1-17; see Jn 1.21). Although Petersen is seemingly not concerned with canonical order (enabling him even to shun canonical labels), an assumption of canonical order reappears in a comment reflecting the order of the books in the Christian community for whom Petersen is reading these texts.

Canonical order, then, slips in and out of the discussion in historical-critical studies and sometimes highlights one canonical order over another. While historical-critical scholars recognize the Hebrew canonical order for Joshua, Judges, Samuel and Kings and recognize the imposition of Ruth in that order, they just as quickly ignore Hebrew canonical order by making Deuteronomy the introduction of their so-called Deuteronomistic History. The role Deuteronomy plays as the conclusion of Torah is dismissed. Such a new canonical re-ordering creates not only an introduction to the Deuteronomistic History but also a Tetrateuch to replace the Torah.

There is another way in which Noth's thesis regarding the Deuteronomistic History ignores Hebrew canonical order. The second part of the Hebrew canonical order does not end with Kings. The four prophetic scrolls known as the Latter Prophets follow it as a continuation. In Christian Bibles, however, 2 Kings is separated and distanced from the four scrolls that give the prophetic section of the canon closure. What difference does it make if a reader reads 2 Kings 25 not as an end but as having a continuation in Jeremiah as the rabbis suggested? Noth saw the Deuteronomistic History as a history of doom and destruction. However, when the rabbis speak about the order of the prophets, they understand the progression from Kings to Jeremiah, Ezekiel, Isaiah and the Twelve as a progression from destruction to consolation.

---

13. Petersen, *Zechariah 9–14 and Malachi*, pp. 1-3.
14. Petersen, *Zechariah 9–14 and Malachi*, pp. 3, 232.

It is interesting, then, that readers of the Torah and the Former Prophets, even historical-critical ones, tend to read these books in ways that reflect the order of books in the rabbinic canon. Readers easily see progression from one book to the other in the Torah and Former Prophets. Critical scholarship has even noticed progression from Deuteronomy to Joshua reflected in those who postulate a Deuteronomistic History or those who speak of a Primary History. It is not difficult to see an order here. But the rabbis also saw order and continuation in the arrangement of books— Joshua, Judges, Samuel, Kings, Jeremiah, Ezekiel, Isaiah and the Twelve— moving the reader from destruction to consolation.

In my reading of the 'Latter Prophets' that follows, I want to read these books in the order suggested by the rabbis—Jeremiah, Ezekiel, Isaiah and the Twelve as a continuation of Joshua, Judges, Samuel, Kings. This way of reading is significant because it does clarify some issues and answer some questions that emerge out of the usual critical way of reading.

Scholars have often noted that Jeremiah shares a lot of stylistic features with the Deuteronomistic History. Observations such as these have, of course, resulted in the scholarly creation of a Deuteronomistic school of redactors who edited Jeremiah, and suggestions have also been made that there may have been a Deuteronomistic redaction of all the books of the prophetic corpus. However, if one reads Jeremiah as following Kings as the rabbis have suggested, then a different explanation of the so-called 'Deuteronomistic' traditions in Jeremiah becomes possible. Just as the successive books/scrolls of Joshua, Judges, Samuel and Kings reflect a common Deuteronomistic style featured in their compilation, so Jeremiah as a continuation of Kings reflects this style of a compilation of materials gathered together on a succession of scrolls read in a particular order. Perhaps it is only the gap in the Christian canonical order separating Jeremiah from Kings that raises the issue of the reappearance in Jeremiah of a style reflected in a series ordered and collected as a whole to form the Deuteronomistic History. If one reads Joshua, Judges, Samuel, Kings as an ordered whole, then perhaps the reader should continue with Jeremiah as an addition reflecting the same style as the rest of the complied material.

Another common problem that has been raised in historical-critical studies is: Why of all the Latter Prophets, are only two prophets—Isaiah (2 Kgs 19.2, 5, 6, 20; 20.1, 4, 7, 8, 9, 11, 14, 16, 19) and Jonah (2 Kgs 14.25)—mentioned in the book of Kings? This question fades away if one understands the prophets as an ordered compilation of scrolls to be read as a whole. In a sense all the prophets are there in the orderly presentation of eight scrolls. The prophets are present in the scrolls as a continuation of Kings; they are not absent.

This way of reading the prophets as an ordered whole offers some interesting solutions to problems that have emerged in historical-critical studies. It also offers an important option related to a semiotics of reading. What the rabbis say about prophetic canonical order presents an alternative to what has become standard practice in reading the Latter Prophets. The standard practice tends to reflect the canonical order in Christian Bibles, which assumes a gap between the Latter and Former Prophets. Standard practice, even canonical criticism, is to read the Latter Prophets as individual literary works unrelated to what comes before or after. This is consistent with a Christian canonical order in which the Latter prophets are separated from one another by Lamentations, Baruch[15] and Daniel. I am not intending to demonstrate that the rabbinic order of the prophets was *the* correct order, that there is indeed a correct order or that this is the correct way to read. We do not have the information to posit normativity.

John Barton comments on how strange the suggestion in the Talmud about the order of the prophets sounds to contemporary readers of the prophets:

> The modern reader is likely to be struck most forcibly by the inadequacy of claiming that Jeremiah 'speaks throughout of destruction' or that Isaiah is 'full of consolation'. But this conceals a feature which is in reality far more startling: the entire failure to grasp that Kings and Jeremiah—history and prophecy—simply belong to different genres. For us the most obvious difference between the 'destruction' at the end of Kings is a record of what has happened, whereas the prophecies whether of weal or woe, in the Latter Prophets are for what still lies in the future. For it to seem natural to ignore that distinction and to treat historical narrative and predictive prophecy as the same kind of thing, the Prophetic scriptures have to be read with concerns different from ours. Once we see that the importance of the Prophets lies, for the rabbis, neither in their accuracy as a record of the past nor in the information they provide about the future, but chiefly in the effectiveness with which they bear witness to God's consistency in remaining true to the character revealed in the Torah—punishing transgression, yet never forsaking his covenant with his people—then we can begin to understand why our distinction between record and prediction, and hence between Former and Latter Prophets, was not functional in the world of the Talmud.[16]

---

15. In the Roman Catholic Canon.

16. John Barton, *Oracles of God: Perceptions of Prophecy in Israel after the Exile* (London: Darton, Longman & Todd, 1986), p. 20.

From the perspective of a semiotics of reading, Barton's comments raise a number of questions about reading these books compiled for a Model Reader. Individual prophetic books are themselves a compiled collage for a Model Reader, as I argued in the last chapter, but canonical order also influences reading. How does the plurality of canonical orders affect our reading of individual books? Does reading prophetic books according to a plurality of canonical orders suggest that one or more of these canonical orderings can only arise because of an aberrant decoding of the books collected and compiled for a Model Reader? As a way of answering these questions I want to take up the thesis of what Philip Davies calls 'the canonizing process' in his *Scribes and Schools: The Canonization of the Hebrew Scriptures*.[17]

2. *The Canonizing Process and the Semiotics of Reading*

The work of Philip Davies, especially his *In Search of 'Ancient Israel'*,[18] has been influential in my own approach to reading prophetic books as literary wholes, that is, separated from the history of their development. Following Davies' thesis that the Israel depicted in the biblical text is a literary construction, I have argued that it is difficult to use that literary portrayal as an actual past against which to plot the development of prophetic books, as many redaction critics do:

> Just as many have become critical of the conception of an Israel encoded in the sources of the historical narratives, conscious of itself, and writing its history as it evolved through time, so we need to become critical of the conception of the Book of the Twelve as encoding its own redactional history.[19]

Davies appears to support the position I have taken. He says,

> Concern with history extends well beyond 'Histories of Israel'; it permeates (though decreasingly) the bulk of exegetical work. Consider how many scholarly works deal with the historical dating and context of parts of biblical literature, or with the historical reconstruction of 'Israel's traditions'. How many commentaries on Isaiah, for instance, concern themselves with what Isaiah thought, what was really happening in his time, what advice he gave to Ahaz and to Hezekiah, what later writers added to his words, when

17. Davies, *Scribes and Schools*, p. 14.
18. Philip R. Davies, *In Search of 'Ancient Israel'* (JSOTSup, 148; Sheffield: JSOT Press, 1992).
19. Conrad, *Zechariah*, p. 16.

they added them, and so on? Necessary to all such speculation is some kind of historical outline, and not just a sequence of dates but a *Gestalt*, an image of a society in which certain beliefs and certain kinds of behaviour govern. Such a lavishly detailed portrait is impossible to construct from elsewhere.[20]

However, having critiqued traditional biblical studies in his *In Search of 'Ancient Israel'*, Davies, in a later book, *Scribes and Schools*, essentially uses the same historical-critical techniques to reconstruct the canonical process by tracing the development of what he calls 'Hebrew canons'. It will be my contention that Davies has constructed ancient Hebrew scribal community/communities in a way that is not dissimilar to the way traditional critical scholars have constructed 'ancient Israel'. Davies' thesis regarding canon as a process is important to me because of what it suggests for a semiotics of reading. It is less convincing in its attempt to map this multi-faceted process.

It will be helpful to review some of the broad features of Davies' views on the canonical process in general and in particular how it relates to books that are now part of the Torah and Prophets in the Hebrew canonical order. Rather than speak of canon in terms of an outcome, as, for example, the rabbinic Masoretic canon with its threefold division into Torah, Prophets and Writings, Davies' strategy in his *Scribes and Schools* is to speak about canonizing as an ongoing process. It is significant that this canonizing process be understood as generating 'all kinds of canons which, as the process continues, can assume different shapes over time or between different groups'.[21] Furthermore, 'the production of a single closed list of authoritative writings' should not be understood as 'the inevitable end product of this ongoing process'.[22] However, this canonizing process does comprise

> a sequence of stages from the creation of texts, through transmission, and discrimination to form lists. Though one stage tends to lead naturally to another, so that we can speak of a sequence of processes, even when the production of final canonical lists does not result, we can, and should speak of a canonizing process.[23]

Much of his book is taken up in describing this canonical process in general and in particular with 'suggestions' about 'the history of canonizing in

    20. Davies, *In Search of 'Ancient Israel'*, p. 30.
    21. Davies, *Scribes and Schools*, pp. 8-9.
    22. Davies, *Scribes and Schools*, p. 9.
    23. Davies, *Scribes and Schools*, p. 10.

Judaism' based on 'a study of some parts of the Jewish scriptural canon (and of other works once canonized)'.[24]

While there may have been a plurality of scribal communities, it is not clear to me that study of parts of the Jewish scriptural canon can give us insight into the actual history of canonizing in Judaism. In other words, my criticism of Davies' 'reading' of the Jewish scriptural canon is similar to my criticism of historical-critical reading cited above. These texts can give us no more insight into the actual process of canonizing in Judaism then they can give us insight into an actual Israel. To make use of Davies' term, what we encounter is a 'fiction'. When these 'biblical' texts mention 'books', they are not giving us unproblematic information about actual 'books' but 'fictional' books that need to be understood in the narrative context of the texts we are reading. The mention of books in the narrative may reflect something about the authoritative role that written texts play as sources of authority in the ancient world out of which the texts emerged, but they are not a direct and unproblematic link to actual books or an actual canonizing process.

It will help if I illustrate my point by reviewing what Davies has to say about what he calls the 'Mosaic canon'. When he speaks about the Torah, he does not want to speak about a process of canonization as an inevitable evolutionary development leading in a straight trajectory to the Torah of the rabbinic canon. Rather, he wants to speak about a fluid canonizing process resulting in a plurality of canons, including individual books which themselves can be understood as a canon. On the one hand, he understands this process as proceeding without direction—a ship without a transcendental helmsman. Yet when he speaks about his canonizing process it sometimes sounds like Childs' 'literary and theological force' transmuted into an intellectual force concerned with collecting and organizing books. In describing why the 'law' came to be collected around the figure of Moses, he says,

> We are not concerned in this book, of course, with the processes of composition or with tradition-history of the individual scrolls... What we can attempt, however, is *to explain the force behind the collection and organization of the materials. There seems to have been a desire to give a complete account of the deeds and the words of the man who created the nation*, not from any disinterested historical or biographical motive, but from an etiological one: to give an identity to an *ethnos*, the Judeans. An enormous

24. Davies, *Scribes and Schools*, p. 14.

amount of scribal activity was expended on compiling an account of the work of the nation's founder.[25]

This *'force'* behind the collection or this seeming *desire* appears here as ungrounded as Childs' 'literary and theological force'. Davies is aware of the need to establish these claims. He says,

> When and where did all this happen? Why should a founder for the nation need to be discovered and so extensively written up? These questions are, of course, all interrelated. But it is important to discover the chronological framework in order to answer them. The outline of an answer to both questions can be achieved by looking at Deuteronomy.[26]

But can Deuteronomy deliver the answer to these two questions?

Davies thinks that Deuteronomy can provide an answer in three different ways. First, he says that Deuteronomy is 'the only book to call itself a "*torah* book"' and hence it 'may provide a clue to the final naming of this canon':[27]

> The laws of Deuteronomy are clearly referred to as 'this *torah*' in its introductory and concluding material. Indeed, Deuteronomy is the only place in the Pentateuch where the term 'scroll of *torah*' occurs. Elsewhere, chiefly Leviticus, we find a *torah* for specific practices such as offerings (Lev. 6.2, 7, 18), or leprosy (e.g., Lev. 14.2). But Deut. 28.58 reads: 'the words of this *torah* written in this book'. Moses is said to have written it down (31.9, 24) and had it placed in an ark. This identification as *the* scroll of *torah* carries over into Josh. 1.7-8, where Joshua is instructed not to depart from the 'scroll of the *torah*' which 'my servant Moses commanded', and reads out this 'scroll of the *torah* of Moses' at a covenant ceremony in (8.30-35). In 2 Kings 22–23 a 'scroll of the *torah*' (22.8) or 'scroll of the covenant' (23.2) is said to have been found in the temple and made the basis of another covenant ceremony and a religious reform.[28]

There are problems, however, with the way in which Davies is reading a history of the canonizing process out of this passage. According to Deuteronomy, 'this *torah*' was written in a book by Moses (Deut. 31.9, 24). If Moses is not an actual character in this passage but a fictional character, as

---

25. Davies, *Scribes and Schools*, p. 93 (my emphasis).

26. Davies, *Scribes and Schools*, p. 93.

27. Davies, *Scribes and Schools*, p. 93. In this chapter he speaks about the '*torah*' not as growing out of actual law but as a theory about 'what ought to happen, or ought to have happened, in an ideal Israelite society. Accordingly, law is a mode of social philosophy, or of theocratic idealizing' (p. 90).

28. Davies, *Scribes and Schools*, p. 93.

Davies would understand him, then why is 'this torah' in the book Moses wrote any more actual than Moses himself? Why is 'this book of the *torah* of Moses' not also simply understood as part of the narrative fiction?[29] Furthermore, his use of the phrase 'scroll of the torah' is rather misleading. The word scroll occurs nowhere in Deuteronomy. For scroll, one would expect the phrase, מגלת־ספר, as in Jeremiah 36 (e.g. vv. 2, 4). The written text referred to in the passages Davies cites in Deuteronomy, Joshua and 2 Kings is not a 'scroll', a מגלת־ספר; it is simply a ספר. I have argued elsewhere that the meaning of ספר does not necessarily equate with what we understand to be a 'book' or a 'scroll'. It can be used for a wide variety of items that are written (letters, marriage contracts, etc.).[30] To translate 'scroll of the *torah*' for ספר־תורה is to introduce the historical notion of a canonical collection and ordering of material on an actual scroll when ספר may be functioning quite differently in a fictional narrative.[31]

Second, Davies thinks that the book of Deuteronomy 'affords sufficient clues to enable it to be dated'. He says,

> Deuteronomy retains a separate identity as *torah* even until the time of ben Sira (end of the third century B.C.E.). In 24.23 this writer mentions 'the scroll of the covenant of Elyon, the law that Moses commanded us'. The reference to 'covenant' *makes one think of Deuteronomy*. Indeed, ben Sira seems to regard this book as exclusively the *Mosaic* law, while his reference elsewhere to 'law of the Most High' (39.1) refers either to other scrolls or perhaps to something not in a fixed textual form at all.[32]

Again, why are we thinking of real books such as Deuteronomy only? And why should a reference to 'covenant' *'make one think of Deuteronomy'*? Why can the 'book of the covenant'[33] not make one think of 'the book of the covenant' written down and read out by Moses at the ceremony of covenant making in Exod. 24.4-7? 'The book of the covenant' does not unproblematically refer to an actual book but can just as easily refer to a book in a narrative that constructs Moses as well as the books he writes and reads out. Both works are narrative fictions taken up and read by later

---

29. This is the kind of question that Davies himself asks when some scholars begin to read David and Solomon as actual individuals.

30. See my article, 'Heard But Not Seen: The Representation of Books in the Old Testament', *JSOT* 54 (1992), pp. 45-59 (54-55).

31. I argue in 'Heard But Not Seen' that the 'book of the law/covenant' does not refer to actual books but is a rhetorical feature of the text itself (pp. 45-59).

32. Davies, *Scribes and Schools*, p. 94 (my emphasis).

33. Again, the reference to 'scroll' is problematic here.

'authors'. Davies' discussion about the distinction between 'the book of the covenant' and 'the books of the law' in 1 and 2 Maccabees[34] perpetuates the historical-critical problem of finding 'the actual' in historical narrative that I discussed in Chapter 2. To move from historical narrative to actual history, including the actual history of the canonical process, is far more problematic than Davies suggests in his discussion of that process.

Finally, his third argument is that the ideology of Deuteronomy points us toward a motivation for the creation of a Mosaic canon.[35] To substantiate this claim he invokes Martin Noth's thesis regarding a Deuteronomistic History in which Deuteronomy originally served as the opening of a historical work followed by Joshua, Judges, Samuel and Kings, written according to the ideology of Deuteronomy. To invoke Martin Noth overlooks the problem that Roland Boer has clearly demonstrated regarding Noth's Deuteronomistic History. Boer understands Noth's Deuteronomistic History itself to be a creation growing out of the German culture reflecting the genre of the historical novel current in Noth's own time rather than a literary genre of the ancient world.[36]

Davies, however, following Noth, says that 'Deuteronomy may have enjoyed a promiscuous life during its canonical career'.[37] But it is not difficult to see that Noth has constructed the Deuteronomistic history out of his own world of Christian canonical order. It is in Christian Bibles that Deuteronomy can be quite promiscuous. Noth's own academic community as a recent scribal community can be seen as the place where Deuteronomy can shift between a Tetrateuch/Pentateuch and a Deuteronomistic History. In the twentieth-century Christian world, Deuteronomy, wedged between Numbers and Judges, can seemingly go in two directions at the same time. A Tetrateuch, a Pentateuch, a Deuteronomistic History (without the book of Ruth) are all there together. Readers can decide to read in whatever way and whatever order they choose as modern day canonizers. Noth's decision on how to read does not so much reflect an ancient canonical process as it does a twentieth century one in which collecting and re-ordering continues. It is easy to see that in Noth's canon, the Deuteronomistic History ends in doom and destruction because in the Christian

---

34. Davies, *Scribes and Schools*, p. 94.

35. Davies, *Scribes and Schools*, p. 93.

36. Roland Boer, *Novel Histories: The Fiction of Biblical Criticism* (Playing the Text, 2; Sheffield: Sheffield Academic Press, 1997), p. 102.

37. Davies, *Scribes and Schools*, p. 94.

canonical order there is a gap between 2 Kings and the Latter Prophets. Noth's canon did not have the continuity the rabbis suggest in Jeremiah, Ezekiel, Isaiah and the Twelve leading from destruction to consolation.

One does not need Noth's Deuteronomistic History, which detaches Deuteronomy from Numbers, to explain the ideology of Joshua through to 2 Kings.[38] Deuteronomy does not need to be cut off from the Pentateuch and constructed as a beginning of a new canonical order if one reads as the rabbis did. Rather, the prophets can be understood in a Talmudic order so that, to quote Barton again, 'they bear witness to God's consistency in remaining true to the character revealed in Torah—punishing transgression, yet never forsaking his covenant with his people'.[39] The point I am making here is that Noth's re-ordering does not provide insight into an ancient canonical processing of this material for reading. It tells us more about a contemporary canonical order. Davies should see Noth as a twentieth-century scribe continuing the canonical process of 'archiving' books in different canonical orders.

None of us can ever read the canon and understand the canonical process from the beginning. We must always start at some canonical outcome or end as Noth himself did. Clearly it is possible to continue canonical processing by compiling the texts in different order. Such canonical processing never ends. In what follows I am interested in looking at canonical outcomes, ancient compilations, as the basis for a reading. There is no reason to discontinue (re)arranging and (re)ordering books, but that process will put us in touch more with our own tastes than with received canonical orders that may be more difficult to savor.

In his discussion of the prophetic books, Davies again invokes Noth's Deuteronomistic History to explain how Deuteronomy was once attached to Joshua through to 2 Kings to form 'a distinct collection' as 'a single "work" spread over a number of scrolls'. These scrolls came together as part of a 'canonizing process' and because of archiving came to form a 'historical sequence'.[40] 'The scroll of Isaiah probably came into existence by processes of commentary and supplementation'; Jeremiah, which occurs in two editions, and

> seems to have grown from within rather than, as with Isaiah, from supplementation; Ezekiel was in fact probably composed as an extended literary

38. I would add Jeremiah.
39. Barton, *Oracles of God*, p. 20
40. Davies, *Scribes and Schools*, p. 112.

work from the outset...by a writer creating a prophetic character; the collection of Twelve on one scroll is a perfect illustration of a canon.[41]

Isaiah, Jeremiah, Ezekiel and the Twelve, he suggests, were each singly canonized, before they were put together and finally linked to the historicized books.

Davies' portrayal of this canonizing process has by and large taken over historical-critical reconstruction of the literature transferring what historical critics have said about the history of the text to the description of a canonizing process. He has abandoned the notion that these techniques will present us with the development of the literature portrayed against the historical background of an actual Israelite community. But can techniques of inquiry designed to produce one set of results be so easily transferred? In criticizing the way scholars have used historical reconstruction of the literature to give us insight into an historical Israel, Davies has said that 'necessary to all such speculation is some kind of historical outline, and not just a sequence of dates but a *Gestalt*, an image of a society in which certain beliefs and certain kinds of behaviour govern'.[42] Changing the *Gestalt* will not change the capability of the well worn techniques of historical criticism to produce actual history whether that be of 'ancient Israel' or 'scribal communities' from literature that now makes up a variety of Christian and Jewish canons.

3. *Reading: Order and Unity*

I have written an extended critique of Davies here because I want to build on the important insights that can be gained from his discussion of scribal communities in his *Scribes and Schools*. Davies' thesis is informative in the way it helps us understand the production of canonical literature. However, the important insight I have gained from Davies is in how to read prophetic literature rather than how to understand any actual canonical processing. How biblical books reached canonical ends is not information that is available to contemporary readers. What is available are books and canonical orders that have resulted from a canonical process of collecting, compiling and archiving.

To read one of the Latter Prophets as a book is to read it as a collection archived and arranged with attention given to order. To read the Latter

41. Davies, *In Search of 'Ancient Israel'*, p. 116.
42. Davies, *In Search of 'Ancient Israel'*.

Prophets according to a canonical arrangement such as the rabbinic canon is to read a series of scrolls as an ordered whole. One could choose to consider this ordering as random and continue the process of re-ordering. This is what I essentially learned to do as a historical critic. However, what I have been trying to do in *Reading Isaiah*, in *Zechariah* and in a number of recent articles is to pay attention to the order of prophetic books as they have come to us. I take it as a challenge as a reader to understand these books as a whole, as they are. The diachronic history of these books is not a process that is available to us as readers. Attempting to uncover such a process, as is the case with Martin Noth, may more likely result in the continuation of a canonical process resulting in new canonical order (a Tetrateuch and a Deuteronomistic History) rather than the uncovering of earlier stages of that process. Anyone interested in reading these texts as an expression of some ancient community needs to pay attention to the order and arrangement that has been received.

Sometimes we discover different orders in different books, as is the case with Jeremiah. I suspect that many of the books we read had a greater plurality of orders than the ones that have come to us. When books have different orders they should be understood as different books. Different meanings emerge out of a different order.

In a semiotics of reading prophetic books, I am concerned with paying attention to order not as redaction critics do, to understand the history of their development, but with the purpose of understanding how they were ordered for their Model Reader. I may inevitably be involved in aberrantly decoding what Eco calls 'closed texts'; but to read this way is to recognize what Eco calls the limits of interpretation. It is to give attention to structure and shape.

As a way of bringing this chapter to a close and as an introduction to my reading of the prophetic books that follows, it might be helpful for me to address an issue that has emerged in recent discussions about prophetic books. It has become commonplace for scholars to speak about the 'unity' of Isaiah and other prophetic books such as the Twelve. David Carr has written an article, 'Reaching for Unity in Isaiah' in which he has argued that 'excessive confidence in the existence of…complete unity in biblical texts—and our need to find it—can blind us to the unresolved, rich plurality built into texts'.[43] I think the key phrase here is 'complete unity'. What constitutes unity in any literature is not an absolute norm but a cultural

43. David Carr, 'Reaching for Unity in Isaiah', *JSOT* 57 (1993), pp. 61-80 (80).

convention. When I speak of the unity of Isaiah or any other prophetic book, I am not speaking of the sort of unity evident in contemporary literature authored by a single individual. I understand unity to be an organizational unity arising in the collecting, cataloguing and archiving of material evident not only in prophetic books but in canonical order. I am assuming that prophetic books are something like a collage that has been organized and given an organizational unity by a scribal community.[44] As a reader I am particularly interested in looking for that encoded 'unity'.

In the next chapter I want to look at superscriptions at the beginning of prophetic books as codes for reading them. In a general form-critical sense, in Gunkel's terms, all prophetic books begin with a superscription. However, the specific formulation of these superscriptions is important for the reader to understand how to read what follows. I will be particularly interested in the differences among 'the words of Jeremiah', 'the vision of Isaiah', 'and it happened…I [Ezekiel] saw visions of God', and the superscriptions found in the Twelve at its beginning and throughout the scroll.

44. On the issue of the different cultural conventions for defining what constitutes unity and conventions of readings see John Barton, 'What is a Book? Modern Exegesis and the Literary Conventions of Ancient Israel', in Johannes C. de Moor (ed.), *Intertextuality in Ugarit and Israel* (Oudtestamentische studiën, 40; Leiden: E.J. Brill, 1998), pp. 1-14.

Chapter 4

OPENING PROPHETIC BOOKS

The words of Jeremiah, the son of Hilkiah, from the priests who were in
Anathoth in the land of Benjamin, to whom the word of Yahweh came in
the days of Josiah, the son of Amon of Judah, in the thirteenth year of his
reign. (Jer. 1.1-2)

And it happened in the thirtieth year in the fourth month, on the fifth day of
the month, and I was among the exiles by the river Chebar, the heavens
were opened and I saw visions of God. (Ezek. 1.1)

The vision of Isaiah son of Amoz, which he saw concerning Judah and
Jerusalem in the days of Uzziah, Jotham, Ahaz and Hezekiah, kings of
Judah. (Isa. 1.1)

The word of Yahweh which came to Hosea, son of Beeri, in the days of
Kings Uzziah, Jotham, Ahaz and Hezekiah of Judah, and in the days of King
Jeroboam, son of Joash of Israel. [The] beginning of Yahweh spoke [was]
with Hosea. (Hos. 1.1-2a)[1]

In the last chapter I argued that reading prophetic books as the products of
a canonizing process like that described by Philip Davies should alert the
reader to pay close attention to order and arrangement. Prophetic books do
not possess the kind of unity that we expect in single authored works. The
books are the result of collecting, arranging and archiving of materials
brought together by scribes. To read a prophetic book paying heed to *a*
final shape given to a prophetic book prompts the reader interested in that
shape to look for the codes or signs employed to give shape to collected
material—to pay attention to *a* canonical outcome. This canonical end will
reflect not only the present form of single books but also the ordered
arrangement of books to form a whole. In my case I am interested in the
order and arrangement of the prophets as described by the rabbis and the
present form of the single prophetic books of the Hebrew canon that

---

1.   This is a literal translation of an awkward Hebrew phrase, which is discussed
in more detail on p. 87.

comprise that ordered whole. Whether I am reading the single prophetic
books that the rabbis read is not something about which I can be certain.

By reading a final canonical outcome, I am not suggesting that this outcome is a normative one—that it is *the* outcome resulting from some theological driving force. I am simply interested in the way a Model Author
constructed prophetic worlds reflected in the shape given to the books
t(he)y compiled. It is equally important to read other canonical outcomes
with the purpose of seeing how different canonical shapes reflect different
ways of understanding this literature. Canonical processing continues into
our own time with new arrangements such as the Tetrateuch, the Hexa-
teuch and the Deuteronomistic History. My particular interest in the rabbinic order is that it is often a neglected order for reading this material.
Contemporary critical studies tend to be influenced by Christian canonical
order that separates the Latter Prophets from the Former Prophets and reads
these collections as two separate canonical arrangements. Such studies are
also inclined to treat the Latter Prophets as single books and not as a
canonical collection.

1. *Form and Prophetic Books*

My focus is on reading the texts that we have come to label the Latter
Prophets as a continuation of the Former Prophets. It is not too difficult to
see how the Latter Prophets in some canonical orders can be separated
from the Former Prophets and understood as an independent collection. It
is also not difficult to see why they are read as individual books. The form
and shape they receive are distinctive. The Latter Prophets focus on individual prophetic characters who are introduced at the beginning of the
'book' with what we have come to call a superscription. Formally, these
superscriptions set these prophetic 'books' apart from the Former Prophets
that precedes them.

Three of the 'books' constitute entire scrolls (Jeremiah, Ezekiel and
Isaiah)—מגלת־ספר, to borrow a term from Jer. 36.2, 4, and so on. Twelve
of the 'books', each with its own superscription, are collected together on
one scroll, the Twelve. I will refer to each of these as a 'book' (ספר)
although this term is used only in the superscription of Nahum (1.1), 'the
ספר of the vision of Nahum'.

However, simply to make a general observation about form—that they
all begin with a superscription—would be to dismiss the distinctiveness of
the 15 superscriptions that introduce the 'books'. It is possible to under-

stand the particular formulations of the superscriptions as codes addressed to a Model Reader signaling how to read the collection that follows. Furthermore, I will suggest that the superscriptions are an important encoded sign for the reader of how to read Jeremiah, Ezekiel, Isaiah and the Twelve as an ordered collection and as a continuation of the Former Prophets.

2. *Superscriptions and Dates*

In order to see how the superscriptions can be understood as scribal signs indicating how the scrolls are to be read, I want to look first at dating in the superscriptions. Six of the prophetic books make no reference to dating (Joel, Obadiah, Jonah, Nahum, Habakkuk and Malachi):

> The word of Yahweh that came to Joel son of Pethuel. (Joel 1.1)

> The vision of Obadiah. (Obad. 1)

> And the word of Yahweh came to Jonah son of Amittai, saying... (Jon. 1.1)[2]

> An oracle of Nineveh. The 'book' of the vision of Nahum of Elkosh. (Nah. 1.1)

> The oracle which Habakkuk the prophet saw. (Hab. 1.1)

> An oracle. The word of Yahweh to Israel in the hand of Malachi. (Mal. 1.1)

These superscriptions are quite short, and all of them occur at the beginning of prophetic 'books' that are placed in the Twelve. None of these short undated superscriptions comes at the beginning of a scroll.

Since all the other prophetic books date the characters introduced in the superscription, it will be important to understand the significance of dating in these other books and the significance of a superscription that makes no reference to time. Five of the prophetic books date the characters mentioned in the superscription by relating them to a general period of time with the general phrase 'in the days of' (בימי) kings with no attempt to be more precise.[3] Two refer to kings from Judah and Israel (Hosea and Amos) and three to kings of Judah alone (Isaiah, Micah and Zephaniah):

---

2. The beginning of Jonah contrasts with the beginning of other prophetic books. It reads more like the beginning of a narrative than a superscription. But compare it with the beginning of Ezekiel. Both begin with ויהי.

3. Jeremiah is dated with reference to the Judean kings 'in the days of' Josiah, Jehoiakim and Zedekiah. However, in Jeremiah one is given more precise information about time: 'in the thirteenth year of his [Josiah's] reign'; 'until the end of the eleventh year of King Zedekiah'; and 'until the captivity of Judah in the fifth month'.

> The vision of Isaiah, the son of Amoz which he saw concerning Judah and Jerusalem in the days of Uzziah, Jotham, Ahaz and Hezekiah, kings of Judah. (Isa. 1.10)

> The word of Yahweh which came to Hosea, son of Beeri, in the days of Kings Uzziah, Jotham, Ahaz and Hezekiah of Judah, and in the days of King Jeroboam, son of Joash of Israel. [The] beginning of Yahweh spoke [was] with Hosea. (Hos. 1.1-2a)

> The words of Amos, who was among the shepherds from Tekoa, which he saw concerning Israel in the days of Uzziah, king of Judah and in the days of Jeroboam, the son of Joash, king of Israel, two years before the earthquake.[4] (Amos 1.1)

> The word of Yahweh that came to Micah of Moresheth in the days of Jotham, Ahaz, and Hezekiah of Judah, which he saw concerning Samaria and Jerusalem. (Mic. 1.1)

> The word of Yahweh that came to Zephaniah, the son of Cushi, the son of Gedaliah, the son of Amariah, the son of Hezekiah in the days of King Josiah, the son of Amon of Judah. (Zeph. 1.1)

Four of these superscriptions are found in the collection of 'books' in the Twelve and the other is found in Isaiah, which precedes the Twelve in the Rabbinic canonical order. Four of the prophets (Isaiah, Hosea, Amos and Micah) are associated with kings in Judah,[5] in what is portrayed in the narratives in the Former Prophets as the period of Assyrian threat before the emergence of Babylon. The dating of Zephaniah associates him with Josiah at the time of the emergence of Babylonia as a world power. These books, then, are dated in time to the days before the Babylonian threat to Judah and Jerusalem's future.

The remaining superscriptions (Jeremiah, Ezekiel, Haggai and Zechariah) date prophets with more precision:

> The words of Jeremiah, the son of Hilkiah, from the priests who were in Anathoth in the land of Benjamin, to whom the word of Yahweh came in the days of Josiah, the son of Amon of Judah, *in the thirteenth year of his reign*. It also came in the days of Jehoiakim, son of Josiah, the king of Judah and until *the end of the eleventh year* of Zedekiah, the son of Josiah of Judah, until the captivity of Jerusalem *in the fifth month*. (Jer. 1.1-3)

---

4.   This reference in Amos concerning the time interval before an earthquake is a detail that does not characterize the other prophets who are dated generally with reference to Judean and Israelite kings.

5.   Hosea and Amos also mention in their superscriptions Jeroboam, a king of Israel.

And it happened in the thirtieth year, in the fourth month, on the fifth day of the month, and I was among the exiles by the river Chebar, the heavens were opened and I saw visions of God. On the fifth day of the month (it was the fifth year of exile of King Jehoiachin), the word of Yahweh came to the priest Ezekiel son of Buzi, in the land of the Chaldeans by the river Chebar; and the hand of Yahweh was on him there. (Ezek. 1.1-3)

In the second year of King Darius, in the sixth month, on the first day of the month, the word of Yahweh was in the hand of Haggai, the prophet, to Zerubbabel, son of Shealtiel, governor of Judah, and to Joshua son of Jehozadak, the high priest. (Hag. 1.1)

In the eighth month, in the second year of Darius, the word of Yahweh came to the prophet Zechariah, son of Berechiah, son of Iddo, the prophet. (Zech. 1.1)

This increased precision has the effect of presenting these prophetic figures as inhabiting a better-known period of time and of placing the other prophets in a more distant and less well-known period of time. Each of these prophetic 'books' also provides more precise dating throughout the 'book'.

Although not all the superscriptions of prophetic 'books' make a reference to time, it is significant that each of the four prophetic scrolls—Jeremiah, Ezekiel, Isaiah and the Twelve—does make such a reference to time at the beginning of the scroll. If these four scrolls of the Latter Prophets are archived as a collection, these references to time can be understood as codes suggesting to the reader how the four prophetic scrolls represent a continuation of the Former Prophets, which are also ordered in temporal sequence. The scrolls of the Former Prophets also begin with reference to time by citing well-known figures from Israel's past, just as the superscriptions of the Latter Prophets make reference to Judean and Israelite kings:

And it happened (ויהי) after the death of Moses, the servant of Yahweh that Yahweh said to Joshua, the son of Nun, the assistant of Moses, saying… (Josh. 1.1)

And it happened (ויהי) after the death of Joshua that Israel asked Yahweh, 'Who will go up for us to the Canaanite at first to fight him?' (Judg. 1.1)

And there was (ויהי) a certain man from Ramathaim, a Zuphite from the hill country of Ephraim and his name was Elkanah[6] the son of Jeroham, the son of Elihu, the son of Tohu, the son of Zuph, an Ephramite. He had two

---

6. The father of Samuel.

wives; the name of the one was Hannah, and the name of the other Penin-
nah. Penniah had two children, but Hannah had no children. (1 Sam. 1.1-2)

And King David was old, advanced in years… (1 Kgs 1.1)

These four scrolls, grouped together in a series, advance a narrative following a sequence of time from the death of Moses to the destruction of
Jerusalem and the beginning of Babylonian exile. Kings ends with the
account of the end of the monarchy in Judah with its last kings Josiah,
Jehoiakim, Jehoiachin and Zedekiah. Three of these kings (Josiah, Jehoiakim and Zedekiah) are mentioned in the superscription of Jeremiah. As
the rabbis say, the scroll of Jeremiah continues the account of the destruction at the end of Kings. It does this by supplementing the account in Kings
with 'the words of Jeremiah'.

Jehoiachin is not mentioned in the superscription of Jeremiah, perhaps
because within the book Jeremiah is portrayed as being much more
actively involved with Jehoiakim and Zedekiah. However, in the 'book' of
Jeremiah, Jehoiachin is mentioned in ch. 52, which repeats in a slightly
different form the ending of 2 Kgs 24.18–25.30. This repetition is significant because Jeremiah 52 ends with the release of Jehoiachin from prison
(52.31-34), the setting for Ezekiel's 'visions of God' when 'the word of
Yahweh came to Ezekiel during the fifth year of the exile of Jehoiachin'
(Ezek. 1.2). That Jeremiah 52 is functioning as a transitional chapter at the
end of the book of Jeremiah is supported by the scribal note at the end of
Jeremiah 51, 'until here the words of Jeremiah' (עד הנה דברי ירמיהו).
This phrase repeats the phrase at the beginning of Jeremiah—'the words of
Jeremiah' (דברי ירמיהו) bringing closure to the main emphasis of the
scroll of Jeremiah before moving on to Ezekiel. The 'book' of Ezekiel
moves the course of events ahead to a new time and to a new place—
Babylon at the time of Jehoiachin.

Haggai and Zechariah, the two other prophetic books that share the
feature of precise dating with Jeremiah and Ezekiel, bring the chronology
to an end in Jerusalem when temple reconstruction has begun at the time
of the Persian king Darius (Hag. 1.14; 2.18). Temple construction seems
to be complete in Malachi when the rabbinic prophetic canon ends. It is
significant that at the closing of this collection the reader is exhorted,
'Remember, the *torah* of my servant Moses, the statues and ordinances
that I commanded him at Horeb for all Israel' (Mal. 3.22 [Eng. 4.4]). This
reference at the close of the prophetic canon recalls the opening of the prophetic canon 'after the death of Moses' (Josh. 1.1), which exhorts Joshua
to obey the *torah* of Moses:

Only be strong and very courageous, being careful to act in accordance with all the *torah* that my servant Moses, commanded you; do not turn from it to the right hand or the left, so that you may be successful wherever you go. This book of the *torah* shall not depart out of your mouth; you shall mediate on it day and night, so that you may be careful to act in accordance with all that is written in it.[7] (Josh. 1.7-8)

To summarize, I am suggesting that the superscriptions at the beginning of the scrolls of Jeremiah and Ezekiel indicate an arrangement of material that continues the chronological ordering found in the Former Prophets. The superscriptions advance the 'history' of Yahweh with his people Judah/Israel. 'Jeremiah's words' are commentary on the 'history' of destruction found at the end of Kings. Ezekiel advances the outline of the story in time and place from Jerusalem to Babylonian exile where reconstruction is envisaged. The dating in Haggai and Zechariah brings a closure to the series of 'events' narrated in this collection of scrolls to the time of the Persian king Darius. Furthermore, this ordered canonical whole at its beginning and end makes reference to the *torah* of Moses with which this collection appears to be closely linked.

But how do Isaiah and the beginning of the Twelve fit into this ordered arrangement of scrolls? They both begin with superscriptions that appear to disrupt this chronological order with an allusion to a more vaguely remembered past in the days of Uzziah, Jotham, Ahaz and Hezekiah, kings of Judah (Isa. 1.1; Hos. 1.1).[8] These are kings who reigned at least a century earlier than the kings mentioned in Jeremiah and Ezekiel. To answer the question about how Isaiah and the beginning of the Twelve fit an ordered continuity in the collection of the prophetic scrolls, it will be necessary to take another look at the superscriptions, and this time to focus on matters other than explicit references to dating.

3. *Vision and Visions*

A clue for understanding how the superscription in Isaiah might suggest continuity with Ezekiel in the chronological ordering of scrolls can be

---

7.   I will look more closely at 'book of the *torah* (covenant)' in the prophetic collection in Chapter 5 since the prophetic collection is concerned with this lost and found book and the consequences of its being lost and found. The prophets are ordered and arranged as commentary on God's character revealed in the *torah* disclosed to Moses. I will discuss the significance of the mention of Elijah at the very end of Malachi (3.23-24 [Eng. 4.5-6]) in Chapter 8.

8.   Hos. 1.1 also mentions that this was the time of Jeroboam of Israel.

found in the meaning of the phrase 'the vision (חזון) of Isaiah'. To determine the meaning of that phrase, it will be important to compare and
contrast the meaning of 'the vision of Isaiah' in Isa. 1.1 with 'the visions
(מראות) of God' in Ezek. 1.1. It will also be important to look at חזון in
the two other superscriptions, both of which occur in the Twelve. In
Obad. 1 the superscription is simply 'the vision (חזון) of Obadiah', while
in Nahum the superscription is slightly longer in length, 'An oracle concerning Nineveh, the "book" of the vision (חזון) of Nahum of Elkosh'.
Also, significant for this discussion is the command Yahweh issues
Habakkuk to 'write a vision (חזון)' (2.2-3).

   The phrase 'the visions (מראות) of God' occurs three times in Ezekiel.
In addition to 1.1, it also occurs in 8.3 and 40.2. These three occurrences
have often been cited as indications of the structure of the book as a whole[9]
and in that sense they suggest temporal sequence in Ezekiel's world.
These three references are all accompanied by a lengthy and detailed
description of what Ezekiel sees (1.1–3.15; 8.1–11.25; 40.1–48.35). It is
important for our discussion to point out that everything he sees is taking
place in his present world. He may be transported from Babylon to Jerusalem in 8.1–11.25 and from Babylon to the land of Israel in 40.1–48.35 to
see things, but what he sees in the 'visions' (מראות) is portrayed as contemporaneous with his own experience of time in exile.

   He looks and he sees (ראה)[10] things and the things he sees are now
(הנה)[11] taking place. What he sees in 1.1–3.15 sounds bizarre to a contemporary reader for the description of what he sees is the appearance of 'the
glory of God'. This appearance is dated to 'the thirtieth year in the fourth
month, on the fifth day of the month' when he was 'among the exiles by
the river Chebar' (Ezek. 1.1). He does not see God in some other world or
place but in his own world and in his own specifically designated time. In
8.1–11.25 he sees things taking place in the temple in Jerusalem, including
Yahweh's departure from the temple (11.22) and all those things that he
saw were taking place in his own time, 'in the sixth year, in the sixth
month, on the fifth day of the month' (8.1). In 40.1–48.35 he sees the city
and temple measured for restoration and the return of Yahweh to the
temple (43.3-4). These things were happening 'in the twenty-fifth year of

   9.   Ellen F. Davis, *Swallowing the Scroll: Textuality and the Dynamics of Discourse in Ezekiel's Prophecy* (Bible and Literature Series, 21; Sheffield: Almond Press,
1989), p. 11.
   10. See, e.g., Ezek. 1.4; 8.2; 40.4.
   11. See, e.g., Ezek. 1.4; 8.2; 40.5.

our exile, at the beginning of the year, on the tenth day of the month, in the fourteenth year after the city was struck down, on that very day…' (40.1). The 'visions of God' that Ezekiel sees are about events taking place in Ezekiel's present world.

I will argue that 'the vision (חזון) of Isaiah' is different from Ezekiel's 'visions (מראות) of God'. While it is customary to translate both חזון and מראה as 'vision', they are encoding different information for the Model Reader of these two texts. The significant difference is that that 'the vision (חזון) of Isaiah' concerns a future time, not a contemporaneous time as do Ezekiel's 'visions (מראות) of God'. Furthermore, 'the vision' (חזון) of Isaiah is more than a matter of seeing things in the present; it is also a document (ספר), written down for another time. In order to make these points about a חזון, I want to begin by looking at the חזון of the prophet Samuel in 1 Samuel 3.

1 Samuel 3 is the story about Samuel, 'a trustworthy prophet of Yahweh' (3.20) at the time when he was just a boy ministering with Eli (3.1) at the temple in Shiloh (3.21). The story tells us that this was a time when 'the word of Yahweh' (דבר יהוה) was 'rare' (יקר),[12] and further qualifies this by saying that 'in those days vision (חזון) was not a frequent occurrence'.[13] It is important to point out here that 'vision' (חזון) and 'the word of Yahweh' (דבר יהוה) are paralleled in this passage. I will want to come back to this equation later on in the discussion. Here I simply want to make the point that while a חזון may be a דבר יהוה, it is clear from the superscriptions that not every דבר יהוה is necessarily a חזון. For example, Ezekiel's 'visions (מראות) of God' and 'the words (דברי) of Jeremiah' are both identified in the superscriptions as 'the word of Yahweh' (יהוה דבר, Jer. 1.2; Ezek. 1.3).

After informing the reader that Eli's eyesight was diminishing so that he was no longer able to see—perhaps, in this way, also offering a reason for the rarity of חזון in those days—the narrative tells us that Samuel was lying down in 'the temple of Yahweh' (3.3) in Shiloh (3.21) near the ark of God. Here the narrative is setting the stage for Samuel to receive a 'vision' in the temple.

This setting for the reception of a חזון in a temple is significant—it helps to further clarify the distinctiveness of the superscriptions in prophetic

---

12. This word also carries with it the connotations of 'precious' or 'costly', that is, something 'highly valued'.

13. נפרץ is used here in the sense of 'being burst forth'.

books.[14] Ezekiel cannot and does not have a חזון because he is in exile where he does not have access to the temple. What he sees, 'מראות of God', appear(s) to him in a foreign land by the river Chebar (1.1) or in his house (8.1).[15] While Yahweh enables him to see at first abominable practices in the Jerusalem temple resulting in Yahweh's departure from the temple and later to see Yahweh return and a man with a 'blueprint' for city and temple reconstruction, his 'visions (מראות) of God' originate in Babylon. They do not arise from his presence in the temple. What he sees is not a חזון. The superscription in the 'book' of Jeremiah concerns 'the words of Jeremiah'. What follows is not a חזון. Jeremiah also does not have a חזון because he is barred from entering the temple. Significantly, in Jeremiah's address in the temple, he quotes Yahweh as saying that in the past he had destroyed his temple in Shiloh (Jer. 7.8-15), the place where Samuel in this story is about to receive a חזון. In a similar way he will destroy the present temple in Jerusalem in which the people put their trust.

While Samuel is lying down in the temple, Yahweh calls his name, 'Samuel, Samuel', and Samuel replies, 'here I am' (הנני, 1 Sam. 3.4). One is reminded of Isaiah, who also heard Yahweh speak when he saw Yahweh in the temple in Jerusalem and responds with the same words, 'here I am' (הנני, Isa. 7.8). This incident in Samuel, however, unlike the occasion in Isaiah, comes in the story as a way of demonstrating Samuel's inexperience, so that he becomes confused. Not realizing that Yahweh is calling him, he goes to Eli, whom he mistakenly thinks is summoning him. The narrative reports that 'Samuel did not yet know Yahweh' and that 'the word/thing of Yahweh (דבר יהוה) had not yet been revealed to him' (3.7). Here 'the word of Yahweh', about to be made known to Samuel, is a חזון (3.1). After Eli realizes that it is Yahweh who is calling Samuel, Eli says to Samuel, 'Go, lie down; and if he calls you, you shall say, "Speak, Yahweh, for your servant is listening"' (3.10). Samuel carries out Eli's instructions and when he responds to Yahweh who calls him again, Yahweh reveals to him a חזון:

> See (הנה), I am about to do a thing (דבר) in Israel that the two ears of everyone who hears will tingle. On that day I will carry out everything which I spoke concerning Eli and his house from beginning to end. For I have declared to him that I will judge his house forever because of the

14. Later I will show the significance of the prophet Nathan's words to David about the temple to be built in Jerusalem which is described as a חזון in 2 Sam. 7.17 and 1 Chron. 17.15.

15. Ezek. 40.1 does not specify a particular setting in Babylon.

iniquity that he knew his sons were blaspheming for themselves, and he did not restrain them. Therefore I swear to the house of Eli that the iniquity of the house of Eli will not be expiated forever. (1 Sam. 3.11-14)

The important observation about this חזון of Samuel is that what he beholds is a 'thing' (דבר) of Yahweh about the future. He is not seeing things happening in his present world, as was Ezekiel, but a thing that will happen in the future, 'on that day'. The way דבר is used in this חזון suggests that what is revealed to the prophet is not just a 'word' of Yahweh but the 'thing' itself. The prophet sees the future 'thing of Yahweh' (דבר יהוה) in the חזון.

At the end of this episode the narrator informs us that Samuel lay there until morning and was afraid to tell 'the vision' (המראה) to Eli (3.15). But Eli insists that nothing should be hidden from him. This narrative comment raises the question: Why does the narrator use the word מראה rather than חזון for what Samuel has just seen? A possible explanation is that the story has been about the boy Samuel who is a novice. He did not originally recognize that Yahweh was summoning him. It is possible that the narrator, by using the word מראה, is sustaining the notion of the inexperience of Eli and the rarity of a חזון in those days. It is also possible to understand that מראה is a term for 'vision' that can be used with a broader range of meaning than חזון. While a חזון may be a מראה not every מראה is a חזון. I will argue shortly that, because a חזון is a 'vision' about a 'דבר' of Yahweh' for a future time, it is written down. A חזון, unlike a מראה, is a vision that is also a writing, a ספר.[16] A much more likely explanation for the use of מראה here is that the narrator is presenting Samuel, the inexperienced and frightened prophet, in his eagerness *to tell* the vision (מראה) to Samuel. He is not originally intent on writing it down as a חזון. Perhaps, the novice Samuel does not know that what he has just encountered in the temple needs to be written down as a חזון for future reference.

That Samuel did eventually write down the חזון may be the meaning of the narrator's comment that comes at the end of the story. 'Yahweh was with him and he [Samuel] did not cause any his [Yahweh's] words to fall (הפיל) to the ground' (3.19). Not causing words to fall to the ground may suggest that they were written down in order to be consulted for future

16. In Chronicles a vision is understood as something written, but here the writing seems to be concerned with writing down the words/things (דברי) of kings. See 2 Chron. 32.32, which says, 'And the rest of the words/deeds of Hezekiah and his good deeds, are they not written in the vision (חזון) of Isaiah, the son of Amoz the prophet in a book of the kings of Judah and Israel?' See also 2 Chron. 9.29.

reference as confirmation of an earlier חזון of Yahweh. This appears to be the significance of the similar phrase about not allowing Yahweh's words to fall to the ground used by Jehu with reference to Elijah in 2 Kgs 10.10. Elijah is no longer present at this time but has been taken up into the heavens in a chariot of fire. After the sons of Ahab have been killed (2 Kgs 10.1-9), fulfilling a דבר יהוה that came to Elijah earlier (1 Kgs 21.28-29), Jehu says, 'Know then that the word of Yahweh will not fall to the earth which Yahweh spoke concerning the house of Ahab. And Yahweh has done what he spoke *by the hand of* his servant Elijah' (2 Kgs 10.10). As I will argue below, to speak 'by the hand of' (ביד) is to speak by means of something written and carried in the hand.[17] Yahweh's words will not fall to the earth when his דבר is written down, and this future about which Yahweh speaks comes to fulfilment.

Other superscriptions of 'books' in the Latter Prophets support the notion that a חזון is a vision about some(thing) (דבר) that Yahweh has decreed about the future[18] and that is written down. While the חזון of Obadiah (Obad. 1) makes no mention of writing, his חזון is about Yahweh's report about Edom's future destruction and the future rescue of exiles of Israel and Jerusalem. However, Nahum's חזון is an 'oracle/burden' (משא) as well as a book (ספר) concerning the future fate of Nineveh (Nah. 1.1). This חזון of Nahum is something that can be carried 'in the hand' in written form as an oracle/burden (משא), a document (ספר).

חזון as something written down gains further support from Habakkuk. The superscription of Habakkuk identifies what follows as 'the oracle (משא) which Habakkuk the prophet saw (חזה)'. What Habakkuk sees is the coming of the Chaldeans whom Yahweh is raising up. That this 'oracle' is to be understood as a חזון, like Nahum's oracle, and that it is also something that is written, is clear from an order Yahweh gives to Habakkuk later in the 'book'. In Hab. 2.2-3, Yahweh says to Habakkuk:

Write (כתוב) *the vision* (חזון),
   make it plain (ובאר) on tablets (הלחות)
   in order that a reader (קורא) may run with it.[19]
For a vision (חזון) is yet for an appointed time (למועד);
   and it will breathe out for the end,

---

17. See Hos. 12.11 (Eng. 12.10), which associates vision as something 'in the hand' of the prophets. Yahweh says, 'I spoke to the prophets; it was I who multiplied vision (חזון) and by the hand of (ביד) the prophets I will bring destruction'.

18. See Ezek. 7.13 where a חזון appears to be about an inevitable future.

19. NRSV inexplicably translates 'so that a runner may read it'.

it will not lie.
If it lingers, wait (חכה) for it;
for it will surely come,
it will not tarry (יאחר).

This instruction to Habakkuk supports the notion that a חזון is something written about what Yahweh has decreed about the future, and additionally that a חזון may be delayed so that it may be necessary to wait (חכה) for it to come to fruition.[20] The notion of waiting further substantiates the identification of a חזון as something that is for the future rather than a vision of something that is immediately present, as were Ezekiel's 'visions of God'.

This discussion of חזון suggests how 'the חזון of Isaiah' in Isa. 1.1 can be understood as a code for the Model Reader of the book of Isaiah. It is a sign of how a reader can read Isaiah as a scroll that follows Ezekiel in series of scrolls ordered chronologically. Isaiah's חזון was something 'he saw (חזה) concerning Judah and Jerusalem in the days of Uzziah, Jotham, Ahaz and Hezekiah, kings of Judah'. However, his חזון was not about the days of these former Judean kings. His חזון was a 'vision' about another time. It concerns Judah and Jerusalem in the time of consolation and restoration following exile, the period that follows what Ezekiel saw in the visions of God about Yahweh's return to Jerusalem and the plans for the reconstructed city and temple.

It will be necessary to speak in more detail about Isaiah's 'vision' and how it relates to this prophetic 'book' as a whole in Chapter 7. However, there are features associated with the materials collected and arranged on this scroll that fit with the notion of a vision as it has been outlined above. The vision of Isaiah is a 'thing' (דבר) of Yahweh concerning the future of Judah and Jerusalem. A scribal notation, and what follows in 2.1-4, supports this notion:

The thing (דבר) that Isaiah son of Amoz saw (חזה) concerning Judah and Jerusalem.

In days to come
the mountain of Yahweh's house
shall be established as the highest of the mountains,
and shall be raised above the hills;
all the nations shall stream to it.

---

20. See Ezek. 12.22, 23, 24 and 27, in which the proverb quoted there—'The days are prolonged, and every vision (חזון) comes to nothing'—seems to be a play on the notion delay and waiting.

Many peoples shall say,
  'Come, let us go up to the mountain of Yahweh,
  to the house of God of Jacob;
that he may teach us his ways
  and that we may walk in his paths'.
For out of Zion shall go forth *torah*
  and the word of Yahweh from Jerusalem.
He shall judge between the nations,
  and shall arbitrate for many peoples;
they shall beat their swords into plowshares,
  and their spears into pruning hooks;
nation shall not lift up sword against nation,
  neither shall they learn war any more.[21]

Like Samuel, Isaiah has his vision in the temple, although this is in the temple in Jerusalem, not Shiloh. 'In the year that King Uzziah died, I saw Yahweh sitting on a throne, high and lofty, and the hem of his robe filled the temple' (6.1). Also, like Samuel he hears Yahweh speaking. Yahweh, however, is asking a question rather than calling his name: 'Then I heard the voice of Yahweh saying, "Whom shall I send, and who will go for us"' (6.8). Also like Samuel, Isaiah responds 'Here I am' (הנני) and further declares 'Send me!' (6.8). That Isaiah's 'vision' is for another time and not for his own time is clear from the way Yahweh speaks to Isaiah. According to Yahweh, the vision is for the future and, like the vision of Habakkuk, it will be delayed (6.9-13):

Go and say to the people:

'Keep listening, but do not comprehend;
  keep looking, but do not understand.
Make the mind of this people dull,
  and stop their ears,
  and shut their eyes,
so that they may not look with their eyes,
  and listen with their ears,
and comprehend with their minds,
  and turn and be healed'.
Then I said, 'How long, O Yahweh?' And he said:
'Until cities lie waste without inhabitant,
  and houses without people, and the land is utterly desolate;
until Yahweh sends everyone far away,
  and vast is the emptiness in the midst of the land.

21. This 'word of Yahweh' about the future is similar to that in Mic. 4.1-4, a prophetic text that is concerned not just with Jerusalem but also with Samaria.

Even if a tenth part remain in it,
> it will be burned again,
like a terebinth or an oak
> whose stump remains standing when it is felled.
The holy seed is its stump.

For Isaiah, this is a time of writing down and waiting, as it was for Habakkuk. In 8.16-17 Isaiah's gives a command: 'Bind up the testimony, seal the *torah* among my disciples. I will wait (חכיתי[22]) for Yahweh, who is hiding his face from the house of Jacob and I will hope (וקויתי) in him'. That Isaiah's vision is a written document for another time is also clear from two other passages in the book. In 29.11-12 the incomprehensibility of Isaiah's vision for people of his own time is reiterated:

> The vision (חזות) of all this has become for you like the words of a 'book' (ספר). If it is given to those who can read, with the command, 'Read this', they say, 'We cannot, for it is sealed'. And if it is given to those who cannot read, saying, 'Read this', they say, 'We cannot read'.

Another passage in Isaiah, which shares vocabulary with the command to Habakkuk to write down his vision (Hab. 2.2-3), is Isa. 30.8-11:

> Go now, write (כתבה) it [the vision[23]] before them on a tablet (לוח)
> > and inscribe it (חקה) in a book (ספר).
> so that it may be for the time to come (ליום אחרון)
> > as a witness forever.
> For they are a rebellious people, faithless children,
> > children who will not hear the *torah* of Yahweh;
> who say to the seers, 'Do not see';
> > and to the prophets, 'Do not prophecy to us what is right;
> speak to us smooth things,
> > prophesy illusions,
> leave the way, turn aside from the past
> > let us hear no more about the Holy One of Israel'.

Isaiah, then, following Ezekiel in the rabbinic canon, can be read as continuing chronological order. 'The words of Jeremiah' continue the account of Babylonian destruction at the end of Kings and are words addressed to the community in Jerusalem at that time. The 'visions of God' that Ezekiel sees are about events taking place in exilic times associated with and

---

22. Here the same Hebrew verb meaning 'to wait', חכה, is used in both Isaiah and Habakkuk.

23. For a fuller discussion of reading and writing the vision of Isaiah, see my *Reading Isaiah*, pp. 117-53.

following the destruction of Judah and Jerusalem. What Isaiah saw in the days of the Judean kings, Uzziah, Jotham, Ahaz and Hezekiah was a חָזוֹן; it was for another time, a time of consolation and return following Ezekiel's visions of Yahweh's return to Jerusalem. This חָזוֹן was something people in his own time could not understand. Their eyes were blind and their ears were deaf to this דָּבָר of Yahweh because Isaiah's חָזוֹן was for another time.

4. *Word and Words*

Before looking at how the opening of the 'book' of the Twelve can be understood to fit the chronological ordering of scrolls in the rabbinic canonical collection, I want to look more closely at the superscription in the 'books' of Jeremiah and Amos. These 'books' contain the only two superscriptions that begin with the phrase, 'the words of'. What does the phrase 'the words of Jeremiah' or 'the words of Amos' signal to the reader about how to read the collection that follows in Jeremiah or Amos? Although it has become conventional to speak of 'visions' in Jeremiah and Amos, what follows in both books is not the same as 'vision' (חָזוֹן) or 'visions (מַרְאוֹת) of God'.[24]

When Yahweh shows things to Amos and Jeremiah, what they see are mundane things which serve as metaphorical images of Yahweh's words. What Jeremiah sees is sometimes encapsulated in puns as in 1.11-12 where he sees 'a branch of almond (שָׁקֵד)' as an expression of Yahweh's words: 'You have seen well for I am watching (שֹׁקֵד) over my word to perform it'. In a similar way, although not as a pun, Jeremiah sees a 'boiling pot, tilted away from the north' as visual imagery of Yahweh's words about disaster that shall come out of the north (1.13b-16). In like manner,

---

24. The word מַרְאֶה (including its plural form מַרְאוֹת) does not occur in either book. חָזוֹן occurs only in Jeremiah where it is used to refer to 'visions' that are false. In response to Jeremiah's observation that the prophets who are telling the people that they will see peace rather than sword or famine (14.13), Yahweh responds (14.14): 'The prophets are prophesying a lie in my name; I did not send them and I did not command them and I did not speak to them. A deceptive vision (חָזוֹן), worthless divination and deceitfulness of their own mind they are prophesying to you.' In the well-known chapter on the false prophets (Jer. 23), Yahweh says to Jeremiah, 'Do not listen to the words of the prophets who are prophesying to you; they are causing you to become vain. A vision (חָזוֹן) of their own mind they speak, not from the mouth of Yahweh. They are the ones who say continually to the ones who spurn [what] Yahweh spoke. "Peace will be to you"' (23.16-17a).

Amos sees a basket of summer fruit (קָיִץ), a metaphorical pun suggesting Yahweh's words, 'The end (הַקֵּץ) has come upon my people Israel; I will never again pass by...' (8.2). Likewise, locusts eating the latter growth (7.1-2) and a plumb line (7.7) are visual expressions of Yahweh's words. It is in this sense of seeing things as metaphorical expressions of Yahweh's words that we should understand the expression 'the words of Amos...which he saw (חזה)', which occurs in the superscription to the book.[25] Amos and Jeremiah see things in their world as visual expressions of Yahweh's words. The superscriptions containing the phrase 'the words of' signal that what is important in both books are 'words' not 'visions'.

To understand what is meant by the phrase 'the words of' and how it can be further distinguished from a חזון or a מראות, I want to look first at its significance in the superscription of Jeremiah. That Jeremiah is a prophetic book concerned with 'words' (דברים) is evident in the simple observation that the plural form, 'words', occurs in the book about 85 times. This use is substantially more frequent than in other prophetic scrolls. In Isaiah it is used twelve times, none of which is in reference to the words of Isaiah, although it is used seven times to refer to the words of the Rabshakeh or the words of Sennacherib (36.12, 13, 22; 37.1, 4, 6, 17). In Ezekiel, 'words' occurs seven times and refers to the words of Ezekiel only on two occasions (33.31, 32). In the book of the Twelve, 'words' occurs twelve times: three times in Amos (1.1; 7.10; 8.11) and only one other time to refer the words of a prophet (Hag. 1.12).[26]

In the superscription to Jeremiah, 'the words (דברי) of Jeremiah' (1.1) are identified as 'the דבר of Yahweh' (1.2), just as 'the vision Isaiah' (1.1) is understood as 'the דבר of Yahweh' (2.1) and 'the visions of God' that Ezekiel sees (1.1) are also understood as 'the דבר of Yahweh' (1.2). 'The דבר of Yahweh' appears to be a broad category encapsulating a variety of things: חזון, מאָרות of God and דברים. Unlike Isaiah's חזון, which is for another time and only dated with the general reference 'in the days of Uzziah, Jotham, Ahaz and Hezekiah, kings of Judah', 'the words of Jeremiah' are given a specific date from the eleventh year of King Josiah until the eleventh year of King Zedekiah. These words of Jeremiah are for his own time just as 'the visions of God' in Ezekiel were understood as 'the דבר of Yahweh' for very specific times during the exile.

---

25. I will look at Amos 9, a different kind of seeing, in my discussion of 'the words of Amos', which follows.

26. It occurs in Zech. 7.7, 12 and 8.9 to refer to 'the words of the former prophets'.

'The words of Jeremiah' receive clarity from the canonical context, which provides for the reader additional detail about the period of time from the thirteenth year of Josiah until the eleventh year of Zedekiah. If we understand the superscription of Jeremiah to be a scribal notation directed to the Model Reader indicating how to read what has been ordered and collected together in a series of scrolls, then it is possible to understand 'the words of Jeremiah' as a verbal connection pointing back to what has preceded in the canonical collection. In other words, the phrase, 'the words of Jeremiah', signals how to read what follows by connecting it with what precedes it in canonical order.

I have already noted that the superscription of Jeremiah mentions three of the kings whose actions are depicted at the conclusion of Kings (Josiah, Jehoiakim and Zedekiah). This mention suggests a link in time with the 'events' portrayed at the end of the preceding 'book' of Kings. Furthermore, the 'book' of Jeremiah also appends ch. 52, repeating 2 Kgs 24.18-25, in which Jehoiachin is mentioned. This repetition forms a link with Ezekiel's 'visions of God' dated at the time of the exile of Jehoiachin. These references to kings and dates in the superscriptions, as I have argued, represent scribal codes for the Model Reader concerning how the prophetic scrolls are ordered in a chronological arrangement. Isaiah's חזון, then, follows Ezekiel's מראות of God as 'the דבר of Yahweh' depicting the coming about of the plans for restoration Ezekiel sees. So also Jeremiah's words can be interpreted as concluding Yahweh's unfinished words for Judah and Jerusalem that come at the end of Kings.

2 Kings 22 and 23 are concerned with 'the words' of another prophet, Moses, written in 'the book of the *torah*/covenant'. Important for canonical design is the reference to this book of Moses found at the very beginning of the collection in Joshua and at the end of the collection in Malachi:

> Only be strong and very courageous, being careful to act in accordance with all the *torah* that my servant Moses commanded you; do not turn from it to the right hand or to the left, so that you may be successful wherever you go. The book of the law (ספר תורה) shall not depart out of your mouth (פיך); you shall meditate on it night and day, so that you may be careful to act in accordance with all that is written in it. For then you shall make your way prosperous, and then you shall be successful. I hereby command you: Be strong and courageous; do not be frightened or dismayed, for Yahweh your God is with you wherever you go. (Josh. 1.7-9)
>
> Remember the torah of Moses, my servant, which I commanded him in Horeb concerning all Israel. (Mal. 3.22)

At the very end of the prophetic collection of scrolls there is a scribal notation addressed to the reader, 'Remember the teaching of my servant Moses, the statutes and ordinances that I commanded him at Horeb for all Israel'. The reference to the *torah* of Moses, then, comes at the beginning, the middle and the end of the rabbinic collection of prophetic scrolls extending from Joshua to the end of the Twelve and is significant for understanding this ordering of scrolls.

The end of Kings and the beginning of Jeremiah come at a central point in the prophetic collection of scrolls as a kind of chiasmic high point concerned with the words of Moses and the words of Jeremiah. The end of Kings is about a time of destruction and devastation rather than the prosperity and success that Yahweh had promised Joshua, saying that the *torah* should 'not depart from your mouth (פיך)'. At the time of destruction of Judah and Jerusalem Yahweh says to Jeremiah, 'I have put my words in your mouth (פיך)' (Jer. 1.9).

In order to see more clearly how the phrase 'the words of Jeremiah' fits this high point in the collection, I want to look more closely at 2 Kings 22–23 concerning the words of Moses written in the book of the *torah*/covenant[27] mentioned there. According to this well-known story, 'the book of the *torah*' (ספר תורה) was found (22.8) in the course of renovations that were being carried out on the temple at the instructions of Josiah, king of Judah. When the king heard the words of this book of the *torah*, he commanded that enquiries be made of the prophetess Huldah concerning the book and learned that because he was penitent he would not see the disaster to befall the place. He read the book to all the people and made a covenant with Yahweh (22.11–23.3). In 13 verses suggesting quick and decisive action by Josiah, reference is made to 'the words' of the book seven times (22.11, 13 [twice], 15, 18; 23.2, 3). After making the covenant he carries out a reform, destroying cultic personnel and cultic objects throughout Judah and Israel and commanding the people to keep the Passover. In doing these things Josiah 'established the words of the *torah* that were written in the book that the priest Hilkiah found in the house of Yahweh' (23.24).

The significance of 'the words of this book of the *torah*/covenant' and its importance for understanding 'the words of Jeremiah' and the canonical order of prophetic books is to be found in what is said in the story

---

27. The book has two designations in 2 Kgs 22–23: 'the book of the *torah*' (22.8, 9, 11) and 'the book of the covenant' (23.2, 21).

following Josiah's actions, not in the actions themselves. The narrative tells us that 'nothing like this Passover was practiced in the days of the judges when they judged Israel and for all the days of the kings of Israel and Judah' (23.22), apparently because 'the book of the *torah*/covenant' had become lost. This observation about the absence of the practice of Passover for all those days matches an absence in what is reported in the canonical ordering of prophetic scrolls. 'The book of the *torah*/covenant' is absent from the stories reported. As we have seen, it is present at the beginning of Joshua, and Joshua is not to let it disappear from his lips (1.8). It has a continual presence in the 'book' of Joshua. Joshua's actions in building an altar are governed by it (8.31), the people continue to be exhorted to follow its stipulations (8.34; 23.6), and it continues to be the basis of covenant making (24.26). But then there is no further reference to it in the story until the time of Josiah.[28]

This very absence serves to highlight the significance of its reappearance toward the end of Kings. It will not appear again until reference is made to the *torah* of Moses at the end of the collection (Mal. 3.22 [Eng. 4.4]). A reader might be led to think that the actions of Josiah would represent a closure or an end. Indeed, Josiah established 'the words of the *torah* that were written in the book that the priest Hilkiah had found in the house of Yahweh' (2 Kgs 22.24). Yet there is an ominous note following these actions of Josiah in 2 Kgs 23.24-26:

> Yet, Yahweh will not turn from his great burning anger with which his anger was kindled against Judah concerning all the vexations by which Manasseh had made him indignant. And Yahweh said also I will remove Judah from my presence just like I removed Israel and I will reject this city which I chose, Jerusalem and the house which I said, my name will be there.

This verse is significant for understanding the two prophetic books to follow. In Jeremiah Yahweh rejects the city and in Ezekiel he rejects the temple and removes his presence from Judah.

But what is the significance of 'the words of Jeremiah' in all this? The answer I think is to be found by taking a look at the origin of 'the words of the *torah*/covenant' in 2 Kings. One does not hear of its origin in the

---

28. There is a reference to it in 2 Kgs 14.6, a narrative comment that Amaziah 'did not put to death the children of the murderers; according to what is written in the book of he *torah* of Moses, where Yahweh commanded, "The fathers shall not put to death for the children, or the children be put to death for the fathers; but every man shall die for his own sin"'.

prophetic canon. To understand its origin, it is necessary to look at another canonical collection, the Torah. The origin of the book of the *torah*/covenant is found in Exod. 24.3-7, in an original ceremony of covenant making like the later covenant of Josiah:

> And Moses came and he declared to the people all the words (דברים) and all the judgments, and all the people answered with one voice and said, 'All the words (דברים) which Moses spoke we will do. And Moses wrote (ויכתב) all the words of (דברי) Yahweh... Then he took the book of the covenant (ספר הברית) and he read (ויקרא) in the ears of (באזני) all the people, and they said, 'Everything which Yahweh spoke we will do and we will obey'.

These actions of Moses in speaking, writing and reading 'words' of Yahweh are matched in Jeremiah, as numerous scholars have observed in the past. Jeremiah also speaks, writes down and reads the 'words' of Yahweh, as he does in Jeremiah 36.[29] Jeremiah is a Moses-like prophet who speaks, writes down and reads Yahweh's words addressed to a community that will experience the destruction of the temple and the city as announced in 2 Kgs 23.26-27. Jeremiah is concerned with the words of Yahweh—words that have not been appeased by the actions of Josiah to establish all the words of the book of the *torah*/covenant. The phrase 'The words of Jeremiah', then, introduces a book concerning the words of Yahweh that explains why Judah and the temple will meet with destruction. What follows in Jeremiah is not a חזון of what Yahweh will do in some distant future, or מראות of God enabling Jeremiah to see Yahweh's movements or the movements of others, but the speaking, writing down and reading out of Yahweh's words giving justification for the destruction and the exile about to take place.

Of course, as many have pointed out in the past, a prophet like Moses was anticipated in the Torah. Yahweh says to Moses in Deut. 18.18, 'A prophet like you, I will raise up for them from the midst of their brothers and I will put my words in his mouth (ונתתי דברי בפיו) and he will speak to them everything that I command him'. This future action of Yahweh announced in the days of Moses is a present reality in the call of Jeremiah (1.9), 'Behold I have put my words in your mouth' (הנה נתתי דברי בפיך).

To summarize the discussion, I have argued here that 'the words of Jeremiah' can be understood as linking Jeremiah in an ordered way with

---

29. In Jeremiah, of course, reading and writing is done through the scribe Baruch.

the preceding book of Kings. As a prophet like Moses, Jeremiah speaks, writes down and reads out the words of Yahweh. He explains why Yahweh's anger was not appeased by Josiah's actions to establish the words in the book of the covenant (see 2 Kgs 23.26-27) and explains why Jerusalem will be destroyed and the people sent into exile.

I will look in more detail at reading and writing in Jeremiah in Chapter 6. Here I want only to point out that the words of Jeremiah bring him into conflict with the temple and royal authority. Jeremiah 36 is the classic instance of this conflict. In this chapter Jeremiah dictates words of Yahweh to Baruch who writes them on a scroll to be read out in the temple. In time the dictated words were finally read to the king, Jehoiakim, who cut the scroll into pieces and threw the pieces into the fire. Yahweh asks Jeremiah to write another scroll and to say the following to King Jehoiakim (36.29-31):

> Thus Yahweh said, you burned this scroll saying, 'Why have you written in it saying, "The king of Babylon will surely come and he will destroy this land and he will exterminate humans and animals"'. Therefore, thus Yahweh said concerning Jehoiakim, king of Judah, 'He will not have anyone to sit on the throne of David and his corpse will be thrown out in the heat of the day and in frost of the night. And I will punish him and his offspring and his servants for their iniquity. I will bring on them and the inhabitants of Jerusalem and to [every] man of Judah the entire calamity that I had spoken to them but they did not listen.

The conflict with authority experienced by Jeremiah is similar to the conflict with authority experienced by Amos. In Amos 7 it is reported that Amaziah, the priest in Bethel, reported 'words' of Amos to the king, Jeroboam, just as the temple officials reported Jeremiah's words to the king, Jehoiakim.[30] Amaziah says, 'Amos has conspired in the middle of the house of Israel against you. The land is not able to contain all his words' (7.10). At the end of his encounter with Amaziah, Amos announces the calamity that will befall Jeroboam and Israel. What he says about Jeroboam is strikingly similar to what Jeremiah says about Jehoiakim. Notice that the words of Amos against Jeroboam (7.16-18) are based on a quotation of Jeroboam's words, just as Jeremiah's words against Jehoiakim are based on a quotation of Jehoiakim's words:

---

30. The book of Amos does not make it explicit that these were words that Amos had written down in a book.

And now hear the word of Yahweh,[31] you who say, 'Do not prophesy against Israel and do not preach[32] against the house of Isaac'. Therefore thus Yahweh said,

'Your wife will practice prostitution in the city
and your sons and your daughters will fall by the sword.
Your land will be parcelled out by a measuring-line,
and you will die in an unclean land
and Israel will surely go into exile away from its land.

Both Amos and Jeremiah are prophets whose 'words' announce 'the end' of kingdoms. Jeremiah's 'words' are about Judah's end and Amos' 'words' are about Israel's end. Significantly, the account of Amos' encounter with Amaziah and Jeroboam closes with visual imagery dramatically announcing the end of Israel (8.1-3):

Thus Yahweh showed me, and there a basket of summer fruit. And he said, 'What do you see Amos?' And I said, 'A basket of summer fruit (קָיִץ)'. And Yahweh said to me, 'The end (קֵץ) has come upon my people Israel. I will not pass through it another time. They will howl in distress the songs of the temple on that day, says the lord Yahweh. The corpses will be many, hurled out in many places. Be quiet!'

The phrase 'words of' (דברי), which occurs only in the superscriptions of Jeremiah and Amos, then, suggests that these prophetic 'books' are about prophets who announce the final destruction of the kingdoms of Judah and Israel. Again Yahweh's words at the end of 2 Kings (23.27) resonate with the role of these two texts in the prophetic collection: 'I will remove Judah also out of my sight, as I have removed Israel [in the time of Amos]; and I will reject this city that I have chosen, Jerusalem, and the house of which I said, My name shall be there'.

Although it was a different Jeroboam (the son of Nebat, not the later Jeroboam the son of Joash) and although it was not Amos but a different man of God who went from Judah to Bethel, the words about this incident in 2 Kgs 23.15-18 resonate with the encounter of Amos and Jeroboam:[33]

Moreover, the altar at Bethel, the high place erected by Jeroboam son of Nebat, who caused Israel to sin—he [Josiah] pulled down that altar along

31. Here 'the דבר of Yahweh' concerns 'words' (דברים), not a 'vision' (חזון) or 'visions (מראות) of God'.

32. The word here is from the root נטף, which means 'to drip', perhaps suggesting a plurality of words falling from the mouth of Amos like water in a heavy storm (see Judg. 5.4).

33. The incident here refers to 1 Kgs 13.

with the high place. He burned the high place, crushing it to dust; he also burned the sacred pole. As Josiah turned, he saw the tombs there on the mount; and he sent and took the bones on the altar and defiled it, according to the word of Yahweh that the man of God proclaimed, when Jeroboam stood by the altar at the festival; he turned and looked up at the tomb of the man of God had had predicted these things. Then he said, 'What is that monument that I see?' The people of the city told him, 'It is the tomb of the man of God who came from Judah and predicted these things that you have done against the altar at Bethel'. He said, 'Let him rest; let no one move his bones'. So they let his bones alone, with the bones of the prophet who came from Samaria.

5. *The Beginning of Speaking*

I have argued that the superscriptions at the beginning of prophetic 'books'—Jeremiah, Ezekiel, Isaiah and the Twelve—are an indication of how to read these books arranged in canonical order. The chronological sequence of Jeremiah, Ezekiel and Isaiah continues the sequential arrangement of Joshua, Judges, Samuel and Kings. Jeremiah's 'words' (דברי) announce the end of Judah and the temple in Jerusalem; Ezekiel's 'visions of God' (מראות אלהים) allows him to see Yahweh's abandonment of the temple and the city of Jerusalem as well as the 'torah' as a kind of blueprint of restoration; and Isaiah's 'vision' (חזון) in the days of Uzziah, Jotham, Ahaz and Hezekiah envision future restoration following Babylonian destruction. The end of the Twelve in the more precisely dated times of Haggai and Zechariah portray the time of temple restoration when messengers such as Malachi ('my messenger') emerge.

I have also maintained that the superscriptions suggest what is distinctive about each of these scrolls. They are a code to the reader of how to read what follows. What follows in Jeremiah are the 'the words (דברי) of Jeremiah', in Ezekiel 'visions (מראות) of God' and in Isaiah 'the vision (חזון) of Isaiah'.[34] These codes suggest among other things a different way of 'seeing' the דבר of Yahweh.

This coded information at the beginning of the larger scrolls of Jeremiah, Ezekiel and Isaiah is reflected in similar prophetic genres or *Gattungen* that come at the beginning of ספרים that make up the Twelve. 'The words of Jeremiah' has its parallel in 'the words of Amos'. 'The vision of Isaiah' has its parallels in the visions of Obadiah, Nahum and Habakkuk, and

---

34. In the following chapters I will look at the larger structural organization of each of the books in light of the superscription.

probably also Joel, Micah and Zephaniah. Ezekiel's 'visions of God' is somewhat unique. However, the 'visions of God' that happened (וַיְהִי) to Ezekiel (1.1) are matched by what happened (אוֹיְהִי) in the story of Jonah (1.1). Yahweh, who appeared to Ezekiel in the foreign city of Babylon, also is present with Jonah in the foreign city of Nineveh.

While I have spoken about some of the individual 'books' in the scroll of the Twelve and how it brings a closure to the chronological sequence, I have not spoken about how it opens. The Twelve opens with a superscription that introduces Hosea: 'The word of Yahweh which came to Hosea, son of Beeri, in the days of Kings Uzziah, Jotham, Ahaz and Hezekiah of Judah, and in the days of King Jeroboam, son of Joash of Israel' (Hos. 1.1). This opening is followed by a phrase in 1.2, תְּחִלַּת דִּבֶּר־יְהוָה בְּהוֹשֵׁעַ, that can be translated literally as '[The] beginning of Yahweh spoke was with [or, by means of] Hosea'. I understand this phrase to be a scribal notation for the Model Reader suggesting how to read what follows on that scroll. The significance of this phrase is sometimes obscured in translations such as the NRSV, where it is read as a dependent clause in a continuing sentence, 'When Yahweh first spoke through Hosea, Yahweh said to Hosea…' However, I read it by itself, separated from what immediately follows; and this reading receives support from ancient readers such as the Masoretes[35] as well as more recent commentators.[36]

'[The] beginning of Yahweh spoke [was] with Hosea' can be understood as a kind of introductory sentence for the Twelve as a whole. The Hebrew word translated 'beginning of' is often used to mean the first in a series of occurrences. For example, at the beginning of the book of Judges, it is used to refer to Judah, who 'will go up first' to fight against the Canaanites (Judg. 1.1; cf. 20.18). But it is also used to refer to the first in a series of visions (Dan. 8.1; cf. 9.21), the first in a series of pitching tents (Gen. 13.3), the first in the series of times that Jacob's sons went to Egypt to buy

---

35. The Masoretes, Jewish scholars of the fifth to the tenth century responsible for preserving the Hebrew text, inserted a *pisqa'* between Hos. 1.2a and 1.2b, that is, a punctuation mark requiring a major pause. Their reading, then, would not support the continuation of the sentence as in the NRSV. On this point see Francis I. Andersen and David Noel Freedman, *Hosea: A New Translation and Commentary* (AB, 24; Garden City, NY: Doubleday, 1980), p. 154.

36. See, e.g., Francis Landy, *Hosea* (Readings: A New Biblical Commentary; Sheffield: Sheffield Academic Press), p. 21, and Hans Walter Wolff, *Hosea: A Commentary on the Book of the Prophet Hosea* (trans. G. Stansell; Hermeneia; Philadelphia: Fortress Press, 1974), pp. 8, 12-13.

bread (Gen. 43.20; cf. 43.18), the first in a series of harvests (2 Sam. 21.9; cf. Ruth 1.22), the first in a series of attacks in a battle (2 Sam. 17.9), and so on.

At the beginning of the Twelve, then, the reader is informed that Yahweh's initial speaking was with Hosea. We have already seen that Haggai, Zechariah and Malachi, with their more specific dating, bring the ordered arrangement of scrolls to an end by dating these figures in the time of the Persian king Darius. The scroll of the Twelve, then, coming at the end of the prophetic collection, represents the beginning and the end of Yahweh's דבר to Jeremiah, Ezekiel, Isaiah and the Twelve Minor Prophets. It begins with Hosea and ends with Malachi.

There is one other feature that distinguishes the Twelve from Jeremiah, Ezekiel and Isaiah. The Twelve gives a distinctly northern orientation to its depiction of prophetic characters. I will return to discuss in more detail the ordered arrangement of the Twelve and its relation to the previous collection of scrolls in Chapter 8.

6. *In the Hand*

A significant feature beginning to emerge in the discussion is the important role of writing in prophetic books. Writing is a central feature of the prophetic activity described in the texts themselves. A חזון, as we have seen, is something that is to be written down (כתב) for another time. It is a document (ספר) and an oracle (משא), which perhaps should be understood in its literal sense, as a 'burden', as something to be carried. Both 'the words of Moses' and 'the words of Jeremiah' are to be written in a 'book' (ספר).[37] Ezekiel is ordered by Yahweh to take 'the scroll' (המגלה) offered to him and to eat it (Ezek. 3.1-3). This 'written' character is a central feature of prophetic books.

I will look more closely at the prophets and writing in later chapters, but now I want to consider the phrase, 'in the hand of' (ביד). This phrase occurs in two of the superscriptions (Hag. 1.1 and Mal. 1.1), and I think that this phrase also refers to writing. Communication can take place when something written is 'in the hand' so that it can be carried elsewhere and read. The superscription of Haggai concerns 'the דבר of Yahweh' which was 'in the hand of (ביד) Haggai the prophet' (Hag. 1.1). The superscription to Malachi describes the 'book' as 'an oracle (משא), the דבר of Yahweh to Israel in the hand (ביד)' of Malachi. Two passages, one from

---

37. In the case of Jer. 36 the writing is referred to as a 'scroll' (מגלת־ספר).

Samuel and one from Esther, illustrate how communication takes place when a written document is carried 'in the hand'. For example, in 2 Sam. 11.14 we are told that 'David wrote (ויכתב) a letter (ספר) to Joab and sent (וישלח) it by the hand of (ביד) Uriah'. In this context 'by the hand of' means instrumentality, that is, the means by which the letter was sent. But the phrase also connotes something concrete to be carried in the hand, a letter. In Est. 3.12-13 we are told that the scribes (ספרי) of the king were summoned and 'all the king commanded was written (נכתב)...and letters (ספרים) were sent (ונשלוח) by the hand of (ביד) runners (הרצים) to all the king's provinces'.[38] In this passage as well ביד connotes both instrumentality, 'by the hand of', and 'concreteness', 'in the hand of'. What these two passages suggest about communication ביד is that communication is carried out *by means of* a document that is actually carried *in the hand*, which can be read aloud.[39] The phrase 'in the hand of' used in these two superscriptions can be interpreted to underscore the importance of writing in prophetic books. I will look more closely at the use of this phrase in the Twelve later, especially as it relates to the phrase 'in the hand of the former prophets' in Zech. 7.7.[40]

8. *Summary and Conclusion*

In this section I have examined the superscriptions of prophetic books as providing 'codes' for the Model Reader to understand how to read the material collected and ordered on the scrolls that follow. Jeremiah is to be read as 'the words (דברי) of Jeremiah', Ezekiel as 'visions (מראות) of God', Isaiah as the vision (חזון) of Isaiah and the Twelve as a collection of occasions on which Yahweh spoke beginning with Hosea giving a northern orientation to the collection and bringing the prophetic collection to

38. This passage has parallels with Hab. 2.2 where a reader will run, that is, Habakkuk's vision is to be disseminated by couriers like the edict of the king in Est. 3.12-13.

39. See also 2 Kgs 19.23; Jer. 29.3; Isa. 37.24.

40. I will consider this phrase in light of the numerous passages where Yahweh 'speaks' (דבר) 'by the hand of' (ביד) prophets. See Exod. 9.35; Lev. 10.11; Num. 17.5 (Eng. 16.40); 27.23; Josh. 20.2; 1 Kgs 8.53, 56. Related phrases are 'Yahweh commanded (צוה) by the hand of Moses' (Exod. 36.13; Lev. 8.26; Num. 15.2; 36.13; Josh. 21.2, 8; Judg. 3.4; Neh. 8.14; 9.14; 2 Chron. 33.8), '(Yahweh) gave (נתן) by the hand of Moses' (Neh. 10.30 [Eng. 10.29]). The phrase 'from the mouth of (מפי) Yahweh by the hand of Moses' (Num. 4.37, 45, 49; 9.23; 10.13; Josh. 22.9) suggests dictation. See also Lev. 26.46; 2 Chron. 34.14; 35.6).

closure in the time of the Persian king Darius. When read in the Talmudic order of Joshua, Judges, Samuel, Kings, Jeremiah, Ezekiel, Isaiah and the Twelve these collected scrolls also depict an ordered sequence of time from just 'after the death of Moses' to the beginning of temple restoration at the time of Darius. In the next chapters, I want to look at the order and arrangement within each scroll rather than at the order and arrangement of the scrolls themselves.

There are a number of general observations that I want to make about these scrolls that will be important for the remaining discussion in the following chapters. First, as a whole, the prophetic collection is a kind of 'history'. The 'data' for this history, however, appear rather unusual to a contemporary reader for they involve 'the דבר of Yahweh' concerning what he communicated in 'words' (דברי) and 'visions' (מראות) to some prophets in their own time and in 'vision' (חזון) to some prophets about a later time. All that time, for the present Model Reader, however, is presented as a past time. Joshua, the Judges, the kings of Israel, Judah and Persia, Jeremiah, Ezekiel, Isaiah and the Twelve Minor Prophets are all figures of the past. All this rbd of Yahweh is about the past. This is important for reading. For example, the recurring phrase כה אמר יהוה is a clear past tense, which convention has come to translate 'Thus says Yahweh', invoking a theological rather than a grammatical appeal to a 'prophetic perfect'. This material, however, is not about present tense speaking. It records what Yahweh said in the past periods of time depicted in the prophetic books.

Second, it will also be important to understand that this 'דבר of Yahweh' is intrinsically associated with writing: the words Yahweh spoke to Moses are in 'a book of *torah*/covenant' (ספר תורה/ברית), Jeremiah's words are written in a scroll (מגלת־ספר) and other writings (ספרים), Isaiah's vision and those of Nahum, Habakkuk and others are written down as a חזון, and the דבר of Yahweh can be 'in the hand' (ביד) of prophets such as Haggai and Malachi as written words. To read the prophetic canon is not only to encounter the written words themselves but texts that thematize the importance of the written word.

Third, the temple is the center of activity. It is a place from which Jeremiah is barred and his words read out; it is a place at which Ezekiel sees his 'visions of God' and it is a place of Isaiah's חזון. Even the northern temple at Bethel figures prominently. There Amos' words are judged to be a conspiracy against Jeroboam, and from there representatives of Bethel come to inquire of Zechariah (Zech. 7.1).

Fourth, and finally, I want to conclude by emphasizing again the central role of text reception in my interpretive agenda. I have read these texts from the point of view of the Model Reader. However, to read these texts is not to read a contemporary text created by an individual as a single composition. Prophetic books are collections of material available to the scribe who arranged this material into ordered collections as a literary collage. Movement can be abrupt. However, to conclude that one should ignore the present order of a compiled text is to proceed as a contemporary scribe to rearrange and reorder the material. The way some scribe(s) in the past ordered materials is important, and what comes before and what comes after is as significant for interpreting scribal compilations as it is for understanding literature that achieves a different kind of unity through individual composition. Communication through compilation, order and arrangement is as significant as communication through composition. When I read this material I may not read it with the ease I read contemporary literature, but reading material compiled for an ancient Model Reader requires that I read taking account of what has come before and what comes after. It is to read with a concern for textual limits. In the next chapters, I will be interested in the limits that order provides for communication even though the distance from that original composition makes reconstruction of the scribal codes highly problematic.

Chapter 5

THE WORDS OF AMOS AND JEREMIAH:
READING JEREMIAH IN LIGHT OF AMOS

Yahweh roars from Zion,
    and utters his voice from Jerusalem. (Amos 1.2)

Yahweh will roar from on high,
    and from his holy habitation utter his voice. (Jer. 25.30)

I have been suggesting that prophetic books coded for a Model Reader are associated with compilational rather than compositional unity. The openings of prophetic books provide information concerning how to read the arrangement of material that follows. In this chapter I want to read Jeremiah in light of Amos to further elucidate the significance of prophetic books that begin 'the words of' (דברי).

The fact that Amos and Jeremiah share identical openings is not a coincidence. By reading intertextually, I want to show how these two books with matching beginnings illumine each other and share common features in the compilational order that follows. This common superscription alerts the reader to the possibility that these two books are in the same genre. Although form criticism in a traditional sense dealt with genre (Gunkel's *Gattung*) as small units, I want to extend the notion of genre to its more common literary use to suggest a type of written composition.

1. *Amos and Jeremiah: Prophets to the Nations*

The same phrase, 'the words of', as I suggested in the previous chapter, introduces the only two prophets who announce the end of a nation: Amos and Jeremiah. Amos announces the end of Israel, and Jeremiah announces the end of Judah. When read in conjunction, each book throws light on the other. Both 'books' can be understood as containing 'the words of' prophets to the nations. To be a prophet to the nations means to announce not only the immediate downfall of either Israel or Judah but also the consequences that Yahweh's voice roaring in warfare will have for all the nations of the land (ארץ).

After the superscription in Amos 1.1, Amos' words are immediately quoted:

> And he said,
>   'Yahweh will roar (ישאג) from Zion,
>   And from Jerusalem he will utter his voice (יתן קולו)
> The pastures (נאות) of the shepherds (הרעים) wither,
>   and the top of Carmel dries up'.

While there appears to be some connection with the similar verse in Joel 3.16,[1] the more interesting connection is with Jer. 25.30-31:

> And you will prophesy against them *all these words*, and you will say to them:
> '*Yahweh will roar* (ישאג) *from a height* (ממרום)[2]
>   and from his holy dwelling (וממעון) he will utter his voice (יתן קולו).
> He will loudly roar (שאג ישאג) against his pasture (נוהו),
>   shouting like the ones who tread on grapes
>   against all the inhabitants of the earth.
> Noise [of battle] is coming against the ends of the earth
>   for Yahweh has a legal case (ריב) among the nations;
> he is entering into controversy against all flesh;
>   the guilty he will put to the sword,
>   a saying of Yahweh.'

Both passages use similar language about Yahweh 'roaring' and 'uttering his voice' to identify 'the words' that Amos and Jeremiah are to speak against the nations. It is significant to note that Amos refers specifically to Zion and Jerusalem as the place where Yahweh roared and uttered his voice. The location in Jeremiah is more vague, referring only to 'a height' and to Yahweh's 'dwelling place'. This difference reflects the different situation of each prophet. Although Amos speaks his words in the Northern Kingdom, the prophetic books make it clear that Yahweh is dwelling in Zion/Jerusalem at that time. Jeremiah speaks his words at a time when Yahweh is abandoning his temple in Zion/Jerusalem—a time when the place of Yahweh's presence is more ambiguous.

In Jeremiah 25, Yahweh's voice is associated with a legal case (ריב) that he has brought against the nations. While there is no reference to a

---

1.   I will look at this connection later in Chapter 8 when I consider the compilation of the Twelve. I will also argue in Chapter 7 that Joel shares features more clearly related to Isaiah and other prophets of חזון than it does with prophetic books that begin 'the words of'.

2.   'Height' is used in the phrase, 'the height of Zion' in Jer. 31.12.

רִיב in Amos, the announcement of Yahweh roaring and uttering his voice is followed by words of Yahweh against the nations, outlining the crimes they have committed and the punishment that will ensue (1.3–2.16). The nations mentioned in Amos are Damascus, Gaza (and the other Philistine cities, Ashdod, Ashkelon and Ekron), Tyre, Edom, Amon, Moab, Judah and Israel.

I want to come back to this passage in Amos (1.3–2.16), but first it is important to look in more detail at the parallel passage in Jeremiah because it provides details that help clarify some problems of interpretation in Amos. Jeremiah makes it evident that the consequence of Yahweh's roaring voice is total warfare against all the nations, resulting in total devastation of the land (אֶרֶץ, 25.10). The end of Judah means the end of all the nations. To bring about this universal military operation, Yahweh will use the human power of 'all the tribes of the north' including King Nebuchadrezzar of Babylon (25.9). Yahweh is acting because Judah did not obey Yahweh's words but instead pursued the gods of the other nations with repercussions not only for Judah but for all the nations of the land (אֶרֶץ).

The words of Jeremiah in ch. 25 amplify the sound of Yahweh's roaring and bellicose voice going out from the height of his dwelling place by describing the outcome for the nations. The call narrative at the beginning of Jeremiah identifies his vocation as a prophet 'over nations and over kingdoms' (1.10). The full description of this appointment is not given until ch. 25, near the middle of the scroll:

> The word of Yahweh[3] that came to Jeremiah concerning all the people of Judah in the fourth year of Jehoiakim, the son of Josiah, king of Judah. It was the first year of Nebuchadrezzar, king of Babylon. Jeremiah the prophet spoke to all the people of Judah and to all the inhabitants of Jerusalem, 'From the thirteenth year of Josiah, the son of Amon King of Judah until this day. This twenty-three years the word of Yahweh has come to me. I spoke to you early and continually but you did not listen.' (25.1-3)

This refusal to listen to Jeremiah is typical of the past behavior of the people:

> Yahweh sent to you all his servants the prophets early on and continually but you did not listen and you did not incline your ears to listen to what they said: 'Turn, each one, from his evil way and from your evil deeds and

---

3. 'The דְּבַר of Yahweh' here concerns 'the words of (דִּבְרֵי) Jeremiah' announced in the superscription (see also 25.30). This is not a 'vision' (חָזוֹן) or 'visions (מַרְאוֹת) of God'.

dwell in the land which Yahweh gave to you and to your fathers from long ago and for a long time to come. Do not go after other gods to serve them and to bow down to them. Do not provoke me to anger with the work of your hands and I will not cause you harm.' But you did not listen to me, a saying of Yahweh, so that you provoked me to anger with the work of your hands so that harm will come to you. (25.4-7)

The consequence of the people's failure to listen to Yahweh's call to return from their evil practices of following the gods of the other nations, the work of their hands, is that they will *not* continue to dwell in the land. The ramifications extend even to the other nations who will be driven from their land:

> Therefore, thus Yahweh of hosts has said, 'Because you did not listen to my words, I am now about to send and bring all the tribes of the north, a saying of Yahweh, and Nebuchadrezzar, king of Babylon, my servant. I will bring them against this land (אֶרֶץ) and against its inhabitants and against all these surrounding nations'. (25.8-9a)

What is envisaged here is complete annihilation of all the inhabitants of the אֶרֶץ as at the time of Joshua, an era of Yahweh's utter destruction (חֶרֶם) of all the inhabitants of the land:

> I will totally destroy them (וְהַחֲרַמְתִּים) and I will make them a desolated waste, an object of derisive hissing, and a ruin forever. I will cause to cease among them the sound of rejoicing, the sound of merriment, the voice of the bridegroom, the voice of the bride, the sound of the millstone and the light of the lamp. The whole of this land will become a desolated waste and a ruin and these nations will serve the king of Babylon 70 years. (25.9a-11)

In Jeremiah ch. 25 the imagery of the nations who experience this devastating wrath of Yahweh's anger is that they will drink from 'the cup of the wine of wrath' which Jeremiah will take from the hand of Yahweh and offer to them (25.15). This cup, Yahweh's sword, which he is sending from all the tribes of the north and from King Nebuchadrezzar, will make the nations stagger like drunkards who fall in their own vomit and will not be able to rise (25.16, 27).

The nations are listed in Jeremiah as they are in Amos, but the list of the nations in Jeremiah, unlike Amos, comes before rather than after the words announcing that Yahweh will roar from Zion and utter his voice from Jerusalem. The nations mentioned in Jeremiah, however, do not include Israel, for whom Amos has already announced a final devastation and that is portrayed as already having been accomplished in 2 Kgs 23.27. In the collection of prophetic books Amos announces the end of Israel; Jeremiah announces the end of Judah. Jeremiah becomes a prophet to the nations when he takes the cup from Yahweh's hand and makes the nations drink. These nations are:

> Jerusalem and the cities of Judah and its kings and princes to make them a ruin and desolated waste and for derisive hissing and a curse like today; Pharaoh king of Egypt and his servants and his princes and all his people; all the עֶרֶב;[4] all the kings of the land of Uz; all the kings of the land of the Philistines (Ashkelon, Gaza, Ekron and the remnant of Ashdod); Edom; Moab; the Ammonites; all the kings Tyre; all the kings of Sidon; all the kings of אִי,[5] which is the region across the sea; Dedan, Tema, Buz and all with shaven temples; all the kings of Arabia[6] who dwell in the desert; all the kings of Zimri; all the kings of Elam; all the kings of Media; all the kings of the north (the ones far and the ones near; one after another); all the kingdoms of the land (אֶרֶץ) which is on the face of the ground (אֲדָמָה). And the king of Sheshak will drink after them. (25.18-26)

The last king mentioned in this list is the king of Sheshak. Sheshak appears to be a cryptogram for Babylon (see 51.41). That Babylon is mentioned here in the list of kings to drink of 'the cup of the wine of wrath' is important because Nebuchadrezzar, the Babylonian king, is from a nation that itself will drink, get drunk, fall in its own vomit and not rise again. The coming destruction of the king of Babylon was already anticipated in Jeremiah's words:

> And it will happen after 70 years are ended, I will punish the king of Babylon and that nation, a saying of Yahweh, because of their iniquity. And the land of the Chaldeans I will make it an everlasting devastation. And I will bring against that land *all the words which I have spoken against it, everything written in this book which Jeremiah prophesied against all the nations.* Because many nations and great kings will make them slaves also, and I will make them repay according to their deeds and according to the work of their hands. (25.12-14)

As a prophet appointed to the nations, Jeremiah's words concern all the nations and total devastation of the land. *Words* are like weapons in the hand of Jeremiah. The destruction they will wreak is as devastating for these kings as for the kings that Joshua destroyed in taking the land, as described in the beginning of the prophetic corpus. The list of kings in Jeremiah mirrors the list of kings Joshua defeated (Josh. 12.1-24) when

---

4.   The meaning of this Hebrew word meaning 'evening' is not clear in this context.
5.   Possibly means 'coastland'.
6.   The phrase is repeated.

Joshua took the whole land (11.23). With new Joshua-like figures, Jeremiah and Amos, Yahweh is again conducting war against all the kings of the land.

The destruction of all the land is described in Jeremiah, as in Joshua, as overwhelming. This destruction is 'now' about to begin as Jeremiah speaks:

> Thus Yahweh of hosts said,
> 'Now (הנה) disaster is moving on from nation to nation,
>> And a great tempest[7] will be roused from the remote parts of the land (ארץ)'.
>
> The fatally wounded ones of Yahweh on that day will be from one end of the land (ארץ) to the other end of the land (ארץ). They will not be lamented; they will not be gathered; and they will not be buried. They will be dung on the surface of the ground (אדמה).
>
> Wail, shepherds, and cry out;
>> be in mourning majestic ones of the flock;
> because your days for butchering and your...[8]
>> have been fulfilled;
>> and you have fallen like a desired vessel.
> Flight has ceased for the shepherds,
>> and escape for the majestic ones of the flock.
> A voice! Shepherds are crying out,
>> and the majestic ones of the flock are wailing!
> Because Yahweh is violently destroying their pasturage (מרעיתם),
>> and the peaceful pastures (נאות) have been made silent.
>> from before the fierce anger of Yahweh.
> Like the lion he left his lair
>> because their land has become a desolate waste
> from before his fierce oppression,
>> from before his fierce anger. (25.32-38)

It is possible to show even closer affiliations between Jeremiah and Joshua reflected in the way Jeremiah is addressed and in the shape and organization of the book. However, I now want to return to Amos and look at 'the words of Amos' in light of what we have seen in 'the words of Jeremiah'.

Amos is dated rather generally, as are all the prophets at the beginning of the Twelve. Amos begins with the general phrase 'in the days of Uzziah...and in the days of Jeroboam'. However, there appears to be an attempt in the superscription to be more precise. Just before Amos' words

---

7. Compare Amos 1.18.
8. The meaning of the Hebrew is not clear.

introduce Yahweh's roaring voice against the nations, there is the notation that this was 'two years before the רעש' (1.1). This Hebrew word is normally rendered 'earthquake' on the basis of 1 Kgs 19.11-12 and Zech. 14.5. In both passages a רעש associated with the appearance of Yahweh is described in imagery that evokes the sounds of an earthquake.[9] However, in light of Amos' role as a Joshua-like prophet engaged in announcing Yahweh's words of total warfare against the nations, it is possible that this word should also carry its other connotations—the rumbling noise of warfare and not the rumbling of an earthquake.[10] As the rumbling of warfare, it is a fitting introduction to the verses that follow concerning Yahweh's bellicose voice against the nations. In Nah. 3.2 and Jer. 47.3 רעש is used for the rumbling noise of the wheels of a war chariot.[11] Even more significant for understanding the meaning of רעש in Amos 1.1 is its use in Jeremiah. In Jer. 10.22 רעש refers to the rumbling noise of warfare from 'the land of the north'—Yahweh's sword against all the nations of the land—that will make the cities of Judah 'a desolation' and 'a lair of jackals'. Also, in Jer. 8.16 the imminent approach of the army from the north can be heard with snorting horses and neighing stallions, and it is reported that the whole land quakes (רעשה כל־הארץ). In light of this intertextual connection with Jeremiah, then, I understand that in Amos the 'two years before the רעש' anticipates the coming רעש of battle when Yahweh will defeat all the nations of the land.

'The words of Amos', then, in the days of Uzziah and in the days of Jeroboam came two years before 'the rumbling noise' of the chariot wheels of warfare:

> Yahweh will roar (ישאג) from Zion,
>   And from Jerusalem he will utter his voice (יתן קולו).
> The pastures (נאות) of the shepherds (הרעים) wither,
>   and the top of Carmel dries up. (Amos 1.2)

---

9.   In 1 Kgs 19.11-12 Yahweh's appearance to Elijah is accompanied by a great wind with mountains splitting and rocks breaking up. Zech. 14.5 refers to the רעש in the time of Uzziah in the description of how Yahweh will create a valley in the Mount of Olives.

10.   The word can be used for any sort of loud rumbling. For example, in Ezek. 3.12-13 it is used for the 'rumbling' of the wings of the creatures that appeared to Ezekiel to be brushing together. In Ezek. 37.7 it is used for the 'rumbling' of the bones coming together.

11.   See Isa. 29.6, which seems to associate the rumbling of warfare with the rumbling of an earthquake.

These words in Amos reverberate with the words of Jeremiah. Yahweh's 'roaring' and uttering his voice recalls Jer. 25.30. Pastures (נאות) and shepherds (הרעים) are precisely the metaphors used to describe the land, the kings and the other officials that Yahweh was laying waste to in Jer. 25.34-38.

To read 'the words of Amos' in light of 'the words of Jeremiah' enables one to gain a perspective on what has been a recurring problem in translating the phrase that introduces the words against the nations in Amos 1.3, 6, 9, 11, 13; 2.1, 4, 6:

> Thus Yahweh said,
> 'For three transgressions of [a nation],
>   and for four, I will not cause *it* to return (אשיבנו)'.

The problem of interpretation is that the pronoun '*it*' does not have a clear referent in Amos. However, in light of Jeremiah 25, the 'it' can be understood to be 'the cup of the wine of wrath' from which all the nations will drink. The 'it' refers to the inevitable disaster for the shepherds (the kings) and the pastures (the lands) of each of the countries mentioned. The NRSV translation of the pronoun 'it' as 'punishment' picks up the meaning of the pronoun with its ambiguous antecedent. In light of Jeremiah 25 the coming punishment can be seen as inevitable. It cannot be revoked because it has already begun:

> And it will come about if they refuse to take the cup from your hand to drink, then you will say to them, 'Thus Yahweh of hosts said, "You will surely drink because now in the city which is called by my name, I am beginning to bring disaster and you will surely be punished.[12] You will not go unpunished because a sword I am calling against all the inhabitants of the land"', a saying of Yahweh of hosts. (Jer. 25.28-29)

Furthermore, in light of Jer. 25.31, the words of Yahweh against each of the nations in Amos can be understood in terms of a legal dispute (ריב). In Amos, unlike Jeremiah, the crimes of the nations are detailed specifically. And so, Damascus

> threshed Gilead with threshing sledges of iron (1.3),

Gaza

> carried into exile entire communities, to hand them over to Edom (1.6),

---

12. The verb here, נקה, can have the meaning of completely plundering a place.

Tyre

> delivered entire communities over to Edom and did not remember the cove-
> nant of kingship (1.9),

Edom

> pursued his brother with the sword and cast off all pity; he maintained his
> anger perpetually, and kept his wrath forever (1.11),

the Ammonites

> ripped open pregnant women in Gilead in order to enlarge their territory
> (1.13),

and Moab

> burned to lime the bones of the king of Edom (2.1).

The punishment to be carried out on each of these nations is announced by a recurring formula about Yahweh sending a fire that, among other things, will destroy the 'strongholds' (אַרְמְנוֹת) of the nations. The war imagery is pervasive (1.4, 7, 10, 12, 14; 2.2). In some instances more details about the punishment are given, including exile, with the inhabitants of those places being 'cut off' or taken away (1.5, 8, 14; cf. 2.3). The important observation for our purposes here is that in Amos Judah will escape exile. For Judah, the sentence is only that Yahweh 'will send a fire on Judah, and it will devour the strongholds of Jerusalem' (1.5); there is no mention of exile.[13] The 'crime' committed is that Judah has 'rejected the *torah* of Yahweh and has not kept his statutes', and that it has 'been led astray by the same lies after which their ancestors walked' (2.4). The escape of Judah from total destruction at this time is clear from Kings. Not until the end of the reign of Josiah does Yahweh decide to remove Judah from his presence as he had removed Israel (2 Kgs 23.27). Not even Josiah's 'establishment of all the words of the *torah* written in the book' that Hilkiah found (23.24) will prevent Yahweh from removing Judah and Jerusalem from his presence. Indeed, as the words of Jeremiah make clear, during the time of Josiah's successor, Jehoiakim, Judah continued to reject Yahweh's *torah* (see Jer. 6.19; 9.12 [Eng. 9.13]; 16.11; 26.24; 32.23; 44.10-11).

The 'words of Jeremiah' announce the end of Judah, removing it from Yahweh's presence (see Jer. 44.10-11); so also 'the words of Amos'

---

13. Punishment that does not include cutting off the inhabitants of the land and taking them into exile is also found for Tyre and Edom.

announce the end of Israel. Amos' words indicate how and why Israel was removed from Yahweh's presence. From 2.6 to the end of the book, the words of Amos compile the 'crimes' of Israel. The end is dramatically summoned up in the image of famine:

> Now days are coming, a saying of the lord Yahweh,
>   when I will send a famine in the land.
> Not a famine for food and not a thirst for water,
>   but for hearing *the words of* (דבר־י) Yahweh.
> They will stagger from sea to sea,
>   and from north to east.
> They will rove about seeking the word of Yahweh,
>   but they will not find it. (Amos 8.11-12)

No *words of* Yahweh for those staggering (נוע),[14] having tasted 'the cup of the wine of wrath' will be found. Prophecy itself has ended for Israel.

The book of Amos, does not close, however, without hope for the future. A future is envisaged in the restoration of 'the booth of David' (Amos 9.11). Here there are strong parallels with Jeremiah. Jeremiah sees hope in a branch of David who will be raised up to execute justice and righteousness (23.5; see 33.17-36). Moreover, as the book of Jeremiah closes, it foresees the restoration of Israel's pasture (נוהו) and Mt Carmel (50.18), bringing luxurious growth to what was withered and dried up by Yahweh's roaring voice in Amos 1.2. Having made these intertextual links with Amos, I now want to return to look at the compilation of Jeremiah in more detail.

2. *Jeremiah as a Prophet and a Warrior*

Jeremiah appears in the middle of the rabbinic order of prophetic scrolls, like Joshua at the beginning of the collection, as a figure involved in the warfare of Yahweh to annihilate all the nations of the ארץ. In Jeremiah, Yahweh will clean out the land (25.29) so that there will be no one to inhabit it among the nations (25.9-11). Unlike Joshua, however, Jeremiah is not a member of the community to whom Yahweh is giving the land, but a member of a community, Judah, from whom Yahweh is taking it away.

A further difference between Jeremiah and Joshua is that Joshua had in front of him the 'book' (ספר) of the *torah* of Moses. According to Josh. 1.7-9, this book was not to depart from the mouth of Joshua; he was to meditate on it day and night so that his way would be prosperous in the land. In the prophetic collection of scrolls, however, that 'book of the

---

14. See Isa. 29.9; Ps. 107.27.

torah/covenant' went missing after the time of Joshua and was not found until the days of Josiah (2 Kgs 22–23) in the time of Jeremiah. Even, then, however, though Josiah established the words of 'the book of the *torah*' (2 Kgs 23.24), Yahweh determined to remove Judah from his sight just as he had earlier removed Israel (23.27). 'The book of the *torah*/covenant' will not result in Judah's prosperity in Jeremiah's time. The book appears to go missing again after the time of Josiah. Yahweh now determines to put words in the mouth of Jeremiah who himself will write 'books' (סירים, Jer. 25.13; 29.1; 30.2; 36.2, 32; 45.1; 51.60-63). The time of Jeremiah is not a period for meditating on the words of 'the book of the *torah*/covenant'.

Jeremiah's situation is dramatically different from that of Joshua in one final way. Jeremiah, unlike Joshua, does not make a magnificent entry across the Jordan into the promised land, leading the people who had escaped from the Egyptians. Rather, he himself is taken ignominiously to the land of Egypt (42.18–43.7).

Despite differences, the parallels are remarkable. Like Joshua, Jeremiah is addressed as a warrior involved in the battle that leads to the land's devastation. The language of warfare used at the beginning, middle and end of the book helps the reader to understand the design of the book and the compilation of 'the words of Jeremiah'. It will be helpful if I outline the main features of my understanding of the 'fear not' language used as comfort to a warrior.

In an earlier book, *Fear Not Warrior: A Study of 'al tîra' Pericopes in the Hebrew Scriptures*, I outlined conventional language associated with warfare. I argued that the phrase 'fear not' (אל־תירא)[15] is used in conventional language (a *Gattung*) to give comfort to a warrior before an impending battle.[16] I understood the *Gattung* not in the normal form-critical sense as an indication of an oral setting (a *Sitz im Leben*), but in what I now describe as a semiotic sense: as coded information used by the Model Author for the reader. Normally, the formula 'fear not' is followed by what I called the 'object of fear'—the enemy—introduced with מן or מפני. A reason why the warrior should not be afraid follows next. In defensive

---

15. Depending on the situation, the phrase was used in the plural, אל תיראו. In other situations, particularly situations of offensive rather than a defensive warfare, different words of assurance were used, such as אל תחת.

16. While this language was most frequently used to describe Yahweh's words of comfort to his warriors (e.g. Joshua), it was also used in the Hebrew Bible for when one human being addresses another as a warrior. See 1 Sam. 23.17; 2 Sam. 9.7; 13.28; and 2 Kgs 25.24//Jer. 40.9-10.

situations the explanation is usually introduced by כִּי ('because, for'), but in offensive situations the imperative רְאֵה ('see') or the particle הִנֵּה ('now, behold') is used. The reason not to fear is expressed in the first person. The form concludes with the orders formulated in the second person. The basic structure of this conventional language can be outlined as follows:

Assurance
'Fear not' (אַל־תִּירָא)

Object of Fear
מִן or מִפְּנֵי used to refer to the enemy

Basis of Assurance
כִּי, רְאֵה or הִנֵּה used before the reason not to fear (formulated in the first person)

Orders
(formulated in the second person)

Two illustrations of this basic structure used to address Moses and Joshua before a battle are Deut. 3.2 (and the parallel Num. 21.34):

Assurance
Do not fear (אַל־תִּירָא)

Object of Fear
him (אֹתוֹ),

Basis of Assurance
for (כִּי) I have given him and all his people and his land into your hand.

Orders
And you shall do to him as you did to Sihon, king of the Amorites, who dwelt at Heshbon.

and Josh. 10.8:

Assurance
Do not fear (אַל־תִּירָא)

Object of Fear
them (מֵהֶם),

Basis of Assurance
for (כִּי) I have given them into your hand;

Orders
there shall not a man of them stand before you.

In my study I considered variations to this basic form reflecting changes in textual setting, but it is not necessary to discuss those variations here.[17]

Although my study of conventional language associated with 'fear not' was a form-critical study, my aim was different from the conventional form-critical goal of scholars such as Gunkel. I was interested in understanding how the conventional language associated with comforting a warrior before a battle illuminated the textual setting in which the form was used (its *Sitz im Text*). My focus was not on an oral setting (a *Sitz im Leben*) outside the text. In light of the semiotic orientation of my current approach, I now understand that my former study of conventional language associated with 'fear not' concerned codes that a Model Author used in constructing a text. Jeremiah is addressed with conventional 'fear not' language to comfort a warrior in the Jeremiah 1.

After the superscription, 'the words of Jeremiah' begin when Jeremiah says, 'And the word/thing of Yahweh came to me' (ויהי דבר יהוה אלי). This phrase will occur two more times in this chapter (vv. 11 and 13).[18] Its use here introduces the task to which Jeremiah has been appointed. 'Before I formed you in the belly I knew you, and before you came out from the womb I caused you to be set apart [that is, I consecrated you]. I made you a prophet to the nations' (1.5). This vocation and the enormity of its consequences, as we have seen, become clear to the reader mid-way through the book in Jeremiah 25:

> Because thus said Yahweh, the God of Israel to me, 'Take this cup of the wine of wrath from my hand and make all the nations to whom I send you drink it. And they will drink and they will stagger and they will act insanely from before the sword that I am sending among them. (25.15-16)

That Jeremiah will be instrumental in making the nations of the ארץ suffer devastation so that all the land will be cleared out makes Jeremiah's objection to his appointment as a prophet to the nations more understandable: 'And I said, "Alas, my lord, I do not know speaking [that is, how to speak]", because I am a boy' (1.6). Jeremiah's objection that he is only a boy is an understatement in light of the consequences of his task.

Yahweh is about to bring utter destruction to the land and to all the nations round about. Yahweh says, 'I will totally destroy them (והחרמתים) and I will make them a desolated waste, an object of derisive hissing, and

---

17. See Conrad, *Fear Not Warrior*, pp. 34-37, for a summary of the elements of this conventional language, and for a fuller discussion of the form as it occurs in the Former Prophets and in the Torah see pp. 5-37.

18. It also occurs in 2.1 and is used throughout Jeremiah.

a ruin forever' (25.9b). Because Jeremiah is to speak Yahweh's words in the total warfare against the nations, Yahweh answers Jeremiah's objection by addressing him with language typical of the address to a warrior preparing for battle. The conventional language of warfare characterizes the rest of the chapter from 1.7-19.

In Jer. 1.7-8 Yahweh addresses Jeremiah as a warrior before an ensuing battle. Yahweh's language in 1.7-8 is similar to that seen elsewhere (8.1-2; 10.8; 11.6), where Joshua is comforted before a battle, and can be outlined as follows:[19]

> *Orders*
> 'Do not say, "I am only a boy"; for you shall go to everyone to whom I send you, and you shall speak whatever I command you.
>
> *Assurance*
> Do not fear (אל־תירא)
>
> *Object of Fear*
> them (מפניהם),
>
> *Basis of Assurance*
> because (כי) I am with you to rescue you', a saying of Yahweh.

The *Orders* Jeremiah receives as a warrior are not like the more conventional orders given to a warrior such as Joshua who is ordered, 'you will hamstring their horses and burn their chariots with fire' (Josh. 11.8). Jeremiah is ordered to fight with words, echoing the superscription that this is a scroll about 'the words of Jeremiah'. The action and words of Yahweh that follow in 1.9-10 further strengthen the initial address to Jeremiah as a warrior (1.7-8). They give Jeremiah additional assurance that he need not be afraid:

> And Yahweh stretched out *his hand* (ידו) and touched my mouth, and he said to me,
> '*Now* (הנה), I have put *my words* (דברי)
>   in your mouth.
> *See* (ראה) I am making you a governor (הפקדתיך)[20] today over
>   nations and over kingdoms,
>   to pluck up and to pull down;
>   to destroy and to tear down;
>   to build and to plant.'

19. I have simplified the structure as it appeared in *Fear Not Warrior*, p. 40.

20. The same verb is used elsewhere (Jer. 40.5, 7, 11; 41.2, 10, 18; 2 Kgs 25.23) for the appointment of Gedaliah as governor after the king, Zedekiah, was taken captive.

Yahweh is stretching out his hand here to put words, the weapons of this warfare, into the mouth of Jeremiah. The action of Yahweh touching Jeremiah's mouth supports the assurance to Jeremiah not to be afraid.

The words Yahweh speaks, introduced by הנה and ראה, take the form of a *Basis of Assurance*. Furthermore, the formulation with הנה and ראה is typical of offensive engagements.[21] The words of comfort are given to Jeremiah because of Yahweh's initiative to wage war.

That Yahweh stretched out *his hand* and touched the mouth of Jeremiah suggests connections between this passage and Jer. 25.15. When read together these passages illuminate one another. In Jer. 25.15 Yahweh says to Jeremiah, 'Take the cup of this wine of wrath from *my hand* (ידי) and make all the nations to whom I send you drink it'. In light of 1.9, in which Yahweh stretched out *his hand* (ידו) and touched the mouth of Jeremiah, it becomes clearer what Jeremiah's role will be as a prophet to the nations. He will make the nations drink the cup of the wine of wrath by speaking all the words that Yahweh puts in his mouth. Jeremiah will be a prophetic warrior by uttering words. That he is appointed governor over nations and kingdoms also echoes Jeremiah 25, where Jeremiah's task—to make the nations drink 'the cup of the wine of Yahweh's wrath'—will result in their total devastation (25.9-11). Jeremiah as Yahweh's governor will be in control. The power will be in the words that come from his mouth.

Jeremiah 1.11-12 further strengthens the assurance given to the warrior-prophet Jeremiah not to be afraid. In these verses Jeremiah is directed to 'see'. The motif of seeing, as I indicated earlier, is typical of the language associated with offensive battles. What Jeremiah sees becomes a basis for his not fearing:

> The word of Yahweh came to me, 'What are you seeing Jeremiah?' And I said, 'a branch of an almond tree (שקד), I am seeing'. And Yahweh said to me, 'You have done well to see because I am watching (שקד) over my word to do it'.

This visual image of an 'almond branch', which is a pun for 'watching', assures Jeremiah that Yahweh will do his 'thing' (דבר), that is, that he will not only put his words in the mouth of Jeremiah but will also enact those words.

To summarize, I have pointed out that vv. 7-8 of Jeremiah present words typical of address to a warrior before battle. In Jer. 1.9-10 are reasons not to fear. The words are introduced by the particle הנה and the imperative

21. Conrad, *Fear Not Warrior*, p. 35.

רֽאָה, both of which are typical of offensive warfare. These additional words reinforce and supplement Yahweh's address to Jeremiah not to fear. Jeremiah 1.11-12 is a visual image of an almond branch further assuring Jeremiah that he is not to fear, for Yahweh is watching over the placing of his words in Jeremiah's mouth to ensure that his words will be accomplished.

The following diagram indicates the structure of 1.7-12. It also shows how this part of the structure forms a chiastic pattern with 1.13-19, verses that still need to be discussed. While the first part of this chiastic structure focuses on all the nations, the second part focuses on Jerusalem and Judah. The structure can be outlined as follows:

   A.   Address to Jeremiah as a warrior against the nations. (1.7-8)
     B.   Yahweh's actions giving assurance. (1.9-10)
       C.   Visual imagery giving assurance. (1.11-12)
       C′.   Visual imagery giving assurance. (1.13-14)
     B′.   Yahweh's actions giving assurance. (1.15-16)
   A′.   Address to Jeremiah as a warrior against Judah. (1.17-19)

The second part of this chiastic structure (C′) begins with visual imagery, which also serves to give assurance to the warrior Jeremiah not to be afraid:

> And the word of Yahweh came to me a second time,[22] 'What are you seeing?' And I said, 'A boiling pot, I am seeing, and it is facing from the north'. And Yahweh said, 'From the north the calamity has been opened against all the inhabitants of the land (אֶרֶץ)'. (1.13-14)

Jeremiah is not to be frightened of this imagery of the boiling pot facing from the north because it suggests that Yahweh has already begun to bring calamity to the land from the north. The reader is reminded of Jeremiah 25, where Yahweh will bring calamity to 'all the tribes (מִשְׁפָּחוֹת) of the north' (25.9). Indeed, 'the tribes of the north' are referred to directly in the next verses (1.15-16 = B′). These words take the conventional form associated with the basis of assurance, and here the words are introduced by the typical words הִנֵּה and כִּי:

22. This is actually the fourth time that the phrase דְּבַר יְהוָה אֵלַי is used in this chapter. It also occurs at the beginning of 2.1. As it is used here, it is referring to the chiastic structure as I have outlined it. It concerns the second time visual imagery has been seen by Jeremiah reassuring him not to be afraid. The different uses of the phrase דְּבַר יְהוָה in this chapter and the next (1.2, 4, 11, 13; 2.1; 4) support the observation I made in the previous chapter that this phrase is used in a general sense for communication from Yahweh.

> Because (כִּי), behold I (הִנְנִי) am about to call all the tribes (מִשְׁפְּחוֹת) of the kingdoms of the north, a saying of Yahweh. They will come and each one will place his throne at the entrance of the gates of Jerusalem, against all the surrounding walls, and against all the cities of Judah. And I will speak my judgments against them concerning all their evil by which they have for-saken me. They have made sacrifices to other gods, and they have bowed down to the works of their own hands.

These words are also linked with Jeremiah 25 where Judah and Jerusalem are among the nations to drink of 'the cup of the wine of wrath':

> And I took the cup from the hand of Yahweh, and I made all the nations to whom Yahweh sent me drink it: Jerusalem, and the cities of Judah and all its kings, its princes, to make them a devastation and a waste… (25.17-18)

This unit ends in 1.17-18 (A') as it began in 1.7-8 (A), with the typical formulation of words addressed to a warrior before a battle:

Orders
> But you, you will gird up your loins, and you will arise, and you will speak to them everything which I command you.

Assurance
> Do not be dismayed (אַל־תֵּחַת)[23]

Object of Fear
> before them (מִפְּנֵיהֶם),

Basis of Assurance
> lest I dismay you before them. And I am now (הִנֵּה) making you today a city of fortification, and an iron column, and bronze walls against all the people of the land (אָרֶץ). They will fight against you but they will not pre-vail over you because (כִּי) I am with you, a saying of Yahweh, to rescue you.

Here, as in 1.7-8, the *Orders* to Jeremiah are to speak everything that Yahweh commands. Jeremiah's weapons will be words. The *Basis of Assurance* is somewhat peculiar because of the threat to Jeremiah if he does not follow orders. Such a threat is not typical of this kind of address to a warrior, but it does anticipate other threats Yahweh makes to Jeremiah in response to Jeremiah's complaints about his situation at those times when the situation makes him afraid (e.g. 12.5; 15.19-21).

To summarize the discussion, then, Jeremiah's appointment as a prophet to the nations (1.5) is followed in 1.7-19 with conventional language that

---

23. The phrase אַל־תֵּחַת is used in the *Assurance* as well as אַל־תִּירָא. See Josh. 8.1-2; Deut. 1.20-21; 31.7-8.

addresses Jeremiah as a Joshua-like warrior. The enormity of the envisaged warfare can be seen when Jeremiah's role as a prophetic warrior is read in light of Jeremiah 25. Yahweh has proclaimed warfare against the land and all the neighboring nations. This warfare is similar to that which he conducted against the nations at the time of Joshua when he gave Israel the land. Jeremiah, then, is a prophetic warrior who represents the reversal of Joshua's triumphant conquest of the land. Not only is he a member of the community of Judah that will lose the land, but at the end of the book he returns to Egypt.

The significant connection between the end of the book of Kings and Jeremiah relates to the time of Josiah when 'the book of the *torah*/covenant' was found in the temple. After finding this book, Josiah made a covenant with Yahweh in order to do 'all the words of this covenant that were written in this book' (2 Kgs 23.3). However, although Josiah 'established the words of the law that were written in the book that the priest Hilkiah had found in the house of Yahweh' (23.24), Yahweh still did not turn from his fierce wrath (23.26). Yahweh determined to remove Judah from his sight as he had earlier removed Israel. The general outline of this end in Kings is briefly mentioned in the stories surrounding the last kings of Israel: Jehoiakim, Jehoiachin and Zedekiah (2 Kgs 24–25). In the collection of scrolls that follows, the 'book' of Jeremiah provides '*the words*' from the roaring voice of Yahweh where Jeremiah as a Joshua-like warrior will fight as a warrior of Yahweh.

Unlike Joshua, Jeremiah lacks a book on which to meditate. Because of the words Yahweh puts in Jeremiah's mouth, Jeremiah himself will write books. One of these books is mentioned in connection with his 'fighting words' against the nations in Jeremiah 25. Yahweh says in 25.13, 'I will bring against that land all my words which I have spoken against it, everything which is written in this book which Jeremiah prophesied against all the nations'. Jeremiah's words are not only for speaking; they are also for writing. What is 'this book'? Indications are that it is a book *other than the one we are reading*. But where is this book? And what happened to the book of the *torah*/covenant that Josiah found?

3. *Compiling the Words of a Warrior-Prophet*

This portrayal of Jeremiah as a warrior speaking Yahweh's words announcing an end to Judah and all the nations of the land provides the background for reading of Jeremiah as a compilational unity. A few observations about

Jeremiah as a whole[24] will help to clarify my reading. First, conventional language of comfort to a warrior using the recurring phrase 'fear not' (אל־תירא) encountered in the first chapter of Jeremiah does not recur until the end of the book (30.10-11; 40.9-10; 42.9-11; 46.27-28). Its reappearance is associated with the end that has also come to Judah when some of the inhabitants of the land are taken into exile in Babylon and others are attempting to escape to Egypt, taking Jeremiah with them. Second, the implications of Jeremiah's role as a prophet and the reasons for Yahweh speaking words of comfort as he did to Joshua before a battle do not become clear until mid-way through the book (Jer. 25) when Jeremiah is to make the nations, including Judah, drink from the cup of Yahweh's wrath. Third, Jeremiah's interactions with Jehoiakim and Zedekiah do not commence until 21.1, where they are clearly dated. Fourth, all the material in the book up to Jeremiah 21 should be associated with the earlier period of Josiah. Not only is Jeremiah's call dated from the thirteenth year of the reign of Josiah (1.2), but also a reference is made to the days of Josiah in 3.6. Furthermore, Jeremiah's preaching of 'the words of the covenant' (Jer. 11), a covenant re-established in the days of Josiah, fits this Josianic context.

In my reading, (1) the superscription (1.1-3), (2) Jeremiah's preaching the covenant in ch. 11, (3) the elaboration of Jeremiah's task as a prophet to the nations in ch. 25, and (4) the appearance of the language of address to a warrior that comes toward the end of the book are key markers indicating how the book can be read as a compilational whole. When I read from the superscription to Jeremiah preaching the covenant (Jer. 11), from the covenant to Jeremiah's taking the cup to make the nations drink (Jer. 25), and from Jeremiah's taking the cup from Yahweh's hand to the reappearance of the language of address to a warrior (especially in 40.9-10),[25] I see that at every stage along the way the words of Jeremiah announce the coming warfare 'from the tribes of the kingdoms of the north' (1.15) with an ever growing intensity and passion until Yahweh's war with Judah and the nations is over.[26] In this growing fervor Jeremiah himself becomes

24. I need to reiterate here that I am reading the MT of Jeremiah, I am not attempting to read Jeremiah in a different manifestation, such as the LXX, nor am I interested in what I think is an impossible task of attempting to reconstruct an original *Vorlage*.

25. Conventional language of address to a warrior actually is found as early as 30.10-11. Here it is addressed to the future community in Babylonian exile and is repeated in 46.27-28.

26. I am not claiming that this configuration was an original scribal intention, but that it arises out of my reading, paying attention to textual limits of a received order.

more and more engaged in the battle as a participant in the fighting, a warrior engaged in the battle by wielding words. His life itself is increasingly put in danger so that the reason Yahweh addressed him as a warrior prior to military engagement becomes more and more obvious. The collection and arrangement of 'the words of Jeremiah' are designed in a literary sense to lead inevitably to Yahweh's final removal of Judah from his sight as anticipated in 2 Kgs 23.27.

4. *From the Superscription to Preaching the Covenant (Jeremiah 1–11)*

After the superscription and the appointment of Jeremiah as a prophet to the nations, the collected material in chs. 2–11 can be read as words of Jeremiah against the background of Josiah depicted in 2 Kings 22–23. By making this observation I am not suggesting that there was an 'actual' Josiah who 'actually' did all the things attributed to him in 2 Kings 22–23. Nor am I proposing that there was an 'actual' Jeremiah who 'actually' proclaimed the words attributed to him in Jeremiah 2–11. I am reading 2 Kings 22–23 as a narrative, which provides a literary setting for the reader who reads 'the words of Jeremiah' as a 'book' that follows Kings in canonical order. The opening of the book of Jeremiah itself suggests such a link with the 'events' of Josiah when it announces that 'the word of Yahweh came in the days of King Josiah son of Amon of Judah, *in the thirteenth year of his reign*'. The book of Kings in its portrayal of Josiah focuses on events associated with the discovery of 'the book of the *torah/ covenant*'. This is dated in '*the eighteenth year of King Josiah*' (2 Kgs 22.3), that is, five years after the book of Jeremiah says that the word of Yahweh came to him.

The beginning of the book of Jeremiah (2.1–4.2) collects words directed primarily to Israel (the Northern Kingdom). In this section Judah is in the background (see 2.28) and will only become prominent in 4.3. That Jeremiah should be directing words to Israel in the north is consistent with the activities of Josiah narrated in 2 Kings 23 that also involved Israel. Josiah burns the high altar at Bethel and 'the high places that were in the towns of Samaria'; slaughtering all the priests of the high places before he returns to Jerusalem (2 Kgs 23.15-20).[27]

---

27. This section of 2 Kings speaks (in 23.16-18) about the earlier Jeroboam and a prophet from Judah at the time of the emergence of Judah and Israel as separate kingdoms. However, this incident does have overtones with the later Jeroboam and Amos,

Israel is not described in 2 Kings 23 as an independent kingdom with its own kings and prophets but more like a place where there has been a famine 'of hearing the words of Yahweh' (Amos 8.11). Indeed, Israel is depicted as having come to an end as Amos' words had earlier proclaimed (Amos 8.1-3). Yahweh is reported as saying in 2 Kgs 23.26-27 that he had already removed Israel from his sight and that he would also remove Judah from his sight (2 Kgs 23.26-27). These words of Yahweh in 2 Kings help explain the transition in focus from Israel to Judah in Jeremiah. Yahweh is about to remove Judah from his sight as he had earlier removed Israel.

Jeremiah is ordered by Yahweh in 2.2 to go and proclaim in Jerusalem that he remembered 'the devotion of your youth'. The identity of the community addressed is clarified in 2.4 as 'the house of Jacob and all the families of the house of Israel'. This is a community that defiled the land after Yahweh had brought the people up from the land of Egypt. This is a community that had forsaken Yahweh (2.13, 19) so that the fear of Yahweh is no longer in Israel (2.19). Therefore Israel has become a waste. It has experienced the roaring voice of Yahweh announced in Amos' words. Israel has already experienced what is coming to Judah:

> Lions have roared (ישאגו) against it;
>   they have uttered their voice (נתנו קולם).
> Its land (ארצו) they have made a waste (לשמה);
>   its cities are in ruins, without an inhabitant. (Jer. 2.15)

While the verbs are in the plural and are here referring to the nations who carried out the destruction of Israel, the vocabulary is identical with that used for Yahweh's roaring and uttering his voice from Zion/Jerusalem in Amos 1.2 (cf. Jer. 25.13).[28]

Judah makes a first appearance, outside the superscription, in 2.28 suggesting that it, like Israel, has many gods.[29] While the focus remains on Israel at this point in Jeremiah, it begins to fade as Judah increasingly comes into focus. Chapter 3 concerns Yahweh's divorce of Israel. This divorce did not stop her running after other gods (lovers), and by doing this

---

another prophet from Judah. The earlier Jeroboam and the earlier prophet from Judah appear to the reader who knows the 'book' of Amos as a clone of the later Jeroboam and Amos, the later prophet from Judah.

28. The image of a devastated land without inhabitants uses vocabulary and imagery associated with the consequence of Yahweh's roaring and uttering his voice, given fuller description in Jer. 25 (see 25.30).

29. The image of Judah's gods being as many as the towns of Judah or the streets of Jerusalem will come up again.

she has polluted the land. This imagery makes sense in light of 2 Kings 23, where Josiah is in Israel pulling down the sacred sites associated with other gods. In 3.6-10 the words concerning what Yahweh said to Jeremiah at the time of Josiah are recorded. What he says to Jeremiah is consistent with what he said at the time of Josiah when he announced that he would remove Judah from his sight just as he had removed Israel (2 Kgs 23.26-27). The passage (Jer. 3.6-10) suggests that Judah has not learned from Israel even though Yahweh had removed Israel from his sight:

> Yahweh said to me in the days of Josiah, the king: 'Have you seen what disloyal Israel has done? She has gone up on every high mountain and under every green tree and she was a harlot there. And I said, 'After she has done all these things to me, she will return'. But she did not return. Her treacherous sister Judah saw it. And I saw that for all the reasons apostate Israel committed adultery, I sent her away. And I gave her bill of divorce to her. But her treacherous sister Judah did not fear, and she went and she was a harlot. And it happened that she played the harlot so frivolously, and she polluted the land and she committed adultery with stone and tree. And also in all this her treacherous sister Judah did not return to me with her whole heart, but with deception.

Here there is no mention of the end of Judah—no bill of divorce. However, the description of Judah's pursuit of other lovers, other gods, is described as being worse than that of Israel. The announcement of Judah's final doom will intensify in Jeremiah after this chapter. The collection of words concerning Israel in Jeremiah 3 closes with calls for Israel to return (3.11-14). That this is not a present expectation is clear; a distinct future is indicated for Israel and Judah when there will be a return to Jerusalem (3.15-18). There is even a reference to the things the returnees will say on Israel's return (3.19-25). This return to the land will be from the north (Babylon), not from the south (Egypt). The notion of eventual rescue from the north is another feature of the book of Jeremiah. Appended words about a future time of restoration typically follow collections of Jeremiah's words announcing doom. Such an organization is evident also in Amos where words of future restoration suddenly conclude a collection of words of unrelenting doom (9.11-15).

After one final offer for Israel to return in 4.1-2, the focus shifts to Judah and a call for its inhabitants to open their hearts to Yahweh in order that they not experience his wrath as a burning fire (4.3-5). Beginning with 4.5-8 and in regular intervals until 10.22, mention is made of the prospect of war coming from the north (6.1-8, 27-28; 10.22). These bellicose rumblings from the north are not yet a fulfilled threat in the literary world of

Jeremiah. The advance of war from the north is presented as imminent. The particular military threat in these early chapters remains unidentified, becoming associated with the king of Babylon only later (20.5). The warfare from the north is near at hand but not present. In this section of the arrangement of 'the words of Jeremiah', Jeremiah's own voice remains in the background. At the time of the Judean king Josiah, the narrative background for understanding these words at the beginning of Jeremiah (chs. 2–22), the war with Babylon had not yet begun.

The collected words about the war coming from the north pick up and anticipate what is said in Jeremiah 25 about Yahweh's total warfare against nations. Judah, as one of the nations on whom Yahweh has declared war, will be a decimated land emptied of all its inhabitants by the tribes of the north (25.9). If one reads the words about the impending warfare from the north (4.5-8; 6.1-8, 27-28; 10.22) in the order in which they are arranged in Jeremiah, one can hear, even as a reader, the army advancing closer and closer. The words themselves create panic.

In 4.5-8 trumpets are to be sounded, and people are to take refuge in fortified cities because Yahweh is about to bring calamity from the north. Notice here that the army described as a lion from its thicket and a destroyer of nations has: *risen up* (עלה), *departed* (נסע) and *set out* (יצא) to make the land a waste and the cities of Judah a devastation.

In 6.1-8, the calamity (רעה) and great destruction (שבר גדול) are *leaning over and looking down* (נשקפה) from the north. Again trumpets are to be sounded and standards raised.

The army, which has *risen up* (עלה), *departed* (נסע) and *set out* (יצא), and which is *leaning over and looking down* (נשקפה) from the north, can now itself be seen in 6.22-23. *See* (הנה), a people *is coming* (בא) from the north. Mention of the bow and javelin in the hands of this cruel people underscores the fact that they can now be seen.

The army is heard in 10.22:

> A noise (קול)! A report (שמועה)! Behold, its coming (הנה באה)! A great rumbling (רעש)[30] from the land of the north to make the cities of Judah a desolation, a lair of jackals.

While there is no mention of the north in 8.16, this great rumbling from the north in 10.22 is vividly described as an oncoming army from the north:

---

30. This is the word used in Amos 1.2 that I argued should be understood as the quaking of an oncoming army.

The snorting of horses (נשמע) is heard from Dan;
　at the sound of the neighing of their stallions the whole earth quakes (רעשה).
They have come and devoured the land and all that fills it;
　the city and all who live in it. (Jer. 8.16)

The army with its rumbling noises of destruction can already be heard in Israel, in Dan.

While the book of Jeremiah is a compilation of 'the words of Jeremiah'—a collection rather than a composition—that compilation read as a collage does create a picture for the reader. One can see a picture of an advancing army when one configures 'the words of Jeremiah' in 4.3–10.22 as being spoken in the days of Josiah. These are the days when the Babylonian army has not yet arrived in Jerusalem, which it did in the later time of Jehoiakim, Jehoiachin and Zedekiah (see 2 Kgs 24.1). The army will appear for the first time in Jeremiah in 20.5. When reading 'the words of Jeremiah', attention to order and arrangement enable literary links to be made.

I want to make a few other observations about the compilation of Jeremiah's words in Jeremiah 2–11. From 2.1–4.2 the words focus on Israel with a gradual shift to Judah. Judah comes to central focus in 4.3 with Israel falling into the background (cf. 5.11). These words about Israel and Judah attain fuller meaning when they are read in connection with 2 Kings 22–23 concerning Josiah, given that the dating of the superscription positions Jeremiah in the time of Josiah. But the words also attain expanded meaning when they are read in connection with what comes after: Yahweh's announcement of total warfare against all the nations of the land.

My intention in these concluding remarks on Jeremiah 2–11 is not to be exhaustive but to make a few additional observations about how meaning emerges by configuring the text in light of what has come before and what comes after. First, in 4.7 the army setting out from the north is depicted as a lion (אריה). The purpose of this departure is 'to make your land a waste; your cities will be in ruins without an inhabitant' (לשום ארצך לשמה עריך תצינה מאין יושב). What is anticipated for the future of the land, the cities and the inhabitants in Judah is what has already occurred in Israel as is stated in 2.15: 'The lions *have roared*; they *have uttered* their voice; they *have made* his [Israel's] land a waste; his cities are in ruins, without an inhabitant' (וישיתו ארצו לשמה עריו נצתה מבלי ישב). What has happened to Israel will happen to Judah. The same point is being made here that was made at the end of 2 Kings where Yahweh announced that at the time of Josiah in 2 Kgs 23.27: 'I will remove Judah also out of my sight, as I have removed Israel; and I will reject this city that I have chosen, Jerusalem, and the house of which I said, My name shall be there'. That Judah has acted similarly to Israel so as to be expelled from Yahweh's sight is also a motif in the words of Jeremiah that came at the time of Josiah (3.6-10). The image of the lion's roaring and uttering its voice, even though it here appears to refer to the nations bringing destruction, re-inforces the image of the 'lion' Yahweh who will roar and utter his voice bringing destruction and devastation to the land, the cities and the inhabitants (25.30).[31]

Second, in ch. 7 Yahweh orders Jeremiah to go, stand at the gate (הִשְּׁעַר) of the house of Yahweh and proclaim the word of Yahweh to all 'the people of Judah'. Later in the collection Jeremiah will be ordered again to go to the temple, this time at the beginning of the reign of Jehoiakim. He is asked to move beyond the gate and to stand in the court (חָצֵר) of the house of Yahweh (26.1) and this time his proclamation is 'to all the cities of Judah'. Interestingly, on this second occasion, Jeremiah's orders come immediately after Yahweh has declared war on all the nations of the land (ch. 25). As a warrior-prophet Jeremiah has moved from the outside to the inside, from the gate to the court. I will look at the relationship between Jeremiah's first words spoken at the gate of the temple (ch. 7) and his second temple 'sermon' (ch. 26) later in this chapter. However, I now want to show how this first sermon (ch. 7), like the rest of the words in Jeremiah 2–11, gain perspective by looking back to the depiction of Josiah in 2 Kings and ahead to Yahweh's declaration of war in Jeremiah 25.

After accusing the people of disobedience and telling them not to trust in the temple—because in the past Yahweh destroyed his temple at Shiloh —Yahweh says, 'I will cast you out (וְהִשְׁלַכְתִּי) of my sight (מֵעַל פָּנַי), just as I cast out all your brothers, the offspring of Ephraim' (Jer. 7.15). Yahweh is reported to have said at the time of Josiah, 'I will remove (אָסִיר) Judah from my sight (מֵעַל פָּנַי) just as I have removed Israel' (2 Kgs 23.27). Yahweh's words spoken by Jeremiah at the end of the sermon, however, also anticipate Yahweh's words when he declares war later in Jeremiah 25. In 7.34 he says, 'And I will bring to an end the sound of mirth and gladness, the voice of the bride and bridegroom in the cities of Judah and in the streets of Jerusalem; for the land shall become a waste'. In 25.10-11 Yahweh says, 'I will banish from them the sound of

---

31. Of course, according to Amos 1.2 (cf. 3.8), Yahweh's voice had roared earlier announcing Israel's end.

mirth and the sound of gladness, the voice of the bride and bridegroom…
This whole land shall become a ruin and a waste…'

Third, in Jeremiah 11 Jeremiah is proclaiming 'the words of this covenant'. Again it is not too difficult to see this proclamation as looking back
to the covenant Josiah made after discovering 'the book of the covenant'
in the temple:

> And the king went up to the house of Yahweh and every man of Judah and
> all the inhabitants of Jerusalem with him, and the priests and the prophets
> and all the people from the least to the greatest. And he read in their hearing
> all the words of the book of the covenant which was found in the house of
> Yahweh. And the king stood by the pillar and he made a covenant before
> Yahweh to walk after Yahweh and to keep his commandments and his
> decrees, and his statutes with his whole heart and his whole being to
> establish the words of *this covenant* that were written in this book. And all
> the people stood בּ *the covenant* (בבברית…ויעמד). (2 Kgs 23.2-3)

That Josiah went up to the house of Yahweh to proclaim the covenant is
significant in light of the fact that Jeremiah goes to the temple to proclaim
the people's failure (Jer. 7). The phrase used in 2 Kgs 23.3—'and all the
people stood בּ *the covenant*'—is unique in the Old Testament. What does
it mean? Most translations render this phrase in a positive sense such as
the NRSV's 'all the people joined in the covenant'. But it is possible that
the phrase means just the opposite, 'and all the people stood against the
covenant'. The preposition בּ can mean 'against' in some contexts when
used with the verb עמד. This is particularly true in contexts of war (see
Josh. 10.8; 21.44; 23.9), where the phrase is used in the sense that none of
your enemies 'shall stand against you'. If עמד בּ means 'to stand against',
then the meaning of this passage takes on a significantly different meaning:

> And the king *stood beside* (על…ויעמד) the pillar and *he made a covenant*
> before Yahweh to walk after Yahweh and to keep his commandments and
> his decrees, and his statutes with *his whole heart* and *his whole being* to
> establish the words of *this covenant* which is written in this book. But the
> people *stood against* (בבברית…ויעמד) the covenant. (2 Kgs 23.3)

The king takes his stand beside the pillar and *he* makes a covenant with
Yahweh to follow his commandments and statutes with *his* whole heart
and with *his* whole being to establish the words of this covenant which are
written in the book. The passage says nothing about *the people* making a
covenant, nothing about *the people* agreeing to follow the commandments,
decrees and statutes with *their* whole hearts and with *their* whole being.
Rather, they take their stand against the covenant.

Such a reading of the passage fits the context of 2 Kings 23 and Jeremiah 11. After Josiah makes this covenant with Yahweh, the actions of Josiah are reported at a dizzying pace. The passage tells us nothing about the actions of the people. The king does everything:

(1) '*the king* commanded' that all the vessels of Baal be brought out of the temple (23.4);

(2) '*he* deposed the idolatrous priests' (23.5);

(3) '*he* brought the Asherah' (23.6);

(4) '*he* broke down the houses of the male temple prostitutes' (23.7);

(5) '*he* brought all the priests out of the towns of Judah and defiled the high places' (23.8);

(6) '*he* broke down the high places of the gates' (23.8);

(7) '*he* defiled Topheth' (23.10);

(8) '*he* removed the horses that the kings of Judah had dedicated to the sun' (23.11);

(9) '*he* burned the chariots of the sun with fire' (23.11);

(10) '*the king* defiled the high places that were east of Jerusalem to the south of the Mount of Destruction, which King Solomon of Israel had built for Astarte (23.12);

(11) '*he* broke the pillars in pieces, cut down the sacred poles and covered the sites with human bones' (23.14);

(12) '*he* pulled down' the altar at Bethel' (23.15);

(13) '*he* burned the high place crushing it to dust' (23.15);

(14) '*he* burned the sacred pole' (23.15);

(15) '*Josiah* turned' and '*he* saw the tombs' and '*he* sent' and 'he took the bones out of the tombs', and '*he* burned' the bones on the altar, and '*he* defiled' the altar (23.16);

(16) '*he* said, "What is that monument I see?"' (23.17);

(17) '*he* said, "Let him rest"' (23.18);

(18) '*Josiah* removed all the shrines of the high places that were in the towns of Samaria' and '*he* did to them just as *he* had done to Bethel' (23.19);

(19) '*he* slaughtered on the altars all the priests of the high places' and '*he* burned human bones' on the altars (23.20);

(20) '*the king* commanded, "Keep the Passover to Yahweh"' (23.21);

(21) '*Josiah* put away the mediums, wizards, teraphim, idols and all the abominations that were seen in the land of Judah and Jerusalem' (23.24);

(22) The consequence of all these actions is that '*he* established the words of the law that were written in the book' (23.24).

In all of this activity we hear nothing about the actions of 'the people'. In 23.21-23, the people are commanded to keep the Passover to Yahweh. We hear that no Passover had been kept since the days of the judges who judged Israel and that the Passover was now kept. But nothing is said about the actions of 'the people'. Josiah appears to be acting alone. Chapter 23 of 2 Kings reads like the activities of one man who makes a covenant, who himself acts to establish the words of the *torah* written in the book Hilkiah found; it does not read like the reforming zeal of the people. Even the priests of the high places did not go up to the altar in Jerusalem, but ate unleavened bread among their kindred (23.9). The closing statement about this episode in 23.24 makes the activities of Josiah sound like a 'one man show':

> Before him there was no king like him, who turned to Yahweh with all his heart, with all his soul, and with all his might, according to all the *torah* of Moses; nor did any like him arise after him. (23.25)

That it was Josiah who made a covenant with Yahweh while the people stood against the covenant helps explain the negative response by Yahweh in 2 Kgs 23.26-27. Yahweh is still angry because of the provocations of Manesseh and therefore will remove Judah from his sight just as he had removed Israel. In spite of the actions of Josiah, the practices of Manesseh that displeased Yahweh continue. Indeed, when Jeremiah challenges the people to heed the words of the covenant, it is just such a return to actions of the fathers that is evident.

Jeremiah is ordered to speak to 'the people[32] of Judah and the inhabitants of Jerusalem' (11.1). According to my reading of Jeremiah, this proclaiming of the covenant is portrayed against the backdrop of Josiah's reign. It is 'the people' who stood against the covenant, not the king Josiah, and it is to the people that Jeremiah's words are directed; they are not directed to Josiah, the king. Josiah does not become a prominent character in the book of Jeremiah. As a prophet to the nations Jeremiah directs his words against the enemy. That enemy is not Josiah but 'all the people of Judah' and the kings who succeeded Josiah.

The response of the people to Jeremiah's words call for them to be obedient to the covenant confirms my reading of 2 Kgs 23.3: 'All the people stood against the covenant'. They have refused to be obedient to the covenant (23.8). Therefore, Jeremiah says (Jer. 11.9-13),

---

32. The phrase here is אִישׁ יְהוּדָה.

> Jeremiah said to me, 'Conspiracy is found among the people of Judah and the inhabitants of Jerusalem. They have returned to the iniquity of their earlier fathers who refused to listen to my words. They have gone after other gods to serve them. The house of Israel[33] and the house of Judah have broken my covenant, which I made with their fathers.' Therefore, thus Yahweh has said, 'Now, I am about to bring a calamity on them from which they will not be able to escape. They will cry out to me but I will not listen to them. And the cities of Judah and the inhabitants of Jerusalem will go, and they will cry out to the gods to whom they are making sacrifices. But they will never save them in the time of their calamity. Because your gods have become as many as your cities, O Judah, and the number of your streets, O Jerusalem, as many as the altars you set up for shame, altars to sacrifice to Baal.

These words in Jeremiah 11 concerning the covenant can be understood in the context of the covenant that Josiah made in 2 Kgs 23.3. The people did not join in this covenant but stood against it, returning to the iniquity of their fathers like Manasseh, who had turned to other gods. The people continued to provoke Yahweh to anger. Jeremiah's words are here directed not against the king, Josiah, but against the people of Judah.

At the end of these words of Jeremiah concerning the covenant, Jeremiah receives orders in 11.14-17 not to pray for these people. That Jeremiah is moving more and more into open conflict in the battle about to come is evident in his lament about how his words are getting him into trouble. He is like a lamb led to slaughter (vv. 18-20). Yahweh's closing words in this chapter (vv. 21-23), are meant as words of comfort to Jeremiah, but they suggest the dangerous situation into which Jeremiah is being drawn:

> Therefore, thus Yahweh said concerning the men of Anathoth who seek your life saying, 'Do not prophesy in the name of Yahweh and you will not die by our hand'. Therefore, thus Yahweh of hosts said, 'Behold I am about to punish them. The young men will die by the sword. Their sons and their daughters will die by famine. And there will not be a remnant of them, because I will bring a calamity to the men of Anathoth, in the year of their punishment.

I want to summarize my configuration of the words of Jeremiah compiled in Jeremiah 2–11. These are words I understand to be associated with the days of Josiah. According to the superscription, the word of Yahweh came to Jeremiah in the thirteenth year of the reign of Josiah, five years

---

33. It is interesting that Israel is mentioned here because Josiah's actions to restore the covenant extended both to Israel and to Judah.

before it was reported to Josiah that the book of the *torah*/covenant was found in the temple. I read the words in Jeremiah 2–11 against the narrative background of Josiah in 2 Kings 22–23 concerning the discovery of the book of the covenant. This was a time when Josiah—but apparently not the people—made a covenant with Yahweh and established all the words of the book found in the temple in both Israel and Judah. According to the narrative in 2 Kgs 23.27, however, Yahweh had determined to bring about the end of Judah by removing them from his sight as he had done earlier to Israel.

The words of Jeremiah concern how Yahweh is about to bring this end to Judah as he had brought an end to Israel. At the beginning of the compilation, the words focus on Israel with Judah gradually moving into prominence until it becomes the central focus in 4.3. A theme running throughout these chapters is how Yahweh is about to bring a great calamity to the land, the cities and the inhabitants of Judah. This coming end is illuminated by the passage that will come later in Jeremiah 25 when Yahweh announces what it means for Jeremiah to be a prophet to the nations (1.5). Jeremiah will make the nations, including Judah, drink from the cup of the wine of wrath as a warrior engaged in Yahweh's battle. In these collected words at the beginning of Jeremiah (chs. 2–11), however, Jeremiah is a voice in the background; but he is about to become a warrior fighting with Yahweh's words in the forthcoming calamity from the north. Jeremiah 5.14b sums up Jeremiah's situation at the time of Josiah. Yahweh says,

> I am about to put my words in your mouth for a fire
>   and this people are the wood, and it will devour them.

Indeed, 'this people' are the primary addressees of Jeremiah's words in Jeremiah 2–11. He is not speaking against the king, Josiah. The time portrayed in Jeremiah 2–11 is a time when the people have stood against the covenant (2 Kgs 23.3; Jer. 11.9-13). Only at the end of this section, when Jeremiah has spoken to the people at the gate of the temple (7.1-34), and they have refused to adhere to the words of this covenant (11.9-13), does Jeremiah begin to become an active warrior with words as weapons, so that his life is in danger (11.18-21).

I want to close this summary overview of Jeremiah 2–11 by drawing attention to the recurring theme of the *torah* of Yahweh. The passages about the *torah* of Yahweh, along with the attempt to re-establish the covenant (Jer. 11), link this collection of Jeremiah's words with 'the book of the *torah*/covenant' found in 2 Kings 22–23. The theme is that the people have rejected Yahweh's *torah* (6.19; 9.12 [Eng. 9.13]).[34] In 8.8, however, an added nuance is given to the rejection of Yahweh's *torah*. These words follow the portrayal of what Jeremiah spoke to the people of Judah at the gates of the temple, and perhaps that incident should be understood for the setting of these words as well:

> How can you way, 'We are wise',
>   and the *torah* of Yahweh is with us?
> Surely, now it is made for deception[35]
>   [by] the deceptive pen of scribes (ספרים).

This scribal deception is an intriguing statement given the prominence of the book (ספר) found at the time of Josiah and given the fact that Jeremiah is so involved with writing. We will need to return to this point in the next chapter when I consider the importance of reading and writing in the prophetic corpus.

5. *From the Covenant to the Cup of the Wine of Wrath (Jeremiah 12–25)*

The compilation of the words of Jeremiah in chs. 12–25 can be read against the historical background of the kings who come to prominence after Josiah (Jehoiakim, Jehoiachin and Zedekiah) who appear after Jeremiah 21. The foe from the north who had remained anonymous in chs. 2–11 is identified as the king of Babylon (20.4). The words of Jeremiah gathered here are also clarified by looking back to 2 Kings and forward to Jeremiah 25, but the links are not as numerous as they were in Jeremiah 2–11.

I want to focus first on Jeremiah 12–20. Gradually, in these chapters Jeremiah is drawn away from the people of Judah. Jeremiah makes a series of intercessions for his people, but gradually the people of Judah and their kings become his enemy. It also emerges that he is fighting against opposing prophets. Scribal arrangement of materials allows a picture of Jeremiah to emerge. There is not logical development of thought created by the composition of an author but a collage of images creating a picture of Jeremiah's world.

---

34. Yahweh's *torah* is also mentioned in connection with Israel (2.8). In that passage the theme is not rejection of the *torah* as it is in 6.16 and 9.12 for Judah where 'the book of the *torah*' had been found. Rather, in Israel people who handle *torah* did not know Yahweh.

35. MT points it as definite, 'for the deception'.

These chapters come into better view when they are linked with Yahweh's address to Jeremiah as a warrior in 1.17. In that verse he is given rather negative assurance as a warrior: 'Do not be dismayed [that is, broken or shattered] before them, lest I dismay you before them'. The implication is that Jeremiah should not buckle in the face of battle. In many ways the interchange between Jeremiah and Yahweh throughout chs. 12–20 is similarly characterized by this negative tone.

At the end of Jeremiah 11 it is clear that the people have not embraced the words of the covenant but have turned back to the iniquity of their ancestors. Therefore Yahweh gives Jeremiah these orders: 'And you, do not intercede for this people and do not lift up a cry or an intercession because I will not listen when they call to me at the time of their calamity' (11.14). In spite of this instruction not to intercede for the people, Jeremiah repeatedly attempts to do so. Yahweh's response reflects the negative assurance of 1.7. As a warrior-prophet, Jeremiah must speak Yahweh's words, but he must not intercede for the people. The reader is reminded of that other warrior-prophet, Amos, and his initial attempts at intercession over the calamities coming to his people (Amos 7.2-3, 5-6). By the time Amos announces the end of Israel, his intercessions for Israel have also ceased (8.1-3; cf. 8.7-9).

Jeremiah 12.1-4 can be understood as a prayer of intercession seeking justice. The question Jeremiah asks in 12.4 is similar to the questions Amos asked in his intercessions (7.2, 5):

> How long will the land mourn,
>   and the grass of every field dry up
>   as a result of the calamity of the ones who inhabit it?
> The animals and birds are swept away;
>   Because they said, 'He does not look after us'.

Yahweh's response to Jeremiah is not to repent of his actions as he does originally in Amos, but to pose a question suggesting that Jeremiah the warrior is breaking down in the face of battle. The battle is coming, and it will get even worse when the enemy arrives. The implication of the response is that Jeremiah should not be fooled and that he should not intercede:

> If you ran with [the] feet [of humans] and they wearied you;
>   how will you contend with horses?
> And if in a peaceful land you trusted,
>   how will you do with the pride of the Jordan?
> Because even your brothers and the house of your fathers,

> even they have dealt treacherously with you,
>   even they called after you with a loud cry.[36]
> Do not believe in them
>   when they speak to you good things. (12.5-6)

Jeremiah was ordered by Yahweh not to intercede for this people (11.14). However, in the face of threats from his home community (cf. 11.21-23), Jeremiah appears to be crumbling. Yet Yahweh warns Jeremiah that things will get much worse.

Jeremiah will again attempt to make an intercession for Judah in 14.7, and this intercession will also go unheeded by Yahweh. Before turning to those verses, however, it will be important to look at the compiled words that precede this intercession since they help to demonstrate how Jeremiah is becoming embroiled increasingly in Yahweh's warfare against Judah.

The words of Yahweh following his threatening rebuke of Jeremiah at the attempted intercession in 12.7 underscore the drastic action that Yahweh has taken. He says,

> I have forsaken my house;
>   I have abandoned my heritage.
> I have given the beloved of my נֶפֶשׁ
>   into the palm of the hand of her enemy.

The expression 'I have given into the hand' is typical of the conventional language of warfare. Whereas in Joshua the phrase 'I have given [the enemy] into your hand' (see, e.g., Josh. 8.1-2; 10.8) is used to reassure Israel, in Jeremiah this conventional language suggests Yahweh has exceeded even abandonment; he has already placed Judah in the hand of her enemy. The use of כַּף ('palm, flat, or hollow of the hand'), rather than the more usual יָד, suggests that the enemy has Judah strongly in its grasp (see 12.14-17).

Chapter 13 uses imagery depicting the house of Israel and the house of Judah as being as useless as a ruined loincloth because they would not listen to Yahweh's word. The imagery of the loincloth is followed by a reference to a wine-jar filled with wine, which foreshadows the coming cup of the wine of wrath in Jeremiah 25:

> And you will say to them, 'Thus Yahweh said, "Behold I am about to fill with drunkenness all the inhabitants of this land and the kings who sit on the throne of David, and the priests and the prophets and all the inhabitants of Jerusalem"'. (13.13)

---

36. 'Loud cry' for Hebrew מָלֵא.

In 13.19, Judah is described as already having been taken into exile, and in 13.20 there is another reference to those who will come from the north wielding disaster on Jerusalem: 'Lift up your eyes and see, the ones who are coming from the north'.

Chapter 14 contains words of Jeremiah describing a drought as a sign that Yahweh has turned against the people. What we see in this compilation of words is the development of impending disaster and Jeremiah's desperate attempts to aid the people in their plight.

Following the words concerning the drought, Jeremiah makes another intercession for his people:

> Though our iniquities answer against us,
>> act, O Yahweh for your name's sake
> when our apostasies are many;
>> we have sinned against you.
> O hope of Israel;
>> its savior in a time of distress,
> why are you like an alien in the land,
>> and like a traveler turning aside for the night?
> Why are you like a man astonished,
>> like a warrior unable to save?
> But you are in our midst, O Yahweh,
>> we called your name over us,
>> do not forsake us! (14.7-9)

As in the earlier attempted intercessions, Yahweh refuses to accept this intercession and instructs Jeremiah for a second time: 'Do not intercede in behalf of this people for [their] welfare' (14.11).

I want to continue to follow the collection of words in this section because of the picture it enables the reader to create. In 14.13-16, Jeremiah brings to Yahweh's attention that the prophets are saying just the opposite of what he has been saying:

> And I (Jeremiah) said, 'Ah, Yahweh, now the prophets are saying to them, "You will not see a sword, and you will not have a famine because I will give to you a true peace in this place"'. (14.13)

Yahweh responds to Jeremiah:

> The prophets are prophesying a lie in my name. I did not send them, and I did not command them, and I did not speak to them. A false vision, and worthless divination, and the deceitfulness of their own mind they are prophesying to you. Therefore, thus said Yahweh concerning the prophets who are prophesying in my name. 'I did not send them but they say, "Sword and

famine will not be in this land". By sword and famine those prophets will
die. And the people to whom they are prophesying, they will be thrown out
on the streets of Jerusalem because of the presence of the sword and the
famine. And there will be no one to bury them, their wives, their sons and
their daughters, and I will pour out their calamity on them.' (14.14-16)

Following these words Yahweh instructs Jeremiah to say that both the
priest and the prophet travel in the land without knowledge (14.17-18).
This comment by Yahweh about uninformed priests and prophets prompts
another intercession from Jeremiah associating the absence of knowledgeable prophets and priests with Yahweh's complete rejection of his people:

> Have you completely rejected Judah,
>   does your נֶפֶשׁ abhor Zion?
> Why have you struck us,
>   and we have no respite?
> [We] hope for peace,
>   but there is no good thing;
>   for a time of respite but only calamity.
> We know our transgressions, O Yahweh,
>   the iniquity of our fathers,
>   because we have sinned against you.
> Do not condemn us for the sake of your name;
>   do not treat your glorious throne as foolish;
>   remember and do not break your covenant with us.
> Can the idols of the nations cause it to rain?
>   Can the heavens give rain?
> Is it not you, O Yahweh, our God?
>   We hope in you, because you have done all these things. (14.19-22)

Again, Yahweh responds negatively to the intercession saying that even if
Moses and Samuel were in front of him, he would not turn toward his
people (15.1). The reference to the covenant brings a response from Yahweh: 'Send them from my sight (פְּנֵי)' (Jer. 15.1), recalling 2 Kgs 23.27 at
the time when Josiah had made a covenant with Yahweh. He also says,
'and I will make them an object of trembling for all the kingdoms of the
land because of Manasseh, the son of Hezekiah, the king of Judah because
of what he did in Jerusalem' (Jer. 15.4), recalling 2 Kgs 23.26.[37]

At this point Jeremiah's words begin a transition from intercession to
lament. He laments the day of his birth (15.10). He will curse the day of

---

37. See also the similar statement made at the time of Jehoiakim in 2 Kgs 24.2.
There the four nations, the Chaldeans, the Arameans, the Moabites and the Ammonites
relate to the four destroyers mentioned in Jer. 15.3.

his birth later (20.13-18) when he begins to speak of his people as the enemy (20.7-13). The character of Jeremiah that is emerging in this compilation of words is that of a warrior-prophet who must speak Yahweh's words that are incontrovertibly against the people. He offers a lament to Yahweh, but this time the lament is for his own plight. In the subsequent exchange with Yahweh, Jeremiah asks that his enemies be punished. He is alone (15.17). Notice also that in the exchange Jeremiah's appointment as a prophet to the nations (1.4-19) is reaffirmed. There is no more intercession after this exchange between Jeremiah and Yahweh. The people to whom he speaks have become the enemy. Jeremiah says:

> You know,[38]
> Yahweh, remember me and visit me;
>   avenge my persecutors for me.
> In your forbearance do not take me away;
>   know that because of you I suffer scorn.[39]
> Your words were found, and I ate them.
>   Your words became to me a joy, and the delight of my mind;
>   because I am called by your name, O Yahweh, God of hosts.
> I did not sit in the company of merrymakers and I did not rejoice,
>   because of the presence of your hand I sat alone
>   because you filled me with indignation.
> Why is my pain everlasting,
>   My wound incurable, refusing to be healed?
> Alas, you are like a deceptive stream,
>   Waters not trusted. (15.15-18)

Yahweh's answer recalls the negative reassurance of 1.17. It also serves as the reappointment of Jeremiah as a prophet to the nations. The impression is that in earlier turning to intercession for his people, Jeremiah had been turning away from Yahweh:

> Therefore thus Yahweh said,
> 'If you return, then I will return to you.
>   You will stand before me.
> And if you express precious instead of worthless things,
>   then you will be like my mouth.

38. There is no object of the verb here. Should we read this as a simple confession? In a sense, Jeremiah gives up his intercession and says that Yahweh knows what he is doing. Yahweh has overwhelmed him with the power with which he is about to overwhelm Judah and the nations.

39. חרפה can have the meaning of 'haunt of an enemy' (see 1 Sam. 17.26; 25.3).

They should turn to you;
　　you should not turn to them.
And I will make you to this people
　　for a fortified wall of bronze.
They will fight against you,
　　but they will not prevail over you;
because I am with you
　　to rescue you and to deliver you,
　　a saying of Yahweh.
I will rescue you from the hand of the wicked,
　　and I will ransom you from the palm of those who strike terror.' (15.19-21)

The verses that follow this reappointment of Jeremiah to his role of warrior-prophet emphasize his being alone. He is told that should not marry and have children. There will be no future because of the coming devastation (16.1-4). But also he is ordered not to go into the house of mourning, or to take up the cup of consolation (כוס תנחומים, 16.5-8). Jeremiah's role is to take up 'the cup of the wine of wrath' (כוס היין החמה, 25.15). This coming role of Jeremiah is anticipated in Yahweh's words in 16.9: 'I am about to cause to cease from this place before your eyes, the voice of mirth and the voice of gladness, the voice of the bridegroom and the voice of the bride' (16.9). These words repeat, but not verbatim, the words that Yahweh speaks in 25.10 when he declares war on all the nations of the land.

After the reappointment of Jeremiah as warrior-prophet, familiar themes emerge. Jeremiah is to tell the people 'all these words' (16.10). He is to tell them that they have not kept the *torah* (16.11), that they are worse than their ancestors (16.12), that they will be hurled out of the land because they served other gods (16.13), and that only in due course will the people be rescued from the north, not from the land of Egypt as in the days of old (16.14-18).

Jeremiah now speaks. He is no longer making intercession. Rather, he is taking comfort in Yahweh. Jeremiah's words are beginning to sound like Yahweh's words about the coming calamity for the people:

O Yahweh, my strength and my stronghold,
　　my refuge in the day of trouble,
to you nations will come
　　from the ends of the earth and will say,
'Surely, our fathers possessed lies,
　　worthless things with no profit in them.
Is a man able to make for himself gods?
　　They are not gods! (16.19-20)

Yahweh responds with a clear determination to bring an end to Judah. It is as if Jeremiah's words have given vigor to Yahweh: 'Therefore, I am about to teach them; in this time I will teach them by my hand (יָדִי) and by my valor (גְבוּרָתִי) and they will know that my name is Yahweh' (16.21). The use of יָד and גְבוּרָה in this passage comes from the vocabulary of war.

The image that arises in the collage of words in the interchange of Jeremiah and Yahweh in 15.13-21 and in 16.19-21 is that Jeremiah had been nearly broken (חָתַת) and that Yahweh had nearly dismayed Jeremiah before the people. The threat of 1.17 had nearly come about. However, Jeremiah and Yahweh are now speaking with new energy as the war approaches.[40]

In 17.12-13, Jeremiah is again speaking and his voice now sides with Yahweh, not with the people. He is speaking Yahweh's words:

> O glorious throne, exalted from the beginning,
>> the place of our sanctuary,
> O Yahweh, the hope of Israel,
>> all who forsake you will be ashamed.
> The ones who turn away will be written in the land,
>> because they have forsaken the fountain of living waters, Yahweh.

But Jeremiah again requests protection from Yahweh. He requests that Yahweh 'heal him' and 'save him' (17.14). The people seem to be continuing to mock him saying, 'Where is the word of Yahweh? Let it come' (17.15). Jeremiah has not run away from the task although he desires the coming day of destruction (17.16). Yahweh knows what has come from his lips (17.16). He then makes a request, which is interesting because its vocabulary echoes 1.17. This time, however, Yahweh's threatening assurance to Jeremiah that he not be dismayed (shattered), lest Yahweh dismay (shatter) him is directed to the enemy. Jeremiah says, 'let them be dismayed (יֵחַתּוּ), but do not let me be dismayed (אֵחַתָּה)' (17.18a). His words are sounding more and more like the warlike language of Yahweh as he goes on to say, 'Bring upon them the day of calamity, destroy them with double destruction' (17.18b).

Yahweh's reassurance is not with words but with action. Yahweh sends Jeremiah to 'the People's Gate, by which the kings of Judah enter and by

---

40. The renewed certainty of the inevitability of warfare that these passages are building up is supported by the image of the 'iron pen with a diamond point', which stands in marked contrast to the 'lying pen' of 8.8. The image that is beginning to emerge in the collage concerns writing. This will become a major theme beginning with ch. 25.

which they go out, and in all the gates of Jerusalem' (17.19). By following Yahweh's orders and speaking his words, Yahweh will become a refuge for Jeremiah (17.17). In 18.1-17 Yahweh sends Jeremiah to the potter's house to hear more of his words. Again visual imagery evokes words about how Yahweh can change his mind about a nation. That Jeremiah is now in the thick of battle, fighting with words, is evident from 18.18, where an anonymous voice indicates that plots are being made on Jeremiah's life by people who refuse to listen to his words. Jeremiah now speaks to Yahweh, and his words suggest that his former intercession has been changed to threats about the destruction of those who plotted against him:

> Give heed to me, O Yahweh,
>   and listen to the voice of my adversary.
> Can evil be repaid for good?
>   Because they dug a pit for my life.
> Remember how I stood in your presence
>   to speak good concerning them
>   to make your wrath turn away from them.
> Therefore, give their sons over to famine
>   And hurl them to the power of the sword.
> Let their wives become childless and widowed
>   their men be slaughtered in death,
>   their young men struck down by the sword in battle.
> Let a cry be heard from their houses
>   when you bring a marauding band upon them suddenly.
> Because they dug a pit to catch me
>   and laid snares for my feet.
> And you, O Yahweh, you know
>   all their plots against me to kill me.
> Do not forgive their iniquity;
>   do not blot out their sin from your sight.
> May they be tripped up before you.
>   Do [these things] to them in the time of your anger. (18.19-23)

After Jeremiah's initial warlike outburst (17.18), Yahweh told him to go to the gate by which the kings enter to speak his words (17.19) and then to go to the potter's house where he will show him additional words to speak. Yahweh tells him to take a potter's earthenware jug and to go to the potsherd gate and proclaim his words. But now he is to speak those words to the kings of Judah as well as to the inhabitants of Judah. He is to say, 'Thus said Yahweh of hosts, the God of Israel: "I am about to bring a calamity upon this place that the ears of anyone who hears it will tingle"' (19.3). The destruction coming to Judah because of what Manasseh did

(2 Kgs 23.27; 24.3; Jer. 15.4) is getting closer and closer—as indicated when Yahweh echoes what he said at the time of Manasseh: 'Because King Manasseh of Judah has committed these abominations…I am about to bring upon Judah and Jerusalem such calamity that the ears of everyone who hears it will tingle' (2 Kgs 21.10-11).

Jeremiah now enters the temple and speaks in the court (חצר) of the house of Yahweh.[41]

As the engagement intensifies, Jeremiah receives the first blows of battle when Pashhur, the priest, the principal overseer in the house of Yahweh, strikes Jeremiah after he hears him speak these words. He then puts Jeremiah in the stocks (20.1-2). Here things begin to reach a denouement, and when Jeremiah is freed from the stocks in the morning the words of Yahweh he speaks mention the king of Babylon for the first time in the book of Jeremiah:

> …thus says Yahweh, 'I am about to make you a terror to yourself and to all your friends. They will fall by the sword of their enemies and you will see with your eyes. And all Judah I will give into the hand of the king of Babylon. He will take them into exile to Babylon and he will strike them with the sword. And I will give all the treasure of this city; all its products; all its precious things and the treasures of the kings of Judah into the hand of their enemies. And they will plunder them, capture them and bring them to Babylon. And you, Pashhur and all who dwell in your house will go into captivity and they will enter Babylon. And they will die there. And you will be buried there and all your friends to whom you prophesied lies.' (20.4-6)

These are fighting words against Pashhur, who prophesied lies. Jeremiah again laments his plight. Yahweh has enticed him, overpowered him and prevailed. As a result he has become a laughingstock because all he can call out is violence and destruction. Even though Yahweh's word has become a reproach and a source of derision, he cannot hold it in. It has become a burning fire.[42] All this has made him weary. He hears whispering, and all his friends are watching, waiting for him to stumble (20.7-10). The interesting thing about this complaining is that Jeremiah answers it himself with confidence:

> But Yahweh is with me, like a terrifying warrior;
>> therefore, the ones who persecute me will stumble;
>> they will not prevail.

---

41. A fuller description is given in Jer. 26.
42. The words that were about to become a burning fire in 5.14 have now ignited.

They will be greatly ashamed,
　　but they will not gain insight;
　　an eternal ignominy will not be forgotten.
But Yahweh of hosts tests the righteous
　　he sees the heart and mind.
Let me see your retribution on them,
　　because to you I have made known my cause.
Sing to Yahweh,
　　praise Yahweh,
for he has rescued the life of the needy,
　　from the hand of the ones who do evil. (20.11-13)

This section of the book comes to a close, however, with Jeremiah cursing the day of his birth (20.14-18). His total resignation to Yahweh's over-powering might ends on the wish that he had never been born—his wish earlier when he was reappointed as a warrior-prophet (15.10-13).

By ch. 20, Jeremiah has moved into the court of the temple (19.14) and he is now talking with kings. Jeremiah's interaction with kings character-izes most of the words collected in Jeremiah 21–24. However, before looking at those chapters I want to consider the movement that has occurred in the book of Jeremiah up to this point. The collage of Jere-miah's words presents a picture of movement and development, but this is not through developed compositional brushstrokes. There is movement in the collection that a reader can see if attention is paid to order and arrange-ment in reading. Jeremiah has moved from a background voice (chs. 2–11) to active involvement (chs. 12–23), and from siding with his people (chs. 12–14) to siding with Yahweh (chs. 15–20), speaking his words of coming devastation on Judah. Movement has also occurred in relation to the temple. In 7.2 Jeremiah is standing at 'the gate (שַׁעַר) of the house of Yahweh', addressing 'the people of Judah'. By 19.14 he has moved inside to the court (חָצֵר) of the house of Yahweh and is addressing not only all the people but also the kings of Judah (19.3). Unlike Samuel at Shiloh (1 Sam. 3) or Isaiah in Jerusalem (Isa. 6), Jeremiah (and Amos) are not in the temple having vision (חָזוֹן) but are coming from the outside to the temple with words. Those words are embodied in visual imagery around them (in almond branches, boiling pots, loin cloths, potters at work, earthenware jugs, lions roaring, birds in snares, trumpets in the city, locusts consuming the latter growth, fire, plumb lines, baskets of summer fruit, etc.). In fact, one could say that the kind of vision characteristic of Samuel and Isaiah was non-existent in the days of Jeremiah. The only vision (חָזוֹן)

was a lying vision—not a vision sent by Yahweh (14.14).[43] What is radical about the words of Jeremiah (and Amos) is that he comes from outside the temple and challenges authority.

In chs. 21–24, Jeremiah, using words coming from outside the temple, addresses all the kings who rule over Judah at its end (Shallum, Jehoiakim, Jehoiachin and Zedekiah). In the middle of these chapters concerning the last kings of Judah is a section on the prophets (ch. 23) whose visions (חָזוֹן) come from their own mind and whose words should not be heeded (23.16). Jeremiah's words to the kings of Judah surround this chapter on the lying vision of the prophets.

The chapters concerning the last kings of Judah in Jeremiah begin in ch. 21 with a word that came at the time of Zedekiah who had sent an envoy to Jeremiah to inquire (דרשׁ) of Yahweh concerning Nebuchadnezzar who was making war on them. Zedekiah thinks that perhaps Yahweh will make him withdraw. In response, Jeremiah without hesitation and without intercession simply speaks Yahweh's word bluntly and boldly. Jeremiah, the warrior-prophet, is now speaking Yahweh's words, and this chapter clearly shows Jeremiah in the role he is to perform in speaking Yahweh's words about the end. Jeremiah's words in 21.3-8 about the end of Judah are almost as bleak and stark as Amos' vision about the end (Amos 8.1-3). Notice in these words that Jeremiah is communicating what Yahweh said (אָמַר).[44] Yahweh's words are already past tense. He did not need to inquire:

> Thus Jeremiah said to them, 'Thus Yahweh, the God of Israel, has said, "Behold I am about to turn back all the weapons of war which are in your hands and with which you are fighting the king of Babylon and the Chaldeans who are besieging you from outside the wall. And I will gather them in the middle of this city. And I myself will fight in your presence with an outstretched hand and a mighty arm with anger, with furious rage, and great wrath. And I will strike down the ones who live in this city, human and animal. They will die with a great pestilence (דֶּבֶר)."' After these things, a saying of Yahweh, 'I will give Zedekiah, king of Judah, and his servants and the people who survive in this city from the pestilence (דֶּבֶר), from the sword, and from the famine into the hand of Nebuchadrezzar, the king of

43. As we will see, the situation in the חָזוֹן of Isaiah will be different. He comes from the temple where he sees Yahweh and goes out from the temple to kings Ahaz and Hezekiah.

44. As we will see, the entire point about Jeremiah writing down Yahweh's words, which is the main theme of the last part of the book, is that he is recording what Yahweh said.

Babylon and into the hand of their enemy and into the hand of the ones who
seek their life. He will strike them down before the sword. He will not pity
them. He will not spare them. He will not have compassion.' (21.3-7)

One cannot read this passage without being struck by the savagery and
unbounded fury in these words. In addition to human beings, even the
animals are to be struck down. Heinous warfare is being described here. A
play on words, a pun, makes clear that all this is Yahweh's intention. The
people are to die with דֶּבֶר, a pestilence. But since the entire book of Jeremiah is about 'the words of Yahweh', one cannot help but hear also דָּבָר,
word. The 'word' of Yahweh is the 'pestilence' about to overtake the city.

The chapter ends with Jeremiah speaking more words that Yahweh had
said to him. The people are given the choice of remaining in the city and
suffering the 'pestilence' or going into exile (20.8-10). The king[45] is also
given 'half a chance' to execute justice, but it is unlikely because Yahweh
is against him and the image of a forest fire is used to imagine his destruction (20.13-14).

Jeremiah is instructed to go down to the king's house (22.1). Jeremiah,
who had been afraid of his family (11.18-20), is now taking on kings. The
king's identity is unclear. Again the king hears that he is to execute justice
(22.1-6), but this will not happen because 'they have abandoned the covenant of Yahweh their God and they have bowed down to other gods and
served them' (22.9). Now not just the people but kings, unlike Josiah, have
broken the covenant with Yahweh.

The rejection of the covenant by the kings that followed Josiah seems to
be suggested by the words addressed to Shallum, the son of Josiah, who
was taken into exile and will not return (22.11-18). Shallum is contrasted
to his father:

Did not your father eat and drink
    and do justice and righteousness?
    Then it went well for him.
He judged the cause of the poor and needy
    and it went well.
Is that not to know me? A saying of Yahweh.
    But your eyes and your mind [are not on that].
But on your precious possessions,
    on shedding innocent blood
    and on practicing oppression and violence. (22.15b-17)[46]

45. It is not clear which king is being referred to here.
46. As I read these words and think of the animals and the humans in Jerusalem at
the time of Zedekiah, I want Yahweh to listen to his own words.

Jeremiah is now in full flight talking to and about the last kings of Judah. In 22.18-23 he says that one should not lament for Jehoiakim, the son of Josiah, when he is buried with a donkey and thrown out beyond the gates of Jerusalem. Jehoiachin (here called King Coniah) is to be hurled into the land of the Chaldeans and will not return. None of his children shall sit on the throne of David (22.24-30).

This section on the exile of Coniah is followed, as is often the case in Jeremiah, with a selection of words concerning the future beyond the exile (23.1-8). Yahweh will raise up shepherds, who unlike these kings have not scattered the sheep. There will be a righteous branch of David to execute justice. Yahweh, who had brought his people in earlier times from Egypt, will in the future bring his people from the north, from Babylon where he had driven them.

That Israel's future is in returning from Babylon rather than remaining in Jerusalem is the theme of Jeremiah 24. Again, words are associated with visual imagery. Yahweh shows Jeremiah two baskets of figs (good figs and bad figs). This imagery expresses Yahweh's word that the good figs are like those who go into exile in Babylon. The future will be in Babylon, and here is the positive element in Jeremiah's appointment as a warrior-prophet (1.10). In Babylon there will be building and planting, and it is from there that they will return:

> I will set my eyes upon them for good, and I will bring them back to this land. I will build them up, and not tear them down; I will plant them and not pluck them up. I will give them a heart to know that I am Yahweh; that they shall be my people and I will be their God, for they shall return to me with their whole heart. (24.7)

Zedekiah and the people who remain in the land will endure the pestilence/word of Yahweh graphically described in the passage quoted above (21.3-7).

In the midst of these words of Jeremiah, addressed to the kings from the outside world of almond branches, boiling pots and baskets of figs is a section of text labeled 'for the prophets' (לאבאים, 23.9)—for those who get their words elsewhere. The surrounding material (21.1–23.8 and ch. 24) concerns the kings.

Jeremiah feels crushed; his bones shake; and he is staggering like one who has had too much wine because of Yahweh's holy words (23.9-11). This is in contrast to the prophets of Samaria who prophesied by Baal, and even more, the prophets of Jerusalem who have committed adultery. They have run after other lovers and do not speak Yahweh's words. Therefore one should not listen to their words:

> Thus Yahweh of hosts said, 'Do not listen (תשמעו) to the words of the prophets who prophesy to you; they are filling you with emptiness. A vision (חזון) of their own mind they speak, not from the mouth of Yahweh. They are saying continually to the ones who despise me, 'Yahweh spoke. You will have peace.' And to the ones who follow their own hearts they say, 'Calamity will not come upon you'. (23.16-18)

The prophets have not stood in Yahweh's council (סוד), yet they ran (23.21). Yahweh has heard what they are saying (23.25). They are stealing Yahweh's words. They do not have a burden (משא) of Yahweh; instead they have become a burden (משא).

All the language used here—vision (חזון), burden (משא) and running (רוץ) with a vision so that it can be heard (שמע)—pick up the vocabulary of vision (חזון) that I have outlined above in Chapter 4 and have associated with prophets such as Isaiah, Nahum, Obadiah and Habakkuk. I have also maintained that a vision is written down so that a reader may run with it in order for it to be heard (see Hab. 2.2-3). The דבר ('thing'/'word') of Yahweh that is a vision (חזון) is different from the דבר of Yahweh that is 'the words of' (דברי) prophets such as Amos and Jeremiah. How should this difference be understood? Are Isaiah, Habakkuk and the other prophets of 'vision' (חזון) in the prophetic canon to be understood as lying prophets? My answer to that question is 'No', and my reasons will become clearer when I speak of the חזון of Isaiah and other prophets. The difference between Isaiah and Jeremiah is the depiction of the time and the situation. In the days of Samuel at Shiloh and in the days of Isaiah in Jerusalem, Yahweh was in the temple. Prophets could lie down in the temple and have 'vision' (חזון). This is not possible for Jeremiah, nor is it possible for Ezekiel. Yahweh is no longer present in the temple. He has moved out. Prophets in situations like those of Jeremiah and Amos have access to Yahweh's word outside the temple in visual imagery of almond branches, baskets of figs and baskets of summer fruit. Prophets who receive their words this way, unlike the prophets of 'vision' (חזון), write them down and bring them to the temple so that they can be read out. Their words are for the present time. Jeremiah's writing of his words will be the recurring theme in the last part of the book (Jer. 25–51). Vision (חזון) in Jeremiah's time can only be false because Yahweh is not present in the temple to grant it. None of these false prophets could have stood in his council. It was not possible, as the compiled material indicates, to have a

הוון in the days of Jeremiah when Yahweh is abandoning his people by abandoning the temple.

I want to close this discussion of Jeremiah 12–24 by summarizing how I have configured these words of Jeremiah when I read it as a whole, paying attention to order and arrangement and to literary development. Jeremiah is drawn further and further into the battle that Yahweh has announced against the land and all the nations including Judah and all the inhabitants of Jerusalem. In chs. 2–11, Jeremiah, while speaking to the people of Israel, was primarily addressing the people of Judah concerning the impending disaster coming from the north. Jeremiah had not yet at this stage been drawn into the battle, so we hear only the words he spoke. By the end of ch. 11, however, Jeremiah begins to reveal his own involvement when his words are getting him into trouble with the people from his hometown of Anathoth.

Yahweh orders Jeremiah not to intercede for the people (11.14). Ironically Jeremiah intercedes for the people and the land in 12.1-4 and continues to intercede (14.7-9). But Yahweh tells him again, 'Do not intercede for the welfare of this people' (14.11). The interaction depicted here recalls the negative assurance Yahweh gave to the warrior-prophet Jeremiah not to be dismayed lest Yahweh would dismay him because the picture is of Jeremiah being 'dismayed'—buckling under the pressure. He makes one last futile attempt at intercession (14.19-22), but Yahweh will not listen. At this point Jeremiah begins a transformation, and the interchange between Jeremiah and Yahweh (15.15-21) is a kind of reappointment to his role of speaking Yahweh's words as a warrior-prophet. From that point on Jeremiah's words begin to echo the bellicose character of the words of Yahweh directed at the people of Judah, and are prefaced and closed by lament (15.10-12; 20.14-18) as Jeremiah wishes that he had not been born, cursing the day of his birth.

In chs. 2–11, Jeremiah was standing outside at the gate of the temple (7.2). Toward the end of chs. 12–24, Jeremiah is standing inside in the court of the temple and he is speaking to kings (19.14). Also the anonymous foe from the north is identified for the first time as the king of Babylon (20.4). The section ends with words of Jeremiah concerning the kings that succeeded Josiah, the last kings of Israel (chs. 21–24). Significantly, these chapters begin with Zedekiah coming to Jeremiah asking him to intercede (21.2). Having abjured intercession, Jeremiah refuses and simply reports what Yahweh had said. At the end, Jeremiah is speaking the words of Yahweh as his warrior-prophet to the last kings of Judah.

In the middle of these words to the last kings of Judah is a section con-cerning the prophets (23.9-40). As I have indicated, these chapters imply that at the time of Jeremiah, when Yahweh is not present in the temple, prophets cannot have vision. In days like those of Jeremiah the prophet can only receive 'the words of Yahweh' that come to expression in visual imagery around him such as almond branches and baskets of figs. In the days of Jeremiah words are written down and are taken to the temple. These are not like the days of חזון when words were taken from the temple by a reader who would run with them. Jeremiah's time is depicted as a time when prophecy is generated outside the temple.

6. *From the Cup of the Wine of Wrath to the End of the Words of Jeremiah (Jeremiah 25.1–51.64)*

In the first half of the 'book' of Jeremiah, the activity of writing appears only briefly and in the background. When the written word is referred to, the references are to deception. For example, Jer. 8.8 suggests that the *torah* of Yahweh itself may have been made into a lie (שקר) by the false pen (עט שקר) of the scribes (סופרים). Writing appears in such a way as to carry authority, but writing has become deceptive.

It is not only *torah* that appears as deceptive writing, however. Prophetic חזון is also described as false (שקר). In 14.13-14, Jeremiah expresses his concern to Yahweh that the prophets are contradicting him. In opposition to the words of Jeremiah about desolation and destruction, the prophets are informing the people that the famine or the sword will not come. Yah-weh's response is that 'the prophets are prophesying (נבאים) a lie (שקר) in his name', a 'lying vision' (חזון שקר). In 20.6, Pashhur, the person who struck Jeremiah in the temple, is also accused with similar words 'you prophesied (נבאת) a lie (שקר) to them'. In 23.16, the prophets are accused of prophesying (נבאים) a vision (חזון) that comes from their own mind and not from the mouth of Yahweh. They are also 'prophesying a lie' (23.25, 26, 32).

To prophesy (נבא) a vision (חזון) involves writing, so that to prophesy a lying vision is to be engaged with deceptive writing. I argued above that a חזון is something that is written down (see Chapter 4).

In my discussion of the second part of Jeremiah (chs. 25–51), I will argue that 'to prophesy' (נבא) is to communicate through writing. In this section of Jeremiah both 'prophesying' and 'written words' come into prominence. Jeremiah's writing stands in contrast to that of the deceptive writing of the false prophets. In the first half of Jeremiah we heard about the words Jeremiah spoke to Israel and to the people of Judah and its kings. In the second part of the 'book' the activity of prophesying is depicted and that activity concerns what is written, ספרים.

Deceptive writing is an emerging theme in chs. 2–24, and it is interesting that writing becomes a central theme in the last part of the book (chs. 25–51). Prophesying (נבא) involves the use of what is written, a ספר. Written words recorded in a ספר become an important instrument for Jeremiah as a prophet of Yahweh's words. The written words of Jeremiah, like the written words of Moses recorded in ספרים, can be heard even when the prophet is not present.

The written words in 'the ספר of the *torah*/covenant' of the prophet Moses, discovered in the temple by Josiah (2 Kgs 22–23) were written words (22.11, 13, 15, 18; 23.3; 24). They became audible at a much latter time. The book was read to Josiah (22.10), and the king 'heard the words of the book'. When prophetic words are written in books, they can be heard even when the prophet is not there. Even after a book has been lost and found, it can be read and the words become audible at a latter time.

Because Jeremiah's words are recorded in writing they become audible words when they are read even in the absence of the prophet. It is possible that even the ספרים containing the written words of Jeremiah will be lost and discovered just as Moses' ספר was discovered after having been lost. According to my calculations, Jeremiah writes at least nine ספרים in the concluding chapters (chs. 25–51). The existence of these ספרים are not only mentioned in the text but are also depicted as functioning documents in the literary world of the 'book'. They will make brief appearances to the reader and come and go as do literary characters such as kings, priests, prophets, and so on. However, after they appear they just as quickly disappear. As a reader I glimpse Jeremiah's ספרים in the same way I sight the ספר of the *torah*/covenant of Moses in the days of Josiah at the end of Kings. Like the ספר of Moses, Jeremiah's ספרים disappear from the narrative and some of Jeremiah's ספרים are gone forever. The reader, after reading all these words in Jeremiah as a continuation of Kings asks, 'Where are the ספרים of Moses and Jeremiah?'

There is a recurring feature in the way these ספרים appear in Jeremiah 25–51. The text will inform the reader about a ספר containing Jeremiah's words. It will then appear as an operative document moving about in the world of Jeremiah. But then it will disappear. It is present in the text, but then it is gone and we wonder where it is. We imagine we know it, but we have only heard about it. We think we know what it is about, but there have been only allusions to its contents.

a. *The ספר against the Nations (Jeremiah 25.13)*

The first mention of a ספר of Jeremiah is in the middle of Jeremiah 25—a chapter discussed in detail above. This is the chapter in which Jeremiah's role as a cupbearer of wrath to the nations is detailed. Yahweh says:

> I will bring upon *that land* all my *words* which I have spoken against it—everything *written in this book* (ספר) which Jeremiah prophesied (נבא) against all the nations. (25.13)

I contend that this verse connotes the activity of prophesying. When Jeremiah prophesies (נבא), he prophesies written words. The words Yahweh puts in Jeremiah's mouth (1.9) are written down in ספרים and used by Jeremiah 'to prophesy' (נבא). While this chapter does not tell us how Jeremiah's words were written down, we are given information about the process of writing down Yahweh's words later, where Jeremiah uses a scribe (ספר), Baruch. In that situation the words that Yahweh put in Jeremiah's mouth will now come 'from the mouth' (מפי) of Jeremiah (cf. Jer. 36.2-4) to the scribe who transforms them into writing.

However, there are clear indications in 25.13, and in the following chapters (26–28), that Jeremiah 'prophesies' (נבא) against the nations by using 'this ספר' in which words Yahweh had spoken to him are written down. Indeed, the phrase 'everything written in this ספר' in 25.13 is rather curious. The book sounds so definite. It is here, and it isn't. Where is 'this ספר'? The answer is that it is in the text. It has become a textual presence in the same way that Jeremiah is present in the text as a character, and it will appear along with him in the very next chapter (Jer. 26). The words of the ספר are not quoted, but there are allusions to its contents.

Jeremiah 26 concerns an incident that occurred early in the reign of Jehoiakim. Yahweh orders Jeremiah to go and to stand in the court (חצר) of the house of Yahweh. This setting appears to be the same as the one indicated earlier in 19.14 when Jeremiah had an altercation with Pashhur who struck him on the cheek (20.2). In the earlier passage it is stated that Pashhur prophesied falsely (שקר, 20.6). Was this altercation with Pashhur a clash of written words?

In Jeremiah 26, Jeremiah is ordered to speak all the words that Yahweh commands him to the cities of Judah. It may be that they will turn from their evil ways and walk in the *torah* of Yahweh and that they will heed the words of the prophets. If not, then Yahweh says that he will make this house like Shiloh. This allusion to Shiloh recalls words similar to those Jeremiah uttered at the time of Josiah (7.14).[47] Jeremiah is also commanded to say that Yahweh will make Judah a 'curse' (קללה) for the nations of the earth (26.6). To make Judah a 'curse' echoes the previous chapter in which Yahweh says that he will make Judah and Jerusalem drink from the cup 'to make them a desolation and a waste, an object of hissing and a curse' (קללה, 25.18).

We then hear that 'the priests and the prophets and all the people *heard* Jeremiah speaking these words *in the house of Yahweh*' (26.7). When Jeremiah finished speaking all that Yahweh had commanded him to speak to the priests and the prophets and all the people, they become very angry and they say:

> 'You will surely die! Why did you *prophesy* (נבית) in the name of Yahweh, "This house shall be like Shiloh and this city shall be desolate without inhabitant"?' And all the people gathered around Jeremiah in *the house of Yahweh*. (26.8-9)

What the people, the priests and the prophets report Jeremiah to have said here matches the words of Yahweh in the ch. 25 associated the ספר against the nations. Judah and Jerusalem will be a desolation (חרבה) (25.18; cf. 25.11) and without inhabitant (25.10).

What is significant, however, is that the priests, prophets and all the people identify what Jeremiah is doing as prophesying (נבא). I contend that 'prophesying' is not extemporaneous oration; the words he is speaking/prophesying are written words from a ספר. Notice that the priests, the prophets and the people *hear the words* Jeremiah is *prophesying* in *the house of Yahweh*. The next verse (26.10) is crucial. A new audience, 'the officials (שר) of Judah' appear. Interestingly, they also *have heard the words* Jeremiah was *prophesying*, but they were not in the house of Yahweh. They came up to *the house of Yahweh* from *the house of the king*.

> When the officials (שר) of Judah *heard these words*, they came up from the *house of the king* to the house of Yahweh and they sat down at the entry of the New Gate of the house of Yahweh.[48]

If the officials of Judah were in *the house of the king* and came up to take a seat at the entrance of the New Gate of the *house of Yahweh*, then how

---

47. At this earlier time Jeremiah was not standing inside the temple in the court but at the gate.

48. Notice also that they do not go to the court where the priests, the prophets and all the people heard Jeremiah's words. They sit at the New Gate.

did they hear *these words*? Is it not possible that Jeremiah appeared in the *house of Yahweh* with the written words of the ספר against the nations. The officials of Judah have heard the words of Jeremiah not in the *house of Yahweh* but in *the house of the king* because a similar thing happened as took place in the time of Josiah. When the ספר of the *torah*/covenant was found in the days of Josiah, the ספר was taken from *the house of Yahweh* to *the house of the king* and was read to him so that he *heard the words* (22.10-11). This procedure of taking written words from the house of Yahweh to the house of the king is confirmed by a later incident in the 'book' of Jeremiah. In Jeremiah 36, Jeremiah writes another ספר with the help of the scribe, Baruch. After Baruch read it in *the house of Yahweh*, it was taken to *the house of the king* (Jehoiakim) and was read to the king so that he *heard the words* (36.23). In all of these situations written words read in the *house of Yahweh* are taken to *the house of the king* where they are heard when they are read. The major difference between the situation here and the situation at the time of Josiah or the later situation with Jehoiakim, is that the king is not personally involved. Rather, 'officials' of Judah come up from the house of the king to sit in judgment in order to mitigate the situation.

After the 'officials of Judah' take their seat at the New Gate, the priests and the prophets ask that Jeremiah be sentenced to death:

> Then the priests and the prophets said to the officials and all the people, 'A sentence of death for this man because he *prophesied* (נבא) against this city as *you heard with your ears*'.[49] (26.11)

The image here is of a trial with its setting at the gate of the temple. The priests and the prophets appear to be making a public accusation against Jeremiah to the officials of Judah and to all the people. Jeremiah's defense is that it was Yahweh who sent him to prophesy (להנבא) all the words that they heard. Recalling the language of warfare that characterizes the 'book' of Jeremiah as a whole, Jeremiah says, 'Now I am in your hands'. He continues by warning them that if they put him to death, they will be placing innocent blood on themselves and the city and its inhabitants, 'because in truth Yahweh has sent me to you to speak in your ears all these words' (26.15).

---

49. 'To hear with your ears' is a frequent expression associated with texts being read aloud to an audience such as the king. It is used repeatedly, for example, in Jer. 36. The use of this expression provides coded information for reading.

The officials and all the people appear to be acting as a kind of jury. They report to the priests and the prophets, 'This man should not receive the sentence of death because in the name of Yahweh our God he has spoken to us' (26.16). Then some of the elders from the land arose and said that Micah of Moresheth in the days of Hezekiah, king of Judah, had said to all the people of Judah:

> Zion will be plowed like a field;
>> Jerusalem will become a ruins
>> And the mountain of the house will be a wooded high place.[50] (26.18)

They go on to say that Hezekiah had not put Micah to death and that Yahweh had changed his mind about the disaster pronounced against them.

The response from the elders prompts several questions by the reader: 'Who are the elders?' and 'How did they know what Micah said?' The text does not provide us any direct evidence here to answer these questions, but if, as I will show later in Chapter 7, Micah was a prophet of חזון, then what he said would be available in writing. It is written down and available to the elders, those who can read. These exact words of Micah could be quoted with precision because they were in writing.

In my reading of Jeremiah I have been suggesting that Jeremiah's prophecy involves warfare, and I am now pointing out that 'prophesying' this message of warfare involves writing. For a book to be presenting a prophet as focusing on warfare and communicating those words by using writing also fits the social and cultural conventions of the ancient Near Eastern phenomenon of prophecy in general. This point has recently been argued by Hans M. Barstad in an article, 'No Prophets? Recent Developments in Biblical Prophetic Research and Ancient Near Eastern Prophecy'.[51] Barstad says:

> Obviously, we cannot and should not regard these texts [here he is speaking primarily of Jeremiah] as 'historical' in the sense that they tell us 'what actually took place'. On the other hand, it is wrong to classify these stories as 'ahistorical'. Sprung from historical environments long lost to us, all of these stories *reflect* the historical and social surroundings that created them, and illustrate to us the significance of war in ancient Near Eastern societies, and of the role of 'prophets' in times of crisis.[52]

---

50. This verse is repeated in Mic. 3.12.

51. Hans M. Barstad, 'No Prophets? Recent Developments in Biblical Prophetic Research and Ancient Near Eastern Prophecy', *JSOT* 57 (1993), pp. 39-60.

52. Barstad, 'No Prophets', pp. 53-54.

Barstad also goes on to argue that the writing down of prophetic words is more common in ancient Near Eastern prophecy than is often assumed. He says:

> I am not so sure that the taking down in writing did change very much *the nature* of the original prophecies, as some scholars of today seem to believe. The unmistakable parallels between the biblical and the ancient Near Eastern prophetic material clearly attest the contrary. Apparently, because some importance was attached to these words, it became important to secure the message from the deity in the most accurate way possible, or the message had to be taken down in order that it might be delivered to the correct addressee. It is hardly likely that the writing down took place in order to secure the words for posterity.[53]

Barstad's observations of ancient Near Eastern prophecy as cultural background to prophetic books support my reading of Jeremiah. Jeremiah's preaching is not extemporaneous. Words written in ספרים are not recorded for posterity but because of the role that writing will have in the act of prophesying Yahweh's words. When Jeremiah speaks in the court of the temple he is conveying as accurately as possible Yahweh's message, and that is done in writing. Furthermore, the very specific words of Micah are expressed by the elders not because of some remarkable memory but because his words have been written down and are available in writing. Indeed, as I have been arguing, the main feature of Jeremiah 25–52 is the centrality of the role of writing for Jeremiah when he prophesies Yahweh's words. Prophecy is not a frenzied activity in which the deity's words are blurted out only to be later remembered and written down. They are put in writing in order to read/prophesy with precision what Yahweh actually had spoken to Jeremiah.

I am suggesting that the 'book' (ספר) Jeremiah is prophesying is present as a fictive element in the literary world in a manner similar to the way Jeremiah is present in the literary world as a character in the text. I am not proposing that there was an actual book prophesied by an actual Jeremiah from the point of view of the 'historical positivism and naïve empiricism' that has characterized so much of contemporary biblical criticism as Barstad has correctly argued.[54]

I will want to come back to Barstad's important article a bit later, especially as that relates to Jeremiah 36, but now I want to return to the text of Jeremiah. As I indicated earlier, as the book of Jeremiah develops,

53. Barstad, 'No Prophets', p. 57.
54. Barstad, 'No Prophets', p. 44.

Jeremiah is drawn further and further into the frontline of battle, and it is the very activity of prophesying itself that puts him in 'the thick of the action'. Earlier we heard that Pashhur had struck Jeremiah when he stood in the court of the temple (20.1). In this later chapter the priests and prophets are publicly accusing him of sedition and calling for him to be put to death (26.11). That this was no idle accusation is clear from 26.20-23, where there is the report of another man, Uriah the son of Shemaiah, prophesying (וַיִּנָּבֵא) against the city and the land as was Jeremiah. When Jehoiakim and all his warriors (גִּבּוֹרָיו) heard these things, the king ordered that Uriah be put to death. Uriah fled but was pursued as far as Egypt. He was brought back to Judah where Jehoiakim struck him with a sword and 'threw his body in the burial place of the common people' (26.23). That Jeremiah was spared by Ahikam and did not suffer this same fate (26.24) suggests that Yahweh's comforting words to his warrior-prophet at the beginning of the book—'do not be afraid of them because I am with you to rescue you' (1.10)—were spoken with power. Jeremiah did not die in battle.

Before moving on I want to make one final point about Jeremiah's words in the court of the temple (ch. 26). The gravity of Jeremiah's words comparing Yahweh's house in Jerusalem with Shiloh is clear. There used to be חָזוֹן in the days of Samuel at Shiloh (1 Sam. 3). But Yahweh abandoned Shiloh (Ps. 78.60). If Yahweh is not in his house, there can be no חָזוֹן.

However, there is no mention of Shiloh in Jeremiah 25, where the surrounding context appears to make allusions to the contents of the סֵפֶר Jeremiah prophesied against the nations. The absence of a reference to Shiloh in ch. 25 suggests that there must have been more in the סֵפֶר against the nations than the reader knows from the general details contained in ch. 25 itself. While the סֵפֶר against the nations is present in Jeremiah 25 and 26, the reader can only sketchily reconstruct the contents of that text. We hear about it but we do not see it. It has a presence in the textual world, but it is not available for reading.[55] We do not know its exact contents or length.

Chapters 27 and 28 are dated at the beginning of the reign of Zedekiah. The contents of these chapters suggest that the סֵפֶר, which Jeremiah prophesied against the nations (25.13), is still present in the literary world. In 27.3, Yahweh orders Jeremiah: 'Send to the king of Edom, the king of Moab, the king of the Ammonites, the king of Tyre and the king of Sidon

---

55. See my 'Heard But Not Seen', pp. 50-55.

in the hand of (בְּיַד) messengers who have come to Jerusalem to Zedekiah, the king of Judah'. The text is not clear about what Jeremiah is to send. There is no object of the verb. If the present 'book' of Jeremiah is read according to compilational order, then what Jeremiah sends 'by the hand of messengers' is the סֵפֶר, which Jeremiah prophesied against the nations (25.13).[56] It has a presence in the literary picture developing here.

The kings mentioned are included in the list of kings who are to drink from the cup of the wine of wrath (25.21-22). What this chapter indicates is that Jeremiah as a prophet to the nations (1.5) is prophesying by the written word. Just as the סֵפֶר could be heard in the king's house when it was read, so the סֵפֶר can be heard when messengers take it 'in the hand' to the kings of Edom, Moab, Ammon, Tyre and Sidon where it can be read so that the words Yahweh spoke to Jeremiah can be heard even in Jeremiah's absence.[57]

According to Jeremiah, Yahweh is giving the land into the hand of the king of Babylon whose land also will ultimately be taken (27.4-7). This is consistent with the theme of Yahweh's warfare against the nations outlined in 25.8-14. If these nations referred to in ch. 25 do not put their neck under the yoke of the king of Babylon, then they will be punished by sword, famine and pestilence. They also are instructed not to listen to their prophets, diviners, dreamers, soothsayers and sorcerers who are prophesying that they will not serve the king of Babylon (27.8-11). The information about prophets who are prophesying a lie (שֶׁקֶר הֵם נִבְּאִים) is additional information we receive about the סֵפֶר mentioned in 25.13. Prophesying lies is not mentioned in Jeremiah 25.

Jeremiah 27.12-22 goes on to say that Jeremiah is communicating the same message to Zedekiah and the people of Judah that he had conveyed to the kings of Edom, Moah, Ammon, Tyre and Sidon. The king of Babylon will bring devastation to the land, and no one should listen to the prophets who are prophesying (נבא) a lie (שקר).

Jeremiah 28 is an encounter between Jeremiah and the prophet Hananiah. The theme of the chapter is prophesying (נבא) and lies (שפרים). Hananiah is presented as the prophet who prophesies a lie—that the yoke of the king of Babylon will be broken. All this is played out with Jeremiah using visual imagery as a manifestation of Yahweh's words. Hananiah breaks a wooden yoke that Jeremiah is wearing. However, Jeremiah turns that

---

56. See 29.31, where the use of the imperative 'send' without an object clearly refers to a סֵפֶר that Jeremiah sent to the exiles.

57. That messengers carry written documents in the hand has been discussed above.

incident into words about the yoke of Babylon as an iron yoke. The heart of the chapter, however, concerns false prophecy. Who is telling the truth? Jeremiah seems to be setting the criterion for telling the truth in 28.8-9. One will know the truth of a prophet who prophesies peace if it comes about. He says to Hananiah:

> The prophets who came before me and before you from times of old, they prophesied (וינבאו) to many countries and against great kingdoms for war, for famine and for pestilence. The prophet who prophesied (יָנבא) peace, when the word of that prophet came about, then it will be known that the prophet was sent by Yahweh.

A picture is beginning to emerge from the collage of material in Jeremiah 25–28. The picture comes into focus around the words Yahweh had spoken, which are written in the סֵפֶר Jeremiah prophesied (נבא) against the nations (25.13). Prophesying (נבא) a lie (שֶקֶר) is also part of the picture. The criterion that a prophecy of peace is true when the דבר eventuates evokes Deut. 18.20-22. If 'prophesied words' are to stand the test of time in order to demonstrate their truth, then writing is important for determining what actually had been said. Prophesying involves the precision of speaking Yahweh's words, and that precision is associated with writing.

The lying vision of the prophets has to do with Yahweh's absence. He has abandoned Shiloh. He is now not available for intercession in his house in Jerusalem as we learned earlier (11.14; 14.11). There can only be false vision when Yahweh is not present to give it. Any claim about vision when Yahweh is absent from the temple is a delusion. Yahweh's words must come from somewhere else, just as they have come to Jeremiah. They have their origin elsewhere in visual imagery in Jeremiah's world and are brought to the court of the house of Yahweh.

There is another dimension the reader can gain from these chapters on the written words Jeremiah himself prophecies by paying close attention to the use of the verb 'to prophesy'. The verbal form of the root נבא ('to prophesy'), which occurs only in the niphal and hithpael *binyanim*, is not evenly spread throughout the so-called Latter Prophets. It occurs once in Joel (3.1) and twice in Zechariah (13.3-4). In both cases it has to do with prophesying in the future and does not relate to the activity of either Joel or Zechariah. All the other references are found in three books: Jeremiah (over 40 times), Ezekiel (over 30 times) and Amos (six times), and each of these 'books' uses the verb to emphasize that Jeremiah, Ezekiel and Amos are prophesying. The verb נבא is not used in any other of the Latter Prophets. Only in these three prophetic books is the point emphasized that these three individuals are prophesying. In the other prophetic 'books' prophesying appears to be taken as a given.

This concentration of the verb 'to prophesy' is significant for understanding the encoded information available to readers of the books of Jeremiah, Ezekiel and Amos. It is significant that each of these superscriptions—and only these superscriptions—makes the point that the figure mentioned is associated with a group *other* than the prophets. Amos' origin was 'among the shepherds (בנקדים) from Tekoa' (1.1), Jeremiah was 'from the priests (הכהנים) who were in Anathoth in the land of Benjamin' (1.1), while Ezekiel was 'among the exiles' (בתוך־הגולה) and was 'the priest (הכהן) the son of Buzi' (1.1-3). In short, in each book the superscription emphasizes the non-conventional origin of the figure and each book itself repeatedly emphasizes that each of the individuals it refers to (Amos, Jeremiah or Ezekiel) is prophesying. Drawing attention again and again to the act of prophesying highlights the unorthodox character of these 'prophets'.

I will look at Ezekiel in due course, but I reiterate the point I made earlier that for both Amos and Jeremiah 'the words of Yahweh' come from outside the temple in visual imagery. Amos and Jeremiah are not like conventional prophets who receive a חזון in the temple. Both 'prophets' bring 'words' from outside to the temple: Amos to 'the house of El' (Bethel) in Israel and Jeremiah to 'the house of Yahweh' in Jerusalem.

Amos sees his words ('the words of Amos...which he saw', 1.1). Amos' dispute with Amaziah at the 'the house of El' concerning prophesying (נבא) is embedded with a text that tells us what Amos sees (locusts, a fire, a plumb line and basket of summer fruit). What he sees—the end of Israel (8.1-2)—brings him to 'the house of El', and Amos, addressed as a 'seer' (חזה), is told by Amaziah to go to Judah and to prophesy (נבא) there (7.11). Amos' response to Amaziah (7.14) supports the point I am developing here: Amos was not a conventional prophet. Yahweh asked a herdsman and a dresser of sycamore trees to prophesy:

> I am not a prophet
>   nor am I the son of a prophet;
> I am a shepherd
>   and a dresser of sycamore trees.
> And Yahweh took me from following the flocks;
>   and Yahweh said to me, 'Go prophesy to my people Israel'. (7.14-15)

Earlier in the 'book' of Amos (3.2-7), it also appears that 'prophesying' grows out of imagery in Amos' world—people walking together, lions roaring, young lions crying out from the den, birds falling into a snare, snares springing up from the ground, trumpets blowing in the city, disaster befalling a city:

> The lion has roared (שאג);
>> who will not fear?
> The lord Yahweh has spoken;
>> Who will not prophesy (נבא)? (3.8)

As I have argued earlier, this roaring voice of Yahweh provides Amos with words drawn from natural imagery and, like Jeremiah, announces the end of a nation.

There is, however, one relevant difference between Amos and Jeremiah. Even though Amos is not a conventional prophet and is receiving words evoked by what he sees in the natural world in the Northern Kingdom, Yahweh is still present in the temple in Jerusalem. In Amos 1.1, Yahweh 'roars from Zion' and 'utters his voice from Jerusalem'. However, in Jer. 25.30 the specific references to Zion and Jerusalem are missing: 'Yahweh roars from on high (מרון) and from his holy habitation (מעון) he utters his voice'. While these terms may refer to Zion and Jerusalem, they do not do so in an unambiguous way. Although מרון can be used to refer to the height of Zion as it does in 31.12, it can mean any height including the height of heaven. While מעון also can be used for the temple as the holy habitation as in Ps. 26.8, in Jeremiah מעון is used most frequently to refer to desolated cities, including Jerusalem and the cities of Judah, as having become a 'lair' of jackals (9.10; 10.22; 49.33; 51.37), that is, a desolated waste.

The point that is being made in Jeremiah 25–28, chapters associated with prophesying written words, is that Jeremiah is the only contemporary prophet prophesying Yahweh's words. While Amos was standing alone against Amaziah, Jeremiah is standing alone against all the prophets in the land who are prophesying a lie—this includes not only the prophets of Judah but also the prophets of all the nations. Every other prophet can only prophesy a lie since Yahweh is neither present in the temple in Jerusalem nor in any of the other surrounding nations.

For Jeremiah's words to come from outside the temple, however, does not mean that Jeremiah scatters words around Jerusalem and among the nations in extemporaneous outbursts.[58] His words, like the חזון, are written

---

58. To recall the earlier discussion (see above, pp. 73-74). He is like Samuel in that he does not let his words fall to the ground.

down. When he goes to the temple to prophesy, Yahweh's words are written in a ספר and this ספר plays a central role in Jeremiah's prophesying/ speaking.

Such a ספר, however, becomes powerful in a prophetic sense when what the prophet says comes true. In the prophetic compilation of scrolls, the words of Jeremiah the non-conventional prophet are empowered by the book of Kings, which has recorded the events surrounding the king of Babylon, who has taken all the land. The war is over at the end of Kings. The land is desolate and emptied. The people of Judah are in exile. When one turns in the compilation of scrolls to Jeremiah, powerful words, from an unconventional prophet, are encountered predicting the end, and those words are in writing. From Jer. 25.13 to the end of the book we hear about 'written words' in ספרים. Upon reflection, however, the reader asks, 'Where are these ספרים containing the written words?' Like the lost ספר of Moses, which was found in the days of Josiah, but for the reader is lost again, the ספרים of Jeremiah can only be remembered and reconstructed from the only source we have—the prophetic books we are reading. Readers looking for the lost words, as many historical critics have done, look for the ספר of Moses and the ספרים of Jeremiah, reconstructing them. Indeed, the entire historical-critical enterprise has in many ways been a search for the sources—the ספרים that lay buried beneath the 'biblical' texts being read.

b. *The ספרים to the Exiles (Jeremiah 29.1-3; 30.2; 31)*
In these chapters Jeremiah becomes involved in writing ספרים and sending them to the exiles in Babylon. It would be wrong, however, to decode this flurry of activity simply as correspondence. It may be appropriate to translate ספר by the English word 'letter' as many contemporary translations do,[59] but this would only be appropriate in the sense that all Jeremiah's ספרים are letters from Yahweh. To decode these ספרים as different from the 'ספר against the nations' or the ספר Jeremiah dictates to Baruch (ch. 36) would be inappropriate. When Jeremiah sends a ספר by the hand of (ביד) Elasah and Semariah (29.3) to the exiles, he is prophesying. He is doing the same thing as carrying the ספר against the nations into the court of the temple (ch. 26), sending it by the hand of messengers to the nations (27.3-11) and using it in his prophesying at the time of Zedekiah (27.12-28). Writing plays a central role in prophecy and to

---

59. The NRSV, for instance, does this in 29.1, 3, 31.

alter the translation of ‏סֵפֶר‎ from 'book' to 'letter' is to decode aberrantly according to contemporary conventions associated with written texts.

The ‏סֵפֶר‎ sent to the exiles is quoted in 29.4-28. It continues the compilation of material in this part of the 'book' as a presentation of the way Jeremiah uses ‏סְפָרִים‎ when he prophesies. The words of Yahweh are that the exiles are to settle down in Babylon and that the prophets in Babylon are 'prophesying' a 'lie' (29.1-9). There is a reference to a 70-year period after which Yahweh will establish his promise and bring the exiles back to the land (29.10). The reference to 70 years echoes Jer. 25.12, which speaks about the punishment that Yahweh will bring on the king of Babylon after the same amount of time. Where was this promise made? Was it also part of the ‏סֵפֶר‎ which Jeremiah prophesied against the nations? Seventy years hence the people will be able to intercede with Yahweh and he will hear (25.12). This positive message directed to the exiles is followed by a negative message concerning the people who remain in the land of Judah (29.16-23). The people who remain in Jerusalem are like 'rotten figs', and this imagery and vocabulary recall the earlier image of the two baskets of figs (ch. 24).

Jeremiah becomes engaged in a battle with Shemaiah, who wrote to condemn Jeremiah of being a madman (29.24, 27). This accusation gains clarity from the discussion above that Jeremiah is a non-conventional prophet from among the ranks of the priests of Anathoth. The interchange in writing is interesting in 29.24-25. Jeremiah writes in the name of Yahweh to Shemaiah: 'Thus Yahweh of hosts, the God of Israel said, "You wrote ‏סְפָרִים‎ in your own name to all the people who are in Jerusalem and to the priest Zephaniah"'. This writing of Jeremiah gains clarity when read alongside the accusation that Yahweh makes against the prophets prophesying lies—that they claim to prophesy in the name of Yahweh (see 14.14; 23.25). Shemaiah is writing (prophesying) *in his own name*; he is not prophesying in the name of Yahweh.

The chapter ends with Jeremiah writing another ‏סֵפֶר‎ to the exiles saying that Yahweh will punish Shemaiah, the ironically named prophet—his name means 'Yahweh had heard'. Shemaiah has prophesied a lie. Prophesying a lie here includes the ‏סֵפֶר‎ Shemaiah sent to the priest Zephaniah declaring that Jeremiah was a prophesying madman (29.26-28). The content of the ‏סְפָרִים‎ Jeremiah wrote is unclear.

In 30.2 Jeremiah is instructed to write another ‏סֵפֶר‎. These chapters continue to depict Jeremiah as a prophet prophesying by writing. Was this ‏סֵפֶר‎ also sent to the exiles? Are the words that follow in 30.3–31.40 the words written in this סֵפֶר? Were any of these words in the סֵפֶר against the nations? We cannot be sure of the answer to any of these questions.

The words prophesied in this סֵפֶר, however, reverse what appears to be the content of the סֵפֶר against the nations. The land that was emptied will now be filled. A few observations will indicate the tone of these words of restoration. Just as the beginning of the book outlined the end of Israel and Judah, now this סֵפֶר contains words about how Israel and Judah will be restored. Restoration will be from the north, recalling earlier sections of the book (e.g. 24.4-7). Jeremiah had been appointed a prophet 'to pluck up and to pull down, to destroy and to overthrow, to build and to plant' (1.10). In this time of restoration Yahweh will now watch over the community 'to build and to plant' as he had watched over it 'to pluck up and break down, to overthrow, destroy and to bring calamity' (31.28).

The community will be returned from the land of the enemy (31.16). Yahweh uses the conventional language of warfare, similar to the language used to address Jeremiah in his battle with all the nations of the land, as words of comfort to the restored community:[60]

> But you, fear not, my servant Jacob, a saying of Yahweh,
>   and do not be dismayed, Israel.
> Because I am about to save you from afar,
>   and your offspring from the land of their captivity.
> And Jacob will return and have quiet and ease,
>   and there will be no one to make him afraid.
> Because I am with you, a saying of Yahweh,
>   to save you.
> Because I will make an end among all the nations where I
>   scattered you,
>   but will not make and end of you.
> I will chastise you with justice,
>   and I will not leave you unpunished. (30.10-11)

The language of war in these contexts has been modified so as not to give orders to fight but to promise that the community will return in 'quiet and ease'.

This is a time when there will be a new covenant. Yahweh will internalize the *torah* and write it on the hearts of the people (31.33). This appears to be a corrective to the 'lying pen' of the scribes, which has made the

---

60. Here, the community addressed is Jacob/Israel (Jer. 30.10-11; cf. also 46.27-28, where the words are repeated in a slightly different form and are similar to those in Isaiah's חָזוֹן about restoration to Zion—Isa. 41.8-13, 14-16; 43.1-4, 5-7; 44.1-5). I will look at this language in more detail when I deal with Isaiah.

torah lie (שֶׁקֶר, 8.8). There will also be a new Davidic king whom Yahweh will set on the throne. The curious thing about all these comforting words of restoration is that there is no mention of prophets who prophesy (נבא) a lie (שֶׁקֶר).

c. *The* סְפָרִים *of Purchase (Jeremiah 32.10-16)*
Chapter 32 is dated in the tenth year of Zedekiah, the eighteenth year of Nebuchadrezzar, when the king of Babylon was besieging the city. Jeremiah is now imprisoned in the court of the guard in the palace. Zedekiah comes to Jeremiah and asks why he is continuing to prophesy that the city will be given into the hands of the Chaldeans and that to fight against the Chaldeans will only result in failure.

Jeremiah does not respond but buys a field and signs סְפָרִים of purchase (30.10-15). The thrust of the chapter is that after the king of Babylon takes the land there will be a future for those who will return from Babylonian exile. In this sense these chapters continue the theme of restoration in chs. 30–32. These documents are to be placed in an earthenware jar so that they last a long time. This incident recalls the words that had come to Jeremiah associated with an earthenware jar in ch. 19. The act of burying these סְפָרִים will serve as testimony to the truth of Yahweh's words as prophesied by Jeremiah. When they are excavated later at the time of restoration, Jeremiah's prophesying will be seen not to be a lie.

d. *The* סֵפֶר *Dictated to Baruch at the Time of Jehoiakim (Jeremiah 36)*
This chapter contains the well-known story of the scroll (מְגִלַּת־סֵפֶר) that Jeremiah dictated to Baruch: 'Baruch wrote from the mouth of Jeremiah all the words of Yahweh, which he spoke to him on a scroll' (36.4). This happened in the fourth year of Jehoiakim—the same year as the 'סֵפֶר against the nations'. That this סֵפֶר is also described as מְגִלָּה suggests that it is perhaps to be more comprehensive. It incorporates all the words that Yahweh spoke to Jeremiah from the time of Josiah until the time of Jehoiakim in the fourth year. There is no mention of whether it includes the words of the סֵפֶר against the nations (25.13) or material from any of the other סְפָרִים mentioned earlier.

After dictating the scroll, Jeremiah orders Baruch to read it in the temple from which Jeremiah is now barred. He had been able to enter the court to prophesy the סֵפֶר against the nations (Jer. 26) in the fourth year of Jehoiakim, but the reading here takes place a year later: 'In the fifth year of King Jehoiakim…in the ninth month…Baruch read the words of Jeremiah from the scroll in the house of Yahweh' (36.9-10). The scroll is eventually taken to the king's house where Baruch reads it to the officials. The scroll is eventually read to Jehoiakim, who cut it into pieces with his knife and through it into the brazier. The reaction of Jehoiakim and his servants to hearing the words of this סֵפֶר are different from Josiah's response upon hearing the words of the סֵפֶר of the *torah*/covenant. On hearing Jeremiah's words, we learn that 'neither the king, nor any of his servants who heard all these words, was alarmed, nor did they tear their garments' (36.24).

In reaction to Jehoiakim's cutting and burning of the scroll, Yahweh orders Jeremiah to create a second scroll. Jeremiah dictates to Baruch 'all the words of the scroll that King Jehoiakim of Judah had burned in the fire; and many similar words were added to them'. Again we can ask: 'Where is this scroll?' The scroll is present in the text and appears in the next chapter 'in the hand of Jeremiah' (37.2). It is a 'character' in the book.

At the beginning of Jeremiah 37 we are told that neither Zedekiah 'nor his servants nor the people of the land listened to the words of Yahweh which he spoke *by the hand* (בְּיַד) of Jeremiah'. I contend that what was 'in the hand of' Jeremiah was the second scroll that was dictated to Baruch. For Yahweh to speak by the hand of Jeremiah is for Jeremiah to read the words written in the סֵפֶר. This entire section of the book is emphasizing the materiality of Yahweh's words written down in סְפָרִים. The expression that Yahweh spoke *by the hand* (בְּיַד) of Jeremiah suggests the concrete form of communicating what has been written by hand and carried in the hand to be read to the recipient. Just as the סֵפֶר against the nations was 'in the hand of' the messengers to the nations (27.3) and was to be read, and just as the סֵפֶר to the exiles was in the hand of messengers to be read (29.3), I argue that the סֵפֶר read by Baruch in the fifth year of Jehoiakim was also 'in the hand of' Jeremiah in the time of Zedekiah. Yahweh was able to speak when what is in Jeremiah's hand is read.

The materiality of communication in Jeremiah recalls the materiality evident in passages concerning Moses. Moses is ordered in Exodus 34 to cut tablets of stone, to take them in his *hand* (34.1-5) and to write on them: 'Yahweh said to Moses, "Write (כְּתָב) these words..."' (Exod. 34.27). At the end of the passage we are told, 'Moses came down from Mount Sinai...with the two tablets of the covenant in his hand (בְּיַד)' (34.29). From this passage in Exodus 34 we can gain insight into a recurring phrase in the biblical literature: 'Yahweh spoke (דִּבֶּר) by the hand (בְּיַד) of Moses'.[61] Yahweh speaks when what was carried by the hand of Moses is

---

61. See Exod. 9.35; Lev. 10.11; Num. 17.5 (Eng. 16.40); 27.23; Josh. 20.2; 1 Kgs 8.53, 56. Related phrases are 'Yahweh commanded (צִוָּה) by the hand of Moses' (Exod.

read. Similarly, the frequently recurring phrase 'Yahweh spoke (דבר) by the hand of (ביד) a prophet(s)'[62] suggests that written documents carried by hand, often in the hand of one who 'runs with' the message, become audible as God's spoken words when they are read aloud.

The chapters that follow Jeremiah 37 portray the end of Judah and suggest that all the words written in the ספר that Baruch read in the temple from the time of Josiah until the fourth year of Jehoiakim, words with which the reader is now familiar, have come about. At the very time that Nebuchadrezzar is besieging Jerusalem (37.5), Jeremiah says to Zedekiah: 'Where are your prophets who prophesied to you, "The king of Babylon will not come against you and against this land"?' (37.19).

To understand prophecy as writing is not to maintain that any of these ספרים are actual or that anything said about Jeremiah actually happened. However, to read these texts is to understand that writing is intrinsic to prophecy and is not an act of preservation after the fact. The close association between writing and prophesying fits what we know of conventional practice in the social and cultural world of the ancient Near East, as Barstad has suggested in citing a text from Mari:

> Another matter: Atamrum, the *āpilum* of Shamash came to find me, and he said: Send me a very competent scribe in order that I can make him write down the message the Shamash has sent me for the king...[63]

e. The ספר concerning Babylon's Disaster (51.60, 63)

There is one final ספר that appears in Jeremiah. In 51.60 we are told that Jeremiah wrote on a ספר all the disasters that would come to Babylon. He sent this with Seraiah to Babylon where Seraiah was instructed to read it. After reading it, he was to tie a stone to it and throw it in the middle of the Euphrates—apparently as a sign that Babylon would sink and rise no more (52.6). At that point the words of Jeremiah end.

Again, we do not know the contents of this ספר, but they are undoubtedly alluded to in the preceding material about the judgment coming to the

---

36.13; Lev. 8.26; Num. 15.2; 36.13; Josh. 21.2, 8; Judg. 3.4; Neh. 8.14; 9.14; 2 Chron. 33.8) and 'Yahweh gave (נתן) by the hand of Moses' (Neh. 10.30 [Eng. 10.29]). A phrase 'from the mouth of (פ) Yahweh by the hand of Moses' (Num. 4.37, 45, 49; 9.23; 10.13; Josh. 22.9) suggests dictation. See also Lev. 26.46; 2 Chron. 34.14; 35.6.

62. Sometimes the phrase gives the specific name of the prophet, and the word 'prophet' is sometimes missing. See 1 Kgs 12.15; 14.18; 15.29; 16.7, 12, 34; 17.16; 2 Kgs 9.36; 10.10; 14.25; 17.23; 24.2; 2 Chron. 10.15; Isa. 20.2; 50.1; Ezek. 38.17; Dan. 9.10; Hos. 12.11; cf. 2 Sam. 28.15; 2 Kgs 17.13; 1 Chron. 11.3; 2 Chron. 29.25.

63. Barstad, 'No Prophets', p. 60 (citing AEM I/2 no. 414 [A431+A4883]).

nations (chs. 46–51). In fact, 49.34 implies that some of the words against Elam came from the time of Zedekiah. The materiality of these words is evident not only in the ספר that sinks to the bottom of the Euphrates, but also in the fact that the words concerning Babylon are 'in the hand' (ביד) of the prophet Jeremiah (50.1). The war against Babylon will now be carried out by a 'new weapon of battle' (51.20). The Medes are preparing for war against Babylon (51.28).

To summarize, then, the last part of the book of Jeremiah focuses on the activity of prophesying. Jeremiah, the unconventional prophet from among the priests of Anathoth receives his words from outside the temple in visual imagery from his world. He takes these words to the temple for the prophets, the priests, the people and the kings. These words, however, are not 'off the cuff' remarks but are words that are written down with precision. This very materiality of the written word is important not only for a prophet who speaks in the name of Yahweh but also for a prophet who does not prophesy a lie. By the end of the book, these written words find fulfilment in the events they portend. The king of Babylon has taken the land and emptied it of its inhabitants. Yahweh himself is gone.

For readers of this text who have encountered a series of ספרים at the end of Jeremiah, it is easy to become caught up in the rhetoric of the book. In my reading, ספרים emerge, allusions are made to their content, and then they disappear—the final one at the bottom of the Euphrates. As readers we are tempted to look beneath the surface to discover the underlying ספרים. But when we do, are we not succumbing to the book's own rhetoric? Our only source for all those books in which Yahweh's words took material form are found in Jeremiah. The text is empowered by making these texts alluded to 'present' in the literary world. There is no reason to attempt to reconstruct texts that may have no reality beyond that of their appearance as 'characters' in the book of Jeremiah. At the beginning of the book a Model Author informs the reader that what follows are the words of Jeremiah. Those words are written words, ספרים, just like the ספר readers of the book of Jeremiah have in their hands.

7. *The Battle is Over*

According to Jer. 1.10, after Yahweh reaches out and touches Jeremiah's mouth he says, 'See I have made you a הפקדתיך [governor or overseer?] today'. Whatever הפקדתיך means exactly in this context, it is clear that it implies appointment to a position of some authority. The same verb (hiphil הפקיד) is used elsewhere in Jeremiah (40.5, 7, 11; 41.2; cf. 2 Kgs 25.23)

concerning the appointment of Gedaliah as governor or overseer over the
cities of Judah. Also the related noun פָּקִיד is used to refer to the position
of Pashhur who struck Jeremiah when he entered the court of Yahweh's
house. It is interesting that after Gedaliah has been assassinated, Jeremiah's
words suggest that he is assuming the same power as Gedaliah, the representative of the king of Babylon. When 'all the leaders of the army
which was in the field and their men heard that the king of Babylon had
appointed Gedaliah as governor/overseer' (40.7), they went to Gedaliah
who tired to reassure them. Gedaliah uses the conventional language to
comfort warriors (40.9-10):

Assurance
'Fear not (אַל־תִּירְאוּ)

Object of Fear
to serve the Chaldeans (מֵעֲבוֹד הַכַּשְׂדִּים).

Orders
Dwell in the land and serve the king of Babylon and it will go well for
you.

Basis of Assurance
And I, behold I (הִנְנִי) am living in Mizpah to serve before the Chaldeans
who have come to us.

Orders
But you, gather wine and summer fruits and oil, and store them in your
vessels, and dwell in your cities, which you have captured.'

This is unusual war language, however. The leaders of the army are not to
fight but to settle down in the land and become farmers not warriors.
When Gedaliah is assassinated, leaders of the troops come to Jeremiah.
Here they are described as a small group of survivors. They ask Jeremiah
to inquire with Yahweh about what they should do. Interestingly, now that
Yahweh has already attacked and brought destruction, Jeremiah intercedes
with Yahweh. The answer Jeremiah receives from Yahweh takes the form
of the conventional 'fear not' language of war (42.10-11). The orders
recall the language of Jer. 1.10, when Jeremiah was appointed as a prophet
to the nations, and take the form of a conditional threat that typified
Yahweh's words to Jeremiah in 1.17:

Orders
'If you will only live in this land, then I will build you up and I will not
pull you down; I will plant you and I will not pluck you up; because I am
sorry for the calamity which I did to you.

Assurance
   Fear not (אל־תיראו)

Object of Fear
   (מפני) the king of Babylon of whom you are afraid of him.

Assurance
   Do not fear (אל־תיראו)

Object of Fear
   him (ממנו),

Basis of Assurance
   a saying of Yahweh, because (כי) I am with you to rescue you from his
   hand.'

These leaders of the army, however, distrust Jeremiah's words and he is
taken (against his orders) out of the land and down to the land of Egypt—
the place from which, as he has been saying, there will be no future
because this time Yahweh will deliver his people from the north (43.7).

By the end of Jeremiah, we learn that Jeremiah's battle is over but that
the war has not ended. Yahweh is going to make Babylon a desolate land
by sending the Medes as his new army against Babylon. It is then that the
people of Israel and Judah will return to fill the land again. However, they
will not be returning as warriors in the same way that Joshua had moved
into the land as a warrior. Nor will they experience the hostility that Jeremiah experiences as a warrior-prophet. They will return in a new Exodus
from the north, not from Egypt.

Jeremiah addresses these returnees with conventional language drawn
from warfare. However, the conventional language has been modified.
There is a promise of rescue from the enemy but no orders are given to
fight. These words are found in two places as words of comfort for the
exiles on the promised return (31.10-11; 46.27-28). The words here are
very much like those in Isaiah's חזון (Isa. 41.8-13, 14-16; 43.1-4, 5-7;
44.1-5), and I will look more closely at them when I review the conventional language of war used in Isaiah in Chapter 7.

7. *Summary and Conclusion*

In this chapter I have argued that the expression 'the words of' (דברי)
occurring at the beginning of the 'books' of Amos and Jeremiah encodes
information for the reader. As we have seen, both Amos and Jeremiah
are unconventional prophets, as the superscriptions of these two books
also suggest. Amos is from among the shepherds (נקדים) of Tekoa, and

Jeremiah is from the priests (כהנים) of Anathoth. Their words do not emerge in the temple as vision (חזון), as was the case with Samuel (1 Sam. 3), and, as we will see, as is the case with conventional prophets such as Isaiah. Rather their words emerge in visual imagery (e.g. plumb lines, baskets of summer fruit, almond branches, boiling pots, baskets of figs, etc.). As prophets they bring their words to the temple from the outside. Their words from outside the temple create conflict with temple officials (e.g. Amaziah in the case of Amos, and Pashhur in the case of Jeremiah). Prophets having access to Yahweh's words in the outside world also raises the issue of what it means to prophecy (נבא). Unlike any of the other prophets in the compilation of prophetic scrolls (apart from the other unconventional prophet Ezekiel, whom I will discuss in the next chapter), Amos and Jeremiah thematize the issue of prophecy as an activity. In Amos, prophecy is an issue in his encounter with Amaziah. Jeremiah has similar encounters with Pashhur and Hananiah and other priests and prophets from the temple. In Jeremiah, however, the issue of who is prophesying the truth and who is prophesying a lie is a primary concern (see, for instance, Jer. 23).

Prophesying as an activity is a more clearly developed theme in Jeremiah than in Amos. The last part of Jeremiah (Jer. 25–51) suggests that prophesying has involved writing. To prophesy is to write down the words of Yahweh so that they can be prophesied in the ears of those who hear, that is, those who hear what is read out by the prophets or by scribes, messengers or others who can hold the words 'in the hand' (ביד). Indeed, in this last section of Jeremiah (chs. 25–51), Jeremiah is associated with a succession of ספרים recording the words he speaks. This is important not only because of the role these ספרים play in the activity of prophesying, but also because these written documents containing the words of Yahweh demonstrate their own truth when what they say eventuates (Deut. 18). These ספרים are present as a 'character' in the literary world of the text not unlike the 'character' of Jeremiah himself. Since our only knowledge of these ספרים is the 'book' of Jeremiah itself, the book is empowered with knowing more than the reader can ever know—the content of the writings sometimes quoted but most frequently only alluded to. When readers encounter 'the words of Jeremiah' at the beginning of the book of Jeremiah, they are encountering written words Jeremiah prophesied.

Jeremiah and Amos share a similar responsibility as unconventional prophets. They announce the end of a nation. Amos announces the end of Israel, and Jeremiah announces the end of Judah. In both situations Yahweh is emptying the land of its inhabitants and bringing the land to total destruction. He is casting Israel and Judah out of his sight (2 Kgs 23.27). But it is clear that Yahweh is also abandoning the land. He will move out of his house and leave the land devoid of both human habitation and divine presence. Both Amos (1.2) and Jeremiah (25.30) announce that Yahweh will roar (שׁאג) and utter his voice (נתן קול) and bring about destruction to all the nations of the land. The major difference between the two books is that, for Amos, Yahweh is still in Zion and Jerusalem. Zion and Jerusalem are not mentioned in Jer. 25.30; Yahweh simply roars from a height and utters his voice from what has become the den of jackals.

There is one final point that I want to make about Jeremiah in particular. From the very beginning of the 'book' the vocabulary and imagery are associated with war. Yahweh has declared war on Israel, Judah and all the nations of the land. Jeremiah himself in his role as a prophet to the nations and as the cupbearer of the wine of wrath is addressed as a warrior in language that follows the conventions of giving comfort before entering a battle. In this sense, in the order and arrangement of the rabbinic canon, Jeremiah recalls the beginning of the prophetic canon, the book of Joshua. However, unlike Joshua, Jeremiah will fight as Yahweh's warrior against his people. Also, unlike Joshua, when Yahweh's is victorious, Jeremiah will be transported by the vanquished to the land of Egypt, the place where Yahweh had delivered his people at the Red Sea—now a place of exile not salvation. For Jeremiah, any future salvation will come from the north where all those obedient to Yahweh's word will return from exile.

Chapter 6

'AND IT HAPPENED' TO JONAH AND EZEKIEL:
READING EZEKIEL IN LIGHT OF JONAH

> Then I said, 'I am driven away from your sight;
>   how shall I look again upon your temple?'…
> As my life was ebbing away,
>   I remembered Yahweh;
> and my intercession came to you,
>   to your holy temple. (Jon. 2.5, 8 [Eng. 2.4, 7])

> And the glory of Yahweh went out from upon the threshold of the house,
> and he stood on the cherubim. And the cherubim lifted up their wings and
> they rose up from the earth before my eyes when they went out. The wheels
> were beside them. And they stood at the opening of the eastern gate of the
> house of Yahweh, and the glory of the God of Israel was above them…
> And the glory of the Yahweh went up from the middle of the city, and he
> stood on the mountain at the east. (Ezek. 10.18-19; 11.23)

In the last chapter I argued that the scroll of Jeremiah as a 'book' has its
counterpart in the scroll of the Twelve so-called Minor Prophets in Amos.
Both Jeremiah and Amos are about 'the words' of an unorthodox prophet
originating outside the temple in visual imagery. From a semiotic perspective, one could say that this information is provided as a code by a Model
Author in the superscription at the beginning of each 'book'. In each
instance we are told that what follows concerns 'the words of' either
Amos or Jeremiah and that both of these individuals have their origin and
identity in groups other than 'prophets'. Amos is from the shepherds and
Jeremiah is from among the priests.

In this chapter I want to argue that, in a similar way, the scroll of Ezekiel
as a prophetic 'book' has its counterpart in the scroll of the Twelve Minor
Prophets in Jonah. Both Ezekiel and Jonah begin with the same phrase
'and it happened' (ויהי). These two 'books' are coded differently for the
Model Author than are the 'books' of Amos and Jeremiah. They are to be
read as a narrative sequence and not as 'the words of' (דברי) Ezekiel or
Jonah. Elsewhere in the Hebrew Bible, ויהי suggests the beginning of a
narrative sequence, as it does at the beginning of three of the scrolls of the

so-called Former Prophets (Joshua, Judges and Samuel). In the case of Ezekiel and Jonah, what follows is to be understood as a connected narrative, as something that happened to Jonah and Ezekiel.

To read Jonah and Ezekiel as narrative sequences does not in itself suggest new insight in critical studies of the Hebrew Bible. Jonah has always been understood as a story and some have even referred to it as a *novella*.[1] Also, Ezekiel has always been understood as a well-organized and constructed book about the prophet Ezekiel even in critical scholarship. In her excellent book, *Swallowing the Scroll*, Ellen F. Davis, summarizes in a succinct way the perception in biblical studies of the overall sequential organization of the 'book' of Ezekiel:

> 'Architectonic' seems to be the scholarly epithet peculiar to the book of Ezekiel. The primary object of critical research has been to account for the book's salient feature: its comprehensive design, which appears highly deliberate and distinguishes this work from earlier collections of prophetic speeches. At the grossest level, there is a discernible pattern in the thematic organization of the book, which seems to divide quite sharply into three units: chs. 1–24, pronouncements of Jerusalem's doom; 25–32, oracles concerning the foreign nations; 33–48, promises and visions of Israel's restoration. But equally, there is an overall coherence of style and perspective, maintained by the first person narrative frame which anchors the divine speeches. The book's comprehensive unity is evidenced also at the level of content. Especially significant in this regard is the sequence of three divine visions (1.1–3.15; 8.1–11.25; 40.1–48.35). The divine visions show the point of orientation for the prophet's message: the divine presence (כבוד יי), which appears first in connection with Ezekiel's call; next, in departure from the defiled Temple, thereby both imaging the abandonment to disaster and showing its just grounds; and finally, in reinvestiture of the new Temple in the holy city. Thus one central image serves the threefold function of prophetic validation, theodicy, and promise.[2]

The problem Ezekiel posed for historical-critical scholars was that Ezekiel did not fit the pattern of prophetic books such as Jeremiah or Isaiah. As Davis indicates, it took a long time for scholars to attempt a 'diachronic analysis of the sort which had been applied to other prophetic books'.[3] For

---

1.   Gerhard von Rad, *Old Testament Theology* (trans. D.M.G. Stalker; 2 vols.; New York: Harper & Row, 1965), II, p. 291.

2.   Ellen F. Davis, *Swallowing the Scroll: Textuality and the Dynamics of Discourse in Ezekiel's Prophecy* (JSOTSup, 78; Sheffield: Almond Press, 1989), p. 11.

3.   Davis, *Swallowing the Scroll*, pp. 11-12. See the whole of Chapter 1, 'Framing the Literary Question', which gives an excellent of the critical study of Ezekiel for most of the twentieth century.

the first quarter of the twentieth century, Ezekiel was almost exclusively read as a unified whole, as a scroll written by the prophet.[4] Eventually, however, Ezekiel was made to look like other prophetic books through diachronic analysis. Historical critics exemplified their radical reader-oriented approach to texts ignoring the limits of interpretation, by congregating prophetic books and making them look like one another. The distinctive features of each book were ignored. Each book was hammered into the general shape that the historical-critical scholar had determined to characterize the origins and development of these 'books' as disorganized collections of prophetic words and speeches.

I am taking a position against this generalizing tendency in reading prophetic books. I have been arguing that prophetic 'books' should be read according to the distinctive information provided by the codes at the beginning and throughout each 'book'. Codes such as ויהי and דברי supply distinctive information to the Model Reader concerning how to read what follows. Ezekiel is a narrative sequence about what 'happened' to Ezekiel (ויהי); it is not a scroll concerning 'the words of' (דברי) Ezekiel.

Both Ezekiel and Jonah need to be read as narrative. Although the two books are not identical, I will be focusing first on their similarities as counterpart prophets to Jeremiah and Amos. Both 'books' are about how Yahweh interacts with a 'prophet' in a foreign land—Jonah in Nineveh, the capital city of the Assyrians, and Ezekiel in Babylon. These are the two cities that brought an end to Israel and Judah as announced by Amos and Jeremiah respectively. It is fitting that Ezekiel follows Jeremiah in the compilation of scrolls I am reading. The setting at the end of Jeremiah (Jer. 52) is Babylon, the place where Jeremiah prophesied that the people should go into exile if they wanted to have a future. Jonah is linked to Amos as Ezekiel is to Jeremiah though not as closely. Jonah follows Amos, separated only by Obadiah, in the compilation of scrolls I am reading. According to the book of Kings (2 Kgs 14.25), Jonah is a northern prophet, and according to the 'book' of Jonah, he is in the land of the Assyrians, a people who brought the Northern Kingdom to an end as Amos prophesied.[5]

In both books extraordinary events take place. Jonah is swallowed by a big fish and spewed out on to dry land, and the Assyrians repent of their evil ways. Ezekiel has extraordinary visions of Yahweh in Babylon. He is

---

4. Davis, *Swallowing the Scroll*, p. 12.
5. While Amos is explicit that Israel will 'end', he does not explicitly refer to Assyria as Yahweh's agent in bringing Israel to an end.

tied up and ordered to lie on his side for 350 days and then for an additional 40 days on his other side. While he is bound and unable to speak, he is ordered to 'prophesy' (נבא). The phrase 'and it happened' appears to be an attempt to convince a skeptical reader that it did indeed happen—or, to ask the reader to suspend disbelief. 'And it happened' may have a similar function to that of 'once upon a time' or 'it so happened' in fairy tales. It may signal a prophetic genre in which extraordinary events are to be narrated about a prophet.

Another feature that distinguishes Jonah and Ezekiel from Amos and Jeremiah is the more intimate interchange between Jonah and Ezekiel with Yahweh than characterizes Amos and Jeremiah, where Yahweh remains more distant. Jonah and Ezekiel appear to be in a world where the only other main character is Yahweh. While Amos and Jeremiah are 'speaking' the words of Yahweh, who remains in the background, Jonah and Ezekiel depict a less formal, more accessible aspect to the relationship between Yahweh and the prophet.[6]

1. *Jonah: Not Out of Sight and Presumably Not Out of Mind*

The thing that happened to Jonah is that the word of Yahweh came to him ordering him to rise up and go to Nineveh described as 'the great city'. Jonah is to proclaim (קרא) against it because of its wickedness. As is well known from this familiar story, Jonah does not obey but flees. He goes down to Joppa and pays his fare to take a boat to Tarshish. Yahweh causes a mighty storm on the sea that nearly results in a shipwreck. The ship and its crew are only spared after Jonah is tossed overboard.

This story provides an interesting contrast when read in light of Yahweh's determination in 2 Kgs 23.27 to throw Judah and Israel out of his sight. No matter how he tries, Jonah cannot get out of Yahweh's sight. After a large fish swallows him up, he cries out at the time of his distress and Yahweh hears him. This lament in 2.2-10 captures the significance of this story when it is read intertextually with Ezekiel. In both stories Yahweh interacts with a prophet in a foreign land. And, more significantly, the confidence is expressed that the prophet will again see Yahweh in the temple. When Yahweh hears Jonah (2.3 [Eng. 2.2]), Jonah exclaims:

---

6.   The distance between Jeremiah and Yahweh is created by Yahweh's refusal to listen to Jeremiah's intercession and his less than comforting responses to Jeremiah's complaints. In the end, Jeremiah appears as a lonely figure with Yahweh's words taken to the land of Egypt from which there will be no return to the land.

'Surely, I will again look at your holy temple'. The difference between the story of Jonah and Ezekiel, however, is that Yahweh hears Jonah's prayer *in the temple* (2.7). Ezekiel, on the other hand, will see Yahweh leave the temple. Both Jonah and Ezekiel embody the theme that even in a foreign land Yahweh sees and can be seen. However, seeing and being seen by Yahweh is outrageous and almost surreal. Under more normal situations this encounter with Yahweh takes place in his 'house'; not in a foreign land.

The extraordinary situation of the Jonah story is underscored by Yahweh's instruction to him, 'proclaim' (קְרָא) to Nineveh 'the proclamation' (הַקְּרִיאָה, 3.2). The proclamation is, '40 days more and Nineveh will be overthrown' (3.4). The people and the king believe in a god (not Yahweh) and declare a fast. It is not clear what Jonah is doing when he 'proclaims' (קְרָא) 'the proclamation' (הַקְּרִיאָה). This is the only place in the Hebrew Bible that the word הַקְּרִיאָה is used. Is he reading out (קְרָא) the proclamation (הַקְּרִיאָה)? Whatever he is doing, it is interesting that nowhere in the story does it say that Jonah is prophesying (נִבָּא) in Nineveh and nowhere does he make a proclamation in the name of Yahweh. It is also interesting to point out that the god the people of Nineveh turn to is not identified as Yahweh (3.5).

While the message of the prophetic 'books' such as Amos and Jeremiah is that Israel and Judah have turned away from Yahweh by turning to the gods of the nations who cannot save, the book of Jonah suggests that Yahweh is a powerful deity even in a foreign land. The last chapter of the story of Jonah demonstrates that Yahweh can change his mind about the calamity that he proposes. This story stands in contrast with the message of other prophetic 'books' that Yahweh is wreaking irrevocable destruction on Israel and Judah.

2. *Ezekiel and the* מַרְאוּת *of God*

The thing that happened to Ezekiel was that he had 'visions' (מַרְאוֹת) of God while he was in the foreign city of Babylon among the exiles (1.1). This happened in the fifth year of the exile of Jehoiachin. Ezekiel differs from Jonah in that these visions, like the whole of Ezekiel, are concerned with the fate of Jerusalem and its temple. Unlike Jonah, Ezekiel is not concerned with the destiny of a foreign people.

It is important to point out that the superscription identifies Ezekiel as an unconventional prophet. He was 'the priest', the son of Buzi. Therefore, as readers we are alerted to the more eccentric portrayal of Ezekiel and his activities. However, the emphasis in Ezekiel is not on 'the words' of Ezekiel as it is with the other unorthodox prophets Amos and Jeremiah. Ezekiel has 'מראות of God'. This phrase signals to the reader the unusual way 'the word of Yahweh' will come to Ezekiel.

These 'מראות of God' are to be distinguished from 'the חזון of a prophet', such as the חזון of Isaiah. While חזון is a more normative depiction of the prophetic reception of 'the word of Yahweh', as I will argue in the next chapter, a few observations about the difference between מראות and חזון will be helpful. Significantly, חזון never occurs in the plural, חזונים. For example, even though the חזון of Isaiah is dated over a long period of time as something he saw in the days of 'Uzziah, Jotham, Ahaz, and Hezekiah, kings of Judah', the whole of the scroll in the superscription is identified in the singular as a חזון. Alternatively, the plural מראות of God that Ezekiel saw on three occasions are all dated to a very specific point in time (1.1-3; 8.1; 40.1).

While חזון may involve seeing God, the emphasis is not on a plurality of sightings but on an activity of reception of 'the word of Yahweh'. Furthermore, as I have already alluded to above, a חזון is also something that is written down. While it has become conventional in English to translate both חזון and מראה as 'vision', it is important to understand that as encoded information for the reader of prophetic books, the words mean different things. I maintain, as I argued above in my discussion of 1 Samuel 3, that a חזון is a prophetic activity for the reception of 'the word of Yahweh' by a prophet in the temple. To receive a חזון may involve a מראה of God but the two cannot be equated as encoding the same information.

As a prophetic book, then, Ezekiel is not about a חזון of the prophet, but about visions (מראות) of Yahweh had by Ezekiel in the foreign city of Babylon while he was among the exiles. Ezekiel did not have a חזון in the temple in Jerusalem. In fact, the entire point of the 'book' of Ezekiel when read as a narrative sequence of events is that he could not have a חזון. Yahweh leaves the temple, and by the end of the book plans are being drawn up for its reconstruction and for Yahweh's return to his house in Jerusalem.

Ezekiel, then, when read as a continuation of Jeremiah in the compilation of prophetic scrolls reinforces the recurring theme in the book of Jeremiah about the prophets in Jerusalem in the last days of the kings of Judah as speaking a 'lying vision' (חזון שקר). Yahweh is not in the temple. Therefore, prophets are unable to receive a חזון from Yahweh. They can only have a חזון arising from their own heart (imagination).

Yahweh abandoned the temple in Jerusalem just as he had abandoned Shiloh (Jer. 7.12; 26.9). In fact, Yahweh is in Babylon with the exiles, and Ezekiel has מראות of him there.

As critics have noted, 'the מראות of God' appear at key places through-out the 'book' of Ezekiel and suggest a structure for the 'book' as a whole. Even if we think of Ezekiel as a collage of compiled materials, the book fits the sense of order and organization with which contemporary readers are more familiar. I want to look in more detail at these three sections of the book where 'the מראות of God' occur (Ezek. 1.1–3.15; 8.1–11.25; 40.1–48.35). However, I want to begin my discussion with 8.1–11.25, and then look at 40.1–48.35 before returning to 1.1–3.15.

a. Ezekiel 8.1–11.25
These מראות of God are precisely dated to the sixth year, in the sixth day of the fifth month of the exile, that is, one year later than the original מראות of God. Ezekiel is sitting in his house with the elders before him (8.1). That Yahweh appears in Ezekiel's house makes this appearance extraordinary. Ezekiel will be taken in 'visions' of God from his own dwelling to Yahweh's house in Jerusalem where he can see why Yahweh is abandoning it. He is brought to a very specific place in Yahweh's house:

> ...and the spirit lifted me up between the land and heaven, and brought me
> in מראות of God, to the entrance of the gate of the inner court facing
> toward the north, where the seat of the image of jealousy, which provokes
> jealously. And there was the glory of the God of Israel, like the מראה which
> I saw in the valley. (8.3b-4)

Ezekiel is shown all the abominations that are taking place in the temple. Yahweh even reports to Ezekiel what all the elders are saying, 'Yahweh does not see us, Yahweh has forsaken the land' (8.12). Here we are re-minded of Jonah. But there is a contrast. Yahweh saw Jonah in a foreign land in distress and heard his voice in the temple. Here Yahweh is in a foreign land seeing what is happening in his house in Jerusalem, a place the elders thought he had abandoned.

Ezekiel also sees Yahweh making preparations to destroy all those who had condoned the abominations being practised in the temple of Yahweh (9.1–10.7). Eventually he sees Yahweh leave the temple:

> And the glory of Yahweh went out from the threshold of the house and
> stood on the cherubim. And the cherubim lifted up their wings and rose
> from the land before my eyes when they went out and the wheels were by

their side. And they stood at the entrance of the east gate of the house of
Yahweh. And the glory of the God of Israel was on top of them. (10.18-19)

Ezekiel also sees Yahweh depart from the city:

And the cherubim lifted up their wings and the wheels by their side and
the glory of God was on top of them. And the glory of Yahweh went up
from the middle of the city and he stood on the mountain east of the city.
(11.22-23)

At this point a spirit lifts up Ezekiel and brings him by a מראה to the
exiles in Chaldea. The מראה, then, leaves Ezekiel and he tells all the
exiles what Yahweh had shown him (11.24b-25).

It is significant that, while Ezekiel is seeing all these things in the
temple in Jerusalem, he is ordered to prophesy against the men of the city
who devised iniquity. Yahweh says, ' Therefore prophesy (הנבא) against
them, prophesy, son of man' (11.4). Ezekiel also says that 'it came about
when I prophesied (כנבא) that Pelatiah, the son of Benaiah died' (11.13a).
At that point, like Jeremiah and Amos before him, Ezekiel makes an intercession, 'And I fell down on my face and I cried out with a loud voice, and
I said, "Alas, my lord Yahweh, are you making a full end to the remnant
of Israel?"' (11.13b). Yahweh's response is that, in time, he will bring the
exiles home (11.14-21).

What does it mean for Ezekiel to prophesy (נבא) in this situation? I
want to return to this a little later. But it is important to point out here that
just as Jeremiah came with 'the words' of Yahweh to the temple to prophesy (נבא) against the city (see, e.g., Jer. 26), so Ezekiel is brought to the
temple to prophesy (נבא) against the city (11.5-12). There is a difference,
however. Jeremiah goes to the temple and interacts with individuals who
are there—prophets and priests such as Pashhur and Hananiah. Ezekiel is
brought by Yahweh in 'visions' to the temple. Even though we hear that a
certain Pelatiah died while Ezekiel was prophesying, Ezekiel has no
interaction with this individual or any others. He is presented as viewing
this world rather than participating in it. This raises the question: How is
Ezekiel prophesying in these 'visions of God'?

b. *Ezekiel 40.1–48.35*
These 'מראות of God' come 19 years later in the twenty-fifth year of the
exile. Again they are dated precisely to the beginning of the year on the
tenth day of the month. A new event is also used here to date the 'visions'.
They are dated in the fourteenth year after the city was struck down (Ezek.
40.1). This reference to the city's end is reported earlier in the book:

And it happened in the twelfth year of our exile in the tenth month, on the fifth day of the month, someone came to me from Jerusalem saying, 'the city has been struck down'. (33.21)

It is important to note that in these last 'visions of God' there is no mention of Ezekiel prophesying. Ezekiel says that

the hand of Yahweh was upon me and he brought me there. In מראות of God he brought me to the land of Israel. And he set me down on a very high mountain. And at the south there was on it [something] like the structure of a city. And he brought me there. And there was a man standing at the gate whose appearance was like the appearance of bronze. In his hand there was a linen cord and a measuring line. And the man spoke to me, 'Son of man, see with your eyes and hear with your ears and put in your mind (לבך) everything I am showing you because you were brought here in order to show you. Declare everything which you see to the house of Israel. (40.2-4)

Ezekiel is shown something on this high mountain that seems to resemble a model of a city and he is to put in his mind everything he is shown (40.2-4). What he is shown in the following chapters is a very complex set of measurements for the building of the temple along with directions on how it should function and how to care for it. How he will keep all this in his heart (mind) is something that I want to take up a little later.

In the midst of being shown these precise measurements, he is brought in another מראה to the east gate of this 'model' city. Ezekiel says:

Now the glory of the God of Israel was coming from the way of the east. Its sound was like the sound of mighty waters and the land shone from its glory. And the מראה was like the מראה that I saw, like the vision I saw [sic], when I came to destroy the city. And מראות like the מראה that I saw by the river Chebar and I fell on my face. And the glory of Yahweh entered the house by the way of the gate facing by way of the east. And a spirit lifted me up and brought me to the inner court, and behold the glory of Yahweh filled the house. (43.2-5)

What the reader sees in the previous 'מראות of God' (8.1–11.25) is Yahweh leaving the temple in Jerusalem. Such a departure makes it impossible for there to be a true חזון in the extraordinary days of Jeremiah and Ezekiel when Yahweh was abandoning the temple at the same time he was emptying the land of its inhabitants. In the second set of 'מראות of God' the reader sees a kind of 'blueprint' (צורה) for the restoration of the temple, the city and the surrounding land. The end of the book of Ezekiel *envisions* restoration. One can look forward to the time when Yahweh will again dwell in his house, when prophesying can return to normal. Yahweh is coming home along with the exiles. The return of the exiles is, of course, a major theme in the חזון of Isaiah that follows Ezekiel in the prophetic compositional order of books I am reading.

Ezekiel overhears Yahweh's voice telling him that he intends now to reside in this place forever:

> And I heard someone speaking to me from the house and a man was stand-ing beside me. He said to me, 'Son of man [this] is the place of my throne and the place of the soles of my feet where I will reside in the midst of the sons of Israel forever. The house of Israel will not again defile my holy name—they and their kings by their whoring and by the corpses of their kings when they die… Now let them send far away from me their idola-try and the corpses of their kings, and I will reside in their midst forever. (43.6-9)

Ezekiel is then given the task to make these plans of restoration known to 'the house of Israel'. Notice that Ezekiel is not to prophesy (נבא) these plans but to write them down as the *torah* of the house (temple). Ezekiel is depicted as returning from his extraordinary role as a prophet to his normal role as 'the priest' who was among the exiles by the river Chebar (1.1). Ezekiel is like Moses who receives new *torah* about the house in which Yahweh will dwell forever:

> You, son of man, declare to the house of Israel the house [that is, the temple]. May they be ashamed of their iniquities and let them measure the proportion(s). And when they are ashamed of everything that they have done, make known to them the plan of the house, its arrangement, its exits and its entrances and its entire plan—all its statutes, all its plan and all its teachings. *Write* (וכתב) before their eyes so that they will keep its entire plan and all its statutes and they will do them. This is the *torah* of the house. On the top of the mountain its borders all around surround the holy of holies. Behold this is the *torah* of the temple. (43.10-12)

Additional instructions are given about temple practice and, like Joshua, Ezekiel is given instructions about parceling out the land (chs. 45–48).

These strategically placed 'מראות of God' in the book of Ezekiel guide the reader through a sequence of narrative events. The reader is moved from the extraordinary times of Yahweh's abandonment of the temple to the issuance in writing of a new *torah* for temple construction and the restoration of the land. Ezekiel also returns from his extraordinary role as a prophet to his role as a priest 'writing' *torah*. I want now to turn to the first set of 'מראות of God' in Ezekiel 1–3 because those 'visions' depict Ezekiel in his extraordinary role as a prophet.

3. *Ezekiel and Prophesying*

After the lengthy and complex description of Yahweh's appearance in 'מראות of God' in 1.4-28, Yahweh informs Ezekiel that he is sending him to a rebellious house (2.1-7). He tells Ezekiel not to be afraid, and there are components here of language to address a warrior. But that language has moved more into the background so that Ezekiel's role will not be that of a warrior-prophet.

The instructions to Ezekiel in 2.8–3.3 provide the reader with a depiction of the role of Ezekiel that distinguishes it from the role of Jeremiah:

> And you, son of man, hear what I am speaking to you. Do not be rebellious like the rebellious house. Open your mouth and eat what I am giving to you. I looked and there a hand was stretched out to me, and there was in it a scroll (מגלת־ספר). And he spread it before me and it was written on the front and on the back, and written on it was lamentations, moaning and woe. And he said to me, 'Son of man, eat what you find, eat this scroll and go speak to the house of Israel'. And I opened my mouth and he fed me this scroll. And he said to me, 'Son of man, your belly will consume [it] and you will satisfy your stomach with this scroll which I am giving to you. And I ate it and it was in my mouth like honey for sweetness.

This situation in which Ezekiel eats the scroll containing written words can be contrasted with a similar situation in Jeremiah. In order to highlight the contrast, I will recall in summary form the relevant features of Jeremiah that have already been discussed in the last chapter. In Jer. 1.9, Yahweh reaches out and touches the mouth of Jeremiah and says, 'I have put my words in your mouth'. We are informed by Jeremiah later in the book that he ate Yahweh's words (15.16). This motif of Jeremiah eating words of Yahweh occurs in that part of the Jeremianic collage where the picture emerges of Jeremiah assuming his task as a warrior-prophet. He has stopped interceding with Yahweh on Judah's behalf, laments the day of his birth, and begins to speak the bellicose words of Yahweh. At this point in the book Jeremiah says:

> Your words were found, and I ate them.
>> And your words became to me a joy,
>> and the pleasure of my heart,
> because I am called by your name,
>> Yahweh, the God of hosts. (15.16)

As I indicated above, in Yahweh's response to Jeremiah, he reappoints Jeremiah to his role as a warrior-prophet (15.19-21). From this point on, Jeremiah, who has eaten Yahweh's words, will be like Yahweh's mouth.

'If you bring forth [or cause to go out] (תוֹצִיא) what is precious rather than worthless, you will be like my mouth' (15.19). As Yahweh's mouth, Jeremiah takes on the identity of Yahweh and is called by his name.

I have argued above that for Jeremiah to speak as Yahweh's mouth involved writing down what Yahweh had spoken to him so that he could prophesy by reading Yahweh's words. To serve as Yahweh's mouth required the precision of reading what was written; not extemporaneous outbursts of speech. Indeed, the entire last section of Jeremiah has to do with the materiality of Yahweh's words written down in סְפָרִים. These סְפָרִים were used when Jeremiah prophesied.

On two occasions Yahweh orders Jeremiah to write a scroll (מְגִלַּת־סֵפֶר) by dictating to the scribe Baruch the words Yahweh put in his mouth (36.2, 28). He never asks Jeremiah to eat a scroll. Only the words are ingested. When words come from the mouth of Jeremiah in dictation (36.6, 32) and reading, he has become like Yahweh's mouth (15.19).

Ezekiel, on the other hand, is asked to consume a scroll on which words are already written (2.9-10). Although he is never told to write a scroll containing the words of Yahweh spoken to him, he does engage in writing. He is instructed to write down, as a kind of record, the name of the day when the king of Babylon laid siege to Jerusalem (24.2) and to write on sticks as a symbolic act of reunification of Judah and Joseph (37.16). Toward the end of the book he is asked, as a priest, to write the plan (תוֹרָה) or *torah* of the temple that he was shown. Nowhere, however, is Ezekiel asked to write down the words of Yahweh or to be his mouth. Ezekiel is not depicted as prophesying the written words of a מְגִלַּת־סֵפֶר in the same way as Jeremiah.

The strange situation in Ezekiel appears to be that when his mouth is opened to speak for Yahweh, the words already emerge as written words. To use a contemporary analogy, Ezekiel appears like a ventriloquist's doll with the exception that Yahweh, the ventriloquist, does not need to throw his voice. The words are already written and in the stomach like the pre-recorded words of a doll that speaks when the string is pulled. Ezekiel the priest who prophesies has ingested the scroll Yahweh offered to him and is presented as a passive prophet. This passivity distinguishes him from the warrior-prophet, Jeremiah, who, as the mouth of Yahweh, more actively participates in reading and dictating scrolls and other סְפָרִים.

In order to give additional clarity to this portrayal of Ezekiel as a passive prophet, I want to review in more detail the text following Ezekiel's ingestion of the scroll in 3.4-27. Yahweh says to Ezekiel, 'Go to the house of Israel and you will speak my words to them' (3.4). These words of action are deceptive. By the end of the chapter the reader is made aware of Ezekiel's restriction in both movement and speech. Ezekiel is going nowhere: 'And you, son of man, they have placed cords on you and I will bind you with them and you will not go out in their midst' (3.25). Interestingly, the word for cords (עבותים) is also used for the cords or chains on a priest's breastplate (Exod. 28.14, 22; 39.15). Is Ezekiel being bound up with the decorative chains that were placed on him as a priest? If that is the case, the subject confusion between 'they have placed' and 'I will bind' becomes clear. Yahweh will bind Ezekiel with priestly chains that were placed on him when he became a priest. Ezekiel is bound and not able to go out into the midst of the people. When he goes, he does not initiate the action. He is brought in 'visions of God' to the temple in Jerusalem (8.1-4; 40.1-4).

Ezekiel is not only immobile, he has also been made speechless: 'Your tongue I will cause to cling to your palate, and you will be speechless, and you will not be able to rebuke them because they are a house of rebellion' (3.26). Ezekiel, who is told to go and to speak in 3.4, is bound and unable to speak in 3.25-26. Furthermore, he will be told repeatedly throughout chs. 4–39 to prophesy (נבא).

How will Ezekiel, bound and with his tongue clinging to his palate, go, speak and prophesy? The final verse in this chapter (3.27) begins to provide some clarity:

When I speak you (ובדברי אותך), I will open your mouth and you will say to them, 'Thus the lord Yahweh has said, "The one who hears let him hear, and the one who ceases [to hear], let him cease [hearing]".'

The phrase ובדברי אותך is not particularly clear. Normally, the object of the verb דבר is 'words' (דברים) or 'song' (שיר), or some other noun that has to do with speaking. One does not expect a person or a personal pronoun to be the object of the verb. The matter is resolved in some translations by reading (אות) as the preposition (את) meaning 'with'. However, the consonantal spelling with the vowel letter ו, makes such a translation more difficult. I think that the intention of the text is to be found in its literal translation, 'When I speak "you" [Ezekiel], I will open your mouth'. What this means will achieve clarity if we evoke an image growing out of the literary world of prophetic books.

That image will become apparent if we go back to the beginning of ch. 3 and follow what is said in 3.5 after the instruction to Ezekiel to 'go' and 'speak'. Yahweh says that Ezekiel is to go and speak Yahweh's words 'because not to a people of unintelligible speech and difficult language are you being sent (שלוח) but to the house of Israel'. The first thing to notice here is the passive participle form. Ezekiel is 'being sent'. The second thing to observe is that he is not being sent to a people with a foreign language but to the house of Israel. If we read these words in light of our discussion of Jeremiah an interesting image begins to emerge.[7] Ezekiel, the bound and speechless prophet sent to the house of Israel, is sent as a ספר with the words of Yahweh already written within him. Just as Jeremiah had sent ספרים as a way of prophesying in the court of the temple and in Babylon to the exiles, so Yahweh is sending Ezekiel as a ספר for the purposes of prophesying. Ezekiel is an unorthodox prophet in whom the scroll of Yahweh's words has been internalized.[8] The bound and speechless Ezekiel will be opened like a scroll when Yahweh opens his mouth. The very cumbersome phrase, 'When I speak you, I will open your mouth', is an image that depicts the passive Ezekiel. He is not depicted as writing and sending scrolls as did the active Jeremiah. Ezekiel himself is a scroll being sent to the house of Israel whom Yahweh reads by opening his mouth so that the written words within can be heard even by the rebellious house who refuses to hear. Indeed, this notion of internalizing the words of Yahweh in the heart, on the scroll within, is evident from 3.10. Yahweh says to Ezekiel, 'Son of man, all the words which I speak, receive in your heart and hear with your ears'.

It is as a מגלת־ספר that Ezekiel can be understood as prophesying in Jerusalem where he was taken by Yahweh. In the 'visions of God' in 8.1–11.25, Ezekiel says that while he was sitting in his house 'the hand of the lord Yahweh fell upon me there' (8.1). Furthermore, a figure that looked like a human being stretched out a hand, lifting him by the hair on his head, and bringing him in visions to Jerusalem. Ezekiel is taken by the hand to Jerusalem just as the ספרים Jeremiah sent were taken in the hand by messengers to foreign countries and to the exiles in Jerusalem. Ezekiel can prophesy in Jerusalem (11.4, 13) when Yahweh opens his mouth and the written words within Ezekiel, the scroll, are prophesied even to those who refuse to hear.

---

7.   A connection with Jonah is also suggested in the following verse (3.6). If Yahweh sent him to a people whose words he could not understand, 'they would listen to you'. Of course, it is just such a people of foreign tongue, the people of Nineveh, to whom Jonah spoke and who listened to him.

8.   The image here of the internalization of Yahweh's words reminds me of the time that Jeremiah envisioned when the *torah* would be within the people and written on their hearts (Jer. 31.31-34).

In many ways my reading of Ezekiel has affinities with Ellen Davis's reading. She understands that in Ezekiel's muteness, prophecy has moved from a basic oral to a written medium. She recognizes that 'from the eighth century, writing was a feature of prophecy, not only for transmission and publication at scribal hands...but also apparently as a means of illustration and emphasis within the original act of pronouncement...'[9] She goes on to say, however, that the difference between the earlier prophets and Ezekiel is

> that Ezekiel was a fundamentally literate mind, i.e., his patterns of thought and expression were shaped by habits of reading and writing. Therefore it was through him that Israelite prophecy for the first time received its *primary* impress from the new conditions and opportunities for communication created by writing.[10]

Later in her presentation she draws a further distinction between Ezekiel and the other prophets:

> ...if Ezekiel is, like earlier prophets, a public figure, nevertheless he has taken a step back from direct confrontation with an audience as the essential dynamic of prophetic communication. *He formulates his speech in such a way as to facilitate a kind of engagement whose essential medium is not the person of the prophet but the text.*[11]

My main difference with Ellen Davis is that I see Ezekiel, as a character in the book, becoming the text. I do not agree that the prophetic books themselves present us with the data to reconstruct what was happening to prophets like Isaiah, Jeremiah or Ezekiel as actual prophets. These characters themselves are the products of the scribal creations in which they appear as characters. The 'scrolls' that depict them do not provide us with material to reconstruct an actual development of prophecy in ancient Israel.

To identify Ezekiel as a prophet who has internalized the scroll helps explain the sustained first person narration of the book. The scroll ingested by Ezekiel was not allowed to become lost, but the written words within have come spilling out on the pages encountered by the reader. Over and over again in the book the phrase 'the word of Yahweh came *to me*' occurs.[12] The reception of the word is a very private and personalized

---

9. Davis, *Swallowing the Scroll*, p. 38.
10. Davis, *Swallowing the Scroll*, p. 39.
11. Davis, *Swallowing the Scroll*, p. 127 (my emphasis).
12. It occurs in 6.1; 7.1; 12.1, 17; 13.1; 14.1, 12; 15.1; 16.1; 17.1, 11; 18.1; 20.2; 21.6, 12, 21; 22.1, 17, 23; 23.1; 24.1, 20; 25.1; 27.1; 28.1, 11; 29.17; 30.1, 20; 31.1; 32.1, 17; 33.1, 23; 34.1; 35.1; 36.16; 37.15; 38.1.

affair in Ezekiel. The 'word of Yahweh' does not come to Ezekiel in the external visual imagery of Amos and Jeremiah, nor is it received as a חזון in the temple.

The 'word of the Yahweh' stops coming to Ezekiel after ch. 40 when Ezekiel again returns to the role of priest by writing down the '*torah* of the temple'. In this resumed role, writing becomes a very public affair. Yahweh says that when they are ashamed of all that they have done, Ezekiel should make known to them the plan of the temple and 'write [it] down before their eyes (וכתב לעיניהם) that they may keep the plan' (43.11). In this section of the book we have moved from the unorthodox Ezekiel internalizing and embodying the prophetic scroll to Ezekiel the priest writing down the '*torah* of the house' (43.12).

To think of Ezekiel as a scroll recalls the observation of Davis (cited above) that Ezekiel has withdrawn from public interaction with an audience. He is not portrayed as a figure moving around in the literary world he occupies but as an object to be moved and pointed in a particular direction. The reference to his being bound reinforces the picture of Ezekiel as a stationary object. When he is instructed to prophesy, he is oriented to a position and words come out of his mouth as words emerge from an opened scroll. Interestingly, when he is ordered to prophesy he is not told to go anywhere. Repeatedly he is simply told, 'set your face (שים פניך)' toward a person place or thing 'and prophesy against (ונבאת על) it'.[13] He is to set his face toward the siege of Jerusalem (4.7), the mountains of Israel (6.2), the daughters of your people (13.17), the south, against the forest land of the Negeb (21.2), Jerusalem, against the sanctuaries and the land of Israel (21.7), the Ammonites (25.2), Sidon (28.21), Pharaoh, king of Egypt (29.2) and Gog (38.2). Other times he is simply commanded, 'prophesy' (11.4; 13.2; 21.14, 19, 33; 30.1; 34.2; 36.1, 3, 6; 37.4, 7, 9, 12; 38.14; 39.1).

4. *Ezekiel and False Vision*

The theme of true and false prophecy is a motif in Ezekiel as it was in Jeremiah. However, unlike Jeremiah, who dictates Yahweh's words unto written scrolls, a scroll on which words are already written is given to Ezekiel to consume so that the written word is inscribed within him. Ezekiel does not write a מגלת־ספר to ensure authenticity and as the basis of

---

13. In 4.7 the phrase is תכין פניך.

prophesying through reading. The authenticity of Yahweh's words is ensured in another way so that they do not become confused with the false
vision (חזון) of the prophets. Yahweh's words are read out directly when
Ezekiel's mouth is opened. There can be no chance of deception. In order
to see this in Ezekiel, it will be important to look at those passages in
Ezekiel concerning the חזון of the prophets.

Reference to חזון occurs for the first time in Ezek. 7.13. In this passage
חזון is not used of any particular prophet. Rather, it appears to refer generally to the future end, the disaster that is coming. The חזון in this passage
equates with the course of events Yahweh has determined for the future,
that is, as something that is already certain. Yahweh has set the future in
action by the חזון, and 'it will not return'. (I will discuss this feature of a
חזון in the next chapter on Isaiah and the prophets of vision.)

While חזון is used in this general way in Ezekiel to speak about the
future, the book of Ezekiel is never identified as a חזון. In fact, later on in
the chapter (7.26), the point is made that חזון is not available from the
prophet. The picture depicted here is of an extraordinary time when nothing is proceeding normally:

> Disaster upon disaster will come,
>   and there will be rumour after rumour.
> They will seek a vision from a prophet,
>   *torah* from a priest,
>   and counsel from an elder.
> The king will mourn,
>   the prince will be clothed in devastation,
>   and the hands of the people of the land will tremble.
> According to their way I will deal with them,
>   and with their own judgments I will judge them.
> And they will know that I am Yahweh. (7.26-27)

The motif of 'false vision' (חזון שקר) *à la* Jeremiah is developed in
12.21–13.23. This passage is significant because it further permits insight
into why the scroll has become internalized in Ezekiel and into the meaning of the odd phrase 'when I speak you, I will open your mouth'. The
following proverb is identified as current in the community portrayed in
Ezekiel's time: 'The days will be prolonged, and all vision has perished'
(12.22). It is interesting to read this proverb in conjunction with what the
people, whom Ezekiel saw in 'visions of God' in the temple in Jerusalem,
said: 'Yahweh does not see us; Yahweh has forsaken the land' (8.13).
There can be no vision if Yahweh is not in the temple to give it. What
the people are saying here also confirms the notion that there can be no

'vision' in the time of Ezekiel; Yahweh is not in the temple because he has forsaken the land.

Yahweh, however, says that he will put an end to this proverb and that Ezekiel is to tell the house of Israel the following, which I have translated quite literally:

> The days are near and the thing of every vision because there will not again be any lying vision (חזון שקר) and flattering divination in the house of Israel. Because I (Yahweh) will speak the word [or thing] that I will speak, and it will be done. It will not be postponed again. Because in your days, O rebellious house, I will speak a word [or thing] and I will do it, a saying of the lord Yahweh. (12.23b-25)

The claim being made here is that there will not again be a lying vision (חזון). Vision like that referred to earlier in 7.13 is about to eventuate.

The other notion that is developed here is contained in the phrase 'I will speak the word that I will speak' (אדבר את אשר אדבר דבר). The situation is different in the time of Ezekiel than it was for Jeremiah. Jeremiah was Yahweh's mouth and he spoke for Yahweh when he read what was written in the books he dictated. Ezekiel is not the mouth of Yahweh. Rather, as a prophet, speechless and bound, he will be the means by which Yahweh speaks; Yahweh opens Ezekiel's mouth and speaks through him. There will be no more 'false vision' emerging out of the prophet's own heart (imagination), because Yahweh's written words, already swallowed, are inside Ezekiel (3.10). This contrast between Ezekiel, the scroll, and the prophets who prophesy 'false vision' will become more obvious in the next chapter when Ezekiel is ordered to prophesy against the prophets.

The חזון, then, is spoken by Yahweh himself by opening the mouth of Ezekiel. This is not like the חזון of Isaiah or Habakkuk, which is written down. The חזון comes immediately to expression from Yahweh himself when the mouth of Ezekiel, the scroll, is opened.

In 12.27-28, Yahweh reports what the people of Israel have been saying:

> Son of man, now the house of Israel is saying, the vision that he sees is for many days [ahead] and for distant times he prophesies. Therefore, say to them, 'Thus the lord Yahweh has said, all my words—a thing (דבר) which I speak—will not be postponed again, and it will be done', a saying of the lord Yahweh.

While vision is understood as something that one waits for, the point of this passage is that vision will not be delayed—as something to wait for—but is imminent.

In 13.1-23, Ezekiel is ordered to prophesy against the prophets of Israel who are prophesying out of their own heart (imagination) (13.2, 17). They could therefore give only 'lying vision' (13.7). In these extraordinary times Yahweh's words either come in visual imagery (to Jeremiah, who was one of the priests from Anathoth) or are internalized (in Ezekiel, the priest among the exiles). Yahweh speaks the חזון directly when 'he speaks Ezekiel by opening his mouth'. The thing (דבר) he speaks will not be delayed; it is about to happen.

5. Compiling Ezekiel

As the superscription suggests, the organization and arrangement of the material in Ezekiel is less difficult for the contemporary reader to understand than the organization and arrangement of the material in Jeremiah. The character of the compilation of materials in Ezekiel is indicated by the superscription beginning with ויהי, which suggests that what follows is a narrative sequence of events. As Davis has indicated,[14] the book has normally been seen as falling into three units: chs. 1–24, pronouncements of doom on the house of Israel; chs. 25–32, pronouncements of doom against the nations and chs. 33–48, promises about Israel's restoration. I agree with this general understanding of the structure, but I would refine it a bit more: chs. 1–7, in which Ezekiel internalizes the scroll and begins to prophesy; chs. 8–11, in which Ezekiel prophesies in Jerusalem; chs. 12–24, in which Ezekiel prophesies doom to the house of Israel; chs. 25–32, in which Ezekiel prophesies against the nations; chs. 33–39, in which Ezekiel prophesies restoration; and chs. 40–48, in which Ezekiel the priest writes down the '*torah* of the temple'.

Each of these divisions is accompanied by the description of a particular event or events. Chapters 1–7 are introduced by the visions of God that come to Ezekiel in exile by the river Chebar (chs. 1–3); chs. 8–11 by the visions of God that come to Ezekiel in his house (8.1-4); chs. 12–24 by the spirit's return of Ezekiel to the exiles in Chaldea (11.22-25); chs. 25–32 by the announcement that the king of Babylon has laid siege to the city (24.1-3) and the admonition that Ezekiel is not to mourn the death of his wife (24.19-24); chs. 33–39 by the announcement that the city has fallen (33.21-22); and chs. 40–48 by 'visions of God' that transport him to a high mountain in Israel.

---

14. Davis, *Swallowing the Scroll*, p. 11.

I want to look in a bit more detail at one of these events associated with the organization of the book. In 33.22-24 it is reported that in the twelfth year of exile a fugitive escaped from Jerusalem and came to report 'the city has fallen'. It is at this point that Ezekiel's mouth was opened and he could speak. When the city of Jerusalem was defeated, it was no longer necessary for Ezekiel to remain speechless. What Yahweh had made Ezekiel prophesy had come about. It is at this very point that it will become evident to the people that 'the priest' Ezekiel has been a prophet in their midst.

6. *Summary and Conclusion*

The books of Jonah and Ezekiel are about prophets in a foreign land. God sees Jonah in Nineveh, and Ezekiel sees God in Babylon. Although Jonah laments that he may never see God again in the temple, Yahweh hears his prayer in the temple. However, Ezekiel sees Yahweh leave the temple and only sees plans of temple restoration and Yahweh's future return. Jonah sees a foreign people, the people of Nineveh, listen to Yahweh's 'proclamation', proclaim a fast and don sackcloth. An alien people turning to Yahweh, a foreign deity, is in contrast with the people of Israel who turned away from Yahweh to the gods of the nations.

The story in Ezekiel has its setting in a different time than that of Jonah. Ezekiel, like Jeremiah, is living in an extraordinary time. It is a time when Yahweh has left the temple so that there can be no חָזוֹן. In such a situation the חָזוֹן of a prophet can only be a lie. Prophets such as Ezekiel can only receive the דָּבָר of Yahweh in extraordinary ways. Jeremiah, the prophet who came from the priests in Anathoth, like Amos, who came from the shepherds in Tekoa, received his words in visual imagery. Yahweh placed his words in Jeremiah's mouth so that when Jeremiah consumed them, he could speak as the mouth of Yahweh. For Jeremiah, the writing down of these words in סְפָרִים became the basis of his prophesying. The reception of the 'word' of Yahweh is different in Ezekiel. The scroll containing the written words of Yahweh is consumed and internalized by Ezekiel so that there is a more intimate and controlled connection between Yahweh and Ezekiel's mouth. Ezekiel has been rendered mute and can only speak when Yahweh opens his mouth as if it were a scroll. Yahweh makes Ezekiel speak. As Yahweh states in the 'book' of Ezekiel, 'When I speak you, I will open your mouth' (3.27).

In Ezekiel, the priest *cum* prophet has become a written text, a מְגִלַּת־
סֵפֶר. For that reason the reader encounters the scroll of Ezekiel in sustained first person narration. This first person narration is evident from the very beginning of the scroll and is used even in the superscription (1.1). Ezekiel is the only prophetic 'book' to begin in this way.

How should the reader understand this portrayal of Ezekiel as a scroll? What was the author encoding for the Model Reader in this image? Why is Ezekiel, the unorthodox prophet, a priest? And why is he not just a priest, but '*the* priest'? The answers to such questions are not immediately clear to a contemporary real reader. Perhaps they never will be. The only way to answer these questions is to read the text of Ezekiel and other texts from the Bible and the ancient Near East intertextually. To use Eco's somewhat confusing terminology, perhaps this closed text will always remain open to aberrant decoding. To read in such a way as to pay attention to the limits of interpretation inscribed in the text does not mean that the reader will arrive at a determinate meaning. Not only will we not know fully how to read what we see, but we will also not know fully what we are failing to see when we read.

I have argued that the visions of Ezekiel demarcate significant divisions in the book. While in the first set of visions (1.1–3.15) Ezekiel becomes a scroll so that he can prophesy to the house of Israel, the last set of visions (40.1–48.35) presents Ezekiel again as 'the priest' writing the *torah* of the temple. Here the writing is not internalized as for the prophetic Ezekiel, but is externalized and written by the priestly Ezekiel before the eyes of the people (43.11).

The book ends with Ezekiel seeing the pattern or plan for the restoration of the temple, the city and the land of Israel. As such, it provides a transition to the return of the exiles depicted in the חָזוֹן of Isaiah. Isaiah, set in the days in the days of Jotham, Uzziah, Ahaz and Hezekiah, was not an unorthodox prophet. Isaiah's חָזוֹן was in the temple: 'I saw my lord sitting on a throne, high and lifted up, and his train filled the temple' (Isa. 6.1). Isaiah did not receive 'words' in visual imagery as did Jeremiah, nor did he have מַרְאוֹת of God as did Ezekiel. His access to the divine was by more orthodox means. I now want to look at Isaiah and the other prophets of חָזוֹן.

Chapter 7

THE 'VISION' OF ISAIAH:
READING ISAIAH IN LIGHT OF THE OTHER PROPHETS OF VISION

Hear, you peoples, all of you;
    listen, O land, and all that is in it
and let the lord Yahweh be a witness against you,
    the lord from his holy temple. (Mic. 1.2)

Hear, O sky, and give ear, O land;
    for Yahweh has spoken:
I reared up children and brought them up,
    but they have rebelled against me. (Isa. 1.2)

Hear this, O elders,
    give ear, all inhabitants of the land. (Joel 1.2)

Before beginning the discussion of Isaiah, who I understand to be an orthodox prophet, it will be useful to review what I have argued about 'unconventional prophets'. I have argued that Amos, Jeremiah and Ezekiel are
unconventional prophets. The superscriptions point this out by indicating
that the identity of each of these figures is associated with some group
other than prophets: Amos with the shepherds of Tekoa, Jeremiah with the
priests who were in Anathoth, and Ezekiel the priest with the exiles. The
location of these three prophets in unconventional circles is matched by
the way each of these three books employs the verb 'to prophesy' (נבא) to
identify the activity of Amos, Jeremiah and Ezekiel. Of the approximately
80 uses of this verb in the Latter Prophets, the verbal root occurs only
three times elsewhere (once in Joel [3.1] and twice in Zechariah [13.3-4])
and in these three instances it is not used to identify the activity of Joel or
Zechariah as 'prophesying'. The frequent use of the verb 'to prophesy' in
Jeremiah (over 40 times) and in Ezekiel (over 30 times) is aligned with an
emphasis that these two prophets are indeed prophesying. The use of the
verb 'to prophesy' highlights the non-conventionality of these two figures.
The two books are overstating what would be obvious for more conventional prophets.

Significantly also, both Jeremiah and Ezekiel prophesy against the prophets who, they claim, are prophesying a 'lying vision' (חזון שקר); but it is not suggested that the book of Jeremiah or the book of Ezekiel is a חזון.[1] I have argued that the extraordinary circumstances depicted in Jeremiah and Ezekiel help explain this situation. There can be no חזון in the time of Jeremiah and Ezekiel because Yahweh has abandoned the temple. Any claim that a prophet has had a vision, therefore, must be a lying claim, necessarily arising out of the heart (imagination) of the prophet himself. It cannot be a חזון from the mouth of Yahweh. The exceptional situation of divine absence from the temple requires extraordinary prophetic figures who receive the word of Yahweh in unconventional ways.

1. *What is* חזון?

When we turn to Isaiah and the prophets of vision, the use of the verb 'to prophesy' has dropped out of the picture. Prophets of vision are assumed to be engaged in a conventional activity—not in an unexpected social role requiring persuasive overstatement. For reasons I will set out below, I consider the prophets of vision, other than Isaiah, to be Joel, Obadiah, Micah, Nahum, Habakkuk and Zephaniah.

During the course of the discussion in earlier chapters, I have made a number of observations concerning a חזון, and it will be helpful to pull some of these observations together here. A חזון is a דבר of Yahweh received in the temple (see 1 Sam. 3). It can also be referred to as an 'oracle' (משא), as it is in Nah. 1.1 and Hab. 1.1.[2] It is a writing, a ספר (see Nah. 1.1), that a reader may run with presumably as a messenger (Hab. 2.2).[3] It may occur repeatedly over a period of time so that a prophetic book such as Isaiah covering a period of 'vision' in the days of Uzziah, Jotham, Ahaz and Hezekiah can be referred to in the singular, as with the חזון of Isaiah (see Isa. 1.1).

Habakkuk 2.1-3 is the most succinct statement about the reception of חזון:

---

1. The same holds true of course for Amos. Nowhere does the book claim to be the חזון of Amos.
2. The oracle seems to be used in this way in Jer. 23.33-40, in the chapter concerned with false prophets and lying חזון (23.16).
3. The notion of royal messengers as runners is evident in Jer. 51.31. See also Jer. 23.21, which concerns prophets who ran even though Yahweh had not sent them.

Write (כתוב) the vision (חזון),
   make it plain (ובאר) on tablets (הלחות)
   in order that a reader (קורא) may run with it.[4]
For a vision (חזון) is yet for an appointed time (למועד);
   and it will breathe out for the end,
   it will not lie.
If it lingers, wait (חכה) for it;
   for it will surely come,
   it will not tarry (יאחר).

In the context of Habakkuk it is important to observe that חזון arises out of Yahweh's answer to questions that Habakkuk poses to Yahweh. That Yahweh is answering Habakkuk's questions highlights the difference between this normal situation and the extraordinary situation in Amos and Jeremiah where intercession ends because Yahweh refuses to answer. While the text of Habakkuk does not explicitly identify the temple as the setting for the interaction of question and answer, the connotations of a temple setting are suggested by 3.1, 19.

2. חזון, *Identity and Time*

Before beginning my reading of Isaiah and other prophets of vision, I want to look at two other features of a חזון, which distinguish this conventional genre of prophecy from the unconventional genre represented by Amos, Jeremiah and Ezekiel. The first distinguishing feature is that a prophetic book identified as a חזון places less emphasis on the figure of the prophet. Prophets engaged in conventional forms of prophecy are figures who fall into the background so that in the prophetic book the 'vision' takes center stage. This is clearly the case in Isaiah.

In *Reading Isaiah*, I observed that as a character Isaiah plays an insignificant background role in the book of Isaiah:

> The name 'Isaiah' occurs just 16 times in the Book of Isaiah. In contrast, the name 'Jeremiah' occurs 131 times in the book that bears his name. This difference is even more striking because, whereas the name 'Jeremiah' is distributed throughout the book, the name Isaiah' is restricted to the three so-called superscriptions (1.1; 2.1, and 13.1) and to three third person narratives (chaps. 7, 20, and 36–39). But even in these three narratives the name is concentrated primarily in chapters 36–39, where it occurs 10 times; it occurs only once in chapter 7 (v. 3) and twice in chapter 20 (vv. 2, 3). These figures alone indicate that whereas the persona of Jeremiah is a

---

4. NRSV inexplicably translates 'so that a runner may read it'.

central focus of attention in the Book of Jeremiah, as past critics have observed, this is not the case in the Book of Isaiah. Isaiah only briefly appears 'onstage' as a character, and even in those appearances his character does not dominate in the way Jeremiah's character does.[5]

I also noted that even though Ezekiel's name only occurs twice, Ezekiel is present throughout the book as a narrative voice speaking in the first person singular.[6]

The reason for this contrast is now clearer to me than it was when I wrote *Reading Isaiah*. Both Jeremiah and Ezekiel have such a strong presence in the books that bear their names because each of them is the central issue. 'The words of Jeremiah' and what happened to Ezekiel concern unconventional prophets in extraordinary times. This contrast provides insight for the reader of a חזון such as the חזון of Isaiah. The importance of the book of Isaiah is more centrally focused on the חזון Isaiah saw than on the prophet himself. Indeed, this is true of all the other prophets of vision, most of whom appear only as a name in the superscription (Joel, Obadiah Micah, Habakkuk and Zephaniah).

The other distinguishing feature of a חזון relates to time. For unconventional prophets such as Amos, Jeremiah and Ezekiel, historical allusions in the book about the present situation of the prophet provides historical background for understanding the 'words of' (דברי) Amos and Jeremiah or 'the visions (מראות) of God' that happened to Ezekiel. Amos and Jeremiah's words and Ezekiel's visions of God relate primarily, although not exclusively, to their own time. Prophetic books of unconventional prophets 'prophesying' (נבא) in extraordinary times depict the activity of these prophets as relating to events surrounding the life and times of these prophetic figures themselves. For Amos, Jeremiah and Ezekiel, not only the figures of the prophets but also the 'historical' background of the prophets are significant for understanding their 'words' or 'visions'. This is so much the case with the unconventional Jonah that the entire book has become not a collection of his 'words' nor 'visions of God', but simply a depiction of the historical background surrounding his prophetic activity.

The situation with the conventional prophet Isaiah and other conventional prophets of חזון is significantly different. Not only does the portrayal of the prophet recede into the background but also the significance

---

5.   Conrad, *Reading Isaiah*, p. 34. I noted that in 52.1 Jeremiah refers to Zedekiah's grandfather and not to the prophet. I further noted that within the narrative of chs. 36–39 Isaiah is not mentioned in ch. 36.

6.   Conrad, *Reading Isaiah*, p. 35.

of the portrayal of a present historical background of prophetic activity
subsides. The emphasis in depicting historical background in the prophetic
books of vision is on the reception of the חזון. An חזון concerns a period
of time in the future; its meaning and significance are not for the prophet's
own present. To understand a חזון to be about the future helps clarify the
recurring feature of a חזון as ushering in a time of 'waiting'. The 'vision'
is for another time; it is not directed primarily to the present time of the
prophet himself. The future orientation of a חזון helps the reader interpret
the motif in the book of Isaiah that the community of the prophet Isaiah
is blind and deaf to the חזון in the days of Uzziah, Jotham, Ahaz and
Hezekiah. Isaiah's community cannot understand the חזון because it is for
another time. As we will see, it is a future community, alluded to in the
חזון itself that will open its eyes and ears to see, hear and understand the
'vision'. Isaiah can only wait in expectation for that day.

3. *Narratives and Structure in Isaiah*[7]

In prophetic books of חזון the depiction of the prophet's historical background is significant for portraying the context in which the prophet
receives the 'vision'. The narratives in the book of Isaiah should be understood in this way. The superscription's reference to the חזון, which he saw
in the days of Uzziah, Jotham, Ahaz and Hezekiah, kings of Judah' (1.1),
suggests the time of origin of the 'vision', not the situation to which the
'vision' is addressed.

That the narratives in Isaiah are functioning as the context in which
the prophet *receives* the 'vision' rather than as the situation to which the
'vision' is addressed explains why my reading of Isaiah diverges from
what has been the traditional historical-critical reading of Isaiah. An interpreter is not required to create a Second or Third Isaiah to read the book of
Isaiah. A reader who encounters חזון as a semiotic code can read Isaiah's
'vision' as relating to a time in Isaiah's future. His vision, to which his
community is blind and deaf, will gain clarity in the future. The narrative
events associated with the depiction of Isaiah's *reception* of 'vision'—

---

7.   This chapter is developed out of earlier published research. See my 'The Community as King in Second Isaiah', in James T. Butler, Edgar W. Conrad and Ben
Ollenburger (eds.), *Understanding the Word: Essays in Honor of Bernhard W. Anderson* (JSOTSup, 37; Sheffield: JSOT Press, 1985), pp. 99-111, 'The Royal Narratives
and the Structure of the Book of Isaiah', *JSOT* 41 (1988), pp. 67-81, and *Reading
Isaiah*, pp. 34-51.

during the Assyrian rise to power—portray a time of waiting and expectation. Much of the 'vision' of Isaiah is for another time—at the end of Babylonian hegemony.

As a way of understanding the narrative as depicting a historical context for the *reception* of Isaiah's חֲזוֹן, I want to focus on two narratives in which Isaiah interacts with kings—Ahaz in ch. 7 and Hezekiah in chs. 36–39. I will refer to these as 'royal narratives'. My argument will be that these two narratives provide key markers in the text for configuring Isaiah as a literary collage.

These royal narratives are also important in light of my previous discussions of Jeremiah and Ezekiel concerning 'lying vision' (חֲזוֹן שֶׁקֶר) in which prophets speak peace where there is no peace (see Ezek. 13.10, 16). In these two royal narratives, Isaiah speaks words of comfort to both Ahaz and Hezekiah that can generally be characterized as speaking peace. The portrayal of Isaiah interacting with kings is quite different from the portrayal of false prophets in Jeremiah and Ezekiel. In the days of Ahaz and Hezekiah, unlike the days of Jeremiah and Ezekiel, Yahweh was present in the temple in Jerusalem. Isaiah is a prophet of 'vision' but, because Yahweh is present in the temple, he does not prophesy 'lying vision' even though he speaks peace.

An examination of the similarities between the two narratives in the following paragraphs can serve as a starting point for a discussion of how they aid the reader in configuring the collage of words that surround them. The two narratives reflect the same type-scene and contain the same sequence of motifs:[8]

1. Each narrative begins by indicating how an invading army has entered the territory and represents a threat to the city of Jerusalem. In the Ahaz narrative two kings working in alliance with one another threaten the city—Rezin king of Syria and Pekah

---

8. The following discussion is taken from pp. 38-39 of my *Reading Isaiah* (Augsburg/Fortress Press, 1991). Used by permission. My ideas here grow out of the important observations of Peter R. Ackroyd on these two narratives. He has pointed out the relationship between the two royal narratives in the book of Isaiah and has made the methodological suggestion that scholars take note of the function the narratives have in their present position in the book. However, he saw a diachronic relationship between these two narratives, whereas my analysis is synchronic. See his 'Isaiah 36–39: Structure and Function', in W.C. Delsman *et al.* (eds.), *Von Kanaan bis Kerala: Festschrift für Prof. Dr. Dr. J. P. M. van der Ploeg O.P. zur Vollendung des siebzigsten Lebenjahres am 4 Juli 1979* (AOAT, 211; Neukirchen–Vluyn: Neukirchener Verlag, 1982), pp. 16-20.

king of Israel. They 'came up to Jerusalem to wage war against it, but they could not conquer it' (Isa. 7.1). In the Hezekiah narrative the Assyrian king Sennacherib poses a threat to the city: 'And the king of Assyria [Sennacherib] sent the Rabshakeh from Lachish to King Hezekiah at Jerusalem, with a great army' (36.2).

2.   The locus of activity for the threat to Jerusalem is the same in both narratives: 'the conduit of the upper pool on the highway to the Fuller's Field' (7.3; 36.2). The detail suggests that this place represented a strategic location for the defense of the city.[9]

3.   The narratives indicate that when the respective kings were informed of the invading army, they were greatly distressed. The Ahaz narrative notes: 'When the house of David was told, "Syria is in league with Ephraim", his heart and the heart of his people shook as the trees of the forest shake before the wind' (7.2). The Hezekiah narrative reports: 'When King Hezekiah heard it, he rent his clothes, and covered himself with sackcloth, and went into the house of the Yahweh' (37.1).

4.   In response to this military threat to Jerusalem and the panic of the king, Isaiah comforts the king by using conventional language of war using the phrase 'fear not'. In the Ahaz narrative Isaiah speaks directly to the king (7.4-9), and in the Hezekiah narrative the words are communicated through Hezekiah's servants (37.6-7).

5.   In each narrative the king is offered a sign (אוֹת) as confirmation that Yahweh's word will come to pass, so that the present threat will end (7.10-16; 37.30-32). Hezekiah is given an additional sign (38.7) and requests yet another (38.22).

6.   Although in both narratives the king and the city are spared, each passage ends on an ominous note. Isaiah predicts at the end of each narrative that a far greater catastrophe is to be expected from another invading king. In the Ahaz section of the book, the king of Assyria poses the future threat. He is mentioned in the explanation of the sign 'Immanuel' (7.15-17) and in one of the four pericopes beginning 'in that day' (7.20) which close the narrative and suggest the future ravaging of the country by the Assyrians and their king. The Hezekiah narrative ends with Isaiah's oracle concerning the coming catastrophe for Jerusalem and its kings from the king of Babylon, when Hezekiah's treasures will be

---

9.   Isa. 7 adds the further detail that this place was at the end of the conduit.

carried to Babylon and some of his sons will be made eunuchs in the palace of Babylon (39.6-7).

The two narratives themselves seem to be following a conventional form. In a traditional form-critical sense they represent a common *Gattung*. However, I am interested in the *Sitz im Text* of this *Gattung*, that is, how it provides insight into the structure of Isaiah as a literary collage, and the important role it plays in the way I have configured the text. I understand that the royal narratives act as textual frames useful for constructing the meaning of what comes before them and what follows them.

The first thing I want to look at is the use of the conventional language of warfare, indicated by the formula 'fear not'. Whereas this conventional language was used to comfort the prophet Jeremiah as a warrior-prophet, announcing Yahweh's words concerning the end of Judah and all the nations of the land, the prophet Isaiah speaks words of Yahweh to the king to comfort him because he is terrified of an invading army. The words addressed to Ahaz facing attack by Rezin king of Aram and Pekah king of Israel are:

> Be on guard, be quiet, do not fear (אל־תירא) and do not let your heart be faint from before of these two smoldering stumps of firebrands, because of the fierce anger of Rezin and Aram the son of Remaliah. Because Aram—with Ephraim and the son of Remaliah—has plotted calamity against you saying, 'Let us go up against Judah and let us lay it open for ourselves and we will make Tabeel king in its centre'. Thus says the lord Yahweh, 'It will not arise and it will not happen because the head of Aram is Damascus and the head of Damascus is Rezin. And in 65 years Ephraim will no longer be a people. And the head of Ephraim is Samaria and the head of Samaria is the son of Remaliah. If you do not believe, then you will not be established.' (7.4-9)

The structure of the language is a bit more complex here than in the texts that were considered in Jeremiah. As I argued in *Fear Not Warrior*, this is because the setting has changed. These words are used to comfort a king, and for that reason I have referred to them as 'Royal War Oracles'. I argued that a king, who is comforted with a Royal War Oracle, was either given orders not to fight or a promise that Yahweh would fight for him. I am not interested here in looking in a detailed way at the change of structure in the language of war but in how its use in this royal setting contrasts with its use in Jeremiah.[10] Isaiah is comforting Ahaz with words which

---

10. See my *Fear Not Warrior*, pp. 52-62, where I discuss the different structures of texts using the phrase 'fear not' to comfort a king facing a military invasion.

suggest that he will not be threatened by an invading army. In the book of Jeremiah, Jeremiah the warrior-prophet himself was comforted by 'fear not' language when he announced Yahweh's words to the people of Judah and its kings that the land would be totally devastated from an invading army from the north.

Similar language is sent by Isaiah to Hezekiah through his servants when they come to inquire of him in the face of the invasion by Sennacherib and his Assyrian army:

> Do not be afraid (אל־תירא) because of the words which you heard, with which the servants of the king of Assyria reviled me. Now I am putting in him a spirit, and he will hear a report and he will return to his land; and I will cause him to fall by the sword in his land. (37.6-7)

It is interesting to point out here that the words of Sennacherib were frightening the king in the same way that Yahweh's words of Jeremiah alarmed those who heard him speaking them in the temple. Perhaps we should understand Jeremiah's role as warrior-prophet speaking the words of the invading King Yahweh to be like that of the Rabshakeh who instilled fear into the king by speaking words from the Assyrian king (36.4-10). By using the formula כה אמר, the Rabshakeh was introducing Sennacherib's words as Jeremiah who, stood in the temple, was introducing Yahweh's words:

> Thus (כה) the great king, king of Assyria said (אמר), 'What is this trust in which you have confidence? Do you think that mere words are strategy and power for war? On whom do you now rely that you have rebelled against me?' (36.4-5)

In these two narratives concerning Ahaz and Hezekiah, then, Isaiah is comforting kings with Royal War Oracles from Yahweh, saying that the king should not fear because Yahweh will deliver them from enemy invasion. That Isaiah is acting in a conventional role is supported by other ancient Near Eastern texts in which prophetic figures like Isaiah speak similar words using the phrase 'fear not' to comfort a king facing an invading army.

For example, in response to a threat of war created by a military alliance, Zakir the king of Hamath and Lu'ath, in the eighth century BCE, seeks the aid of the deity in the face of military threat to his kingship. The god Be'elshamayn answers Zakir through seers with words that are very much like those that Isaiah speaks to Ahaz and Hezekiah:

Do not fear for I made you king, and I shall stand by you and deliver you from all [these kings who] set up seige against you. [Beʻelshamayn] said to me: [*I shall destroy*] all these kings who set up [*a siege against you and made this moat*] and this wall which…[11]

Other similar texts concerning the Assyrian kings Ashurbanipal and Esar-haddon further support this conventional use of language using the formula 'fear not' to comfort a king before a military threat.[12]

By pointing out these parallels, I am arguing that Isaiah in these royal narratives is portrayed in a role that is consistent with the cultural context of the ancient world. These parallels provide the reader with information that helps support the picture of Isaiah emerging in the way I am configuring the literary collage. Isaiah is a conventional prophet engaged in an expected role in his interaction with kings facing military invasion. I am not arguing that Isaiah is an actual prophet, or that the book of Isaiah provides us with information that tells us what actually happened in the interaction between Isaiah and the two kings, Ahaz and Hezekiah. Although the Zakir stele is dated in the eighth century BCE, I am not intending to argue that this is a demonstration of the authenticity of Isaiah as an eighth-century prophet. Rather, as a reader, I can bring this intertextual insight from the stele of Zakri to my reading as providing information for identifying textual codes. I am assuming that the author expected his or her Model Reader to know the conventional roles of prophets and kings. In particular,

11. The text is translated with notes by Franz Rosenthal in *ANET*, pp. 655-56. The text also appears in Hugo Gressman (ed.), *Altorientalische Texte und Bilder zum Alten Testamente* (Berlin: W. de Gruyter, 1926), pp. 443-44. The words are written on a stele set up by the king in connection 'with the dedication of a statue of Ilu-Wer, an avatar of Hadad'. The opening words announce that it was Zakir who set up the stele. After Zakir identifies himself in the first person he goes on to say how Barhadad, the son of Hazael, king of Aram, formed an alliance of kings against him: 'Barhadad, the son of Hazael, king of Aram, united [seven of] a group of ten kings against me: Barhadad and his army; Bargush and his army; the king of Cilicia and his army; the king of ʻUmq and his army; the king of Midh and his army. [All these kings whom Barhadad united against me] were seven kings and their armies. All these kings laid siege to Hatarikka. They made a wall higher than the wall of Hatarikka. They made a moat deeper than its moat.' The situation described here involving an alliance of kings is similar to that of Ahaz in Isa. 7, which also, interestingly, involved a king of Aram. In response to this threat of war created by the military alliance, Zakir, like Hezekiah (37.2-4), seeks the aid of the deity. He says, 'But I lifted up my hand to Beʻelshamayn and Beʻelshamayn hear me. Beʻelshamayn [spoke] to me through seers and *diviners*.'

12. For a fuller discussion of these texts and a more detailed analysis of the language see my *Fear Not Warrior*, pp. 57-62, 153-59.

I am surmising that a Model Reader would have understood the significance of the conventional 'fear not' formula associated with a prophetic figure announcing God's words of comfort to a king facing military threat.

Isaiah, however, is not speaking peace when there is no peace. Both narratives end with Isaiah suggesting that the present peace will not be an enduring one. An enemy will come who will bring even greater destruction. At the end of the Ahaz narrative, Ahaz refuses to ask for a sign from Yahweh, so Yahweh sends him a sign that a young woman has conceived. The message is that before the child is old enough 'to refuse evil and choose the good, the land before whose two kings you are in dread will be deserted' (7.16). The reader who has read the book of Kings, already knows that the land of King Pekah, the land of Israel, has been deserted (2 Kgs 18.9-12; cf. 23.27) and that this military defeat and exile was accomplished by Sennacherib, king of Assyria.

The words suggesting deliverance from the king of Israel and the king of Aram whose lands will be deserted is accompanied by the threat that the emptying of these lands will ultimately bring military destruction to Ahaz and the people of Judah:

> Yahweh will bring against you [Ahaz] and against your people and against the house of your father days which have not come since Ephraim departed from Judah, the king of Assyria. (7.17)

The remaining part of the ch. 7 (vv. 18-25) contains imagery depicting that day. This predicted threat of Assyrian invasion is already present in the conditional orders given to Ahaz in the words associated with the 'fear not' formula: 'If you do not believe, then you will not be established (7.9).

The day the king of Assyria invades Judah does come and is depicted in the book of Isaiah at the beginning of the Hezekiah narrative: 'And in the fourteenth year of king Hezekiah, Sennacherib, the king of Assyria, came up against all the fortified cities of Judah and captured them' (36.1). If we read the material surrounding these narratives as the 'vision' (חזון) of Isaiah, then we can begin to see how the book of Isaiah has been compiled. The conventional prophet Isaiah is not a prophet whose חזון is focused on announcing the end. The unconventional prophets, Amos and Jeremiah, announce this destruction. Isaiah is a prophet who announces comfort and consolation. Those words of comfort and deliverance are announced in the חזון of ch. 10, a chapter that depicts Assyria as the rod of Yahweh's anger (vv. 12-19). He addresses the people as if they were a king by using the conventional 'fear not' language of comfort, the language of a Royal War Oracle:

Therefore, thus says the lord Yahweh of hosts, do not be afraid (אל־תירא),
my people who dwell in Zion, of the Assyrians when they will beat you
with a rod and lift up a staff against you in the way of the Egyptians. Because in a very little while my indignation will come to an end, and my
anger will be directed to their destruction. Yahweh of hosts will wield a
whip against them, as when he struck Midian at the rock of Oreb; his staff
will be over the sea, and he will lift it as he did in Egypt. On that day his
burden will be removed from your shoulder, and his yoke will be destroyed.
(10.24-27)

Notice how this requires waiting: 'in a very little while my indignation
will come to an end'. That waiting does come to an end for the people of
Judah in the Hezekiah narrative where Yahweh defeats the Assyrian king,
who is forced to withdraw to his land, and delivers them from Assyrian
invasion.

However, it is important to see that the Hezekiah narrative also ends
with Isaiah's announcement to Hezekiah of a far worse catastrophe that is
coming. This time it will result from an invasion by the Babylonians.
Isaiah says,

Hear the word of Yahweh. Now days are coming and everything that is in
your house and everything that your fathers have stored up until this day
will be carried to Babylon. Yahweh said, 'Not a thing will be left'. And
some of your sons who were born to you will be taken away and they will
become eunuchs in the palace of the king of Babylon. (39.5-8)

The deliverance from the Assyrians will ensure only immediate peace as is
clear from Hezekiah's response: 'Then Hezekiah said to Isaiah, "The word
of Yahweh that you have spoken is good". For he thought, "There will be
peace and security in my days"' (39.8). However, the task of Isaiah, the
conventional prophet, is *not* to announce the end of Judah. If one reads
according to the rabbinic canonical order, it was the unconventional prophet Jeremiah who announced the Babylonian destruction of Judah and the
temple. Isaiah's role, according to the rabbinic arrangement of prophetic
scrolls, is to announce consolation. Just as he had consoled the people of
Judah saying that they would be delivered from the Assyrians, addressing
them with a Royal War Oracle using the conventional 'fear not' language
of comfort normally addressed to the king (10.24-27), so he uses similar
words of comfort for the people in Babylonian exile (41.8-16; 43.1-6;
44.1-5):[13]

---

13. For a more detailed discussion of he structure of this language see my *Fear Not
Warrior*, pp. 79-107.

> But you, Israel, my servant,
>   Jacob, whom I have chosen,
>   the offspring of Abraham, my friend...
> Fear not, for I am with you. (41.8, 19)

> Fear not, you worm Jacob,
>   You insect Israel!...
> Fear not, for I am with you. (43.1, 5)

> Fear not, O Jacob, my servant. (44.2)

To read Isaiah this way, following Jeremiah and Ezekiel in the canonical order, helps make sense of the rabbinic observation about Isaiah:

> Let us see again. Isaiah was prior to Jeremiah and Ezekiel. Then why should not Isaiah be placed first?—Because the book of Kings ends with a record of destruction and Jeremiah speaks throughout of destruction and Ezekiel commences with destruction and ends with consolation; therefore we put destruction next to destruction and consolation next to consolation.[14]

Reading the books in this order also enables one to see in Isaiah's חזון, Ezekiel's *torah* of temple rebuilding, the beginning of consolation following destruction. One must wait for this 'vision' of Isaiah that he saw in the days of Uzziah, Jotham, Ahaz and Hezekiah.

In these two narratives (Isa. 7 and 36–39), then, Isaiah is portrayed as a prophet of comfort and consolation. He does, however, suggest that the deliverance of both Ahaz and Hezekiah from military invasion is only temporary. The deliverance will be followed by a far greater invasion, first by the Assyrians, and then by the Babylonians. An interesting feature of the book of Isaiah is how it uses language conventionally used to comfort a king ('fear not') to comfort the people (10.24-27; 41.8-16; 43.1-6; 44.1-5). The shift of emphasis from royalty to the people suggests that kingship itself is coming to an end and that the people in a 'democratized' sense assume the position of royalty.[15]

I have already argued that these two narratives can be viewed in the Isaianic collage as indicators of order and arrangement. Isaiah's warning of Assyrian invasion at the end of the Ahaz narrative links up with the depiction of Assyrian invasion at the beginning of the Hezekiah narrative. In what follows, I want to build on these observations about the place of

---

14. *Baba Batra* 14b-15a (translation from Lieman, *The Canonization of Hebrew Scripture*, p. 52).

15. For a fuller account see my 'The Community as King in Second Isaiah', pp. 99-111.

these two royal narratives in the Isaianic compilation, in particular how they provide textual frames for reading Isaiah's 'vision'.

4. *Re-Reading the Book of Isaiah*

When I wrote *Reading Isaiah* in the 1990s, I also understood these same two royal narratives as playing a central role in the book as a whole.[16] In that earlier book I considered Isaiah largely in isolation from the larger prophetic collection. In this present study and other more recent studies, I have been reading prophetic books intertextually to see how they can illuminate one another.[17] This intertextual approach has led me to modify my understanding of Isaiah's compilational unity as originally presented in *Reading Isaiah*.[18]

I will argue below for a tripartite division of חֲזוֹן in Isaiah. As I will show, however, this division is different from the more conventional division of the book into three Isaiahs (chs. 1–39, 40–55 and 56–66). I will also argue that this division is important for understanding the literary effect of the ordered arrangement of materials rather than underlying sources.

At the beginning of the book of Isaiah, חֲזוֹן is used in the singular to refer to the multiple occasions on which Isaiah receives חֲזוֹן. Isaiah's 'vision' was not singular and did not happen at one point in time but occurred over a period of time during the days of Uzziah, Jotham, Ahaz and Hezekiah.[19]

---

16. In that book I spoke of the 'unity' of Isaiah, and, while I did not intend to speak of *compositional* unity, I can understand how my use of the term 'unity' could have been interpreted in that way.

17. See, e.g., *Zechariah*, pp. 17-18, and 'The End of Prophecy', pp. 65-79. See also Robert P. Carroll, 'Intertextuality and the Book of Jeremiah: Animadversions on Text and Theory', in J.C. Exum and D.J.A. Clines (eds.), *The New Literary Criticism and the Hebrew Bible* (JSOTSup, 143; Sheffield: Sheffield Academic Press, 1993), pp. 55-78.

18. See pp. 117-53. My present study, which has focused on the beginning of prophetic books as codes for the Model Reader, has given me the opportunity to reconsider the significance of חֲזוֹן. In light of my present study, I understand חֲזוֹן to be encoding information about everything that follows. I do not advance the notion that the חֲזוֹן of Isaiah is a book within the book in quite the same way as I did in *Reading Isaiah*. There are books within the book of Isaiah, but these 'writings' are multiple.

19. I, therefore, no longer see Isaiah's 'vision' to be a singular incidence associated with a portion of the book (Isa. 6–39) as I did in *Reading Isaiah* (see pp. 155-56).

As I will argue, the narratives in the book associated with kings, Uzziah in ch. 6, Ahaz in chs. 7–8[20] and Hezekiah in chs. 36–39, demarcate the times of the reception of Isaiah's vision. They indicate: (1) the 'vision' he had at the time when king Uzziah died (chs. 1–6);[21] (2) the 'vision' he had at the time of the Syro-Ephraimite alliance of kings during Ahaz's reign (chs. 7–35), and (3) the 'vision' he had at the time of the Assyrian king Sennacherib's invasion during Hezekiah's reign (chs. 36–66).

In the remaining part of this chapter, I want to look at these three time-frames and read them intertextually with similar books of vision from the Twelve. Before doing that, however, I want to review briefly the overall structure of Isaiah's compilational unity as I now see it. Some of the observations I made about the relation of the parts of Isaiah to one another in *Reading Isaiah* need to be redefined in light of my present understanding of the tripartite division of Isaiah's חזון.

In order to show the significance of this threefold vision in Isaiah, it will be helpful to contrast it with the overall structure I presented in *Reading Isaiah*. I understood Isaiah 1–5 and 40–66 as material depicting a community of survivors who had a speaking voice in the text as a recurring and often interruptive 'we'. Isaiah's vision (chs. 6–39) was understood as a book within the book of Isaiah. Isaiah wrote down his vision (8.16) because it was for another time. The people in his own time were deaf and blind to its significance (6.10). Isaiah would wait (8.17). The end of this waiting is depicted at the end of the book (chs. 40–66) in chapters concerned with the reception of the vision.

At this time the 'vision' of Isaiah, which is written down for another time, is read out (40.6). This is a time when the blind can see and the deaf can hear. It is also the time that Yahweh brings the nations to trial, challenging them to match his power. He announced long ago what has now occurred. But the gods of the nations can show no similar power. They are idols made of wood and stone. Yahweh can prove that what he announced long ago has taken place or is about to occur because he has witnesses, Jacob/Israel, one who can attest to the 'vision' of Isaiah, which took place long ago in the days of Uzziah, Jotham, Ahaz and Hezekiah.

In that 'vision' (chs. 6–39), Yahweh announced a military plan against all the nations and that plan began to reach fulfilment in the time of Hezekiah when he overthrew the Assyrian king Sennacherib. The community of

---

20. Ahaz is not mentioned in ch. 8, but the chapter continues the narrative of ch. 7 by focusing on the Assyrian invasion.

21. Isa. 1.1 is, of course, the superscription for the scroll.

survivors (chs. 1–5; 40–66) are now waiting for the final narrative of fulfilment of Yahweh's plan. Yahweh will successfully carry out his plan to wage total warfare against all the nations, including Babylon. (I also argued that the Babylonian community of survivors is not a historical community but any community of subsequent readers suffering exile and oppression.)

I now want to look more specifically at each of the units of the threefold division of Isaiah's חזון in order to show how my earlier reading of Isaiah has been modified. The major difference between my earlier and my present reading is that, whereas I had read the central section of Isaiah as the 'vision' of Isaiah addressed to a present community of survivors depicted in chs. 1–5 and 40–66, I now see the whole of Isaiah as a tripartite division of Isaiah's 'vision'. Chapters 1–5 and 40–66 are also understood as the vision of Isaiah. However, each of these three divisions of Isaiah's חזון needs to be read in light of one another and in order. They build on one another and create an increasingly clearer picture of what Isaiah saw in the days of Uzziah, Jotham, Ahaz and Hezekiah. While the community in the days of Uzziah was deaf and blind to Isaiah's vision, the book presents that 'vision' in increasingly sharper focus. In the following discussion I will also show how these three divisions of Isaiah's vision both illuminate and are illuminated when they are read intertextually with other prophetic books of vision in the Twelve.

5. *The First Section of the Vision of Isaiah (Chapters 1–6)*

The book of Isaiah opens 'the חזון of Isaiah…which he saw (חזה)' (1.1) but is followed by a command to hear, 'Hear (שמעו), O sky, and give ear (והאזיני), O land, because Yahweh has spoken (דבר)' (1.2). Later in the chapter there is another command to hear, 'Hear (שמעו) the word of Yahweh, rulers of Sodom. Give ear (האזינו) to the *torah* of our God, people of Gomorrah' (1.10). This shift from 'seeing' to 'hearing' may come as a jolt to a contemporary reader who expects a description of what is seen in 'vision' rather than a command to hear.

The opening of Ezekiel represents a dramatic contrast to the opening of Isaiah: 'The heavens were opened, and I saw (ואראה) visions (מראות) of God', is followed by a description of what Ezekiel saw: 'I looked and behold (וארא והנה)…' (1.4). The entire first chapter of Ezekiel is a rather bizarre description of what he saw, 'the appearance of the likeness of the glory of God' (1.28). Only at the end of the chapter does Ezekiel hear:

'When I saw (וָאֶרְאֶה) it, I fell on my face and I heard (וָאֶשְׁמַע) a voice speaking (מְדַבֵּר)' (1.28). Hearing in Ezekiel is a private affair; he hears a voice speaking to him. In contrast, Isaiah's 'vision' is followed by a public call for the land and the sky to hear.

How is the reader to understand a 'vision' like Isaiah's that moves so quickly from seeing to hearing? The answer to this question relates to conventions associated with חָזוֹן. A number of other prophetic books of חָזוֹן in the Twelve provide an intertextual resource. Isaiah is like Obadiah, Nahum and Habakkuk, which are also books of חָזוֹן. As we will see, the books of Joel and Micah have conventional openings following the superscription similar to those in the book of Isaiah. Both Joel and Micah share similar vocabulary about a call to hear. They also share other features with Isaiah suggesting that they also are to be understood as 'vision'.

Habakkuk 2.2-3, as I have already mentioned, represents in summary form the main components of the conventions associated with חָזוֹן. Yahweh's instructions to Habakkuk concerning the חָזוֹן also stress written word for oral proclamation rather than visual: 'Write (כְּתוֹב) the חָזוֹן... so that a reader (קוֹרֵא) may run with it...' In light of Habakkuk, one is prompted to read the opening of Isaiah's 'vision' as a reader calling out to the sky and the land to hear what is being read. Isaiah's vision is for the ear.

The superscription in Nahum also confirms this notion of חָזוֹן as a writing: 'An oracle of Nahum, the book of the vision (סֵפֶר חֲזוֹן) of Nahum...' (1.1). The חָזוֹן of Obadiah gives further support to the close connection between חָזוֹן and hearing. This 'vision' is about a messenger and what is written for reading out: 'We heard (שָׁמַעְנוּ) a report (שְׁמוּעָה) from Yahweh, and a messenger (צִיר) was sent among the nations' (Obad. 1). In light of this intertextual association with חָזוֹן in the Twelve, therefore, I am suggesting that at the beginning of Isaiah we are reading what is written, the חָזוֹן of Isaiah. As a חָזוֹן, it is in written form to be read out; it is for the ear.

The narration of the reception of Isaiah's חָזוֹן comes later in the autobiographical narrative in Isaiah 6, and its placement in the book is important for understanding how to configure the collage. The description of Isaiah's 'vision' is described at the end of the first part of 'vision' and is associated with the year that King Uzziah died (6.1). It functions as a demarcation and time frame for the חָזוֹן in Isaiah 1–5.

Like Samuel, Isaiah sees Yahweh sitting on a throne in the temple (6.1). The appearance of the deity is downplayed. We are given a glimpse of the seraphim, fiery creatures attending Yahweh, but little more. The focus of the chapter is the message that Isaiah is to deliver to the people. He is to stop up their ears and shut their eyes so that they are unable to understand or perceive what is being said (6.9-10). Isaiah is sent with a message (6.8). The vision of Isaiah is not for his own time but for another time. There will be a time of waiting as is typical of חזון:

> Then I said, 'How long, O Yahweh?' And he said:
>   'Until cities lie waste without inhabitant,
> and houses without a human being,
>   and the land is utterly desolate;
> until Yahweh sends everyone far away,
>   and broad is the emptiness in the midst of the land.
> Even if a tenth part remains in it,
>   it will be burned again,
> like a terebinth or an oak
>   whose stump remains standing when it is felled.'
>   The holy seed is its stump. (6.11-13)

The vision in the first part of Isaiah is about this time of desolation of the land:

> Your country lies desolate,
>   your cities are burned with fire
> in your presence aliens devour your land;
>   it is desolate, as overthrown by foreigners,
> And daughter Zion is left like a booth in a vineyard
>   like a shelter in a cucumber field,
>   like a besieged city.
> If Yahweh of hosts had not left us a few survivors,
>   we would have been like Sodom, and become like Gomorrah. (1.7-9)

This חזון concerns a future desolation of the land with uninhabited cities. The 'vision' of total desolation foreshadows the future time of Jeremiah when he gave the cup of the wine of wrath to the nations to drink. That was a time when Yahweh made the land utterly desolate and without inhabitant (Jer. 25.8-11). To read the חזון of Isaiah in connection with the דברי of Jeremiah helps to clarify the distinction between the conventional Isaiah and the unconventional Jeremiah. Jeremiah (like Amos) was seeing visual imagery in his world about imminent events in the contemporary situation when the enemy from the north was already present. Isaiah saw this time of desolation, but he saw it as a future time in a חזון he received long ago in the year King Uzziah died.

The 'vision' compiled in Isaiah 1–5 is not organized cohesively, but it gains some clarity when it is read as a 'vision' of the destruction following the war Yahweh has waged against the nations announced in Jeremiah. The very end of the vision, 5.26-30, is a vision of that coming destruction. Here the roaring (שׁאג) voice of the coming army is reminiscent of the roaring voice of Yahweh in Jer. 25.30:

> He will raise a signal for a nation far away,
>> and whistle to him from the ends of the land,
>> and behold he will come swiftly and speedily...
> His roaring is like a lion,
>> like young lions they roar
> he growls and he seizes his prey
>> and he will escape and there is no one to rescue.
> He will growl over it on that day,
>> like the growling of the sea.
> He looks to the land and now darkness, an adversary;
>> and light is darkness with clouds. (5.26-30)

Intermingled with this 'vision' of a ravaged land is the vision of a failed leadership. Scattered through chs. 1–5 are references to rulers (1.10), princes (1.23; 3.14), judges (1.26), planners (1.26) and elders (3.14). A whole series of leaders is mentioned in 3.1-3 in a pericope suggesting that the total leadership of the community will be eliminated by Yahweh (warrior, soldier, judge, prophet, diviner, elder, captain of 50, dignitary, counselor, skilled magician and the expert in charms). The whole of the land will fall into anarchy when it becomes a heap of ruins and there is no one to rule (3.6-8). The failure of leadership also recalls the failure of leadership in the words of Jeremiah.

But just as Isaiah's words concerning judgment in the Ahaz and Hezekiah narratives contained words of comfort and consolation to the community, so also in this section of the vision there are words of future salvation. It is important to note that this future salvation is associated with the establishment of 'Yahweh's house'. This reference also implies that Yahweh's vision is about a time when he will have abandoned his house as he did in the days of Jeremiah and Ezekiel:

> And it will happen in days to come that the mountain of the house of Yahweh will be established at the top of the mountains and will be raised above the hills. All the nations will stream to it. Many peoples will come and they will say, 'Come, let us go up to the mountain of Yahweh, to the house of the God of Jacob. He will teach us his ways and we will walk in his paths because from Zion will go forth *torah* and the word of Yahweh from Jeru-

salem. He will judge between the nations and will arbitrate between many peoples. They will beat their swords into plowshares and their spears into pruning hooks. A nation will not lift up a sword against a nation, and they will not learn war again. (2.2-4)

The vision, then, is about a future time that extends beyond Yahweh's war against the nations. It will be a time when there will be universal peace (see 4.2-6).

The very beginning of Isaiah's vision in Isaiah 1–5, then, is about the future day of desolation of the land, like that announced by Jeremiah when he prophesied against the nations. However, as a prophet of vision, Isaiah also sees beyond the destruction to deliverance and restoration.

6. *Isaiah 1–6 Read Intertextually with Joel and Micah*

I want to conclude my remarks on the first part of the vision of Isaiah (chs. 1–6) with reference to Joel and Micah. To read these three texts intertextually will further illuminate conventions associated with חזון. The books of Joel and Micah, like Isaiah, open with a call to hear. Also like Isaiah, they speak about the future as a 'vision' of the destruction of the land. The superscriptions of these two books do not use the term חזון but the more inclusive phrase דבר יהוה. Micah does speak of the 'word of Yahweh' as something which he saw (חזה), the same verb used in the superscription of Isaiah.

That Micah and Joel are to be read as חזון is evident in a form-critical sense in that immediately after the superscription there is a command to hear, as in Isaiah. Joel uses the same verbs as in Isaiah: 'Hear (שמעו) this, O elders, and give ear (והאזינו) all the inhabitants of the land' (1.2). Micah is similar to Isaiah and Joel, although the second verb is an alternative verb for listening: 'Hear (שמעו) peoples, all of them, pay attention (הקשיבי), O land, and all that is in it' (1.2). In both texts, following this command to hear, there is a 'vision' of land that will be totally devastated—as is the case in Isaiah.

I want to look more closely first at Joel and than at Micah. As is well known, the book of Joel opens using a plague of locusts as an image of an invading army (1.4) and the imagery is concerned with the devastation of the produce of the land and the animals:

> For a nation has invaded my land,
>   powerful and innumerable;
> its teeth are lions' teeth,
>   and it has the fangs of a lioness.

It has laid waste my vines,
    and splintered my fig trees
it has stripped off their bark and thrown it down;
    their branches have turned white. (1.6-7)

This army is further described in ch. 2 as coming in a future day of Yahweh that encapsulates the devastation of the land:

Blow the trumpet in Zion;
    sound the alarm on my holy mountain!
Let all the inhabitants of the land tremble,
    for the day of Yahweh is coming, it is near—
a day of darkness and gloom,
    a day of clouds and thick darkness!
Like blackness spread upon the mountains
    a great and powerful army comes;
their like has never been from of old,
    nor will it ever be again after them in ages to come.
Fire devours in front of them,
    and behind them a flame burns.
Before them the land is like the garden of Eden,
    but after them a desolate wilderness,
    and nothing escapes them. (2.1-3)

This invasion is like the devastation Amos announces. Amos follows Joel in the rabbinic ordering in the Twelve and shares similar language with Joel about the devastating army in 2.10-11. The land quakes (רגזה) and the sky trembles (רעשו). I argued above that רעש is used in Amos 1.1 to refer to the thunderous noise of an invading army and that this occurs in Amos just before Yahweh roars (שאג) from Zion and utters his voice (יתן קולו) from Jerusalem (1.2). In Joel this quaking of the sky is associated with Yahweh uttering his voice (נתן קולו) at the head of the invading army (2.11).

While this invading army is not clearly identified in Joel, Joel's close association with Amos in the Twelve suggests that the text is referring to the Assyrian army that brought an end to the Northern Kingdom as prophesied by the words of Amos. If this is the case, then one can see in 1.14-16 a parallel to Yahweh's refusal to respond to intercession at the time of Amos. The people are called to 'sanctify a fast and gather in the house of Yahweh, your God and to cry out to Yahweh' (1.14). However, 'there will be no joy or gladness from the house of our God' (מבית אלהינו, 1.16). The use of 'house of our God' rather than 'house of Yahweh' suggests the house at Bethel (בית־אל) where Amos encountered Amaziah and spoke out against Jeroboam.

That Joel 1.14-16 is about the house of Bethel becomes even clearer when read in conjunction with 2.15-16. At this point Joel's vision of a devastated land modulates to words of comfort and consolation. The command in 1.14, 'sanctify a fast' (קְדְשׁוּ צוֹם), and call a solemn assembly in 'the house of our God' now appers as a command: 'blow the trumpet in Zion' and 'sanctify a fast'(קְדְשׁוּ צוֹם) in Jerusalem. It appears that it is from Zion that Yahweh answers the intercession, 'Why will they say among the peoples, "Where is their god?"' (2.17). God hears and becomes jealous for his people (2.18). While the Northern Kingdom has come to an end and Bethel with it, the envisioned future even for the north is in Zion/ Jerusalem in the house of Yahweh there. There is no mention of Yahweh leaving his house in Zion/Jerusalem.

Many of the prophetic books (but not all) in the Twelve, like Amos, have a northern focus. But also like Amos, these books associate the envisioned salvation with a restored Zion/Jerusalem. The remaining portion of Joel contains words of comfort distinctive to Joel but resonating with words of comfort in Isaiah. Yahweh will remove the 'northern army' and drive it into a parched and desolate land. The language associated with the 'fear not' warfare formula is used, but in Joel the words of comfort are addressed to the soil and to the animals who dwell in the land:

> Do not fear (אַל־תִּירְאִי), O soil;
>> be glad and rejoice,
>> for Yahweh has done great things!
> Do not fear (אַל־תִּירְאוּ), you animals of the field,
>> for the pastures of the wilderness are green;
> the tree bears its fruit,
>> the fig tree and the vine give their full yield. (2.21-22)

The future vision of peace in Joel 4.16 (Eng. 3.16) anticipates a future of peace and security from Zion in contrast with the devastation that will be announced by Amos in the prophetic book that follows: 'Yahweh roars from Zion and utters his voice from Jerusalem' in Joel 4.16 (Eng. 3.16) repeats the first half of Amos 1.2. That the sky and the land will quake with the thunderous noise of an invading army (רַעַשׁ) anticipates the end of Amos 1.1. But all this vision in Joel is for a time in the future *after* Amos announces the end of Israel. It is also a time *after* the devastation of the land in Jeremiah's time. According to Joel, in that future time Yahweh will never again allow strangers to move through his holy land (4.17). Yahweh will dwell in Zion (4.14, 21), and Jerusalem will be inhabited forever (4.20).

Micah, according to the superscription, is dated in a similar time to that of Isaiah—during the days of Jotham, Ahaz and Hezekiah.[22] The 'vision' also has a northern orientation. The word of Yahweh that Micah saw concerned Samaria and Jerusalem (1.1). The setting of this vision is the temple where Yahweh will be a witness against all the peoples of the land (1.2). What distinguishes Micah from Joel, however, is that, in Micah, Yahweh is coming out of the temple to bring destruction to the land:

> Because now Yahweh is coming out (יצא) from his place
>   and he will come down and he will trample on the high places of the
>   land,
> and the mountains will melt away under him
>   and the valleys will be cleaved asunder,
> like wax from in front of the fire,
>   like waters poured down a slope. (1.3-4)

The future envisaged here resembles the days of Jeremiah, when Yahweh left his temple to bring devastation to all the land. Yahweh is going out from his place and will tread on all the high places of the land (1.3). He will punish the transgression of Israel (the city of Samaria and its temple) and the transgression of Judah (the city Jerusalem and its temple) (1.5).

Yahweh will bring disaster first to Samaria—Samaria will be a heap in the open country (1.6). This disaster will spread all the way to the gate of Jerusalem (1.12). The momentum of the text is toward Jerusalem. Micah 3 picks up some of the themes I have associated with the time of Jeremiah. The people will cry to Yahweh but he will not answer them (1.4, 7), and the prophets will prophesy peace when they are paid, but it will become a time when there is no חזון (3.6). In due course,

> Zion will be plowed like a field;
>   Jerusalem will become a heap of ruins,
>   and the mountain of the house a wooded height. (3.12)

This is, of course, the verse that certain elders quoted from Micah to defend Jeremiah when he prophesied everything written in the ספר against the nations (Jer. 26.18). According to Jer. 26.18, Micah said these things during the time of Hezekiah. The elders recall that Hezekiah entreated the favor of the Yahweh and that Yahweh changed his mind about the disaster he was about to bring against them (26.19). But when Jer. 26.18 is read in conjunction with Mic. 3.12, an explanation different from that of the elders can be offered. Yahweh did not change his mind. By reading these

---

22. Joel, of course, is given no specific dating.

two texts together Yahweh's action can be understood as delaying the time when Jerusalem will be plowed making it a heap of ruins; he did not change his mind at the time of Hezekiah. The elders who are portrayed as defending Jeremiah misunderstand (Jer. 26.27). Their appeal to Micah as a prophet of vision is no defense of Jeremiah. Rather, Micah's words can be viewed as חזון that, in the literary context, substantiates the words of Jeremiah that Jerusalem will be destroyed. Micah as a prophet of 'vision' receives his 'vision' in a time of waiting and expectation. His חזון is for the future.

Micah, like Habakkuk, laments the perversion of justice (7.1-6). Habakkuk will station himself at the watchpost and station himself at the rampart, where he says: 'I will keep watch (ואצפה)' to see what Yahweh will answer. In a similar way Micah says (7.7):

> And I will watch (אצפה) for Yahweh, I will wait (אוחילה) for the God of
> my salvation, my God will hear me.

There are two other ways in which Micah links with Isaiah as a prophet of vision. These connections also support the notion that Micah's vision of Jerusalem becoming a heap of ruins can be understood differently from that portrayed by the elders in Jer. 26.19. In the next section of this chapter I will argue that in the second division of Isaiah's vision (chs. 7–35), there is a key motif that Yahweh has a plan, announced long ago, about the future destruction of the nations of the land. I will argue that the book of Isaiah suggests that this plan is coming to fruition at the time of Babylonian exile. In a similar way, Micah in his vision also speaks about Yahweh's plan. The plan is also associated with the nation, 'the daughter of Zion', who will be rescued from Babylon (4.10). This community in Babylon should know Yahweh's plan (4.11-12). Micah as a prophet of חזון, like Isaiah, looks beyond the time of the desolation of the land to restoration:

> And now many nations are gathered against you,
>> saying, 'Let her be profaned,
>> and let us gaze on Zion with our eyes'.
> But they do not know the thoughts (מחשבות) of Yahweh,
>> and his plan (עצתו) they do not understand,
>> that he has gathered them like sheaves to the threshing floor.

His vision also shares common words with Isaiah. Micah's words in 4.1-4 parallel, although not exactly, the words in Isaiah (2.1-4). This 'vision' concerns how Yahweh's house will be established so that the *torah* and the word of Yahweh may again go out from the temple in a time when there will be an end to warfare.

Indeed the end of Micah sounds like the third part of the 'vision' of Isaiah (chs. 40–66), for God is seen to be incomparable, to have compassion once again and to be faithful to Jacob as he was in the days of old (Mic. 7.18-20).

To summarize, then, I have argued that the book of Isaiah begins with 'vision' (chs. 1–6) associated with the year that King Uzziah died. This vision is of the future time when Yahweh will have carried out his warfare against all the nations of the land so that the land lies desolate with only a few survivors. As a prophet of חזון, however, Isaiah also envisions a future time of restoration when Yahweh will again be on his holy mountain and warfare will come to an end.

As a חזון, the book of Isaiah shares characteristics with other books of חזון in the Twelve. Significantly, in a form-critical sense, Isaiah, Joel and Micah all begin with a command to hear immediately following the superscription. All three include a vision of desolation of the land; yet all three speak of the house of Yahweh in a restored Jerusalem. While the desolation of the land in Isaiah and Micah is associated with Yahweh's departure from the temple in the time of Babylonian invasion, Joel appears to have a vision of Assyrian invasion—when Yahweh remains in his temple in Jerusalem but abandons the Northern Kingdom.

7. *The Second Section of the Vision of Isaiah (Chapters 7–35)*

In the intertextual reading of the prophetic scrolls of Jeremiah, Ezekiel and Isaiah with the books of the Twelve Minor Prophets, I noted that the books of the Minor Prophets have an orientation toward the Northern Kingdom. The words of Jeremiah are primarily concerned with the end of Judah, while the words of Amos are concerned with the end of Israel. Ezekiel interacts with Yahweh in the foreign land of Babylon, the enemy that devastated the land of Judah, while Jonah interacts with Yahweh in the foreign city of Nineveh, the foe that devastated the land of Israel. The first part of Isaiah's חזון (chs. 1–6) concerns the devastation of Judah following the Babylon invasion, while the 'vision' of Joel concerns the devastation of Israel following the Assyrian invasion.

Given the two themes of Yahweh first abandoning Israel and later abandoning Judah, it should not be surprising that the book of Isaiah contains 'vision' set in the context of the invasions of Assyria and Babylon. I want to turn now to the second section of Isaiah's vision (chs. 9–35), with its narrative setting in the time of Ahaz, anticipating Assyrian invasion (chs. 7–8). Against the background of this same threat of Assyrian invasion, the extraordinary prophet Amos is depicted as announcing the end of Israel. Isaiah in the south, as a conventional prophet of חזון, is portrayed as receiving 'vision' at this same time. However, he is portrayed as delivering words of peace to the Judean king.

Isaiah 7–8 is the narrative that provides the setting for the second part of Isaiah's vision. I have already pointed out that the narrative concerning the deliverance of Ahaz from the invasion of kings from Israel and Aram (Isa. 7) ends with the threat to Ahaz of a far greater catastrophe—the future Assyrian invasion (7.17-25).

In the chapter following the interaction with Ahaz (Isa. 8), Isaiah is depicted as a writer, and his writing concerns Assyrian invasion. The tone of the whole has a legal ambience. What is written is presented as important legal documentation and concerns the recurring theme of Yahweh's plan for the future recorded in the written 'vision'. Yahweh announces long before it happens what will occur in the future. As a prophet of חזון, Isaiah will wait for Yahweh to do what he plans.

At the beginning of ch. 8 Yahweh instructs Isaiah to write. What he is to write has legal connotations (8.1-4), recording what Yahweh tells him before it occurs:

> Take a large tablet and write on it with a man's stylus, 'Concerning The-Spoil-Speeds-The-Prey-Hastens'. And let me take as reliable witnesses for myself, Uriah the priest and Zechariah, the son of Jeerechiah. And I went to the prophetess and she conceived and she bore a son. Yahweh said to me, 'Name him The-Spoil-Speeds-The-Prey-Hastens because before the lad knows how to call "My father" and "My mother", the wealth of Damascus and the spoil of Samaria will be carried away before the king of Assyria'.

This writing is evidence that can later be interpreted in light of events as validating the vision.

Yahweh tells Isaiah that the king of Assyria will sweep into Judah (8.5-8). Isaiah is not to walk in the way of the people, nor fear the coming invasion. In Habakkuk-like fashion (see Hab. 2.2-3), Isaiah, a prophet of חזון, gives the order:

> Bind up (צור) the testimony (תעודה) seal the teaching (תורה) among my instructed ones. I will wait (וחכיתי) for Yahweh who is hiding his face from the house of Jacob and I will hope (וקיתי) in him. (8.16-17)

This testimony, this teaching, appears in the חזון in the following chapters. What we encounter as written words in the second part of the 'vision' is not presented as speech later recorded but as a message that came to its original expression in writing, to be proved correct in the light of subsequent events. Like Habakkuk, Isaiah will wait for the 'vision' to come about.

The legal ambience of Isaiah's written תורה helps to clarify a key point in this second part of Isaiah's vision (chs. 9–35). A central motif concerns Yahweh's plan of destruction against the nations, including Judah. This plan is written down and announced during the time of Ahaz. The significance of this plan will become apparent in the third section of Isaiah's vision when the written evidence will be used in the metaphorical trial that Yahweh will conduct against the nations.

I see a threefold division in the arrangement of the materials. The first section is 'vision' associated with the Judean king Hezekiah and the Assyrian king Sennacherib in Isaiah 9–12. Some of this 'vision' about the future finds narrative fulfilment in chs. 36–39. The second section is 'vision' concerned with Yahweh's plan to wage war against all the nations of the land (chs. 13–27). This plan, also involving Assyria, reaches partial fulfilment in the Hezekiah narrative. It is a plan, however, whose final fulfilment is to take place in a later time, such as the time described in 'the words of Jeremiah', when all the nations will be made to drink of the cup of the wine of wrath. The third section concerns 'vision' associated with failed leadership (chs. 28–35).

a. *Hezekiah and Sennacherib*[23]

Both Hezekiah and Sennacherib are envisaged in the second part of Isaiah's vision. The way these characters are portrayed in the later narrative (chs. 36–39) suggests that this part of Isaiah's vision of the future has been fulfilled. Hezekiah is foreshadowed in the narrative context that provides the narrative setting for the second part of Isaiah's vision (chs. 7–8). The sign offered to Ahaz that a young woman has conceived and will bear a son named Immanuel (whose name means 'God is with us'), presages Hezekiah, later present in the narrative (chs. 36–39). Immanuel is also a theme in ch. 8, indicating that the Assyrian advance will not succeed (8.8, 10). Hezekiah's actions in the *later* narrative (chs. 36–39) demonstrate Yahweh's presence, and it is for that reason that Jerusalem is delivered from the invading Assyrian army. Indeed, Hezekiah's faithful actions, in

---

23. For a fuller treatment of how the depictions of Sennacherib and Hezekiah in chs. 36–39 are anticipated by Isaiah's vision, see my *Reading Isaiah*, pp. 41-46.

contrast to the unfaithful actions of Ahaz, illustrate how he fulfils the name Immanuel. In contrast to Ahaz, who does not bother to ask Yahweh for a sign, Hezekiah not only accepts signs (37.30; 38.7), but also requests a sign (38.22). In contrast to Ahaz, who gives the impression that Isaiah's presence is an unwanted intrusion, Hezekiah, when hearing of the Assyrian intrusion, sends a message directly to Isaiah requesting that Yahweh intervene to rebuke the words of the Rabshakeh (37.4). Even the words of the Rabshakeh, suggesting on the one hand that Hezekiah is misleading the people by saying 'Yahweh will deliver us' (36.18), and on the other hand that Hezekiah is deceiving himself by relying on Yahweh (37.10), portray Hezekiah as believing in God's presence. In contrast to the unfaithfulness of Ahaz implied in the orders, 'if you do not believe (תאמינו), you will not be established (תאמנו)' (7.9b), Hezekiah, in his petition to be healed from his sickness, says that he has walked before Yahweh in faithfulness (באמת, 38.3).

Hezekiah also fulfils Isaiah's vision of an ideal king (9.2-7). The sign given to Hezekiah, 'the zeal of Yahweh of hosts will do this' (37.32), comes at the climax of the description of the perfect king (9.7). Isaiah's 'vision', however, goes far beyond these words of divine presence symbolized in Hezekiah's actions, as is clear from the more glorious picture of peace in Isaiah 11 and 12. Isaiah's 'vision' reaches beyond his own time to even greater desolation and even greater salvation and restoration. As we will see in the third part of Isaiah's vision, salvation and restoration are envisioned as a period of time without Davidic kings.

The Assyrian king in Isaiah 36–39 is portrayed as the fulfilment of the second part of Isaiah's vision concerning Assyria. This is evident in the following ways. First, Yahweh says of the Assyrian king:

> Ah, Assyria, the rod of my anger—
> > the club in the hand of my fury!
> Against a profane nation I will send him,
> > and against a people of my rage I command him.
> To take spoil and seize plunder,
> > to trample them down like the mire on the streets. (10.5-6)

That this vision has been fulfilled at the time of Hezekiah is confirmed by the speech of the Rabshakeh, the messenger of the Assyrian king who said that Yahweh himself had commanded him to attack Judah:

> And now is it without Yahweh that I have come up against this land to destroy it? Yahweh said to me, 'Go up to this land and destroy it'. (36.10)

Second, in the second part of Isaiah's vision the Assyrian king is envisioned as boasting that no gods of any of the other nations prevented him from doing what he has intended:

> Just as my hand reached out to the kingdoms of idols,
>   and their images greater than those of Jerusalem and Samaria,
> Shall I not do the same as I did to Jerusalem and her images
>   As I did to Samaria and her images? (10.10-11)

This arrogant boast of the Assyrian king is spoken through the Rabshakeh in the Hezekiah narrative, when the former says that neither any god of other nations nor Yahweh could deliver Jerusalem out of his hands (36.20; 37.10-12):

> Who [is it] among all the gods of these nations who has saved their country from my hand that Yahweh will save Jerusalem from my hand?

> Do not let your god on whom you rely deceive you by promising that Jerusalem will not be given into the hand of the king of Assyria... Have the gods of the nations delivered them, the nations my predecessors destroyed?

Third, and finally, in middle part of Isaiah's vision, the downfall of the Assyrian king, when he is struck down by a messenger of Yahweh (37.36-38), fulfils the vision anticipated (10.15-19).

The point I am making here is that חזון is about the future. It is written down so that one must wait for it to eventuate. In the case of the invasion of the Assyrian king and its aftermath, the waiting for this part of the vision is portrayed as resulting in Isaiah's time during the days of Hezekiah, and this is depicted in the Hezekiah narrative.

A more significant insight into how חזון, writing and waiting are to be understood in Isaiah is afforded by the the words that Yahweh speaks in his rebuke to Sennacherib (37.22-29). Yahweh says to Sennacherib:

> Have you not heard
>   from a distant time I determined (עשיתי) it?
> From days of old I planned it (ויצרתיה),
>   now I will cause it to happen
> that you should make fortified cities
>   crash into heaps of ruins. (37.26)

This plan regarding Assyria had earlier been recorded in the second part of Isaiah's vision:

> Yahweh of hosts has sworn:
>   'As I have designed (דמיתי)
>   so shall it be;

as I have planned (יעצתי)
  so it shall come to pass;
I will break the Assyrian in my land,
  and on my mountains trample him under foot;
his yoke shall be removed from them,
  and his burden from their shoulders'.
This is the plan (העצה) that is planned (היעוצה)
  concerning all the land;
  and this is the hand that is stretched out over all the nations.
Because Yahweh of hosts has planned (יעץ)
  and who will annul it?
His hand is stretched out,
  and who will turn it back? (14.24-27)

The announcement in Isaiah's 'vision' of Yahweh's plan at the time of Ahaz and its fulfilment in the days of Hezekiah has a significant literary effect: it suggests that nothing happens by chance. Yahweh announces in plans made long ago what is to happen and that announcement is recorded as written testimony in the חזון of Isaiah. The fulfilment of Yahweh's plan concerning Assyria, however, is only partial fulfilment of a plan that is grander in scope. I now want to look in more detail at Yahweh's plan as characterized in Isaiah 13–27.

b. *Yahweh's Plan Against the Nations (Chapters 13–27)*[24]

Recurring throughout the so-called 'Oracles against Foreign Nations' in this second חזון of Isaiah is the theme that Yahweh has announced his plan that he will bring destruction against all the nations of the land. The motif concerning Yahweh's planning is primarily associated with the noun עצה and its related verb root יעץ. But other words are used in association with these to express the notion of what Yahweh is planning and doing (e.g. דמה, יצר, חפץ, פעל, עבדה, עבד, מעשה, עשה). He has 'planned' (דמה, יעץ), 'purposed' (צפן) or 'formed' (יצר) this strategy long ago. History is therefore moving in a predetermined way to accomplish Yahweh's 'plan' (עצה) or 'work' (עבדה, משעה) that he is doing (פעל, עשה, עבד).

This language, especially the noun עצה and the verb root יעץ, often have military connotations and concern the plans or strategies for warfare. They have these connotations in the so-called historical books in the

24. The following discussion is taken from pp. 52-63 of my *Reading Isaiah* (Augsburg/Fortress Press, 1991). Used by permission.

Hebrew Bible (see Judg. 20.7; 2 Kgs 6.8; 2 Chron. 25.17). Of more immediate importance, the verb and the noun occur in both the Ahaz and
Hezekiah narratives in the book of Isaiah, and in both narratives they concern military planning. In the Ahaz narrative, Isaiah tells Ahaz not to fear
Aram and Ephraim who have planned (יעץ) evil against him saying 'Let
us go up against Judah and terrify it, and let us conquer it for ourselves,
and set up the son of Tabeel as king in the midst of it"'. Ahaz should not
fear because Yahweh will not allow this military plan to succeed.

In the Hezekiah narrative, the noun עצה occurs with military connotations in the initial speech of the Rabshakeh, who says, 'Say to Hezekiah,
"Thus says the great king, the king of Assyria: On what do you rest this
confidence of yours? Do you think that mere words are strategy (עצה) and
power for war? On whom do you rely, that you have rebelled against
me?"' (36.4-5). Here the Rabshakeh is saying that successful military
planning requires more than words of rebellion. It requires the aid of
superpowers such as Egypt, although Egypt is only a 'broken reed of a
staff' (36.6).

The point that I am making is that in this second part of Isaiah's 'vision',
Yahweh has announced his military strategy to carry out warfare against
all the nations of the land. This plan was announced ahead of time in
Isaiah's חזון during the days of Ahaz. Yahweh's plan begins to be imple-
mented in the days of Hezekiah when Assyria invades the land and puts an
end to the Northern Kingdom as prophesied 'in the words of Amos'.

I now want to look more closely at the announcement of Yahweh's plan
in the second 'vision' of Isaiah. Associated with the announcement and
fulfilment of Yahweh's plan against the Assyrians (14.24-28; 37.26-27),
discussed above, are argumentative questions as in 14.27: 'For Yahweh
has planned (יעץ) it, and who will annul it? His hand is stretched out and
who will turn it back?' At the time of the fulfilment of that plan in the
Hezekiah narrative, the Assyrian king is challenged with a argumentative
questions and an answer: 'Have you not heard that I determined (עשׂיתי) it
long ago? I planned (ויצרתיה) from days of old what now I bring to pass'
(37.26). The answer to this question is that no one can annul Yahweh's
plan because Yahweh determined it long ago. I understand the question
directed at the Assyrian king in association with Yahweh's announcement
of a military plan involving this king, to be a argumentative device. The
narrative containing a poetic taunt of the king and accented by an argumentative question compellingly supports the theme of the inevitability of

the fulfilment of Yahweh's plan in final victory over all the nations of the land. The Hezekiah narrative functions as a specific instance of the out-working of Yahweh's plan.

The motif of Yahweh's planned strategy of war appears also in the oracle of judgment against Egypt in ch. 19. Yahweh will foil the plan of Egypt, as he did the strategy of the Syro-Israelite alliance, by causing the Egyptians to fight against one another (19.2-4). Significantly, Yahweh's action will incorporate an assault on Egypt's *plans*: 'I will confound their plans' (ועצתו אבלע, 19.3). Yahweh will empty out the 'spirit' (19.3) of the Egyptians and replace it with a 'spirit of confusion' (19.4). The result will be that 'the wise planners of Pharaoh' (חכמי יעצי פרעה) will give 'stupid plans' (עצה נבערה, 19.11). The Egyptian plans will be confused because they run counter to the 'plan of Yahweh' (עצת יהוה) that 'he planned (הוא יועץ) against them' (19.17).

Isaiah 19, like the chapter announcing Yahweh's planned destruction of the Assyrians (Isa. 14), raises argumentative questions. After describing that the 'wise planners' of Egypt will give 'stupid plans' (19.11), Yahweh asks 'the princes of Zoan' and the 'wise planners of Pharaoh' (19.11b-12),

> How can you say to Pharaoh,
>   'I am a son of the wise,
>   a son of ancient kings'?
> Where then are your wise men?
>   Let them tell you and make known
>   what Yahweh of hosts has planned (יעץ) against Egypt.

Here, as elsewhere, Yahweh's plans frustrate the plans of the nations. The Egyptians cannot answer questions about what Yahweh has planned; they are deemed to be deluded fools. They can consult the idols, the sorcerers, the mediums and the wizards (19.3), but to no avail. Here argumentative questions have the literary effect of underscoring the inevitability of Yahweh's plan and the folly of any alternative plan.

The motif of Yahweh's military plan of judgment against the nations also appears in the oracle against Tyre. After announcing the judgment of Tyre, the oracle says:

> Is this your exultant city
>   whose origin is from days of old,
> whose feet carried her
>   to settle afar?
> Who has planned (יעץ) this
>   against Tyre, the bestower of crowns

whose merchants were princes,
　　whose traders were the honored of the land?
Yahweh of hosts has planned it (יעצה),
　　to defile the pride of all glory,
　　to dishonor all the honored of the land. (23.7-9)

Here again a series of argumentative questions has a cumulative effect, leading to the inevitable answer that Yahweh has planned all these things. As the reader follows the motif of Yahweh's plan against the nations, the argumentative questions intensify the persuasiveness of the claim that Yahweh's military strategy will be accomplished. The language of the book is establishing the certainty of Yahweh's plan about the future course of world events.

The last time that Yahweh's plan is mentioned in this second 'vision' is in 25.1-2. This part of the Isaianic collection (chs. 24–27) has been usually understood as 'the Little Apocalypse'. In these chapters, it has been contended can be seen a movement from prophecy to apocalyptic, history to the end of time. However, I do not read this as any more 'apocalyptic' than the sweeping destruction of all the land depicted in Jeremiah 25, when the nations are made to drink of the cup of the wine of wrath.[25]

The description of Yahweh's plan described in Jeremiah 25 is in keeping with his plan concerning Assyria, Egypt and Tyre. However, his plan is described as being against all the land. Here, Isaiah is speaking in the first person praising Yahweh:[26]

O Yahweh, you are my God;
　　I will exalt you, I will praise your name;
For you have done wonderful things,
　　plans (עצות) from long ago, faithful and sure.
Because you have made the city a heap,
　　the fortified city a ruin,
the citadel of aliens from a city;
　　it will not be rebuilt for a long time. (25.1-2)

25. The kind of 'apocalyptic' horror that is presented in this chapter (e.g. 24.1-23) is the kind we experience in the total devastation of our own world (תבל, see 26.9). To translate ארץ as 'land' rather than 'earth', as the NRSV does in this chapter, leads to a reading with a global dimension more characteristic of our own construction of the world than the ancient world constructed by this text. The envisioned destruction of the land in these chapters is no more catastrophic than that imagined in Jer. 25. Indeed, the land 'staggering' in Isa. 24.20 recalls the nations who stagger as a result of Yahweh's wrath in Jer. 25.16.

26. Here Isaiah's vision parallels Hab. 3.

What is to happen in Jerusalem is similar to what Micah has prophesied—the city will become a heap of ruins (Mic. 3.12). Micah also saw the destruction of Jerusalem as the outworking of Yahweh's plan (4.12).

For Isaiah, like Micah (7.7), Habakkuk (2.2) and other prophets of חזון, the fulfilment of vision will require waiting:

> And he will say on that day,
> 'behold, this is our God, we waited (קוינו) for him that he might rescue us.
> This is Yahweh; we waited (קוינו) for him.
> Let us be glad and rejoice in his salvation;
> because the hand of Yahweh will rest on this mountain. (25.9-10)

Similarly in 26.8 we read:

> In the path of your judgments, we wait for you (קוינוך).

In this second vision, Isaiah is portrayed as seeing Yahweh's plans for the future. This includes not only Yahweh's plans regarding Assyria, which were announced and accomplished in Isaiah's own time, but also Yahweh's plans for all the nations of the land. The whole world will suffer catastrophe and this is depicted in very gruesome terms. For example, in 25.10-12, Moab, which seems to be an exemplar of all proud peoples, is described as being 'trodden down in his place, as straw is trodden down in a dung-pit. And he will spread out his hands in the midst of it as a swimmer spreads his hands out to swim; but Yahweh will lay low his pride together with the skill of his hands' (25.10b-11). This and other similar verses of judgment in Isaiah (e.g. the judgment on Babylon that envisages the slaughter of infants and the ravishing of women [13.15-16]) use images that in horror and gruesomeness compete with images of military atrocities in our own time.

This second section of Isaiah's vision, like material in other prophetic books, cannot be read as a singly authored composition with a developed line of thought. Taken together, however, as a literary collage, the material does enable a pattern to emerge of Yahweh working out his judgment against the nations, including his judgment on Judah and Jerusalem. The disclosure of Yahweh's military plan against all the nations helps complete the picture of total desolation that was foreseen in the first vision.

While the motif of Yahweh's plan is not used in the words of judgment against Babylon (13.1–14.21) in the second part of the 'vision', Babylon is included in Yahweh's plan and that will be seen more clearly when we look at the third section of Isaiah's 'vision' (chs. 40–66). However, deliverance from Babylonian oppression is also part of Isaiah's 'vision'

(13.1-3), as is the eventual downfall of the king of Babylon (13.4-21). That Babylon figures centrally in this second section of Isaiah's 'vision' is suggested by the envisioned announcement of the downfall of Babylon. Again in language reminiscent of that in Habakkuk, a watchman is stationed to look and to announce (21.8-9) the downfall of Babylon:

> Fallen, fallen is Babylon
>   and all the images of its gods lie shattered to the ground.
> O my threshed and winnowed one,
>   what I have heard from Yahweh of hosts,
>   the God of Israel, I announce to you. (21.9b-10)

The audience to whom this חזון of Isaiah is announced is not the community of Isaiah's day but a future community that will already have experienced desolation at the hands of the Babylonians. However, it is this plan and its outworkings that Isaiah sees in his חזון. Isaiah records this 'vision' as evidence of Yahweh's power which will be presented (read out) in another time. Yahweh and his power are being defended in this plan and seen in this חזון.

I have been arguing that the second section of Isaiah's 'vision' is the announcement of Yahweh's plan against the nations, including Judah and Jerusalem. This 'vision' is the announcement 'long ago' of the plan that he will bring to fulfilment in an age later than Isaiah's time—an era like that depicted in Jeremiah and Ezekiel. While Jeremiah and Ezekiel are in the middle of the war, Isaiah is 'seeing' that war in an earlier time. For him it is a time of waiting.

c. *A Failed Leadership (Chapters 28–35)*

The picture that emerges in Isaiah chs. 28–35 is that Isaiah (cf. Jeremiah and Ezekiel) sees the problem in Judah and Jerusalem to be one of a failed leadership. It will be helpful to look at the motif of failed leadership in chs. 28–35, part of the second section of Isaiah's vision, in light of the earlier section of his vision in chs. 1–6.[27] Both chs. 1–5 and 28–35 are concerned with the misguided and wrongheaded actions of the ruling elite within the community. In chs. 1–5, scattered reference is made to rulers (1.10), princes (1.23; 3.14), judges (1.26), planners (1.26) and elders (3.14). A whole series of leaders is mentioned in 3.1-3 in a pericope suggesting that the leadership of the community will be removed by Yahweh:

---

27. This section of failed leadership presents in a modified form my earlier reading in *Reading Isaiah*, pp. 122-30.

> Because, behold, the lord Yahweh of hosts,
>   is taking from Jerusalem and Judah
> stay and staff,
>   the whole stay of bread,
>   and the whole stay of water;
> mighty man and the warrior,
>   judge and prophet,
>   diviner and elder,
> the captain of 50,
>   and the man of high position,
> the planner and the wise magician,
>   and the expert in charms.

The problem is not with select leaders within the community, but with the entire leadership. Leadership is characterized by pride and arrogance, as is eloquently stated in 2.12-17, with its series of metaphors of things lofty and superior. Associated with metaphors of the arrogance of leadership is the metaphor of haughtiness of the proud daughters of Zion (3.16-17).

In chs. 28–35, the leaders are likewise presented as arrogant, but also as being wrongheaded and inept. The leaders specified here are the priests (28.7), prophets (28.7; 29.10), scoffers who rule Jerusalem (28.14) and seers (29.10). In these chapters the incompetence of the leaders is associated with drunkenness, as is evident from the opening image of 'the proud crown of the drunkards of Ephraim' (28.1). The theme of the haughtiness of this leadership recurs in this section in the image of the proud and easy-living women of Zion (32.9-12).

The theme of the drunken prophets and priests recalls the imagery of Jeremiah of making the nations drink of the cup of the wine of wrath. References to the prophets who err in seeing (בְרֹאֶה, 28.15) and who deal in lies (כֹּזֵב, 28.15) and falsehood (שֶׁקֶר, 28.15) echo themes of Jeremiah and Ezekiel.

Significantly, chs. 1–5 and 28–35 are stylistically linked: each section contains six oracles beginning with 'woe' (הוֹי).[28] These twelve woes (with the exception of 33.1) are directed against the misguided leadership within

---

28. The 'woes' are found in 5.8, 11, 18, 20, 21, 22; 28.1; 29.1; 30.1; 31.1; 33.1. In his important two-part article ('The Composition of the Book of Isaiah', *JQR* 46 [1955–56], pp. 259-77; 47 [1956–57], pp. 114-38), L.J. Liebreich also identifies chs. 1–5 and 28–35 as two important divisions within the book. He points out the close relationship between these divisions, each with six woes. To explain the structure of the book Liebreich proposes a theory of *Stichworte*, the means the final redactor used to compile the book.

the community.[29] A motif that occurs in the 'woes' both in chs. 1–5 and 28–35 is that of faulty planning. This common element is important because it helps complete the picture that is developing in the Isaianic collage so that we can construe the problem with leaders as one in which they do not consider seriously (because they do not know) Yahweh's plan to wage war against all the nations of the land.

In chs. 1–5, the planner (יועץ, 3.3) is listed with the inventory of leadership that Yahweh will oust (3.1-3), and planners (יעצים) will be restored by Yahweh in the future (1.26). The 'woe' oracles against the leaders show them to be impatient, demanding immediate disclosure and fulfilment of the divine plan:

> Woe to those who draw iniquity with cords of falsehood,
>   who draw sin as with cart ropes,
> who say, 'Let him make haste,
>   let him speed his work (מעשהו)
>   that we may see it;
> let the plan (עצה) of the holy one of Israel draw near,
>   and let it come, that we may know it'. (5.18-19)

The attitude of the failed leadership is that Yahweh should 'make haste' (מהר) and 'speed (חוש) his work' so that his 'plan' (עצה) will come (בוא) and be made known (נדעה). This is in sharp contrast with Isaiah's waiting for Yahweh to accomplish his plan:

> O Yahweh, behold, we will wait (קוינו) for you.
>   Be our arm every morning,
>   our salvation in the time of trouble. (33.2; see also 8.16; 25.9; 26.8)

Woes directed against unsatisfactory planning are also found in the second part of Isaiah's 'vision'. In 28.23-29 a positive statement is made about the planning of Yahweh. Here, agricultural imagery is used to describe the wonder of Yahweh's planning:

> Give ear, and hear my voice;
>   Hearken, and hear my speech.
> Does he who plows for sowing plow continually?
>   Does he continually open and harrow his ground?
> When he has leveled its surface,
>   does he not scatter dill, sow cumin
> and put in wheat in rows
>   and barley in its proper place,

---

29. The woe oracle in 33.1 is directed against Babylon.

and spelt as the border?
For he is instructed aright;
    his God teaches him.
Dill is not threshed with a threshing sledge,
    nor is a cart wheel rolled over cumin;
but dill is beaten out with a stick,
    and cumin with a rod.
Does one crush bread grain?
    No, he does not thresh it forever;
when he drives his cart wheel over it
    with his horses, he does not crush it.
This also comes from Yahweh of hosts;
    a plan is made wonderful
    and excellent in wisdom.

The agricultural imagery recalls Yahweh's failed vineyard, which produced wild grapes (5.4) rather than the good grapes that Yahweh had planned for it (5.1-2). It is suggested that plowing and threshing are done the way they are because Yahweh planned them that way, and it is implied that this plan involves both crushing and the cessation of crushing. The emphasis on Yahweh's planning also points forward to the third 'vision' of Isaiah, which connects Yahweh's plan with the created order of things (cf. 40.12-17).

In Isaiah 29 a Woe Oracle is directed against those who disregard Yahweh's plan. They are confused because they think they can devise their own plan and hide it from Yahweh. Such a thing is as mistaken as misconstruing the potter and the clay:

Woe to those who hide deep from Yahweh their plan (עצה),
    and their deeds are in a dark place,
    and who say, 'Who sees us, and who knows us?'
You are turning things around.
    Shall the potter be regarded as the clay;
that the thing made says to its maker,
    'He did not make me';
or the imagination to the one who formed it,
    'He does not understand'? (29.15-16)

This confusion resulting in the inversion of the order of things recalls the similar theme of a woe oracle in 5.20:

Woe to those who say to the evil, 'good'
    and to the good, 'evil',
who put darkness for light

> and light for darkness,
> who put bitter for sweet
> and sweet for bitter.

The notion that plans of one's own making can be concealed from Yahweh in the dark (hidden 'deep from Yahweh' by those whose 'deeds are in the dark', who ask, 'Who sees us?') echoes visual imagery in another woe oracle in ch. 5:

> Woe to those who are wise in their own eyes,
> and shrewd in their own sight! (5.21)

These woe oracles in what I have called Isaiah's first and second sections of the 'vision' indicate that the חזון of Isaiah develop a sustained theme of reversal. It should not be surprising therefore that a similar woe against those who misconstrue the order of things is found in the third 'vision' of Isaiah. This occurs in 45.1 where potter-and-clay imagery is again used to describe one who confuses the clay of a potter with the potter.

Another woe oracle in the second section of Isaiah's 'vision' is directed against those who, ignoring Yahweh's plan, look elsewhere for a plan to follow:

> 'Woe to the rebellious children', a saying of Yahweh,
>   to accomplish a plan (עצה) and it is not from me;
> to pour out a molten image, and it is not my spirit,
>   in order to add sin to sin;
> the ones who go down to Egypt,
>   and do not ask my advice,
> to take refuge in the protection of Pharaoh
>   who seek shelter in the shadow of Egypt. (30.1-2)

This oracle recalls the denunciation of the Egyptian planners earlier in this second 'vision' of Isaiah (Isa. 19) when Yahweh confused the plans of the Egyptians by emptying out their spirit. It also anticipates the argument in the third section of Isaiah's vision (40.13) that good planning is connected with the spirit of Yahweh.

It will be helpful to summarize my discussion of failed leadership in this second vision of Isaiah. I have argued that it picks up the similar theme in chs. 1–5, which also appears in woe oracles directed against failed leadership. This second vision of Isaiah develops the vision in chs. 1–6. Yahweh has a plan for the future for which Isaiah is waiting. This plan concerns Yahweh's military strategy for waging war on all the nations of the world.

It is only when he accomplishes that plan, which includes reducing Judah and Jerusalem to a heap of ruins, that there will be restoration. The failure of leadership inheres in a failure to understand this plan.

As I have been arguing, however, חזון in Isaiah does not only speak about the destruction and disaster but also of salvation and restoration. Indeed, one might say that for prophets of חזון the emphasis is on salvation. Salvation is more prominent in the prophets of חזון than in Amos or Jeremiah.

This second section of Isaiah's vision also anticipates the third 'vision' in chs. 40–66. While the woe oracles in chs. 28–33 focus on a failed leadership in Judah, the last woe oracle (33.1) is directed against Babylon the destroyer (33.1; see also 21.2). Babylon in this woe oracle is symbolic of all present, inept and unjust power structures. We notice here again that the announcement of the downfall of Babylon entails a period of waiting (33.2).

The second part of the 'vision' looks forward to a time of world peace (chs. 34–35) as I have noted elsewhere in the 'vision' of Isaiah. Yahweh's victory against the pride and aggression of foreign powers will develop upon the aggressive arrogance of the leaders within the local community. Isaiah's vision opens up the vista of the future beyond the time of desolation and destruction with which the vision begins in Isaiah 1. What is viewed here is a world with a new social order, a world without arrogant leaders either domestic or foreign—a world where the people are addressed as royalty.

This envisioned future is the primary focus of the 'third' part of Isaiah's vision, but before turning to that, I want to look at the motif of reading and writing that occurs in this second vision of Isaiah. The emphasis on writing is further evidence of the importance of writing for חזון. I first consider 29.11-12:

> And the vision (חזות) of everything has come to you like the words of the sealed (החתום) book (הספר). If they give it to one who knows the book [that is, is able to read] saying, 'Read (קרא) this', he says, 'I am not able [to read] because it is sealed (חתום)'. And if the book is given to one who does not know the book [that is, is unable to read] saying, 'Read this', he says, 'I am not able to read'.

I contend that these words are referring to the writing down of Isaiah's vision. They echo words in the autobiographical narrative concerning Isaiah's reception of חזון during the days of Uzziah (ch. 6) and especially in the autobiographical narrative that opens the second 'vision' of Isaiah

during the days of Ahaz (ch. 8). That this vision has become like a book
that cannot be read because it is sealed (חתום) reflects what Isaiah said
about his 'vision' in 8.16: 'Bind up the testimony, seal (חתום) the teaching among my instructed ones'. Furthermore, a 'vision' that cannot be
seen is one that cannot be heard. The inability to hear and see the words of
Isaiah is a significant theme of ch. 6: 'Hear and hear, but do not understand; see and see, but do no perceive' (6.9).

The surrounding context of 29.11-12 echoes vocabulary and imagery
from Isaiah 6 and 8. The opacity of Isaiah's message to an audience that
cannot hear or see (6.9) recurs in 29.9-10 in the images of the prophets and
seers who, because they are 'blind drunk', are oblivious to sight and sound.
More significant, however, are the verses following the passage about the
unreadable sealed book (29.11-12). Yahweh is then quoted as saying:

> Because this people (העם הזה) draw near with their mouth (בפיו),
>> and honor me with their lips (ובשפתיו),
>> while their minds (ולבו) are far from me,
> and their fear of me has become a commandment of men
>> who are being trained;
> therefore I will again do incomprehensible things with this people,
>> incomprehensible and extraordinary;
> and the wisdom of the wise men will perish,
>> and the discernment of the discerning men will be hid. (29.13-14)

In these verses in which Yahweh is speaker, the 'you' (plural) of vv. 11-12
has changed to the third person, 'this people'. The change from the second
to the third person connotes a distancing of Yahweh from the community,
anticipating his abandonment of the people that we saw in Jeremiah. Similarly, when Yahweh is quoted as speaking in chs. 6 and 8, the implication
is that Yahweh has detached himself from the community. He refers to the
community as 'this people' (העם הזה) in 6.9-10:

> And he [Yahweh] said, 'Go, and say to this people (העם הזה),
> "Hear continually, but do not discern;
>> see continually but do not perceive".
> Make the mind (לב) of this people grow fat,
>> their ears grow heavy,
>> and their eyes shut.
> Lest they see with their eyes,
>> and hear with their ears,
> and understand with their heart (לב),
>> and turn and be healed.'

See also 8.16:

For Yahweh spoke thus to me [Isaiah] with his strong hand upon me, and
warned me to walk in the way of this people (העם הזה).

Both of these passages suggest that the community is incapable of receiving the חזון of Isaiah; 'this people' is a form of reference that suggests
separation.

The vocabulary concerned with the mouth, lips and heart of this people
in 29.13-14 also recalls the reception of חזון in Isaiah 6. That the *hearts*
(*minds*) 'are far from me' (29.13) echoes the directive given to Isaiah, 'to
make the *heart* (*mind*) of this people fat' (6.10). Furthermore, the couplet
'this people draw near with their mouth / and honor me with their lips'
(29.13) recalls Isaiah's encounter with Yahweh, which required that Isaiah's
mouth and lips be cleansed with a burning coal (6.6-7).

Another passage associating Isaiah's vision with a book is 30.8-11, which
recalls vocabulary and imagery in the narrative from ch. 8. Vocabulary
and imagery similar to those found in 29.11-12 appear in 30.8-11:

And now, go, write it (בכתה) on a tablet (לוח) before them,
 and inscribe (חקה) it in a book (ספר),
and it will be for a day to come,
 for a witness (עד) forever.
Because they are a rebellious people,
 lying sons,
sons who will not hear (שמוע)
 the teaching (תורת) of Yahweh;
who say to the seers (לראים), 'See not' (לא תראו);
 and to the seers (ולחזים), 'Do not see (לא תחזו) for us right things;
speak to us smooth things,
 see illusions,
leave from the way, turn aside from the path,
 let us hear no more of the Holy One of Israel'.

This passage has clear links with 8.16-20, the narrative at the opening of
the second part of the 'vision'. The command to 'write it' on a tablet and
'inscribe it' in a book that it may be a 'witness forever' recalls Isaiah's
command in the earlier narrative: 'Bind up (צור) the testimony (תעודה),
seal (חתום) the teaching (תורה) among my instructed ones' (8.16). The
verbs referring to the preservation of the vision in these two passages—
'write' (כתב), 'inscribe' (חקק), 'bind' (צרר) and 'seal' (חתם)—connote
authority and permanence. Some commentators have suggested that the
verbs in 30.8 seem to be confused.[30] 'To inscribe on a tablet' and 'to write

30. Otto Kaiser, *Isaiah 13–39* (trans. R.A. Wilson; OTL; Philadelphia: Westminster
Press, 1983), pp. 293-94.

in a book' would make better sense than 'to write in a tablet' and 'to inscribe in a book', since 'tablet' (לוח) refers chiefly to something hard such as stone on which inscriptions are made, and since book (ספר) refers to something less substantial on which one writes. This seeming confusion, however, is associated with understanding the language referentially rather than figuratively, that is, if one attempts to read this language as evidence for the actual production of the book of Isaiah or some other book or inscription. The noun 'tablet' in one phrase and the verb 'inscribe' in the other, each of which connotes durability, forces longevity upon transitory writing and perishable scroll respectively. The following line of poetry reinforces this imagery: 'that it may be for a day to come / as a witness forever'.

The word 'witness' (עד) in 30.8 and its counterpart 'testimony' (תעודה) in 8.16 (cf. 8.20), both of which connote legal proceedings and the official and weighty status given to legal transactions,[31] add an undertone of authority to the imagery of permanence. The forensic ambience is augmented by the verb 'to seal' (8.16; 29.11), which can also be used in the sense of 'to attest by sealing' a legal document.[32]

To summarize, then, this second 'vision' of Isaiah fleshes out the opening 'vision' of a land that is desolate with only a few survivors. The devastation of the land is the outcome of Yahweh's plan to wage war against all the nations. For prophets of חזון such as Isaiah, the accomplishment of this plan requires a period of 'waiting', since Yahweh announces these things long before they eventuate. The vision of Isaiah is written down in a 'book/tablet' and is sealed as a legal document. The forensic implications of Isaiah's חזון will become clearer in the third vision when all the nations are on trial and Yahweh prepares to bring the survivors home to Zion/ Jerusalem.

8. *Isaiah 7–35 Read Intertextually with Obadiah and Nahum*

In this section of Isaiah's vision, chs. 7–35, which focuses on Yahweh's plan against the nations, Isaiah is paralleling the חזון of Obadiah and Nahum. While these prophets, however, do not speak of Yahweh's plan

---

31. See, for example, Ruth 4.7-10, where both words occur in the same context of a legal transaction.

32. See, e.g., Jer. 32.10-11 where it is used with a deed of purchase. Notice also here that the transaction took place in the presence of 'witnesses' (עדים). See also Est. 3.12 and 8.8 where the word 'seal' is used in connection with a royal edict.

for total warfare against the nations, they do speak about Yahweh's judgment directed against two specific nations, Edom and Nineveh. In this way they parallel the second section of Isaiah's vision directed against the nations. Unlike Isaiah, however, both of these prophets have a northern orientation.

Obadiah's חזון is directed against Edom and appears to relate to Amos' words of future restoration when the booth of David will possess the remnant of Edom (Amos 9.11-12). The book of Nahum's חזון is directed exclusively against Nineveh, the capital city of the nation that had been Yahweh's instrument for bringing Israel to an end in the time when Yahweh abandoned the Northern Kingdom, which was announced in the words of Amos.

There are themes in these two prophets, however, that resonate with motifs we have encountered elsewhere. For example, in Nahum, Nineveh is questioned because it plots against Yahweh (1.9) and plans (יצא) only calamity (1.11). Implied here is the unsuccessful planning of the nations that is a theme in the second section of Isaiah's vision concerning Egypt and Tyre.

Obadiah's portrayal of Edom as drinking on Yahweh's holy mountain so that 'they shall be as if they have never been' (14-15) recalls imagery in Jeremiah 25 about the nations made to drink of the cup of the wine of wrath. Neither of these two prophets of 'vision', however, speaks about the total warfare of Yahweh, which we see in the חזון of Isaiah and the דברי of Jeremiah.

9. The Third Section of the Vision of Isaiah (Chapters 36–66)

For the reader interested in the compilational unity of Isaiah, it is not difficult to see an underlying structural design on several levels in the book. Comforting words of salvation and deliverance follow impending disaster. When Ahaz is threatened by the invasion from the alliance of the Syrian and Israelite kings, he is comforted with words of assurance promising deliverance. Even the implied threat—'if you do not believe, you will not be established'—and the warning of the coming invasion by the Assyrians (7.17–8.22) are followed by words of assurance that the people will be delivered from this threat (10.24-27). Later, the Hezekiah narrative depicts Hezekiah as escaping the imminent destruction of Jerusalem by the Assyrian king (37.21-38). The ominous warning that the Babylonian king is coming to take all the possessions of Hezekiah and his ancestors (39.5-7) is immediately followed by words of comfort (40.1-2). The words of salvation that characterize the text after ch. 40 in the third 'vision' of Isaiah differ in that there is no longer mention of deliverance for a king of Israel. Nor is there mention of a new external threat from an invading army. The focus (as in 10.24-27) is on the deliverance of the people Jacob/Israel and the place Zion/Jerusalem.

While the book of Isaiah does not avoid words of judgment, the design of the book always highlights deliverance and salvation. The first section of the 'vision' has words of salvation scattered throughout (e.g. 2.1-4; 4.2-6), even though the overall thrust is of devastation of the land. The first section of the 'vision' ends by referring to a nation that will come and bring destruction like a lion seizing its prey (5.26-30). The second section of Isaiah's 'vision' provides the reason for this anticipated calamity. Yahweh has a plan against all the nations of the land and against all the leaders in Judah and Jerusalem. This second section of the 'vision', however, ends with a view of the future as a time of restoration and return to Zion, the once desolated land (chs. 34–35). The third part of Isaiah's 'vision' is dominated by the theme of a future return from the north, a new Exodus, heralding a new beginning for a reinhabited Zion/Jerusalem. The overall design of the book, like the narratives themselves, represents a movement from disaster to restoration.

The distinguishing characteristic of this third part of Isaiah's 'vision' becomes immediately apparent when the opening lines (40.1-2) are compared to the opening lines of the first 'vision' (1.2). What had been the command for an impersonal sky and land to hear and give ear (שמעו, יהאזינו) to what Yahweh says about his rebellious children, who have turned against him leaving the land in a state almost like that of Sodom and Gomorrah, is now a very different decree:

> 'Comfort (נחמו), comfort my people',
>   your God will say,
> 'Speak (דברו) to the heart (mind) of Jerusalem,
>   and proclaim (קראו) to her
> that her warfare is completed,
>   that her iniquity is pardoned,
> that she has received from the hand of Yahweh
>   double for all her sins'.

These commands are not *about* Yahweh's people, as in 1.2, but are to be addressed *to* Yahweh's people and to the heart (mind) of Jerusalem. In 40.2 the words of comfort are words that Yahweh *will say* (יאמר), whereas in 1.2 the command concerns something Yahweh *has already spoken*

(דבר). This comforting, speaking and proclaiming in 40.2 is not for the present, but for the future. The first part of Isaiah's 'vision' is about what Yahweh *has already spoken*. This third section of the 'vision' is about *what Yahweh will say*.

As in 1.2, there is no clear indication of who is to carry out the commands, to 'speak' and 'proclaim'. However, I have argued that if one takes Hab. 2.2-3 as a typical setting for the reception of חזקן, then we should understand that a messenger, a reader, will run with the 'vision' to read it. Such a messenger is identified in 40.9 (cf. 41.27; 52.7) as Zion/Jerusalem, who will be a herald of good tidings (מבשרת). Such a herald of good tidings (מבשר) and proclaiming peace is referred to in Nahum who speaks of this 'messenger' as being on the mountains.[33]

The imagery of the bearer of tidings (מבשרה), who will announce that the warfare is over, again is derived from a military context. For example, in 2 Sam. 18.19-33 the story of Ahimaaz son of Zadok concerns his desire to run to bear the good tidings (בשר) that Yahweh had delivered David from his enemies. How Zion/Jerusalem will be the 'herald of good tidings' is not immediately clear, but it is from the mountain of Zion/Jerusalem that the herald will proclaim the good news that the warfare has ended for the cities of Judah. This messenger will also herald Yahweh's coming to Jerusalem. The identity of this herald becomes clearer in the 'vision' that follows.

I think that we should also see in ch. 40, that Isaiah's reception of חזון has some parallels with his reception of חזון in ch. 6. In both chapters he is unnamed but speaks in a first person singular voice. In both chapters he responds to Yahweh's voice (6.8; 40.6). Rather than reading Isaiah 40 as the call of a 'Second Isaiah', I think that it can be read as another occasion when the character of the prophet Isaiah receives vision.[34] The setting this time is not during the days of Uzziah but during the days of Hezekiah. What is to be proclaimed (read) is the חזון about the fall of Babylon and the return of Yahweh and his people to Zion.

The beginning of this 'vision' (chs. 40–47) focuses on Yahweh's plan to overthrow Babylon—missing in 13.1–14.21—and to accomplish his final triumph against all the nations of the land.[35] Argumentative questions like

---

33. The language here is very similar to Isa. 52.7.

34. For a discussion of the relationship between Isa. 6 and 40 see Christopher R. Seitz, *Zion's Final Destiny* (Minneapolis: Fortress Press, 1991), pp. 196-208.

35. The following is taken from pp. 63-82 of my *Reading Isaiah* (Augsburg/Fortress Press, 1991). Used by permission.

those used in the announcement of Yahweh's plan against the nations in chs. 13–27 occur here as a literary device aimed at persuading the reader of the inevitability of Yahweh's plan. The argumentative questions occur for the first time in 40.12-31. Unlike the questions associated with Yahweh's plan in chs. 13–27, which occur singly and in pairs, the questions here are numerous and occur in quick-fire succession to give persuasive weight to the contention that Yahweh is incomparable and the accomplishment of his plan inevitable.

Each of the five sets of questions in 40.12-31, like the question in the oracle of judgment against Tyre (23.8-9), is followed by an articulated answer.

	Questions	Answer
a.	40.12-14	40.15-17
b.	40.18	40.19-20
c.	40.21	40.22-24
d.	40.25-26a	40.26b
e.	40.27-28a	40.28b-31

These questions and answers in succession function as an argument supporting the inevitability of Yahweh's plan. Furthermore, these questions and answers reiterate points made in the articulation of Yahweh's military plan against the nations (chs. 13–27) and its partial fulfilment in the Hezekiah narrative (chs. 36–39).

a. *Isaiah 40.12-17*

The first set of questions concerns the incomparability of Yahweh as a military planner (40.12-14):

> Who has measured the waters in the hollow of his hand
> > and marked off the heavens with a span,
> enclosed the dust of the earth in a measure
> > and weighed the mountains in scales
> > and the hills in a balance?
> Who has directed the spirit (רוח) of Yahweh,
> > or who is his planner (עצתו) [who] has instructed him?
> Whom did he consult (נועץ) for his enlightenment,
> > and who taught him the path of justice,
> and taught him knowledge,
> > and showed him the way of understanding?

These argumentative questions indicate that Yahweh is incomparable as planner and military strategist and the ultimate creator and authority. As a planner he stands in sharp contrast with the planners of Egypt referred to earlier in the book (Isa. 19). In 19.3, Yahweh says that he will empty out the spirit (רוח) of the Egyptians so that their plans will be confounded. Indeed, the Egyptian planners will give stupid advice (19.11). In contrast, no one can empty out the spirit (רוח) of Yahweh and send his plans into confusion (Isa. 40). Furthermore, Yahweh does not need to consult anyone as the Egyptians did. As has just been learned from the Hezekiah narrative, Hezekiah's success came about because he consulted Yahweh for his military strategy (36.5). Yahweh does not consult; rather, he is consulted by those who are successful in averting military peril.

When nations such as Egypt and Assyria are compared to Yahweh, they are nothing. And that is exactly what is said in the answer that is given to the argumentative questions in 40.12-14:

> Behold, the nations are like a drop from a bucket,
>   and are accounted as the dust on the scales;
>   behold, he takes up the isles like fine dust.
> Lebanon would not suffice for fuel,
>   nor are its beasts enough for a burnt offering.
> All the nations are as nothing before him,
>   they are accounted by him as less than nothing and emptiness. (40.15-17)

b. *Isaiah 40.18-20*

The Egyptians in their confusion consulted idols (19.3). If the nations are nothing to Yahweh—'Who can empty out their spirit and send their plans into confusion?'—then how does Yahweh compare to idols such as those the Egyptians consulted? 'To whom will you liken God, / or what likeness compare to him?' (40.18). For the reader following the compilation of materials in the book of Isaiah, the answer is 'no one'. Hezekiah's prayer of confidence suggests that there is no one like Yahweh: 'Of a truth, O Yahweh, the kings of Assyria have laid waste all the nations and their lands, and they cast their gods into the fire, for they were no gods, but the work of men's hands, wood and stone; therefore they were destroyed' (37.18-19).

The answer to the question in 40.18 reiterates what the Hezekiah narrative demonstrates, namely, that unlike Yahweh, who is successful in warfare, idols of wood and stone have no power.

> The idol! A workman casts it,
>   and a goldsmith overlays it with gold,
>   and casts for it silver chains.

He who is impoverished chooses for an offering
    wood that will not rot;
he seeks out a skilful craftsman
    to set up an image that will not move. (40.19-20)

c. *Isaiah 40.21-24*

The next set of questions poses the central motif concerning Yahweh's plan: because Yahweh is unlike the nations and their idols, he can announce his plans beforehand and bring them to fruition. The questions ask:

Have you not known? Have you not heard (הלוא תשמעו)?
    Has it not been told you from the beginning?
    Have you not understood from the foundation of the earth? (40.21)

These questions echo the argumentative questions posed for the Assyrian king:

Have you not heard (הלוא שמעת)
    that I determined long ago?
I planned from days of old
    what now I bring to pass. (37.26)

For those following the ordering of materials as they are presented in the book, the reasons for the demise of the Assyrian king is clear—he fell victim to Yahweh, mistaking Yahweh's success with his own. The answer given to the argumentative questions in 40.21 suggests that Yahweh blows away earthly princes and rulers as if they were nothing, recalling Yahweh's easy victory over the Assyrian king just described in the Hezekiah narrative:

It is he who sits above the circle of the earth,
    and its inhabitants are like grasshoppers;
who stretches out the heavens like a curtain,
    and spreads them like a tent to dwell in;
who brings princes to naught,
    and makes the rulers of the earth as nothing.
Scarcely are they planted, scarcely sown,
    scarcely has their stem taken root in the earth,
when he blows upon them, and they wither,
    and the tempest carries them off like stubble. (40.22-24)

The reader is aware of what the Assyrian king has not heard. Yahweh has announced his plan long ago and is bringing that plan to fruition. No king can stand in his way.

d. *Isaiah 40.25-26*

The first three sets of questions function to persuade the audience that Yahweh is not like nations or their idols and kings. The incomparability of Yahweh is demonstrated in his predetermined plan against all the nations of the land, a plan that has reached partial fulfilment in the Hezekiah narrative. Answers to these questions reassure the audience and function to assuage any doubts. If Yahweh is not like nations and their idols and kings, then who is like Yahweh?

> To whom, then, will you compare me,
>> that I should be like him?
>> says the Holy One.
> Lift up your eyes on high and see:
>> Who created these? (40.25-26)

Yahweh as creator of the sky echoes the theme of Yahweh's announced victory 'over the host of the sky, in the sky/and the kings of the land, on the land' (24.21). Yahweh is incomparable both in the land and in the sky.

e. *Isaiah 40.27-31*

The last set of questions is directed to Jacob/Israel. The question posed earlier to the king of Assyria ('Have you not heard [הלוא שמעת]?') and echoed in the third set of argumentative questions (40.21) is echoed again in this final series of questions:

> Why do you say, O Jacob,
>> and speak, O Israel,
> 'My way is hidden from Yahweh,
>> and my right is disregarded by my God'?
> Have you not known? Have you not heard (לא שמעת)? (40.27-28a)

The accent on 'hearing' in the recurring argumentative question, 'Have you not heard?', recalls the emphasis on hearing in the Hezekiah narrative.[36] In the interaction among the Assyrian king, Hezekiah and Yahweh (Isa. 36–37), there are repeated references to hearing. In response to the Rabshakeh's initial speech (36.4-10), the servants of Hezekiah ask the Rabshakeh not to speak in the language of Judah when he is in the 'hearing' (literally 'in the ears', באזני) of the people (36.11). In a defiant retort the Rabshakeh stood and called out in the language of Judah, 'Hear...'

---

36. For a discussion of the emphasis on hearing in this narrative as it appears in 2 Kings, see Donna Nolan Fewell, 'Sennacherib's Defeat: Words at War in 2 Kings 18.13–19.37', *JSOT* 34 (1986), pp. 79-90 (84).

(36.13). In this second speech he tells the audience: 'Do not listen to Hezekiah' (36.16). Then 'when Hezekiah heard' (37.1), he sent a message to the prophet Isaiah saying, 'it may be that your God heard the words of the Rabshakeh' (37.4). The text implies that Yahweh has, of course, heard; and in the comforting War Oracle Yahweh says, 'Do not be afraid because of the words that you have heard' (37.6).

At this point the narrative suggests that something is going wrong for the Assyrians. The Rabshakeh 'had heard that the king [of Assyria] had left Lachish' (37.8). This happened because the king of Assyria 'heard' that Tirhakah king of Ethiopia had set out to fight against him, and 'when he heard it, he sent messengers to Hezekiah' (37.9). The messengers say to Hezekiah, 'Behold, you have heard what the kings of Assyria have done to all lands, destroying them utterly' (37.11). Hezekiah then prays to God in which he petitions Yahweh, 'Incline your ear, O Lord, and hear, open your eyes, O Yahweh, and see; and hear all the words of Sennacherib, which he has sent to mock the living God' (37.17). Yahweh does hear and answer Hezekiah with a taunt against the Assyrian king in which he questions the king, 'Have you not heard?' (37.26), and observes 'your arrogance has come to my ears' (37.29). The king who had challenged the power of Yahweh because he had overcome the gods of the other nations is slain worshipping in the temple of Nisroch his god (37.37). The emphasis on hearing is used to represent a strategy of war; boasting before the city walls is a strategy of war to persuade a besieged city to surrender without fighting.[37] Given the military connotations of Yahweh's plan, his argumentative questions concerning his incomparability are an enactment of this strategy of war. The emphasis on hearing has another significance in the book. Earlier in the text, Yahweh has announced his defeat of the Assyrian king. The correctness of that announcement is now proved: he has been slain. That he was slain in the temple of his god further strengthens the case the text is making as it develops: Yahweh is not like the nations and their gods and kings. He has announced his plans long ago and his plans prevail. Those who 'hear' the book have been given a demonstration of Yahweh's ability to accomplish all his plan: what Yahweh has previously announced he has done.

37. See Josh. 2.10-11 and 5.1, where the emphasis is placed on the psychological consequences of *hearing* about the exploits of the invading army. Robert G. Boling refers to this as 'psychological warfare' (*Joshua: A New Translation with Notes and Commentary* [AB, 6; Garden City, NY: Doubleday, 1982], p. 187).

Naming Jacob/Israel in 40.27-28 has an important consequence for the development of the thought of the book. The implication is that Jacob/Israel, unlike the king of Assyria and unlike the nations to whom questions were posed in the announcement of Yahweh's plan, has heard and does know what the king of Assyria did not hear and did not know. Yahweh has announced his plan long ago and is bringing it to fruition. This matter of having heard and having known Yahweh's plan confers special status on Israel among the world's nations on whom Yahweh is planning total warfare. It is at this point that it begins to become clear who will hear what Yahweh *will say* (40.1) and how Zion/Jerusalem will become a herald of good tidings. The community Jacob/Israel will be Yahweh's witnesses so that his 'vision' will be proclaimed from Zion/Jerusalem.

The questions in ch. 40, however, indicate that Jacob/Israel is not entirely persuaded of Yahweh's ability to accomplish his plan and that some within Jacob/Israel may not be persuadable. The text intimates that Yahweh's plan may not be clearly manifest to everyone. In fact, Jacob/Israel is portrayed as contending an opposite case, namely, that Yahweh has hidden himself from Jacob/Israel. To counter this contention the following answer is given:

> Yahweh is the everlasting God,
> > The Creator of the ends of the earth.
> He does not faint or grow weary,
> > his understanding is unsearchable.
> He gives power to the faint,
> > and to him who has no might he increases strength.
> Even youths shall faint and be weary,
> > and young men shall fall exhausted;
> but they who wait for Yahweh shall renew their strength,
> > they shall mount up with wings like eagles,
> they shall run and not be weary.
> > they shall walk and not faint. (40.28b-31)

This answer reinforces the theme of 40.26b that Yahweh is creator of the heaven and the earth. With its references to Yahweh's giving of 'power to the faint' and increasing strength 'to him who has no might', it also alludes to the final announcement about Yahweh's plan in 25.1-5 to provide strength to the poor and needy. The response to the claim that Yahweh has hidden his face is that this is a time of waiting; the weak and powerless will receive strength in the future (40.31). But this time of waiting is also a time for a reader to run with the good tidings that Yahweh has now turned to his people to comfort them.

The questions in ch. 40 are used to build a persuasive argument concerning Yahweh's plan for Babylonia. The imminent demise of Babylon is announced in chs. 41–47, where the motif of Yahweh's plan appears for the last time in the text (46.8-11). Argumentative questions appear in chs. 41–47 interspersed with other material. When read together and in succession, these questions establish that Yahweh is about to fulfil his announced plan to defeat the Babylonians (13.1–14.23). The nations, including Babylon, are as uninformed about the meaning of Yahweh's plan as was the Assyrian king in 37.26 to whom Yahweh posed questions about his plan. When questions are posed to the nations in chs. 41–47 about what is happening, they do not answer—and the implication is that they cannot answer. But Yahweh has witnesses: Jacob/Israel, to whom Yahweh's plan has been made known. The reader also knows of the partial fulfilment of that plan in the Hezekiah narrative. The representation of Jacob/Israel as witnesses helps explain the legal connotations that we have seen above associated with Isaiah's writing down the חזון as testimony for the future.

In the following section I have summarized the material in chs. 41–47 in order to highlight the significance of the argumentative questions. The first questions after ch. 40 are found in 41.2-4. Here the coastlands and the peoples are summoned to come together as if they are being brought to trial, and Yahweh interrogates them with the following questions:

> Who stirred up one from the east,
>> whom victory meets at every step?
>> He gives up nations before him,
>> so that he tramples kings under foot;
>> he makes them like dust with his sword,
>> like driven stubble with his bow.
>> He pursues them and passes on safely,
>> by paths his feet have not trod.
>> Who has performed (פעל) and done (עשה) [this],
>> calling the generations from the beginning? (41.2-4a)

Yahweh answers this question himself, implying that the nations are unable to respond:

> I, Yahweh, the first,
>> and will be with the last; I am he. (41.4b)

The new military event that will be the undoing of the Babylonians is about to occur, and it is Yahweh who has planned it. In response to this new military threat, the uncomprehending scurry around to make idols for protection (41.5-7), apparently in order to consult them, as it was said the

Egyptians would do (19.3). The reader, however, knows that idols are of no protection. This was indicated in the prayer of Hezekiah (37.18-19). The reader also knows that Yahweh is not like an idol (40.18-20), and, for that reason, was able to deliver Hezekiah from the Assyrian king who had defeated only nations whose gods were made of wood and stone. When Yahweh delivered Hezekiah from the Assyrians, he addressed Hezekiah with a War Oracle. In this new situation, with a new conqueror on the scene, Yahweh comforts Jacob/Israel with Royal War Oracles (41.8-13, 14-16). When Jacob/Israel is threatened by military attack, Yahweh, unlike the idols, will deliver his people, who are not like the other nations with their kings.

There follow (1) additional words of comfort (41.17-20), (2) a new trial scene in which the gods this time are to tell what is to happen—however, they are not able to do so because they are nothing (41.21-24)—and (3) an announcement that Yahweh had proclaimed and declared to Zion/Jerusalem what was about to happen (41.25-29). At this time the image of the servant is introduced (42.1-4), and the way the servant is described picks up key motifs associated with Yahweh's military planning. Yahweh, whose spirit cannot be directed (40.13) and who had emptied out the spirit of the Egyptians and sent them into confusion (19.3), will put his spirit in his servant (42.1) who, like Yahweh (40.14), will bring justice to the nations (42.1). This servant, who will have Yahweh's spirit, will be a 'wonderful planner', as was Hezekiah (9.5). The vocation of this royal servant to whom Yahweh will give his spirit (42.5) is further described in 42.5-9. A song is given in praise of Yahweh (42.10-13) because of his actions as 'a man of war' (42.13). Yahweh reiterates his plan to conduct his global warfare (42.1-17), and then a new set of argumentative questions is raised. These questions, like the questions in 40.27-28, are addressed to a community that appears to be characterized as a reluctant servant:

> Hear, you deaf;
>   and look, you blind that you may see!
> Who is blind but my servant,
>   or deaf as my messenger whom I send?
> Who is blind as my dedicated one,
>   or blind as the servant of Yahweh? (42.18-19)

The response to these questions is significant not only because it also contains questions, but also because it is spoken in a first person plural voice, the voice of the community who waits for Yahweh, a community with whom Isaiah identifies (42.23-24):

Who among you will give ear to this,
　　will attend and listen for the time to come?
Who gave up Jacob to the spoiler,
　　and Israel to the robbers?
Was it not Yahweh, against whom *we* have sinned,
　　in whose ways *they* would not walk,
　　and whose law *they* would not obey?

This questioning first person plural voice is important because it under-girds the movement I have been pointing out in the design of the text. The text is shaped so as to present the case persuasively that Yahweh is about to fulfil his plans for the world announced long ago. This first person plural voice now invites the larger community (Jacob/Israel) to 'give ear', 'attend' and 'listen'. Yahweh's question, 'have you not heard?', addressed to the Assyrian king (37.26) and repeated twice in the argumentative questions in ch. 40 (vv. 21 and 28), is now a question that is addressed to Jacob/Israel. The emphatic nature of this question is underscored by the use of the word שׁמע with two of its synonyms אזן and קשׁב. This passage (42.18-25) offers another perspective on the final argumentative questions addressed to Jacob/Israel in 40.27-28. There the questions suggested that the community thought that Yahweh had hidden his face from them. This passage suggests otherwise. It is the community that is blind and deaf (42.18-20) and therefore cannot see and hear what Yahweh is doing in this new phase of his plan. The 'vision' of Isaiah has changed. Whereas the land and the sky are invited to hear about desolation and destruction at the beginning of the book, Jacob/Israel is invited to hear about deliverance and restoration.

The questions challenging the community to hear are followed by Royal War Oracles (43.1-4, 5-7) which give comfort to the servant of Yahweh, the community and Jacob/Israel as they hear the war strategy of Yahweh. The War Oracles are followed by another trial scene (43.8-13) involving the blind and deaf servant of Yahweh (43.8) and all the nations (43.9). The nations are not able to bring any 'witnesses' to testify for them because they are not able to speak about the former things and the things to come. They do not know Yahweh's plan. But Yahweh has witnesses to what he planned long ago and to what he is now bringing to pass:

'You are my witnesses', says Yahweh
　　'and my servant whom I have chosen,
that you may know and believe me
　　and understand that I am he.

Before me no god was formed,
  nor shall there be any after me.
I, I am Yahweh,
  and besides me there is no savior.
I declared and saved and proclaimed
    when there was no strange god among you;
    and you are my witnesses', says Yahweh. (43.10-12)

This passage clarifies why it is important for this community, the royal servant, to hear Yahweh. The people are to keep their ears open to hear Isaiah's 'vision' read. This vision as testimony will enable them to be witnesses to what is happening as the fulfilment of Yahweh's plan for the nations.

Following this passage in which the servant of Yahweh is designated as his witnesses, he says that he is about to defeat the Babylonians (43.14-24). Even though his people have transgressed (43.25-28), he comforts them, as if they were a king, with a Royal War Oracle in which he promises to pour his spirit on their descendants, assuring sound counsel and planning (44.1-5). This last War Oracle is followed by another set of argumentative questions in which Yahweh reiterates the point that he had planned, proclaimed and announced long ago what he is now bringing to pass, and that, unlike the gods of the other nations, he has witnesses to prove it:

Who is like me? Let him proclaim it,
  let him declare and set it forth before me.
Who has announced from of old the things to come?
  Let them tell us what is yet to be.
Fear not, nor be afraid;
  have I not told you from of old and declared it?
And you are my witnesses!
  Is there a god besides me?
There is no rock; I know not any. (44.7-8)

The text then reiterates the main points already raised. There is another attack on the idols who are nothing and whose witnesses neither see nor know (vv. 9-20); a call for Jacob/Israel, Yahweh's servant, to remember (vv. 21-22); a responsive praise to Yahweh (v. 23); and a final passage (vv. 24-28) averring that Yahweh will confirm 'the plan of his messengers' (עצת מלאכיו). In this passage the conqueror who is to carry out Yahweh's plan is mentioned by name (v. 28). He is Cyrus. Yahweh says of him that he is 'my shepherd' and that he will fulfill 'my plan' (חפצי). Just as Hezekiah and Sennacherib were not mentioned in the book by name until Yahweh was about to fulfill his plan concerning Assyria, so Cyrus, the king who is to carry out Yahweh's plan against Babylon, is mentioned by name for the first time here as the book moves toward the final announcement of the fall of Babylon (chs. 46–47). Before 44.28 there are only veiled references to Cyrus (e.g. 41.2).

In ch. 45 Yahweh again mentions Cyrus by name in an extended passage in which Yahweh argues that he is responsible for what Cyrus does (45.1-8). At that point, a woe oracle is pronounced on these who doubt (cf. 40.27-28). They are challenged with the following rhetorical questions, again used to persuade rather than to elicit answers:

> Woe to him who strives with his Maker (יצרו),
>   an earthen vessel with the potter!
> Does the clay say to him who fashions it, 'What are you making (תעשה)?'
>   or [to a woman] 'Your work (פעלך) has no handles'?
> Woe to him who says to a father, 'What are you begetting?'
>   or to a woman, 'With what are you in travail?'
> Thus says the Yahweh,
>   the Holy One of Israel, and his Maker (ויצרו):
> 'Will you question me about my children,
>   or command me concerning the work (פעל) of my hands?' (45.9-11)

The images of 'the potter' and of 'parents' use a variety of the words (יצר, פעל, עשה) associated with the announcement of Yahweh's plan and its accomplishment.

In 45.14-17 the makers of idols are again condemned as confused. This is followed by a passage saying that Yahweh did not speak in secret (45.18-20). At this point another trial-scene appears. The survivors of the nations are asked to make their case and to answer questions after consulting with one another:

> Declare and present your case;
>   let them make plans (יועצו) together!
> Who told this long ago?
>   Who declared it of old?
> Was it not I, Yahweh?
>   And there is no god besides me,
> a righteous God and a Savior;
>   there is none besides me. (45.21)

The nations again cannot answer this question and are invited to come to Yahweh and be saved (45.22-25).

Chapter 46 is another attack on the idols, but this time the idols are mentioned by name as Babylonian gods, as the text moves toward the climax of announcing Yahweh's victory over Babylon. The ineffectiveness of the idols, Bel and Nebo, is suggested in the images of beasts struggling to carry them (46.1-2). These idols are borne by beasts, but it is Yahweh who has borne Jacob/Israel (46.3-4). Again, the point is made that Yahweh is incomparable and that for this reason his plan cannot be thwarted. Here Yahweh mentions for the last time his plan to use a new conqueror to defeat Babylon:

> Remember this and consider,
>   recall it to mind, you transgressors,
>   remember the things of old;
> for I am God, and there is no other;
>   I am God, and there is none like me,
> declaring the end from the beginning
>   and from ancient times things not yet done,
> saying, 'My plan (עצתי) shall stand,
>   and I will accomplish (אעשה) all my purpose (חפצי)',
> calling a bird of prey from the east,
>   the man of my plan (עצתי) from a far country.
> I have spoken, and I will bring it to pass;
>   I planned (יצרתי) and I will do it (אעשנה). (46.8-11)

Chapter 47 concerns the imminent downfall of Babylon. It makes the point that Babylon's planners cannot save it:

> You are wearied with your many planners (עצתיך)
>   let them stand and save you,
> those who divide the heavens,
>   who gaze at the stars,
> who at the new moons predict
>   what shall befall before you. (47.13)

Babylon's planners, like those of the Syro-Israelite alliance, Egypt and Assyria, cannot prevail against Yahweh's plan.

This third 'vision', then, is not a 'vision' of desolation and destruction, which Yahweh *has already spoken*. This vision is about what Yahweh *will say* after that destruction has taken place. This חזון will be proclaimed by Jacob/Israel, who will herald good tidings from the mountain, Zion/Jerusalem. They will be Yahweh's witnesses for they have Isaiah's vision as a testimony to what Yahweh had announced long ago.

The remaining part of the third part of Isaiah's vision concerns the portrayal of the future community and Yahweh's interaction with them. This material cannot be summarized succinctly. Therefore I want to conclude my discussion of this section of Isaiah's vision by making some general observations about the remaining material.

A central theme in this material, already encountered in the discussion above about Jacob/Israel as Yahweh's witnesses, concerns the former things and the new things to come (41.22; 42.9; 43.9, 18; 44.7; 45.21; 46.9; 48.3). In light of my discussion of the prophetic literature read as a collection of scrolls, this new thing should be understood as referring to restoration after Yahweh has cleared the land. The community depicted in this third section of Isaiah has already drunk from the cup of the wine of wrath (כוס היין החמה) prophesied by Jeremiah:

> Rouse yourself, rouse yourself!
>   Arise, O Jerusalem.
> You who have drunk
>   the cup of his wrath (כוס חמתו),
> you who have drunk to the dregs
>   the bowl (קבעת כוס) of staggering. (Jer. 25.15-26)

The community who has experienced the cup of Yahweh's wrath is presented as one that is distant from the ancestors since Yahweh is about to create a new sky and a new land (Isa. 65.17). Abraham (63.16) and Moses (63.11) are depicted as characters from the past who are separated from the present community. The community will be a new community in a restored Jerusalem (51.12; 61.4) with a new name (62.2).

When Isaiah received his 'vision' he wrote it down because the time of the reception of his 'vision' was a time of waiting (8.17). In this new time the period of waiting is over:

> And from long ago, they did not hear (שמעו),
>   and they did not give ear (האזינו),
> there was no one who saw a god besides you,
>   he will work for the one who waits for him. (64.3 [Eng. 64.4])

The two verbs 'hear' (שמעו) and 'give ear' (האזינו) are the same two verbs used to address the sky and the land at the beginning of Isaiah's vision (1.2). The period of waiting is now over for Yahweh is creating a new sky and a new land.

The third part of Isaiah's vision, then, is concerned with the time of restoration after Yahweh has cleared the land. It is a time when the vision of Isaiah can be heard and seen by a community who will be his witnesses for the work he has done and which he announced long ago. Isaiah's vision, which he wrote down in the days of Jotham, Uzziah, Ahaz and Hezekiah testifies to Yahweh's power. He has brought to fruition what he announced in an earlier time.

10. *Isaiah 36–66 Read Intertextually with Habakkuk and Zephaniah*

Both Habakkuk and Zephaniah as prophets of 'vision' have affinities with the third part of Isaiah's 'vision'. While the main motifs of חזון are found in Hab. 2.2-3, חזון is not used in the superscription of either Habakkuk and Zephaniah, nor do they begin with call to hear as do Isaiah, Joel and Micah. They do contain motifs, however, that associate them more clearly with the orthodox prophets of vision than with unorthodox prophets such as Amos, Jeremiah and Ezekiel.

Habakkuk begins with intercession (1.2-4), an intercession that is answered by Yahweh (1.5-11). This intercession and answer stand in contrast to Amos and Jeremiah for whom Yahweh refused to provide answers. Perhaps we should understand from Habakkuk that the role of an orthodox prophet of vision to intercede. The action of Habakkuk, although he is not doing this on behalf of a king, has some parallels with Isaiah's interaction with Ahaz and Hezekiah offering them signs of Yahweh's activity.

Habakkuk's intercession concerns how long violence and destruction leading to injustice will continue. The answer is that Yahweh is about to act through the Chaldeans (Babylonians). As a prophet of vision Habakkuk will wait for Yahweh to carry out his work through the Chaldeans (2.3). The coming destruction by the Babylonians recalls the image of the cup of Yahweh's wrath by which he will make the nations stagger—the same imagery as in Jeremiah and Isaiah.

Habakkuk is a prophet, like Isaiah, who interacts with Yahweh who is in his holy temple (2.20). Also like the third section of Isaiah's vision, Habakkuk contrasts Yahweh with the idol (2.18-19), and also like Isaiah, Habakkuk will wait for the day of calamity to come (3.16).

Zephaniah, like other prophets of vision (Isaiah, Joel and Micah), begins with a picture of total destruction against all the land (1.2-18). The vision here is like that in Jeremiah where all the inhabitants are emptied from the land (25.11). Chapter 2 of Zephaniah are words of judgment offered against the nations. Like Isaiah, Zephaniah also sees the problem with the leaders (3.3-5). For Zephaniah in the days of Josiah, this is also a time of waiting for Yahweh, who will arise as a witness. Like the third section of Isaiah's vision, Zephaniah waits for that day when Yahweh will be a 'warrior who gives victory' (1.17) and delivers a 'fear not' oracle comforting Zion (1.16-20).

11. *Summary and Conclusion*

In this chapter I have looked at Isaiah as a prophet of חזון and have read his vision in conjunction with other prophets of vision (Joel, Micah, Obadiah, Nahum, Habakkuk and Zephaniah). The character of these prophets, unlike the unorthodox prophets (Amos, Jeremiah and Ezekiel), tends to fall into the background. Their words are for another time; the reception of 'vision' initiates a period of waiting.

These prophets are primarily concerned with announcing comfort and consolation and they look forward to restoration. In the collection of prophetic scrolls their role is seen as moving the history beyond the time of destruction to the time when Zion/Jerusalem will be rebuilt. They receive their 'vision' in the temple; they do not see words in natural imagery as do Amos and Jeremiah; nor do they have visions of God in a strange land as does Ezekiel. God's presence, ensuring security for the community, is associated with his presence in the temple. The significance of the temple will become more evident in the next chapter in the discussion of the book of the Twelve.

Chapter 8

'[THE] BEGINNING OF YAHWEH SPOKE [WAS] WITH HOSEA':
READING THE TWELVE IN LIGHT OF THE MAJOR PROPHETS

The word of Yahweh which came to Hosea, the son of Buzi, in the days of
Uzziah, Jotham, Ahaz and Hezekiah, kings of Judah, and in the days of
Jeroboam, son of Joash, a king of Israel. [The] beginning of Yahweh spoke
[was] with Hosea... (Hos. 1.1-2a)

In the second year of Darius, the king, on the sixth month on the first day of
the month the word of Yahweh came in the hand of Haggai, the prophet, to
Zerubbabel, the son of Shealtiel, the governor of Judah, and to Joshua, the
son of Jehozadak, the high priest. (Hag. 1.1)

In the eighth month, in the second year of Darius, the word of the Yahweh
came to Zechariah, the son of Berechiah, the son of Iddo, the prophet,
saying... (Zech. 1.1)

An oracle, the word of Yahweh, to Israel in the hand of Malachi. (Mal. 1.1)

Before beginning my discussion of the Twelve, let me review briefly what
has happened in the three previous chapters. I have been reading Jeremiah,
Ezekiel and Isaiah by focusing on how the openings of these scrolls, their
superscriptions, provide a clue about how to read the collection, order and
arrangement of materials that follow. Superscriptions function as identi-
fiers of genre. Isaiah is to be read as the 'vision' (חזון) of the prophet,
Jeremiah as the 'words of' (דברי) the prophet Jeremiah, and Ezekiel as a
narrative of what happened (ויהי) to the prophet. Isaiah, Jeremiah and
Ezekiel each represents a distinctive collection of materials. The three
should not be grouped together and read as a single genre—as 'the prophetic book'. To allude to the discussion in Chapter 1 on the semiotics of
reading, I have argued that a prophetic book should not be viewed simply
as representing 'the typical' in Gunkel's sense of the task of the form
critic. Evoking Muilenburg's notion of the rhetorical critic makes it necessary to look at each of the prophetic scrolls as distinctive. To read the
prophetic scrolls intertextually as I have done suggests particularity as
well as commonality.

Commonality has already been suggested in relation to Isaiah, Jeremiah and Ezekiel. These books gain clarity when read intertextually with 'books' in the scroll of the Twelve Minor Prophets that share common phrases in the superscriptions—חזון, דברי and ויהי—suggesting similarity in genre. In the case of Isaiah, I also looked at how Isaiah shared other formal characteristics with some of the scrolls that had alternative openings in the superscriptions, which suggested that they, like Isaiah, should be read as 'vision'. However, although 'vision' (חזון), 'words of' (דברי) and 'and it happened' (ויהי) were understood as encoding representative features of prophetic books, each prophetic book was understood in terms of its singularity. Jeremiah was not read as a clone of Amos, Ezekiel as a clone of Jonah, or Isaiah as a clone of the other prophets of vision.

The scroll of the Twelve[1] needs to be read in terms of its particularity illumined by the common features it shares with Jeremiah, Ezekiel and Isaiah. As a prophetic scroll, it is different from these three prophetic books in one obvious way. The materials collected, ordered and arranged on this scroll do not concern a single, individual, prophetic figure. Rather it is a collection of prophetic books representing an assortment of prophetic genres.[2]

---

1.   I am aware that there is some variation in the ordering of books in the scroll of the Twelve. I am reading the canonical outcome represented by the order of the Twelve in the received MT. For variations in canonical order see Paul L. Redditt, 'Recent Research on the Book of the Twelve as One Book', *CRBS* 9 (2001), pp. 47-80 (65-67).

2.   Michael H. Floyd's article ('The מַשָּׂא [*Maśśa*] as a Type of Prophetic Book', *JBL* 121 [2002], pp. 401-22) appeared on my desk just as this manuscript was scheduled to go to press. The article builds on the previous work of Richard Weis ('Oracle', in *ABD*, V, pp. 28-29). Floyd's article is important for my study because he argues for an approach similar to the one I have taken in this book. He understands מַשָּׂא as important information at the beginning of a prophetic book providing guidance for reading a book as a whole (p. 421). He is primarily concerned with this information for 'books' in the Twelve: Nahum, Habakkuk, the two oracles that conclude Zechariah (chs. 9–11 and 12–14) and Malachi. He understands the oracle to indicate genre with its purpose being 'prophetic reinterpretation of a previous revelation' (pp. 409-10). It consists of three parts: (1) 'an assertion…about Yahweh's particular involvement in a particular historical situation', (2) a clarification of 'the implications of a previous revelation from Yahweh' and (3) 'the basis for directives concerning appropriate reactions or responses to Yahweh's initiative, or for insights into how Yahweh's initiative affects the future' (p. 409). Although all of the books representative of this genre in the Twelve have these same three characteristics, they 'are in many ways very different' (p. 421). I also understand that Nahum, Habakkuk, Zechariah and Malachi function differently in the Twelve. As I will argue, later Nahum and Habakkuk can

In the three previous chapters, eight of the prophetic books have been briefly discussed. 'The words of Amos' were understood to share common generic features with 'the words of Jeremiah'. Both prophets are unconventional prophets seeing natural imagery as metaphorical expressions of Yahweh's words. Both prophets receive their words in the outside world and bring them inside the temple to announce the end of a kingdom, including its people and its temple. Amos prophesies the end of Israel; Jeremiah prophesies the end of Judah.

While Jonah and Ezekiel are highly distinctive, both are prophetic narratives about fantastic characters, sharing the common feature that Yahweh appears to a prophet in the land of the enemy. Yahweh appears to Jonah in Nineveh and to Ezekiel in Babylon.

Isaiah as a prophet of 'vision' shares features with other prophets of vision—Joel, Micah, Obadiah, Nahum, Habakkuk and Zephaniah. These prophetic books, set in a distant past, portray Yahweh's plan for the future for Israel and Judah, and for all the nations of the world. It is a time of waiting for 'the word of Yahweh' to come to fruition. While the prophets of vision see destruction and desolation (and this is the sole theme in some), their words are generally characterized as words of consolation. These prophets envision that Yahweh's people will return to prosperity in the land and will have numerous offspring when Yahweh again is present in the temple.

Four of the prophets in the Twelve—Hosea, Haggai, Zechariah and Malachi—were not discussed in the previous three chapters. These are prophets that come at the beginning and end of the Twelve. In Chapter 4, I alluded to one of the distinguishing features of the Twelve. As a whole, the Twelve has a more northern focus than Jeremiah, Ezekiel and Isaiah. The Northern Kingdom, with its plurality of cultic centers at Bethel, Samaria, Gilgal and elsewhere, receives more focused, although not exclusive, attention. The future restoration after the calamity coming to the north is envisioned as centering on Jerusalem.

also be understood as 'vision' in my intertextual reading of them with Isaiah. The oracles at the end of Zechariah and Malachi perform a unique function at the close of the Twelve in a literary world where messengers appear. Floyd's article, then, provides important supplementary information to my own understanding of a מַשָּׂא, which I have understood primarily as a document to be held in the hand. It is important to observe, however, that a מַשָּׂא never comes at the beginning of a scroll. Rather, it identifies sections of a scroll as it does in the Twelve.

1. *The Beginning of Yahweh Spoke*

Hosea begins with a very general superscription that encodes only general information. The phrase, 'the דבר (word/thing) of Yahweh' is a general phrase that can designate 'vision' (חזון), 'the words of' (דברי) or even prophetic narrative (ויהי). The general dating in the days of Uzziah, Jotham, Ahaz and Hezekiah has affinities with the חזון of Isaiah. However, its significant difference when compared with Jeremiah, Ezekiel and Isaiah is that it also provides temporal information by making reference to a king of Israel, 'Jereboam, son of Joash', as does Amos. This coded information, situating the book in the time of a king of Israel, distinguishes Hosea and introduces the northern focus for the Twelve to which I have alluded.

The significant phrase at the beginning of Hosea follows the superscription in Hos. 1.2a—'[the] beginning of Yahweh spoke [was] with Hosea' (תחלת דבר־יהוה בהושע). I discussed this phrase above in Chapter 4 arguing that it should be read as an independent phrase suggesting that Hosea is the first of a series of figures to whom Yahweh spoke. In this sense it is a fitting phrase to introduce the scroll of the Twelve, which collects and arranges a series of twelve prophetic books on one scroll.[3] As the last scroll in the rabbinic canonical order, the Twelve follows Joshua, Judges, Samuel, Kings, Jeremiah, Ezekiel and Isaiah. The Twelve represents not only the beginning of God speaking to prophets but also the end. Prophets disappear in the Twelve, and, as I will show, messengers (מלאכים) emerge in Haggai, Zechariah and Malachi to take their place.

I now want to concentrate on Hosea as the beginning of the collection of the Twelve: 'the beginning of Yahweh spoke'. The book of Hosea is not a חזון as is the book of Isaiah. The collection of materials is not about a distant future but focuses on Hosea's own present situation, primarily concerning Israel. Judah, however, is a recurring and important, although not central theme. Because of this emphasis on the present, Hosea shares themes with Jeremiah and Ezekiel. However, the book is neither like 'the words of' (דברי) Jeremiah announcing the end of a kingdom, nor like 'the visions (מראות) of God' that happened (ויהי) to Ezekiel in a foreign land. Hosea is like Ezekiel in chs. 1–3 in that Yahweh uses him in a personal way to live out Yahweh's 'word'. He even speaks in the first person (Hos. 3) as does Ezekiel. But Hosea is not subjected to manipulation as was the more passive Ezekiel. In the later part of the book, Hosea, like Jeremiah,

---

3.   See also my *Zechariah*, p. 23.

addresses the coming desolation of Israel (and to a lesser degree Judah), but the emphasis is not on Hosea's 'words', nor is Hosea engaged in military confrontation with his own people as enemy, as was Jeremiah. Hosea needs to be read in its distinctiveness as a prophetic book at the commencement of Yahweh's speaking to prophets about the end of Israel and Judah in the Twelve, and in a period chronologically portrayed as prior to Jeremiah and Ezekiel but closely related in time to Isaiah.

2. Divorcing Gomer (Israel)

However offensive the ideology underlying the relationship between Hosea and Gomer,[4] the opening three chapters of Hosea introduce the major theme of Jeremiah, Ezekiel, Isaiah and the Twelve: Yahweh separates himself from his people (both Israel and Judah). This separation is accomplished by his departure from the temples in Israel and Judah where his presence ensured prosperity. He is also sending his people away. Return and restoration will only take place after the period of separation in which the land is made desolate.

As is well known, the first three chapters of Hosea contain (1) a third person narrative about how Hosea is to take a wife of harlotry (זנונים) (1.2b–2.2), (2) a poetic commentary on that relationship (2.3-25) and (3) a first person narrative for Hosea to go again and 'love a woman who has a lover and is an adulteress (מנאפת)' (3.1-5). The cruel, cold-hearted Yahweh as lover depicted in the narrative and poetry of ch. 2 in which Gomer has no voice and remains anonymous in ch. 3, is consistent with the self-centered actions of Yahweh depicted especially in Jeremiah and Ezekiel, where the community is largely silenced. The pornographic-like discipline of the wife and mother is suggested in 2.3-25 where it is threatened that the woman is stripped naked in public (2.5):

> *Lest I strip her naked,*
> *and I expose her like the day of she was born.*
>> And I make her like a wilderness,
>> and I make her like a land of drought,
>> and I kill her with thirst.

This matches the ruthless and heartless desolation of the land of Israel that we encounter, for example, in Jer. 25.9b-10a:

---

4.   Gomer is mentioned by name in 1.3. Whether or not the woman in ch. 3 is Gomer is ambiguous.

> I will totally destroy them and I will make them a desolate waste, an object
> of derisive hissing, and a ruin forever. I will cause to cease among them the
> sound of rejoicing, the sound of merriment, the voice of the bridegroom, the
> voice of the bride, the sound of the millstone and the light of the lamp. The
> whole of this land will become a desolated waste and a ruin.

What is envisaged here is the end of Israel (1.4) and its accompanying
cultic celebrations (2.13-15).

Dispersed throughout the imagery of the wife stripped of her identity
and dying of thirst are expressions of return. This theme is significant for
understanding the Israelite focus of the Twelve, which is viewed from a
southern perspective. Return is associated with Judah and the rebuilding of
the temple, as will become more explicit in the books that conclude the
Twelve: Haggai, Zechariah and Malachi. The envisaged restoration of the
people of Israel under Judean rule is found in two places in Hosea:

> And the sons of Judah and the sons of Israel will be gathered together and
> they will appoint for themselves one head and they will go up from the
> land, for great is the day of Jezreel ('God will plant'). (2.2)

> For many days the sons of Israel will live without a king, without a prince,
> without sacrifice, without pillar and without ephod or teraphim. Afterwards
> the sons of Israel will return and they will seek Yahweh, their God, and
> David, their king, and they will be in awe of Yahweh and to his goodness in
> the latter days. (3.4-5)

The notion that Israel's end has come so that its future is only in Judah
is stated in 1.6b-7, in connection with the name of the child 'not pitied'.
Yahweh says that he will not have pity on Israel 'but I will pity the house
of Judah and I will cause them to be saved by means of Yahweh their God.
I will not save them with bow, or with sword, or with war, or with horses
or with horsemen.'

3. *What is Wrong with Israel?*

The second half of Hosea gathers together poetry highlighting themes
that emerge in the prophetic corpus in the Twelve as well as in Jeremiah,
Ezekiel and Isaiah. The text reads as an introduction explaining what is
wrong with Israel and appears to the reader more as words for the wise
and discerning, as Hos. 14.9 puts it at the end of the book, than as words
about future vision (חזון) or words of (דבר) prophets engaged in conflict
with a present community.

The second half of Hosea opens by announcing a legal dispute (רִיב)
that Yahweh has against the inhabitants of the land (יוֹשְׁבֵי אֶרֶץ). This
dispute recalls the setting for 'the words of' Amos and Jeremiah announcing the end of Israel and Judah and all the nations of the land (see above,
Chapter 5). The punishment for Israel announced later in the book—'I will
send a fire on its cities and I will destroy its strongholds' (8.14)—recalls
the similar sounding phrase in Amos where Yahweh's punishment of the
nations is expressed in similar terms (Amos 1.4, 7, 10, 12, 14; 2.2, 5). The
indictment against Israel is 'that there is no faithfulness, and no loyalty,
and no knowledge of God in the land' (Hos. 4.12). The notion of Israel
pursuing other gods, often characterized as idols, recurs throughout (4.10,
12, 15, 17; 8.4-6; 9.1-2, 10; 12.1; 13.2; 14.8). Unfaithful Israel goes after
these gods forgetting that Yahweh is its 'maker' (עֹשֵׂהוּ, 8.14). That Israel
is not faithful, loyal and knowledgeable about Yahweh has led to swear-
ing, lying, murder, stealing, adultery and bloodshed (4.2)—themes which
also reappear (5.4; 6.7-8; 7.1-16; 10.9, 13; 12.1, 7, 14).

Because of the people's faithlessness, disloyalty and lack of knowledge,
when they seek Yahweh with their flocks and herds to conduct sacrifice,
'they will not find him; he has withdrawn from them' (5.6). The theme
here is that Yahweh has abandoned the temple, as was the case in Jeremiah
and Ezekiel. In Israel this concerns a plurality of temple sites, for example,
Samaria (7.1; 8.4, 6), Gilgal (9.15) and Bethel (10.15; 12.4). In Hosea this
rejection of Yahweh goes back to its roots, to the time of Jacob (12.3-5).
The problem in Israel, as elsewhere in prophetic books, is with the leaders:
kings (5.1; 7.5-7; 8.4; 10.3, 7; 13.10), princes (5.10, 84), priests (3.3-4;
5.1) and prophets (3.4).

While the view of the coming destruction centers on Israel, Judah also
appears—only in a more minor role. Early in the collection of poetry there
is a reference suggesting that attempts should be made to prevent Judah
from becoming guilty like Israel (4.15). Toward the end it is noted that
Judah still remains faithful to the Holy One (12.1), but in the end Judah
appears as one who, like Israel, will stumble (5.5-15; see 6.11; 12.1).

Although prophets are counted among the failed leaders in Israel (10.5),
they are primarily viewed in a positive fashion. Significantly, however,
references are made to the prophets in ways that distance them from Hosea.
The intriguing question this distancing raises is: What is the function of
the book of Hosea in the Twelve and in the rabbinic order of the Latter
Prophets? The fact that Hosea does not fit easily into any of the genres I
have identified suggests the unique role the book of Hosea is playing not

only as an introduction to the Twelve but also as the beginning of God speaking to the prophets.

In Hos. 6.5 the prophets are presented as something quite different from the figure of Hosea himself. They appear as Jeremiah-like prophets who fight with words: 'Therefore I have hewn [them] into pieces by means of the prophets; I killed them by the words (אִמְרֵי) of my mouth'. Likewise the role of the prophets depicted in Hos. 12.11 can also be read as a vocational activity more like that of Isaiah and the other prophets of 'vision'. 'I spoke to the prophets and I multiplied vision (חָזוֹן), and by the hand of the prophets I will bring destruction'. This depiction of prophets suggests to the reader that the book of Hosea is introducing the reader to the prophetic books that are to follow in the Twelve, and to the other prophetic books that are portrayed in their superscriptions as following Hosea in time: Jeremiah, Ezekiel and Isaiah. Following Hosea, to whom Yahweh first spoke, the reader will encounter written words in the hands of prophets—'vision' and 'words' that brought death and destruction to Israel and Judah and other nations in the land.

The separation of Hosea from the other prophetic figures is also suggested by 9.7b: 'the prophet is a fool, the man of the spirit is mad'. Although many commentators understand this verse to refer to Hosea, it can be taken as referring to the prophetic books that follow. This interpretation is supported by the next verse (9.8): 'a watchman of Ephraim present with my God is a prophet'. What is being defined here is not the role of Hosea but the role of the prophets who follow. Another definition of a prophet is found in 12.13: 'By means of a prophet Yahweh brought up Israel from Egypt, and by a prophet he was guarded'. Here the prophet is viewed as a past figure who will, like Moses, bring Israel back to the land through their 'words' and 'vision'.

4. *From Joel to Zephaniah*

I want now to turn to those prophetic figures in the books that follow Hosea in the Twelve and comment on the order and arrangement of the prophetic books within this collection. Since I spoke in some detail in previous chapters about the eight prophetic books that follow Hosea in the Twelve (Joel, Amos, Obadiah, Jonah, Micah, Nahum, Habakkuk and Zephaniah), my comments here will focus on the order and arrangement of these prophetic books, which represent a variety of genres: 'vision', 'words' and narrative.

The first thing to mention is that the eight books following Hosea are primarily 'vision' about the coming end of Israel, Judah and the nations, as well as the return of Israel and Judah. The books, along with Hosea, are arranged according to a chronology suggested by the reference to kings in some of the superscriptions:

Hosea	Uzziah, Jotham, Ahaz, Hezekiah, kings of Judah, Jeroboam, king of Israel
Joel	No kings mentioned
Amos	Uzziah, king of Judah, Jeroboam, king of Israel
Obadiah	No kings mentioned
Jonah	No kings mentioned
Micah	Jotham, Ahaz and Hezekiah
Nahum	No mention of kings
Habakkuk	No mention of kings
Zephaniah	Josiah, king of Judah

Kings are absent from five of the books that, apart from Jonah, are 'vision(s)'. The absence of specific historical setting is understandable, as I argued earlier, because the present situation in which a prophet received his 'vision' is not as significant for reading a prophetic book of vision as one containing the 'words' of a prophet addressed to the prophet's own time. Vision is important, not primarily during the time of its reception but for another time. Those books that do not mention kings in the superscription can be dated in terms of the place they have in the arrangement of books where books preceding and following them give specific information about time.

The setting for the eight books following Hosea roughly parallels the time portrayed as the period in which Isaiah received his 'vision', that is, in the days of Uzziah, Jotham, Ahaz and Hezekiah. The period of time is extended in the Twelve to the time of Josiah (Zeph. 1.1). Apart from the overlap in time between Zephaniah and Jeremiah (the time of Josiah), all the material gathered here is suggested to refer to events prior to the time of the 'words' of Jeremiah and the prophetic narrative about Ezekiel. But because so much of this material is vision, it functions as does Isaiah, to speak about a future time beyond Jeremiah and Ezekiel.

As I argued in the previous chapter, Joel is a vision about Yahweh's warfare against Israel. It is followed by Amos, which announces the end of Israel envisioned in Joel. However, both books see Yahweh's actions coming out of Zion/Jerusalem. The end of Joel (4.16) uses the same language about Yahweh roaring and uttering his voice from Zion/Jerusalem as that found at the beginning of Amos (1.2a). Both Joel and Amos also see future restoration in Judah, not in Israel. For Joel, Judah will be inhabited forever and Jerusalem for all generations because Yahweh dwells there. In Amos, the booth of David (9.11) will be raised up. The important role of Jerusalem/Zion in future restoration is related to a central motif of the Twelve, which focuses on Yahweh's warfare against Israel. That warfare is seen from the perspective of Judah, and future return and restoration will be in the temple in Jerusalem.

The vision of Obadiah follows Amos and envisions the destruction of Edom alluded to in Amos 9.12 at the time of restoration. Jonah, following Amos, plays a similar function in the Twelve to that of Ezekiel in the rabbinic canonical order. After Amos announces the end of Israel, Yahweh makes an appearance to Jonah in Nineveh, the land of the enemy. Similarly, after Jeremiah's announcement of the end of Judah, Yahweh makes an appearance to Ezekiel in Babylon, the land of the enemy.

Micah as a prophet of vision has a northern focus. This book concerns Samaria as well as Jerusalem. The vision of the future extends beyond Joel's vision; Micah has a vision of Yahweh coming out of his dwelling in Zion/Jerusalem (1.3) and destroying it (3.12). Micah sees the desolation of all the land as a consequence of the total warfare Yahweh will conduct against all the nations through his warrior-prophet Jeremiah (7.13).

The prophets of vision end in the Twelve with Nahum, Habakkuk and Zephaniah. Nahum and Habakkuk envision the end of Nineveh and Babylon, respectively—the two nations that Yahweh used as instruments of warfare to bring Israel and Judah to an end. In many ways the visions of Nahum and Habakkuk function in the Twelve as did the oracles against the foreign nations in Isaiah's vision of Yahweh's plan (chs. 13–35). While Zephaniah's vision concerns Yahweh's plan for the nations, it also picks up motifs of the third section of Isaiah's vision in which a 'fear not' oracle is addressed to a restored Zion, promising that warfare has ended (3.16-20).

The Twelve, then, collects a series of prophetic books representing 'vision', 'words' and 'narrative' depicting the warfare that Yahweh will conduct to put an end to Israel and Judah before restoring them to a new land. The focus in the Twelve is on Yahweh's bringing an end to Israel. Significantly, however, its future restoration is seen to be in Judah where Yahweh will dwell in Zion/Jerusalem.

5. The End of Prophecy and the Emergence of Messengers

The Twelve concludes with three books: Haggai, Zechariah and 'My Messenger'.[5] The superscriptions of these three books employ semiotic codes introducing unconventional prophets, more similar to Amos, Jeremiah and Ezekiel, than to conventional prophets of vision such as Isaiah or Micah. However, the role that Haggai, Zechariah and 'My Messenger' perform in the Twelve, and in the collection of the prophetic corpus as a whole, is different from that of the other unconventional prophets, Amos, Jeremiah and Ezekiel. These three figures represent the end of prophecy and the emergence of messengers. The role of the messenger is associated with Yahweh's return to be present in the rebuilt temple. Yahweh will be present in the temple where he will communicate directly through messengers as he did in the days of the patriarchs.[6]

Like Jeremiah and Ezekiel, Haggai and Zechariah begin with superscriptions that give very precise dating:[7]

> In the second year of Darius, the king, on the sixth month on the first day of the month the word of Yahweh came in the hand of Haggai the prophet to Zerubbabel, son of Shealtiel, the governor of Judah, and to Joshua, the son of Jehozadak, the high priest. (Hag. 1.1)

> In the eighth month, in the second year of Darius, the word of the Yahweh came to Zechariah, the son of Berechiah, the son of Iddo, the prophet, saying... (Zech. 1.1)

The significant difference is that the dates of Haggai and Zechariah, unlike those of Jeremiah and Ezekiel, are associated with a foreign king, the Persian king Darius, rather than with Judean kings. Just as the precision in dating in Jeremiah and Ezekiel had to do with the extraordinary role that they would perform—Jeremiah announcing the end of Judah and Ezekiel seeing God in the land of the enemy—so the introductions in Haggai and Zechariah are encoding information about the extraordinary roles they play in the prophetic corpus. While Jeremiah announced the end of the temple, and Ezekiel in his visions saw Yahweh leave the temple as well as

---

5.   For reasons that I will detail later, I understand מלאכי to refer to a task rather than the name of a person, Malachi.

6.   My thesis builds on two earlier articles, 'The End of Prophecy', and 'Messengers in Isaiah and the Twelve'.

7.   The precise dating in Amos is done in a different way. His dating is given as 'two years before the rumble' rather than in terms of the reign of kings.

the plan for temple restoration in a foreign land, Haggai and Zechariah are associated with temple restoration and the return of Yahweh's presence.

I argued above that the extraordinary character of Amos, Jeremiah and Ezekiel was associated with the identification of these figures in the super-scriptions with roles other than that of a prophet (נביא). Amos was from the shepherds of Tekoa, Jeremiah from the priests of Anathoth and Ezekiel the priest from the land of the Chaldeans. It is significant, therefore, in the superscriptions of Haggai and Zechariah that they are clearly linked to the נביאים. Haggai is identified as 'the prophet' (הנביא, 1.1) and Zecharaiah is identified as 'the son of Berechiah, the son of Iddo, the prophet' (בן ברכיה בן עדו הנביא, 1.1). This ambiguous phrase appears to identify Zechariah with his grandfather Iddo, who was 'the prophet'.[8] However, to identify Haggai and Zechariah with the word הנביא is itself extraordinary. Of the 15 prophetic books in the Latter prophets, apart from Habakkuk (1.1),[9] only Haggai and Zechariah are identified in this way.

The unusual use of the phrase 'the prophet' (הנביא) to identify Haggai and Zechariah reminds the reader of the extraordinary use of the verb 'to prophesy' (נבא) in Amos, Jeremiah and Ezekiel. In those books it was constantly employed to identify the activity of these three individuals as 'prophesying' although it was not used this way anywhere else in the prophetic corpus. I suggest that the identification of Haggai as 'the pro-phet' and Zechariah as the descendant of Iddo 'the prophet' is overstate-ment. As a reader, I understand that the Model Author by the use of the phrase 'the prophet' is insisting that these two individuals really are prophets (נביאים). Indeed, Haggai is identified as 'the prophet' five times (1.1, 3, 12; 2.1, 10) and Zechariah is associated with Iddo 'the prophet' twice (1.1, 7).

But why is it important to emphasize the point that these two individuals are 'prophets'? The answer is that in Haggai and Zechariah we meet figures whose role is different from that of any of the other characters we have thus far encountered. These figures are 'messengers' (מלאכים) of Yahweh. This new role as messenger is most significant for understanding Haggai, Zechariah and 'My Messenger' as the conclusion of both the Twelve and the prophetic collection as a canonical whole. At the end of the Twelve, and at the end of the prophetic corpus, Yahweh's messengers are carrying out their tasks in the extraordinary time of temple restoration when Yahweh returns to be present in his temple. This is as unusual as the

8. See my *Zechariah*, p. 46.
9. Habakkuk is also identified as 'the prophet' in 3.1.

roles of Amos, Jeremiah and Ezekiel who were performing their roles at the equally extraordinary time of temple destruction when Yahweh departed from the temple and was no longer present there.

6. *Messengers in the Twelve*

Haggai is referred to as the 'messenger of Yahweh' (מלאך יהוה) in 1.13. He is the only individual clearly designated as a נביא who is also identified as a מלאך. While it has become conventional in biblical studies to refer to prophets as messengers, it is important to emphasize that only in Hag. 1.13 is a prophet (נביא) also designated as a 'messenger (מלאך) of Yahweh'.[10] Nowhere else in the Hebrew Bible is a prophet (הנביא) designated in this way. In light of the prophetic corpus as a whole, then, Haggai is performing an extraordinary role.

The message that Haggai delivers to the people is important for determining the significance of this extraordinary role. The 'message of Yahweh' (מלאכות יהוה) is 'I am with you, a saying of Yahweh' (אני אתכם נאם יהוה). Haggai's message announcing Yahweh's presence stands in contrast to the words of Amos and Jeremiah prophesying the end of Israel and Judah associated with Yahweh's absence—when he had left temple precincts. The literary context surrounding Haggai's message suggests this difference. Whereas the people, including royalty and other leaders, refused to listen to 'the words of Jeremiah', in this case Zerubbabel, the governor, Joshua, the high priest and the remnant of the people began to listen: 'And they listened…to the voice of Yahweh' and to 'the prophet Haggai' (1.12). Listening to the message, 'I am with you', delivered by Haggai, 'the messenger of Yahweh', stirred up the spirit of Zerubbabel, Joshua and the remnant of the people 'and they came and did work on the house of the Yahweh of hosts, their God' (1.14). This happened, according to the book, precisely on 'the twenty-fourth day of the month, in the sixth month' (1.15). Also, according to the book, on 'the twenty-fourth day of the ninth month', the 'foundations of the temple of Yahweh were laid' (יסד היכל יהוה, 2.18). The emergence of 'the messenger' Haggai in the Twelve, and in the prophetic corpus as a whole, concerns the return of Yahweh and the rebuilding of the temple.

---

10. 2 Chron. 36.16 is sometimes seen as a passage equating 'prophets' and 'messengers'. However, in light of my discussion of the emergence of 'messengers' in the Twelve, 2 Chron. 36.16 can be seen as describing two roles: prophets and messengers.

Just as detailed dates are offered throughout the books of Jeremiah and Ezekiel to portray the extraordinary times of temple destruction, so also in the books of Haggai and Zechariah precise dating is given in portrayal of events surrounding temple restoration (see Hag. 1.1, 14b-15; 2.1, 10, 20; Zech. 1.1, 7; 7.1). However, while the dating in Jeremiah and Ezekiel suggest that the events in Ezekiel as following those in Jeremiah, the datings in Haggai and Zechariah sketch a world in which Haggai and Zechariah overlap. The first date in Zechariah (1.1) comes two months after the time Haggai is presented as appearing as the messenger of Yahweh and after work is described as having begun on the house of the Yahweh; it is also one month after Haggai spoke to Zerubbabel, Joshua and the people about the temple in its former glory (Hag. 2.1). The second date in Zechariah (1.7), when messengers begin to appear in the literary world of Zechariah, is, according to Haggai, two months after the foundations of the temple have been laid. This is portrayed in Haggai as a time when prosperity returns and when the temple appears to be in operation (Hag. 2.10, 20).

The two dates in Zechariah are clues for understanding the arrangement of materials in the Twelve at a time when messengers emerge. This world is depicted as one that is distanced from the fathers and from the prophets who are portrayed as characters from the past—'former prophets' (הנביאים הראשנים, 1.1-6). The world in which messengers begin to replace the world of the 'former prophets' is also one in which seeing (ראה) in Zechariah differentiates him from the Former Prophets.

7. The Former Prophets

The theme of the Former Prophets in Zechariah is important for understanding Haggai, Zechariah and Malachi as the conclusion not only for the Twelve but also for the prophetic corpus as a canonical whole. I have argued a number of the prophetic characters are unconventional prophets prophesying in extraordinary times (Amos, Jeremiah, Jonah and Ezekiel). Some of these prophets, especially Amos and Jeremiah, are portrayed as raising considerable controversy among the authorities in their own times. Furthermore, the theme of true and false prophecy, particularly concerning the prophets of false or lying (שקר) vision (חזון) was a prominent motif in both Jeremiah and Ezekiel. This theme regarding the Former Prophets is, therefore, a fitting conclusion to the prophetic corpus.

The theme of the former prophets in Zechariah mirrors a criterion found elsewhere in the Hebrew Bible for determining who is a prophet and who is not. In Deut. 18.15-22, it is envisaged that on some occasion there may be confusion concerning who is a prophet of Yahweh and who is not, and the following basis for making such a determination is given:

> You may say to yourself, 'How will we recognize a word that Yahweh has not spoken?' If a prophet speaks in the name of Yahweh but the thing does not take place or prove true, it is a word that Yahweh has not spoken. The prophet has spoken it presumptuously, do not be frightened by it. (Deut. 8.21-22)

Read from the perspective of this Deuteronomic text, what Yahweh spoke to the 'former prophets' (beginning with Hosea and including all the prophets in the prophetic corpus) has proved true at the later time of Persian rule and messenger presence—the time of Haggai and Zechariah.

> But my words and statutes, which I commanded my servants the prophets, did they not overtake your ancestors? So they repented and said, 'Yahweh of hosts has dealt with us according to our ways and deeds, just as he planned to do'. (Zech. 1.6)[11]

Furthermore, in the Twelve both Haggai and Zechariah gain authority as prophets in their own time because they stand in continuity with the Former Prophets. Indeed, this continuity is made explicit later in Zechariah when the people of Bethel send Sharezer and Regem-melech and their men to inquire about mourning and practicing abstinence. Zechariah's answer to their question is:

> Then the word of Yahweh of hosts came to me: 'Say to all the people of the land and the priests, "When you fasted and lamented in the fifth month and in the seventh, for these 70 years, was it for me that you fasted? And when you eat and when you drink, do you not eat and drink only for your-selves?"' (Zech. 7.4-6).

In continuation of his response to the question put to him by the people of Bethel, Zechariah supports his answer by claiming that his answer is in accord with what the 'former prophets' had proclaimed:

---

11. I understand this relationship with Deuteronomy as an intertextual one; I do not understand it as a result of Deuteronomic redaction. Rather, the text of the Twelve, like any text, makes its readers aware of other texts not only because it is related to other texts at the time of its origin (its pretext) but also at the time of its reception (the readers' context).

Were not these the words Yahweh proclaimed by the hand of former prophets (הנביאים הראשנים), when Jerusalem was inhabited and in prosperity,
along with the towns around it, and when the Negeb and the Shephelah
were inhabited? (Zech. 7.7)

Zechariah is not directly quoting what any of the 'former prophets' said,
but he seeks to ground his answer in the words of the prophets from the
past to whom Yahweh had spoken and whose words were proved true by
subsequent events (cf. Zech. 1.6). His answer receives authority from its
foundation in and continuity with a kind of précis of the past prophetic
messages to show that the present behavior of the people is consistent with
what the 'former prophets' said about the past behavior of the people. In
both cases the people are presented as self-centered.

> The word of Yahweh came to Zechariah, saying, 'Thus says Yahweh of
> hosts: "Render true judgments, show kindness and mercy to one another, do
> not oppress the widow, the orphan, the alien, or the poor; do not devise evil
> in your hearts against one another". But they refused to listen, and turned a
> stubborn shoulder, and stopped their ears in order not to hear. They made
> their hearts adamant in order not to hear the law and the words that Yahweh
> of hosts had sent by his spirit through the former prophets. Therefore great
> wrath came from Yahweh of hosts. Just as, when I [the Hebrew reads "he"]
> called, they would not hear, so when they called, I would not hear', says
> Yahweh of hosts, and I scattered them with a whirlwind among all the
> nations they had not known. Thus the land they left was desolate, so that no
> one went to and fro, and a pleasant land was made desolate.' (Zech. 7.8-14)

Although Haggai and Zechariah are presented as maintaining a continuity with the Former Prophets, prophets are seen to have no future in
this period in which messengers emerge. Zechariah looks forward to a day
when there will be no prophets (13.1-6).

A passage in Zechariah's extended answer to the men from Bethel
(Zech. 8.9-13) links the written words of the former prophets with the
commencement of temple construction. Zechariah says:

> Thus Yahweh of hosts said, 'Let your hands be strong, the ones who hear in
> these days, these words from the mouth of the prophets which were [heard]
> in the day the foundation of the house of Yahweh of hosts was laid, to
> rebuild the temple'. (Zech. 8.9)

According to Hag. 2.18, the foundation of the temple of Yahweh was laid
on the twenty-fourth day of the ninth month in the second year of Darius
(Hag. 2.18).

That Zechariah is referring to written words 'in these days' from the former days of the prophets is evident in the phrase 'from the mouth of' (מפי) the prophets. 'From the mouth' suggests dictation as was noted above in Jer. 36.4, 6, 17, 18, 27 and 32 (cf. Ezra 1.1). These dictated words of the former prophets were heard in the days of the laying of the foundation of the temple. The emphasis here is on what the former prophets said in writing for later reading not on oral proclamation.[12]

There are a number of verbal links associating Zech. 8.9-13 with the passage in Haggai (2.8) regarding the laying of the foundation of the temple. Language in the larger context of Zech. 8.9-13 is reminiscent of the language of Haggai:

1. The phrase 'the day the foundation of the house of Yahweh of hosts was laid to rebuild the temple' is reminiscent of Hag. 2.18, which concerns 'the day that the foundation of Yahweh's temple was laid'. Indeed, the opening of Haggai emphasizes that the time has come 'to rebuild Yahweh's house' (Hag. 1.2). These two phrases in Haggai pick up all the words of the phrase in Zechariah.

2. The phrase 'let your hands be strong' (Zech. 8.9, 13) echoes the thrice repeated 'take courage' uttered to Zerubbabel, Joshua and the remnant of the people (Hag. 2.4). The same Hebrew verb is used in Hebrew for 'be strong' and for 'take courage'.

3. The comforting 'Do not be afraid' (Zech. 8.13; cf. 8.16) is the same phrase used to comfort Zerubbabel, Joshua and the remnant of the people in Hag. 2.5.

4. The reference to the community as 'the remnant of this people' (Zech. 8.11, 12; cf. 8.6) echoes the address of Haggai as 'the remnant of the people' (Hag. 1.11, 14; 2.2).

5. The phrase 'you will be a blessing' in Zech. 8.13 is paralleled by the similar phrase, 'I will bless you' in Hag. 2.19.

6. The description of the days before the foundation of the temple was laid, as a time when there 'was no wages for people or for animals', recalls similar language in Haggai about those who earn wages (1.6) and the deprivation of both humans and animals (1.11).

---

12. The NRSV translates 'from the mouths of the prophets who were present when the foundation was laid'. It renders מפי in the plural ('from the mouths') and understands the relative clause introduced by אשר to refer to the prophets rather than to words. The translation emphasizes 'spokenness' rather than dictation, which is suggested by 'from the mouth of'.

7.   The envisaged change in prosperity, 'there shall be a strong sow-
      ing of peace; the vine shall yield its fruit, the ground shall give
      its produce, and the skies shall give their dew', recalls similar
      language in Haggai about things withheld in the past (1.10-11) as
      well as the envisaged prosperity now that the foundation of the
      temple has been laid (2.18-19).

In the Twelve, then, the prophets are portrayed as being from former times.
They appear in Zechariah's (and Haggai's) world in the form of written
words and law or *torah*. The beginning of temple construction, the time
when the foundation of the temple of Yahweh was laid, marks the occasion
for reading these prophetic words. In many ways the words of the prophets
are a written justification of Yahweh's actions in the past. The appearance
of messengers in the Twelve marks the end of prophecy. The words of the
prophets are now available as written words from the past.

8. *Seeing in Zechariah*

The world depicted in Haggai and Zechariah when the temple is being
rebuilt—a time when the prophets are from former times and messengers
emerge—occasions a different kind of seeing. Zechariah does not have a
חזון, as do Isaiah and the other prophets of 'vision';[13] he does not have
'visions' (מראות) of God in a foreign land as does Ezekiel; nor does he
see the words of Yahweh metaphorically 'written' in natural imagery as do
Amos and Jeremiah. Zechariah says that on the night of the twenty-fourth
day of the eleventh month in the second year of Darius, 'I saw' (ראיתי).
What Zechariah saw is activity and imagery associated with temple
construction. He is not portrayed as seeing 'night visions'. What he sees is
more straightforward.

I can only briefly outline the scenes in Zechariah and what Zechariah
sees depicted in the first eight chapters of the book. I have given a more
definitive reading in my commentary on Zechariah.[14] In that context I
argued that Zechariah's interaction with messengers in these scenes,
including the messenger of Yahweh (Haggai, see 1.11), which takes the
form of question and answer, is one in which Zechariah himself is learning to be a messenger of Yahweh. He is learning from what he sees

---

13.   For a fuller discussion see my *Zechariah*, pp. 58-59. 'Vision' itself is seen as
something that will cease (Zech. 13.4).

14.   See my *Zechariah*, pp. 57-150.

concerning the restoration of Jerusalem and the temple imagery that he sees for the first time. He will emerge as a messenger in ch. 8 when representatives from Bethel come to Zechariah.

The first scenes portray Zechariah outside the temple. He sees horsemen returning from patrolling the land (Zech. 1.1-17), workmen associated with the altar (1.18-21) and a young man measuring the width and length of Jerusalem (2.1-5). In these three scenes Zechariah ceases to be an observer; he becomes an active participant in what he is seeing. Zechariah himself is drawn into Yahweh's presence and communicates directly with him (1.18-21). At the end of these three scenes Zechariah claims that in what is about to happen it will be evident that Yahweh has sent him. When he makes this claim, his words as messenger and the words of Yahweh converge in form and content (2.6-11). This is consistent with the role of the messenger in these scenes, in which messenger presence is tantamount to divine presence.

At the end of ch. 2 and after Zechariah's repeated claim about his special status, there is a call for silence directed to the reader, for Zechariah is about to enter the temple (2.13). In the temple (3.1-10), Joshua is installed as high priest and is charged with special duties by 'the messenger of Yahweh', whom I contend in my commentary is Haggai. In this scene Zechariah begins to act like the messenger of Yahweh when he gives instructions about Joshua's apparel.

When the scene involving Joshua closes, Zechariah is in the temple viewing temple imagery and learning about its significance from the messenger who spoke with him (Zech. 4.1–6.8). The need for such instructtion is necessary because few in the remnant community had seen the temple in its former glory (see Hag. 2.3). The recurring motif associated with temple imagery is that Yahweh is 'the master of the whole land'.

At the end of the scenes in the temple, the horsemen who appeared in the first scene are portrayed as eager to get out to patrol 'the whole earth'. The messenger who spoke with Zechariah indicates that his spirit is at ease with the north country (6.8). This is an important motif in Zechariah, for the reference to the north country signals a change in focus to the north, to Israel, the Northern Kingdom.

After crowns of silver and gold are made for Joshua and Zerubbabel, indicating that it is they who will rule in the restored community (6.9-14), and after Zechariah claims that the temple will be completed, again sustaining his claim that Yahweh sent him (6.15), the book moves two years ahead in time to when Bethel sends representatives to the house of Yahweh to ask a question of the priests and prophets (7.2-3). This reference to Bethel is significant. It emphasizes the northern focus of the Twelve. Bethel was the place where Amos announced the end of the Northern Kingdom in the days of Jeroboam. While the Twelve has this northern focus, the future, as it is presented in the books of 'vision' in the Twelve, is associated with the restoration of Jerusalem and its temple where Yahweh will be present. That the representatives come to the house of Yahweh in Jerusalem after Zechariah has seen and been instructed in the significance of the temple's imagery reinforces the vision of Israel's future in Jerusalem.

Zechariah's answer, as a messenger of Yahweh, concerns Yahweh's mastery over all the land, which is about to eventuate. He concludes by saying that in the days to come 'ten men from nations of every language shall take hold of a Jew, grasping his garment and saying, "Let us go with you, for we have heard that God is with you"'. The whole land has heard the message first spoken by the messenger Haggai, 'I am with you, says Yahweh' (Hag. 1.13).

That men come from Bethel after temple restoration when messengers are again present is important in one other way. The only other reference to a messenger (מלאך) in the Twelve is associated with Bethel at the introduction of the scroll in Hos. 12.5 (Eng. 12.4). This verse about a מלאך who used to appear to the ancestor Jacob/Israel, is part of a larger passage (Hos. 12.3-7 [Eng. 12.2-6]), pertaining to an indictment (ריב) Yahweh has against Judah:[15]

> In the womb he tried to supplant his brother,
>   and in his manhood he strove[16] with a divine being.
> He strove with a messenger (מלאך) and prevailed,
>   he wept and sought his favor;
> he used to find us (ימצאנו)[17] at Bethel,
>   and there he used to speak (ידבר)[18] with us (עמנו).
> Yahweh the God of hosts,
>   Yahweh (יהוה) is his name (זכרו).

15. The incidents in these verses recall occurrences in the life of the patriarch similar to the stories about him in Gen. 25–35.

16. The two verbs עקב ('supplant') and שרה ('strive') are a play on words suggesting the patriarch's two names, יעקב and ישראל.

17. Reading the object suffix here as a first person plural rather than a third person singular to bring it into agreement with the first person plural suffix on the preposition with the following verb, עמנו.

18. I am reading the two imperfect verbs (ימצאנו and ידבר) as eruptive imperfects, that is, to indicate what happened repeatedly in the past.

But as for you, return (תשוב) to your God,
   hold fast to (שמר) love (חסד) and justice (מפשט),
   and wait (וקוה) continually for your God.

There are a number of links between this passage in Hosea, at the beginning of the Twelve, about a messenger that used to appear to Jacob at Bethel and to Haggai and Zechariah, at the conclusion of the Twelve, when messengers again appear. I will briefly discuss these links.

First, the doxology that concludes the allusion to the time of the patriarch Jacob suggests the name Zechariah (זכריה):

Yahweh the God of hosts
   Yahweh (יהוה) is his name (זכרו).

The tetragrammaton as well as the unusual use of זכר rather than שם for 'name'[19] pick up the two components in the name Zechariah (זכריה). Zechariah's very name embodies the doxology accompanying the remembrance of a messenger past. Zechariah's name, 'Yahweh has remembered', links the time of messenger presence in Zechariah with the way Yahweh used to speak by a messenger in the days of the ancestor Jacob. What Yahweh has remembered at the time of Zechariah—that Yahweh is present in his messenger—is presented as something that had come to an end at the time of Hosea but that now has been restored.

Second, these verses in Hosea suggest that prevailing against Yahweh is not only an accusation against the ancestor Jacob but also indictment against the entire community at the time of Hosea for prevailing against Yahweh. The community has lost the messenger presence of its patriarchal past. The messenger 'used to find us at Bethel, and there he used to speak with us'. The community without a messenger presence is directed to return (תשוב) to their God. The call 'to return' is finally heeded when Zechariah reiterates the call of the Former Prophets for the community to return:

Yahweh was very angry with your fathers. Therefore say to them, 'Thus says Yahweh of hosts: *Return* (שובו) to me, says Yahweh of hosts, and I will *return* (אשוב) to you, says Yahweh of hosts. Do not be like your fathers, to whom the former prophets proclaimed, Thus says Yahweh of hosts, *Return* (שובו) from your evil ways and from your evil deeds. But they did not hear or heed me, says Yahweh. Your fathers, where are they? And the prophets, do they live forever? But my words and my statutes,

19. Francis I. Andersen and David Noel Freedman, *Hosea* (AB, 24; Garden City, NY: Doubleday, 1980), p. 615, note this unusual use of זכר.

> which I commanded my servants the prophets, did they not overtake your
> ancestors? So they *returned* (שׁובו) and said, Yahweh of hosts has dealt with
> us according to our ways and deeds, just as he planned to do.' (Zech. 1.2-6)

The summons 'to return' is not heeded until there is again a messenger
presence and this is portrayed as emerging in Haggai and Zechariah.

Third, a מלאך used to be present 'with' (עם) the community at a specific place, Bethel, from a remembered patriarchal past (Hos. 12), and
Yahweh has remembered this past in the time of Zechariah and Haggai.
Messengers of Yahweh again appear. Haggai is concerned with establishing a place for Yahweh by summoning the people to rebuild the temple:
With the message of Yahweh (במלאצות יהוה) Haggai also announces the
presence of Yahweh: 'I am with you (אתכם)' (Hag. 1.13; cf. Hos. 12.5).
Hosea, at the beginning of the Twelve, introduces a time when Yahweh
was no longer present at Bethel as he used to be in the presence of his
messenger at the time of the patriarch Jacob. At the end of the Twelve, in
Haggai and Zechariah, Yahweh returns and again is present in the messengers who begin to appear in that literary world.

The end of Yahweh's indictment in Hosea calls for the community to
wait continually (וקוה...תמיד) for their God. This theme of waiting picks
up an important theme that we have encountered in the prophets of vision.
At the time of Haggai and Zechariah, this waiting is coming to an end.
Yahweh has returned and again is present in his community.

The narrative portrayal of the return of messengers in Haggai and Zechariah has affinities with the third part of Isaiah's vision (chs. 36–66). In
that vision of the restored community, prophets have also disappeared from
the scene. What Isaiah sees in his vision, however, is prior to the time of
Haggai and Zechariah. Messengers are deaf and blind (Isa. 42.19-20)
because the laying of the foundations in order to rebuild the temple is seen
as a future activity (44.26-28). However, in Isaiah, as in the Twelve, the
early times of the ancestors of Israel are remembered as a time when messengers were present (63.8-9).[20]

9. *My Messenger and the Concluding Oracles in Zechariah*

The northern focus of the Twelve is evident from the superscription at the
beginning of Malachi, 'An oracle, the word of Yahweh to Israel in the hand
of my messenger'. The oracle of 'my messenger' continues the arrange-

---

20. For a fuller discussion of these texts see my article 'Messengers in Isaiah and
the Twelve'.

ment of oracles at the end of Zechariah (9.1; 12.1) which, as I have argued in my commentary, *Zechariah*, also have a northern orientation. These oracles represent a continuation of the answer of Zechariah, who has now appeared as a messenger of Yahweh, to the initial inquiry from Bethel.[21] I have argued in my commentary that these oracles concern a disparity between what Zechariah sees in the temple imagery—Jerusalem as the centre where all the people of all the land will recognize Yahweh's presence and present political realities.[22] Imagery of the temple as the centre for all the nations of the land is not recognized by those who reject this message (e.g. the shepherds). These chapters are notoriously difficult to interpret in any detail, and that makes sense semiotically. Here the Model Author is using veiled language to refer to those who stand in opposition to the outcome of the collection of prophetic materials. With such a closed text requiring very specific information on the part of a reader to read the codes, the text is open to aberrant decoding. As a real reader of this text, I must recognize that the kind of specific information necessary is not available to me for reading with any kind of precision. At the end of the Twelve, and at the end of the prophetic corpus, I feel as a reader that I have been drawn into a 'real' world growing out of a prophetic collection of materials that ultimately is closed to me. The major impression I gain from this material is that those who arranged the prophetic material represent an ideological perspective that stands over against that of another community.

At the end of the Twelve, Yahweh says that he will send the prophet Elijah. He is a prophet/messenger who, in the past, blurred the distinction between heaven and earth, when he ascended into heaven accompanied by horses and chariots of fire (2 Kgs 2.9-12). As real readers of this prophetic corpus, we can choose to read this as 'the end' of a world—a literary world which we have inhabited as readers but a world which is long since past. I have chosen to read the text in the prophetic corpus in this way. It ends by looking to a future time when Yahweh will act through his prophet Elijah to come and confirm the ideology associated with Yahweh's presence in Jerusalem.

---

21. See my *Zechariah*, pp. 152-204, especially pp. 152-55.

22. See also Floyd, 'The מַשָּׂא (*Maśśa*) as a Type of Prophetic Book', pp. 418-20, who understands the so-called 'oracles' at the end of Zechariah (chs. 9–11 and 12–14) as explaining the dysfunctional prophecy at the beginning of Zechariah. His arguments about the function of these texts in Zechariah in many ways correlate with my own understanding.

Readers of these words who see them as sacred can choose to read this text as having continuation in subsequent tradition, a text with a future. Jewish and Christian communities have chosen to read this way. In such a situation, meaning does not emerge out of the time of the text's origin but out of a future time. Canonical rearrangement and reordering continue into the present, especially as communities of faith rearrange canonical materials in liturgy and theology. I am not arguing against such a way of reading. However, to read in this way considers vital information about the text's meaning to lie not in the world out of which the text emerged but in the world of the receiving community.

10. *Summary and Conclusion*

Unlike Jeremiah, Ezekiel and Isaiah, each of which center on an individual, the Twelve is a collection of prophetic books incorporating a plurality of individuals. The Twelve is distinctively, although not exclusively, northern in focus. Hosea does not sit easily with any of the major genres of prophetic books and acts as an introduction to the Twelve 'the beginning of Yahweh spoke', also serves as the time frame for understanding the prophetic corpus as a whole. Yahweh first spoke to Hosea about his intention to empty the land. A major theme in Hosea is the call to return.

Following Hosea are books that emulate genres in the collection of the Major Prophets: Isaiah ('vision'), Jeremiah ('the words of') and Ezekiel ('it happened to'). Vision is represented in the books of Joel, Micah, Obadiah, Nahum, Habakkuk and Zephaniah, although the genre is not as clearly identified in the opening superscriptions of all of these books as in Isaiah. 'The words of' Amos, like the words of Jeremiah, announce the end of Israel. 'It happened to' Jonah narrates the appearance of Yahweh in Nineveh, the land of the enemy, mirroring the foreign element in Ezekiel. The whole of the Twelve has a northern focus. Even the last book in the collection (Malachi) is an oracle to Israel. However, in these books restoration has to do with Yahweh's return to Judah and Jerusalem.

The Twelve ends with extraordinary prophets—Haggai, Zechariah and 'My Messenger'. These prophets have to do with the extraordinary situation of temple restoration. This is the period of return, when Jerusalem will be the center of the whole land. Here Yahweh will dwell and all the nations of the land will pay allegiance to Jerusalem because of Yahweh's presence.

The Twelve, however, ends with oracles that appear to be offered by the messenger Zechariah. The oracles suggest conflict in the community, for there are those in the surrounding region that appear not to adhere to the ideology that Jerusalem is the center of the entire land. The texts here are closed for the reader to a clear understanding because information for understanding the conflict is not available.

CONCLUSION

In this study I have read the prophets in the Talmudic canonical order: Joshua, Judges, Samuel, Kings, Jeremiah, Ezekiel, Isaiah and the Twelve.[1] I understand canon in the sense that Philip Davies has defined it—as a process of shaping, arranging and ordering not only individual books but also canonical collections of books (or scrolls). I have not been interested in canon in the theological sense of a singular or normative outcome. Indeed, there is a plurality of canons, and canons continue to be reformed as biblical books are reordered in interpretive uses of them in academic studies and in liturgical use, as well as in translation.

My interest in reading books in a final form according to a canonical outcome grows out of my interest in history. To read books as they are is a way of gaining insight into how some ancient community/communities constructed their 'real' past world. My only access to that world is in the literature these older communities compiled. I am assuming that the compilation of prophetic books and the concomitant creation of a canonical order are purposeful. I understand that communities who created both these texts and canonical order have intended to communicate through the way they have collected, arranged and ordered the material.

Since these texts, in a semiotic sense, are 'closed' texts—that is, texts that are susceptible to aberrant decoding—I have no illusions about reading them the way in which a Model Author intended. However, as a reader I am concerned with textual limits. Only by taking into consideration textual intentionality do I have any hope of reading an ancient text in such a way as to enable it to communicate from the past. Of course, as Eco points out, textual intentionality does not suggest singularity but allows for a plurality of meaning.

As I argued in Chapter 1, our traditional historical-critical approach to the biblical text ironically has often been consistent with a radical reader

---

1. I have read each of these prophetic books in the form in which it appears in the *Biblia Hebraica Stuttgartensia*. I have no way of knowing the form of the books to which the Talmud referred.

response approach. Textual intentionality is disregarded in an effort to recover authorial or source intention, and the texts are beaten into new shapes. Texts are rearranged so that in the end the process of critical biblical study represents contemporary canonical ordering and rearranging. Just as there have been different canonical orders from the Talmudic one I have read, so there are now historical-critical canonical orderings as historical critics have rearranged biblical texts. The whole of the Pentateuch has been rearranged for reading as have the prophetic books such as Isaiah and others. I have no major problem with this kind of reordering. I do have a problem with the notion that this reshaping of texts is an avenue into the past world of ancient Israel rather than a new way of reading biblical texts by creating a new canon.

As I argued in Chapter 8, it is essential that we determine how meaning emerges in the prophetic corpus. As readers we bring all sorts of information to the texts we read. All our readings of the prophetic books in some sense will be anachronistic since we can only read prophetic books in a world that the Model Author could never have imagined. For a very similar reason, as contemporary readers we can also not imagine with any great clarity the world of the Model Author. As readers we can beat texts into new shapes for reading, or we can attempt to enter the world of these texts in the shape(s) they come to us.

It also makes a difference in reading prophetic books to understand that prophecy in the rabbinic canon has an end, at least in a literary sense. So much of our reading, including our historical-critical reading, has treated these texts as if they have a future. Their meaning is determined by that future. This is because these texts have been taken over by communities of faith whose final 'decoding' of them requires information that the Model Author could never have known. To read the prophets from the perspective of future information necessary to understand them is a legitimate theological, but not an historical, way to read.

Because my own community of interpretation is not a theological one, although I learned my historical criticism in a Christian community, I do not feel compelled in my work to read these texts from the perspective of either Judaism or Christianity. For example, historical-critical study of the prophets as it has been employed in Christian theological institutions combines an interest in both the past and future in reading prophetic books. Theological study is study of books seen to have a future in the Christ event. Perhaps it is for this reason that canonical criticism as Brevard Childs has practiced it speaks of 'canon' in the singular. The whole of the historical-critical enterprise on which he rests his canonical reading of biblical texts is heading toward a normative end. Reordering and reshaping texts according to a diachronic process is but another form of the canonical process.

The intention of my reading of prophetic books is to understand them as *past* and as *from the past*. I have attempted to show that we should not think of prophetic books as representing a common genre. 'Vision', 'the words of' and 'it happened' are introducing different kinds of literature about 'prophetic figures' during the extraordinary time in which Yahweh announced an end to his presence with the people in Israel and Judah. Prophets who appear as messengers suggest the extraordinary time when he again determines to be present in the temple in Jerusalem, deemed to be the centre for all the nations of the land.

The construction of this prophetic past encodes the ideology of the scribal community that produced it. As a reader, I want to know more than it is possible for me to know about the disputes represented in the oracles that conclude the canonical order of books I have been reading. There are voiceless ones who appear to dispute the claim about the centrality of Yahweh's presence in the Jerusalem temple. But that is a past story and a past use of these texts to which I have no access.

This past story has been given a future by being rearranged and re-ordered by historical critics. To read the Latter Prophets as separated from the Former Prophets and to read the end of the corpus with the appearance of Elijah, who will soon reappear in John the Baptist in Matthew, as I learned to read them as a Christian, makes it more difficult to read the prophetic corpus historically.

At one point these texts were constructed by a Model Author to communicate to a past community of readers. That community and that past have now disappeared, and our ability to reconstruct the codes necessary to read so as to understand the intentionality of the text constructed by a Model Author is greatly diminished. The task of understanding what these texts meant at the time of their origin has been further complicated because these prophetic books have been taken up and given new canonical orders in which new scribes have authored them for a Model Reader.

If we are to read biblical texts with an interest in learning what they are communicating from an ancient past, then semiotics contributes to the clarity of the theoretical base for interpretation. In past studies my appeal to Fish's reader response theory was important in large part because it helped me to understand the role of communities in interpretation. However, even as I saw myself as a reader-response critic, I steadfastly respected the text as an 'object of study'. Eco's discussion of semiotics has illumined the relationship between reader and text for me by suggesting that it is interaction (albeit, in dealing with ancient texts, the interaction of an 'odd couple', to use a code from the contemporary cultural world) rather than reader control or textual obscurity. Semiotics seems to me to offer a way of interpreting literature that is fundamentally more 'historical' in its aims than is historical criticism. That is, it accepts the text as an artefact of an ancient time compiled by scribes for a Model Reader closely identifiable with 'real readers' in their own time. This artefact, of course, has been subsequently subjected to a complex process of transmission so that we have not even received it 'pristine' from the ancient compiler's hand. As contemporary readers we are far from the Model Reader that the compilers had in mind. Furthermore, the scribes are unlike any Model Author in our own time. However, as a contemporary and real reader of this artefact from the ancient past, I can construct textual meaning guided by compilational order and other textual signals that seem to me to create boundaries within which I can interpret. I believe that 'authorial intentionality' is entirely beyond our grasp. However, 'textual intentionality' refers not to the human mind but to signals and codes that, to some extent, are typical of writing and reading everywhere: order (even disorder), arrangement (even rearrangement), openings and closings. But many of these codes are distinctive to the time and culture in which they were compiled. By reading intertextually, looking for similarities and differences between a given text and other texts from the ancient world—chiefly biblical texts—we can attempt to identify codes that help us to construct meaning from those texts.

If I were to compare historical criticism and my approach in this book, I might say that historical criticism often takes a pot, breaks it, examines the shards, and uses the shards to construct new pots. The approach I prefer is to examine the pot as a whole as I have received it. Even if to my eyes the pot seems somewhat distorted and misshapen in terms of my contemporary expectations of pots, I can look for shapes that may indicate whether it could have been used for cooking or pouring. I can compare it to other pots, looking for the similarities and differences, and discern in what may first appear to be a useless appendage a handle that allows me to hold it and to draw water. I do not claim that this pot is my own or that I could use it in the way it would have been used in an ancient culture. However, I can begin to learn something of the way it could have been used—and this seems to me to be of the greatest historical interest. When applied to texts, this metaphor suggests that historical interest is related to the literary form of the whole. A semiotic theoretical framework allows the reader to interact with the text in its received form with a respect for the differences between text and reader—but allowing the possibility of communication between them. Prophetic books that have been claimed to be 'unreadable' can, in this way, be read. There may be a plethora of readings growing out of this approach; but they all help us to understand both the text and ourselves as readers.

BIBLIOGRAPHY

Ackroyd, Peter R., 'Isaiah 36–39: Structure and Function', in W. C. Delsman *et al.* (eds.), *Von Kanaan bis Kerala: Festschrift für Prof. Dr. Dr. J.P.M. van der Ploeg O.P. zur Vollendung des siebzigsten Lebenjahres am 4 Juli 1979* (AOAT, 211; Neukirchen–Vluyn: Neukirchener Verlag, 1982), pp. 16-20.

Andersen, Francis I., and David Noel Freedman, *Hosea: A New Translation and Commentary* (AB, 24; Garden City, NY: Doubleday, 1980).

Barstad, Hans M., 'History and the Hebrew Bible', in Lester L. Grabbe (ed.), *Can A 'History of Israel' Be Written?* (JSOTSup, 245; European Seminar in Historical Methodology, 1; Sheffield: Sheffield Academic Press, 1997), pp. 37-64.

—'No Prophets? Recent Developments in Biblical Prophetic Research and Ancient Near Eastern Prophecy', *JSOT* 57 (1993), pp. 39-60.

Barton, John, 'Classifying Biblical Criticism', *JSOT* 29 (1984), pp. 19-35.

—' "The Law and the Prophets": Who are the Prophets?', *OTS* 23 (1984), pp. 1-18.

—*Oracles of God: Perceptions of Ancient Prophecy in Israel after the Exile* (London: Darton, Longman & Todd, 1986).

—'What is a Book? Modern Exegesis and the Literary Conventions of Ancient Israel', in Johannes C. de Moor (ed.), *Intertextuality in Ugarit and Israel* (Oudtestamentische studiën, 40; Leiden: E.J. Brill, 1998), pp. 1-14.

—'Reading the Bible as Literature: Two Questions for Biblical Critics', *Literature and Theology* 1 (1987), pp. 135-53.

—*Reading the Old Testament: Method in Biblical Study* (London: Darton, Longman & Todd, 1984).

Berlin, Adele, 'The Role of the Text in the Reading Process', *Semeia* 62 (1993), pp. 143-46.

Boer, Roland, *Novel Histories: The Fiction of Biblical Criticism* (Playing the Text, 2; Sheffield: Sheffield Academic Press, 1997).

Boling, Robert G., *Joshua: A New Translation with Notes and Commentary* (AB, 6; Garden City, NY: Doubleday, 1982).

Brett, Mark G., *Biblical Criticism in Crisis? The Impact of the Canonical Approach on Old Testament Studies* (Cambridge: Cambridge University Press, 1991).

Bright, John, *A History of Israel* (Philadelphia: Westminster Press, 3rd edn, 1981).

Carr, David, 'Reaching for Unity in Isaiah', *JSOT* 57 (1993), pp. 61-80.

Carroll, Robert, 'Inscribing the Covenant: Writing and the Written in Jeremiah', in A. Graeme Auld (ed.), *Understanding Poets and Prophets: Essays in Honour of George Wishart Anderson* (JSOTSup, 152; Sheffield: Sheffield Academic Press, 1993), pp. 81-76.

—'Intertextuality and the Book of Jeremiah: Animadversions on Text and Theory', in J.C. Exum and D.J.A. Clines (eds.), *The New Literary Criticism and the Hebrew Bible* (JSOTSup, 143; Sheffield: Sheffield Academic Press, 1993), pp. 55-78.

Childs, Brevard S., 'The Canonical Shape of the Prophetic Literature', *Int* 32 (1978), pp. 46-55.

—*Introduction to the Old Testament as Scripture* (Philadelphia: Fortress Press, 1979).

Clements, Roland E., 'The Unity of the Book of Isaiah', *Int* 36 (1982), pp. 115-27.

Collins, Terence, *The Mantle of Elijah: The Redaction Criticism of the Prophetical Books* (The Biblical Seminar, 20; Sheffield: JSOT Press, 1993).

Conrad, Edgar W., 'Changing Context: The Bible and the Study of Religion', in E.W. Conrad and T.G. Newing (eds.), *Perspective's on Language and Text: Essays in Honor of Francis I. Andersen's Sixtieth Birthday July 28 1985* (Winona Lake, IN: Eisenbrauns, 1986), pp. 393-402.

—'The Community as King in Second Isaiah', in J.T. Butler, E.W. Conrad and B. Ollenburger (eds.), *Understanding the Word: Essays in Honor of Bernard W. Anderson* (JSOTSup, 37; Sheffield: Sheffield Academic Press, 1985), pp. 99-111.

—'The End of Prophecy and the Appearance of Angels in the Book of the Twelve', *JSOT* 73 (1997), pp. 65-79.

—'The Fear Not Oracles in Second Isaiah', *VT* 34 (1984), pp. 126-52.

—*Fear Not Warrior: A Study of 'al tîra' Pericopes in the Hebrew Scriptures* (BJS, 75; Chico, CA: Scholars Press, 1985).

—'Heard But Not Seen: The Representation of Books in the Old Testament', *JSOT* 54 (1992), pp. 45-59.

—'Messengers in Isaiah and the Twelve: Implications for Reading Prophetic Books', *JSOT* 91 (2000), pp. 83-97.

—*Patriarchal Traditions in Second Isaiah* (doctoral dissertation, Princeton Theological Seminary, 1974).

—'Prophet, Redactor and Audience: Reforming the Notion of Isaiah's Formation', in R.F. Melugin and M.A. Sweeney, *New Visions of Isaiah* (JSOTSup, 214; Sheffield: Sheffield Academic Press, 1996), pp. 306-26.

—*Reading Isaiah* (Overtures to Biblical Theology; Minneapolis: Augsburg Press, 1991 [repr. = Eugene, Oregon: Wipf & Stock, 2002]).

—'The Royal Narratives and the Structure of the Book of Isaiah', *JSOT* 41 (1988), pp. 67-81.

—'Second Isaiah and the Priestly Oracle of Salvation', *ZAW* 93 (1981), pp. 234-46.

—*Zechariah* (Readings: A New Biblical Commentary; Sheffield: Sheffield Academic Press, 1999).

Darr, Katheryn Pfisterer, *Isaiah's Vision and the Family of God* (Louisville, KY: Westminster/ John Knox Press, 1994).

Davies, Philip R., *In Search of 'Ancient Israel'* (JSOTSup, 148; Sheffield: JSOT Press, 1992).

—*Scribes and Schools: The Canonization of the Hebrew Scriptures* (Library of Ancient Israel; Louisville, KY: Westminster/John Knox Press, 1998).

Davis, Ellen F., *Swallowing the Scroll: Textuality and the Dynamics of Discourse in Ezekiel's Prophecy* (Bible and Literature Series, 21; Sheffield: Almond Press, 1989).

Eco, Umberto, *Interpretation and Overinterpretation* (ed. S. Collini; Cambridge: Cambridge University Press, 1992).

—*The Limits of Interpretation* (Bloomington: Indiana University Press, 1990).

—*The Role of the Reader: Explorations in the Semiotics of Texts* (London: Hutchinson, 1981).

—*A Theory of Semiotics* (Bloomington: Indiana University Press, 1976).

Fewell, Donna Nolan, 'Sennacherib's Defeat: Words at War in 2 Kings 18:13–19:37', *JSOT* 34 (1986), pp. 79-90.

Fish, Stanley, Is There a Text in This Class? The Authority of Interpretive Communities (Cambridge, MA: Harvard University Press, 1980).

Floyd, Michael H., 'The נָשָׂא (*Maśśa*) as a Type of Prophetic Book', *JBL* 121 (2002), pp. 401-22.

Frei, Hans W., *The Eclipse of Biblical Narrative: A Study in Eighteenth and Nineteenth Century Hermeneutics* (New Haven: Yale University Press, 1974).

Gottwald, Norman, 'Triumphalist Versus Anti-Triumphalist Versions of Early Israel: A Response to Articles by Lemche and Dever', *CRBS* 5 (1979), pp. 15-42.

Gressman, Hugo (ed.), *Altorientalische Texte und Bilder zum Alten Testament* (Berlin: W. de Gruyter, 1926).

Gunkel, Hermann, 'The Prophets as Writers and Poets', in *Prophecy in Israel: Search for Identity* (trans. J.L. Schaaf; ed. D.L. Petersen; Issues in Religion and Theology, 10; Philadelphia: Fortress Press; London: SPCK, 1987), pp. 22-73.

Hayes, John H., and J. Maxwell Miller, *A History of Ancient Israel and Judah* (Philadelphia: Westminster Press, 1986).

Hobsbawm, Eric, and Terence Ranger *The Invention of Tradition* (repr., Cambridge: Cambridge University Press, 1983).

Hutchinson, John, *The Dynamics of Cultural Nationalism: The Gaelic Revival and the Creation of the Irish Nation State* (London: Allen & Unwin, 1987).

Jameson, Frederic, 'Introductory Note', in *The Ideologies of Theory, Essays 1971–86*. II. *Syntax of History* (THL, 49; Minneapolis: University of Minnesota Press, 1988).

Kaiser, Otto, *Isaiah 13–39* (trans. R.A. Wilson; OTL; Philadelphia: Westminster Press, 1983).

Landy, Francis, *Hosea* (Readings: A New Biblical Commentary; Sheffield: Sheffield Academic Press, 1995).

Liebreich, L.J., 'The Composition of the Book of Isaiah', *JQR* 46 (1955–56), pp. 259-77, and 47 (1956–57), pp. 114-38.

Lieman, Sid Z., *The Canonization of Hebrew Scripture: The Talmudic and Midrashic Evidence* (New Haven: Connecticut Academy of Arts and Sciences, 1991).

Miscall, Peter D., *The Workings of Old Testament Narrative* (SBLSS; Philadelphia: Fortress; Chico, CA: Scholars Press, 1983).

Muilenburg, James, 'Form Criticism and Beyond', *JBL* 88 (1969), pp. 1-18.

Nogalski, James, *Literary Precursors to the Book of the Twelve* (BZAW, 217 ; Berlin: W. de Gruyter, 1993).

—*Redactional Processes in the Book of the Twelve* (BZAW, 218; Berlin: W. de Gruyter, 1993).

Noth, Martin, *The Deuteronomistic History* (trans. J. Douall *et al.*; JSOTSup, 15; Sheffield: JSOT Press, 2nd edn, 1991).

—*The History of Israel* (trans. P.R. Ackroyd; London: A. & C. Black, 2nd edn, 1960: Harper & Row, 1987).

Oden, Robert A., *The Bible Without Theology: The Theological Tradition and Alternatives to It* (San Francisco: Harper & Row, 1987).

Petersen, David L., *Zechariah 9–14 and Malachi* (OTL; London: SCM Press, 1995).

Rad, Gerhard von, *Old Testament Theology*, II (trans. D.M.G. Stalker; 2 vols.; New York: Harper & Row, 1965).

Redditt, Paul, 'Recent Research on the Book of the Twelve as One Book', *CRBS* 9 (2001), pp. 47-80.

Schwartz, Regina M., 'Joseph's Bones and the Resurrection of the Text: Remembering the Bible', *PMLA* 103 (1988), pp. 115-24 (reprinted in Schwartz [ed.], *The Book and the Text*, pp. 40-59).

Schwartz, Regina M. (ed.), *The Book and the Text: the Bible and Literary Theory* (Oxford: Basil Blackwell, 1990).

—*The Curse of Cain: The Violent Legacy of Monotheism* (Chicago: University of Chicago Press, 1997).

—*Remembering and Repeating: Biblical Creation in Paradise Lost* (Cambridge: Cambridge University Press, 1988).

Seitz, Christopher, *Zion's Final Destiny* (Minneapolis: Fortress Press, 1991).

Stibb, Mark W.G., 'Semiotics', in R.J. Coggins and J.L. Houlden (eds.), *A Dictionary of Biblical Interpretation* (London: SCM Press; Philadelphia: Trinity Press International, 1989), pp. 618-20.

Sweeney, Marvin A., *Isaiah 1–4 and the Post-Exilic Understanding of the Isaianic Tradition* (BZAW, 171; Berlin: W. de Gruyter, 1988).

Weis, Richard, 'Oracle: Old Testament', in *ABD*, V, pp. 28-29.

Wolff, Hans Walter, *Hosea: A Commentary on the Book of the Prophet Hosea* (trans. G. Stansell; Hermeneia; Philadelphia: Fortress Press, 1974).

INDEXES

INDEX OF REFERENCES

INDEX OF AUTHORS

JOURNAL FOR THE STUDY OF THE OLD TESTAMENT
SUPPLEMENT SERIES